From Disarmament to Rearmament

Rosemary,

with sincere best wishes

Sheldon Goldberg

FROM DISARMAMENT TO REARMAMENT

The Reversal of US Policy toward West Germany,
1946–1955

Sheldon A. Goldberg

Foreword by Ingo Trauschweizer

OHIO UNIVERSITY PRESS
ATHENS

Ohio University Press, Athens, Ohio 45701

ohioswallow.com

Printed in the United States of America
Ohio University Press books are printed on acid-free paper ♾ ™

27 26 25 24 23 22 21 20 19 18 17   5 4 3 2 1

Library of Congress Cataloging-in-Publication Data
Names: Goldberg, Sheldon Aaron, author.
Title: From disarmament to rearmament : the reversal of US policy toward West
Germany, 1946/1955 / Sheldon Aaron Goldberg ; foreword by Ingo Trauschweizer.
Other titles: Reversal of US policy toward West Germany, 1946/1955
Description: Athens, OH : Ohio University Press, [2017] | Includes bibliographical
references and index.
Identifiers: LCCN 2017026384| ISBN 9780821423004 (hc : alk. paper) |
ISBN 9780821446225 (pdf)
Subjects: LCSH: Germany—History—1945-1955. | Disarmament—Germany—
History—20th century. | United States—Relations—Germany (West) | Germany
(West)—Relations—United States. | World War, 1939-1945—Peace. | Militarism—
Germany. | Military planning—History—20th century. | United States—Military
policy—History—20th century.
Classification: LCC DD257.4 G65 2017 | DDC 355/.03109730943—dc23
LC record available at https://lccn.loc.gov/2017026384

To my late son, Steven Lawrence Goldberg, of beloved memory, who achieved so much in such a short time under great adversity, and to my grandchildren, Rachel, Aaron, and Barrett, to whom I hope this effort will be an example that learning continues throughout one's lifetime.

Contents

Foreword

The North Atlantic Treaty Organization (NATO) is fast approaching its seventieth anniversary and one may conclude that the alliance is showing its age. What started as a Cold War organization aimed at deterring the Soviet Union, first by demonstrating political resolve and then, in the wake of the Korean War, by creating more potent armed forces, has far outgrown its original geographic and strategic dimensions. NATO is now an almost all-European coalition that ties the continent to North America (and vice versa) and even acts far outside of its own territory (for example, in Afghanistan). NATO is facing challenges from Russia in Eastern Europe and could well get drawn into the vortex of Middle East conflicts. In the United States, politicians have repeatedly questioned the purpose of an alliance in which the United States outspends all other members. Today is thus a particularly important moment in time for Dr. Sheldon Goldberg to present a book that invites us to reconsider the foundations of the transatlantic alliance, so that we can weigh its less obvious strengths against its evident problems.

When NATO was founded in 1949, West Germany was not a member, France was the most important American ally on the European continent, and the alliance had no military command structures and very little by way of armed force. Just four months after the original twelve members signed the North Atlantic Treaty in Washington, the Soviets broke the Americans' monopoly on atomic weapons and in short succession China fell to Communism and war broke out in Korea. Whatever NATO was supposed to be, it was no longer sufficient in 1950, and leaders of the alliance readily agreed to install General Dwight Eisenhower as the first supreme allied commander, Europe. They built a headquarters in France as well as regional ones in Norway and Italy, and armed themselves for World War III or, better, the deterrence thereof. In that context, as the United States ramped up its direct investment from just one to six combat divisions in southwestern Germany, and with French and British forces distracted by wars of empire in Southeast Asia, it became clear that a realistic defense posture and credible deterrent could only be attained with a West German army.

This evolutionary, albeit sometimes stumbling process of building an alliance marked a departure from peacetime policies of the United States that had largely adhered to the advice of the Founding Fathers and avoided entangling alliances. Until World War II, Americans had been safely ensconced on the North American continent and in the Western Hemisphere, protected by the expanses of two oceans. With the advent of new enemies and long-range bombers, that sense of security vanished and the advent of atomic weapons made outright military preparedness necessary. The new strategic environment required the United States to project power across those oceans east and west. Containment of Communism and the Soviet Union became the new strategic objective and the NATO alliance one of its means. Sheldon Goldberg's book tells an important piece of that larger story.

Just half a decade after the end of the Second World War, rearming Germany was an almost unthinkable proposition. Strategic calculus was one thing, but political sentiments and intensely fresh and raw memory of the brutality of the recent war were quite another. Germany had occupied seven of the original twelve NATO nations, either entirely or in part, and German air, sea, and ground forces had done much harm to almost all of Europe, Canada, and the United States. Sheldon Goldberg carefully traces the politics, diplomacy, and military decisions on both sides of the Atlantic that made it possible for deep-seated fears and hostility to take a back seat to military necessity. This was not simply a story of the interests of entire nations pitted against one another, but one in which there were deep divisions in the United States (especially between the state and defense departments), France (where leading generals favored German rearmament), Britain, and Germany (where the majority of the people were opposed to taking up arms again so soon after the war). Skillful diplomats, blunt military men, and cagey politicians ultimately worked out a solution, albeit one that took five years to implement from the fundamental decision in autumn 1950 to rearm West Germany to that country's accession into NATO and the standing up of the first postwar German armed forces.

NATO could have taken a very different turn in 1954. For some time, the US government supported French plans for an integrated European Defence Community (EDC), an organization that would have included a close intertwining of armies. The point behind EDC was to prevent a German national army but take advantage all the same of the manpower pool and of the military expertise that generations of Germans had gained in the world wars. It was perhaps never realistic, from a military and cultural perspective, to expect small units from one country to perform well under commanders of entirely different nations. But it seemed in the early 1950s a feasible political compromise, and the administration of Dwight Eisenhower, with the active work of Secretary of State John Foster Dulles, threw its weight behind these plans. For Eisenhower, who had seen the American commitment to NATO grow firsthand, this offered a way to balance fiscally responsible defense expenditures with the need to stand tall in Europe. When it did not come to pass, when the national assembly in Paris voted down the EDC, Eisenhower and Dulles reluctantly lined up behind the proposal of a more conventional alliance structure by Anthony Eden's administration in London. West Germany got its own army and a greater degree of sovereignty, and national autonomy in military matters became a core principle of the alliance for better or worse. The US military would be deployed in Europe in much greater numbers and for much longer than Eisenhower had hoped.

Dr. Goldberg's study blends military, diplomatic, and political history. The dividing lines between these three fields are somewhat arbitrary, and, particularly when we consider strategy in the twentieth or twenty-first century, it is not advisable to emphasize one over the other. Sheldon Goldberg strikes the right balance in his book. *From Disarmament to Rearmament* reminds us how much of recent American history has played out overseas. It provides great insights into the inner workings of alliance building and showcases the expertise of bureaucrats and military officers as well as diplomats and statesmen. Goldberg demonstrates how unlikely that central axis of the NATO alliance, the relationship of the United States and Germany, really was. In 1948, when the first military officers in the United States—as well as, rather surprisingly, in France—raised the specter of German rearmament, it seemed unlikely that a resulting alliance of recent enemies could last. One may ascribe what followed entirely to perceived Soviet aggression, but, somehow, the NATO alliance has persisted well past a time when Europeans assumed the Soviet Union had hostile intentions. And it has now outlived its supposed sole raison d'être by over twenty-five years. In the process, NATO has reinvented itself more than once. Goldberg's study considers the first such transformation as being caused and affected by the United States: the practical military and diplomatic workings of the shift from a political pact to a military alliance.

Ingo Trauschweizer
Cincinnati, Ohio
December 2016

Acknowledgments

This work is the result of a significant amount of research I completed at the ripe young age of seventy-two after finally retiring from forty-six years of military and civil service. I am fortunate to have had the true and constant support of a number of scholars and others who were and remain very important to me. First of all, I need to acknowledge my wife, Waltraud, who like so many other dedicated military wives spent many years accompanying me and moving our family from base to base and country to country throughout my US Air Force career. She then tolerated my long hours and other absences while working for the federal government following my retirement from the air force and then, when I finally retired and we entered our "golden years," stood by as I embarked upon my quest for greater knowledge of military and political history. Next in line is Dr. Jeffrey Herf, who took me under his wing and opened up to me the world of modern European history, especially archival research. His challenge led me on a journey that continues to hold me in awe. Dr. Jon Tetsuro Sumida, a naval historian of renown, made military history more relevant and understandable to me than it had ever been, even after my thirty years of military service, and showed me that it was much more than just generals and battles. He, too, was a most valuable critic and supporter. I also need to thank Dr. Melvyn Leffler for the time he spent with me over a long lunch in Washington, DC, and for the insights he shared regarding US-European policy during the period covered by this book.

Outside of the University of Maryland, where much of my research took place, my thanks go to the archivists of the Modern Military Records

Branch, especially Mr. Richard Boylan, and the archivists of the Diplomatic Branch at the National Archives in College Park, Maryland. All of them were instrumental in teaching me how to use the archive's resources to find those records upon which the majority of this work is based.

Further afield, I must thank Dr. Randy Sowell of the Harry S. Truman Presidential Library, who made my short stay very productive, and Dr. Christopher Abraham at the Dwight D. Eisenhower Presidential Library, who prepared my visit and made my research of pertinent records of the president and his advisors both easy and rewarding. Both of these gentlemen were also extremely helpful in answering questions and providing other information long after I departed.

Gary Trogden and James Tobias at the Center for Military History at Fort McNair were extremely helpful at the beginning and end of my research, especially in finding among their holdings several unpublished documents that contributed significantly to the early chapters. Dr. Gabriele Bosch of the *Militärgeschichtliches Forschungsamt*, Potsdam, Germany, was extremely helpful and not only graciously provided me with references to relevant German literature but also sent me copies of hard-to-find German journal articles via post and as e-mail attachments. I also greatly appreciate David Read, archivist at the Soldiers of Gloucestershire Museum, Gloucester, England, for his help in providing me with biographical information on Brigadier T. N. Grazebrook.

I need to thank Dr. Malcolm "Kip" Muir Jr., who encouraged me to enter the VMI Adams Center Cold War Essay contest, and to the judges who found an abridged version of my chapter on Operation Eclipse worthy of an award. I would also like to thank the officers of Phi Gamma Phi, who selected me to receive a Love of Learning grant. This grant gave me a very welcome impetus to venture outside my comfort zone in College Park, Maryland, and continue my research at the Harry S. Truman and Dwight D. Eisenhower Presidential Libraries.

To both Dr. Mark Mandeles and Harry Yeide, former colleagues, long-time friends, military historians, and authors in their own rights, my gratitude for their thorough reviews and thoughtful comments as I prepared the final manuscript. Last but not least, I extend my sincerest thanks to my very good friend and excellent military historian Dr. Ingo Trauschweitzer, whose scholarly advice, encouragement, and comments on my chapters were invaluable, and who helped me keep my goal in sight.

Acronyms

AAFCE	Allied Air Forces, Central Europe
ACA	Allied Control Authority
ACC	Allied Control Council
ACS	Assistant Chief of Staff
AEAF	Allied Expeditionary Air Forces
ANCXF	Allied Naval Expeditionary Forces
AOR	Area of Responsibility
APG	Advanced Planning Group
BTO	Brussels Treaty Organization
CCMS	Control Commission, Military Staff
CCS	Combined Chiefs of Staff
CENTAG	Central Army Group
CDU	Christian Democratic Union (West Germany)
CFM	Council of Foreign Ministers
CINC	Commander in Chief
CICEUCOM	Commander in Chief, European Command
CINCEUR	Commander in Chief, Europe
CJCS	Chief of the Joint Chiefs of Staff
COMAAFCE	Commander, Allied Air Forces, Central Europe
COMNAVFORGER	Commander, US Naval Forces Germany
COS	Chief of Staff
COSSAC	Chief of Staff to the Supreme Allied Commander
DCS	Deputy Chief of Staff
EAC	European Advisory Commission

xvi	EDC	European Defense Community
	EDC-IC	European Defense Community – Interim Commission
	EDF	European Defense Force
	ETOUSA	European Theater of Operations, United States Army
	EWP	Emergency War Plan
	FRG	Federal Republic of Germany (West Germany)
	FY	Fiscal Year
	GSO	General Staff Officer
	HICOG	High Commissioner for Germany
	HICOM	High Commission
	HQ	Headquarters
	JCS	Joint Chiefs of Staff
	JSPC	Joint Strategic Planning Committee
	JSSC	Joint Strategic Survey Committee
	JWPC	Joint War Planning Committee
	LANDCENT	Land Forces, Central Europe
	LSU	Labor Service Unit
	MAAG	Military Assistance Advisory Group
	MAP	Military Assistance Program
	MDAP	Mutual Defense Assistance Program
	MSB	Military Security Board
	NAC	North Atlantic Council
	NATO	North Atlantic Treaty Organization
	NHT	Navy Historical Team
	NIE	National Intelligence Estimate
	NORTHAG	Northern Army Group
	NSC	National Security Council
	OKH	High Command of the Army (German, World War II)
	OKL	High Command of the Air Force (German, World War II)
	OKM	High Command of the Navy (German, World War II)
	OKW	High Command of the Armed Forces (German, World War II)
	POW	Prisoner of War
	PPS	Policy Planning Staff

RAF	Royal Air Force	xvii
RCT	Regimental Combat Team	
SACEUR	Supreme Allied Commander Europe	
SCAF	Supreme Commander Allied Forces	
SHAPE	Supreme Headquarters Allied Powers Europe	
SHAEF	Supreme Headquarters Allied Expeditionary Forces	
SPD	Social Democratic Party (West Germany)	
T/O and E	Table of Organization and Equipment	
UK	United Kingdom	
UN	United Nations	
USAAF	United States Army Air Force	
USAFE	United States Air Forces, Europe	
USAREUR	United States Army, Europe	
USEUCOM	United States European Command	
USFET	US Forces European Theater	
USSR	Union of Soviet Socialist Republics	
WEU	Western European Union	
WSC	Working Security Committee	

Introduction

On 8–9 May 1945, the entire German military establishment put down their arms and surrendered. Approximately six weeks later, the Potsdam Agreement stipulated that Nazism and German militarism were to be extirpated and Germany's armed forces dissolved in such a way as to permanently prevent their revival or reorganization. Furthermore, because of the nature of German militarism and the crimes committed during the war, German soldiers were reviled and looked upon as criminals. No one wanted to see Germans in uniform again.[1]

But just as wars have their unintended consequences, so too does peace—or at least attempts to maintain peace. For the United States, the desire to maintain the peace following World War II and prevent the Cold War from becoming a "hot" war resulted in a series of these unintended consequences. Rearming Germany was one. The irony of rearming Germany is that it had been agreed by all parties at the Potsdam Conference that Germany should be disarmed and demilitarized and that "all forces and all institutions or organizations which served to keep alive the military tradition [should] be completely and finally abolished."[2] It is clear that the decision to totally disarm and demilitarize Germany stemmed from the failure of the World War I Allies to control German disarmament. The World War II Allies concluded that Germany alone was responsible for that war, and, because of the failure of the restrictions imposed by the Versailles Treaty to cure the symptoms of German militarism, they formed the concept of disarming and demilitarizing a nation without any serious thought given to whether it could, in fact, be done or what the consequences might be.[3]

2   The above notwithstanding, the emerging Cold War caused some, particularly in the US Department of Defense, to think differently. There was universal agreement that Western Europe had to be protected against a Communist takeover. The question that remained was how? Thus, after years of debate within the US government and between it and the governments of its West European allies, a resurrected West Germany was granted full sovereignty and authorized to create a national armed force just ten years after being totally defeated. That this Cold War event could occur at all was primarily due to the reversal of a major US policy decision made long before World War II ended to keep Germany disarmed and demilitarized for generations.

Revisiting the rearmament debate contributes a new perspective to the vast scholarly literature on the Cold War's first decade. It reflects what has been called a real "gap between the disciplines" (meaning diplomatic historians have neglected the military aspects of the period before 1950 while military historians have equally neglected this period's politics).[4] This book endeavors to fill that gap and thus examines both military and political dimensions of the German rearmament process and, with respect to the evidence, goes where others have not. This brings to light (often for the first time) many previously unseen, neglected, or underexamined archival files from the Department of State, the Policy Planning Staff, the Joint Chiefs of Staff (JCS), and the Supreme Headquarters Allied Expeditionary Forces (SHAEF), as well as previously classified histories of the military services, some still unpublished.[5]

While these documents do not change our overall understanding of the era in question, they provide fresh insights to the underlying discussions and rationales that led to the decisions initially made by the Allied Combined Chiefs of Staff and subsequently within the Department of State and the War Department (later the Department of Defense). They also add context to the existing scholarship and depth to understudied issues, such as the lack of US preparedness to defend Western Europe in the face of possible Soviet aggression both before and after the Soviet acquisition of the atomic bomb. Furthermore, they document the genesis of the original plan to disarm Germany and the heretofore unknown US military plans to arm West Germany that began as early as 1948, and provide additional meaning to the later debates over the question of German rearmament between officials of the departments of state, war, and later, defense.[6] Using formerly classified documents, this history describes the efforts of and the obstacles faced by the US military services in planning for the creation of a new German armed force. Lastly, these documents show that while the United States had no intention of incurring a long-term defense commitment in Europe, American officials believed that they had no choice but to make repeated assurances that US forces would remain in Europe as long as needed, both to deter the Soviets and to protect America's European allies against an imagined German revanchism.

This archival focus is not meant to denigrate the plethora of published books and articles that cover this early Cold War period, but rather to fill the literary void on the subject of German rearmament below the policy level and provide new details that illuminate the rationale behind the policies and actions taken. Most of the discussions in the literature on this period focus primarily on the nuclear issue (i.e., America's nuclear monopoly prior to 1949 and the need to rapidly build on that nuclear capability after the first Soviet nuclear test in August 1949). The literature does not mention that the US Army, rapidly demobilized and seen as inconsequential, had not included atomic weapons in its war-fighting doctrine and remained focused on large formations and a need to conduct a war of attrition.[7] While it was eventually agreed that German troops would be needed on the ground to help defend Western Europe, the discussions, debates, and actual planning for German rearmament that took place within the War Department (later the Pentagon) prior to 1949 are simply absent from the literature.[8]

What the literature does cover is the belief that German rearmament would require an end to the occupation, a step that would make the Federal Republic of Germany (FRG) not only independent but also stronger. This, in itself, was feared as an invitation for a Soviet attack, one that some felt could not be resisted.[9] France also feared a strong Germany, despite evidence that some French leaders had realized as early as 1945 that Germany would have to be rearmed to ward off the emerging Soviet threat. Even Field Marshal Bernard Montgomery, chairman of the Western Union Military Committee, stated in late 1948 that a rearmed Germany should be admitted to the WEU and later to NATO. French WEU staff officers were of the same mind.[10] However, despite all the words that have been written on the subject of German rearmament, still missing is a comprehensive narration of how the military services planned for it, how it was viewed by Congress, what actions they took to speed up or impede this rearmament, and under what conditions it finally took place.

Despite the key role played by the rapid disarmament and demilitarization of Germany following World War II, there is little in the literature

4   about the two-year-long disarmament planning process that became Operation Eclipse or about its outstanding results. None of the several long and detailed articles on posthostilities planning for Germany even mention Operation Eclipse (with one exception), and the official histories of the World War II period only mention it briefly, if at all.[11]

Aside from the several texts that inform us that President Eisenhower was a strong supporter of the European Defence Community (EDC), as was his secretary of state, John Foster Dulles, little is really known about Eisenhower's initial opposition to EDC and his subsequent conversion to favor of it when he was Supreme Allied Commander Europe (SACEUR), or how deeply he became committed to it as president. Nor has much been written about how his support impacted US policy to make the success of the EDC a cornerstone of US European policy. Similarly, while the literature underscores Dulles's threats of an "agonizing reappraisal" of US policy toward Europe should the EDC fail, there is no real narrative in the literature of his everyday thoughts about the EDC or of his discussions with Eisenhower about the EDC or German rearmament.[12]

One reason there are so few details on the process of disarming and demilitarizing Germany is that when most of the history covering that period was written and documented, many of the key State Department and Defense Department papers had not been declassified and were simply not available to researchers. Since their declassification, both time and interest have passed, so a number of documents that can add depth and detail to the narrative are now available but remain largely untouched.

Discussions on rearming West Germany can be broken into two chronological periods, the first from the end of the war on 8–9 May 1945 until 12 September 1950, the day Secretary of State Dean Acheson presented the US demand that West Germany be rearmed to the British and French foreign ministers, and the second from 13 September 1950 until 9 May 1955, when the FRG was admitted to NATO as a fully sovereign nation following its earlier admission to the WEU (along with Italy), an expanded Brussels Treaty Organization. For the first of these periods, archival research is necessary because until 1948, with the exception of rumors and innuendo published in a number of American and European newspapers, there is no mention of arming West Germany in the literature covering that period.[13] For the second period, archival research is still necessary to fill in the gaps that remain in the large number of books on German rearmament published after 1950.

The various agencies in Washington responsible for formulating pre-surrender and posthostilities policies for Germany were slow to act on the need for posthostilities planning. They were plagued by serious divisions and fundamental differences in outlook. In addition, the State Department and the War Department were greatly at odds with one another over the role Allied military forces should have during the occupation. The resulting US posthostilities planning process, albeit thorough and extremely broad in its coverage, was overly bureaucratic, cumbersome, and to some degree duplicative. Much of this can be understood by realizing that posthostilities thinking was, aside from the obvious task of disarming German forces, focused on establishing military government there to restore law and order initially, eventually establishing civil government in the liberated areas, and enforcing the terms of Germany's surrender.[14]

From the end of the war until the September 1950 unilateral US demand that West Germany be armed (despite the outbreak of the Korean War), the official US position regarding Germany was that it should remain disarmed and demilitarized. The September 1949 Occupation Statute stated explicitly that not only would the newly created Federal Republic of Germany remain disarmed and demilitarized but that all military-related areas of scientific research, industry, and even civil aviation would remain circumscribed, if not totally forbidden. In this regard, the Tripartite Military Security Board was created to ensure that the demilitarization of Germany continued.[15] This Allied position was actually welcomed in many quarters of Germany. For example, in the fall of 1950, before German interior minister Gustav Heinemann resigned from the cabinet, he told Chancellor Konrad Adenauer that "since one of the noblest Allied war aims was to disarm us and keep us disarmed into the future, and the Allies have done everything during five years of occupation to make the German military despicable . . . and to educate the German people about military attitudes, it is therefore not for us to either search for or offer military measures."[16] Heinemann also invoked God, opining that "after God had twice dashed the weapons from the hands of the Germans they should not reach for them a third time."[17]

However, as early as 1946, it was becoming clear to both the United States and Great Britain that a defeated, apathetic, and virtually prostrate Germany was no longer to be feared, while their erstwhile ally, the Union of Soviet Socialist Republics (USSR), was changing into a potential threat. The changes taking place in that relationship spawned fears that unless the USSR were contained (an effort that could only be successful with

6   a rearmed Germany), a third world war would erupt. This created quite a dilemma, however, as the act of rearming Germany might instigate the very aggression it was meant to prevent.[18]

While the initiative to arm the FRG in 1950 came from the United States, the plan was not conceived in a vacuum. Both Great Britain and France, the United States' main NATO allies, had also been considering the matter. But while the objectives of the NATO allies were the same (containment of possible German revanchism and deterrence of Soviet advances), the means were not. Each nation found itself at times working at cross-purposes to the others and even resorting to deception as the perceptions of political realities and strategic imperatives demanded. As a result, the United States lost both the initiative and control of the process of rearming West Germany.

The United States' objectives for the 1950 decision to arm the Federal Republic, aside from the goal of strengthening the defense of Western Europe against the perceived Soviet strength, were twofold: to bind the western half of the divided German nation to the West by forming a West German army within an integrated West European edifice, and to withdraw US occupation forces from the European continent. The actual outcomes of the 1950 decision to rearm—a West German "national" army and US commitment to a virtually permanent presence in Western Europe—were completely at odds with those objectives. While the United States wanted a rearmed Germany, it did not as a matter of national policy want a national German army. Despite long-held plans to remove US forces from Europe—to build down as the Germans built up—the United States was forced to assuage European fears of a resurgent Germany by promising an open-ended commitment to keep significant US forces on the continent.[19] The subsequent failure of the EDC in 1954 forced the United States into a "double containment" situation, where the United States would now be called upon to protect Western Europe against a Soviet invasion on the one hand, and to protect all of Europe against a possible resurgent Germany on the other.[20] Furthermore, faced with a fait accompli, the United States' pledge to retain an open-ended commitment of military forces was made in order to regain its lost initiative and leadership of the Alliance. The NATO treaty imposed no requirement on any member nation to station troops either on the continent or in Germany; therefore (discounting altruism as a motive), the US commitment was made to balance its military imperatives with political realities. Regaining the initiative in and leadership of the Alliance would do just that.[21]

Conventional wisdom attributes the arming of the FRG to the Korean War. Robert McGeehan writes that "the German rearmament question was among the most important, and frustrating, concerns of American diplomacy during the postwar period" and that rearmament was the result of a unilateral US decision in the summer of 1950 following the outbreak of the Korean War.[22] While this statement is true in regard to the timing of the decision and that it was unilateral, one cannot deny that in reality the issue of rearming the Germans had roots going back as early as 1948 and possibly even 1947.[23] That said, there can be no question but that the hostilities in Korea, seen by the West as blatant Soviet-backed aggression, gave a greater urgency to the issue of rearming Germany and caused West European nations to make a U-turn regarding their own rearmament thoughts and view the use of German manpower and resources as imperative.[24]

In this book, I document US Army plans to rearm West Germany that began as early as 1947 as well as discussions that took place between the departments of state and defense prior to the formal presentation of the US decision on 12 September 1950. As alluded to above, many of the existing histories have failed to fully indicate that in some instances, particularly in the early period of the Cold War, military-diplomatic actions were taken without strategic guidance or even a strategic consensus. One key purpose of this history is to draw together these heretofore ignored or underemphasized aspects of this issue, such as the delaying tactics used by the British and the French to slow the German rearming process down. This provides a more detailed and nuanced picture of this key episode in the first decade of the Cold War.

In the view of US political and military leaders, the Soviet threat had been growing since 1944 and took on greater urgency following the 1948 Czech coup, the Berlin Blockade that same year, and the Soviet detonation of an atomic bomb in the late summer of 1949.[25] For these reasons, five years after the war's end, US policy, which had initially supported disarming and demilitarizing Germany, changed direction. Prior to these events, President Harry S. Truman had stated on record that he planned to reduce the US military presence overseas and wanted to cut an additional $5–$7 billion from the $13.7 billion defense budget. These events, however, intervened and led to the promulgation of NSC 68 and a massive US rearmament program, and caused the president and Secretary of State Acheson, both disposed to keeping Germany disarmed, to bend to the fear in Europe resulting from the Korean War and the urgings of the Joint Staff

8   to strengthen the defense of Western Europe. They reversed course and began to favor a German contribution to that defense.[26]

In addition, before 1950, the desire to arm the FRG was deeply imbedded in an international, politico-military conundrum that followed two separate but related paths from 1948 until the late summer of 1950. The differences were not in the fundamental goals but in the tactical approaches to the same goal.[27] The State Department saw the threat and sought to strengthen Western Europe by unifying it politically and economically, thereby creating a mechanism by which a rehabilitated Germany could be reintegrated into Western Europe without posing a threat to the peace and stability of its neighbors. As mentioned above, the State Department wanted Western Europe to be a third power, capable of saying no to the United States and the USSR. Only once that was accomplished, some State Department officials thought, could one raise the question of arming Germany. It was not that the leading officials of the State Department were adamantly against seeing Germany armed; they just wanted to decouple this issue from other issues they deemed more important and less risky.[28] They believed that in this manner, the Soviet threat could be held at bay.

Defense officials likewise believed that the reconstruction of Western Europe and the need to strengthen its economy took precedence over rearmament and preparing for a possible war against the Soviet Union. Because strategic planners believed the Soviet Union would not risk a war with the United States, their planning was more of a theoretical exercise.[29] Nonetheless, the Department of Defense faced a number of challenges to that assumption during this period. The first Soviet nuclear bomb test and the Communist takeover of China, for example, provided reason to suspect that a powerful coalition might be forming that could threaten US national security. Furthermore, the USSR army outnumbered the US Army in terms of manpower due to the United States' postwar demobilization, caused by a limited budget. The army was also dealing with the threat of additional reductions, caught in an interservice rivalry with the air force and the navy for money and resources as well as roles and missions, and associated with the relatively weak West European powers, who were still recovering from the ravages of World War II. In light of these circumstances, and because they needed to rapidly devise a strategy to defend Western Europe, the War Department chose the path advocated by the JCS and sought a solution that would utilize the manpower and highly regarded fighting expertise that the recently defeated Germany could provide, placing German boots on the ground as quickly as possible.[30]

In addressing these issues, US policymakers and the administration were confronted with several difficulties. First, gaining popular approval for this decision would require reversing American attitudes that had been held throughout the war years about the Soviet Union (erstwhile ally) and Germany (erstwhile enemy). Second, US policymakers needed to find a way to rearm Germany in a manner that would "deter the Russians but not scare the Belgians" while at the same time ensuring that the new German army would not be able to act independently and threaten the peace of Europe again.[31] Third, the United States had to convince its European allies to strengthen their own defensive capabilities. Finally, the American public had to be convinced that the preservation of democracy and the "American way of life" required the long-term presence of US military forces on the European continent.

The situation with the USSR worsened, causing the United States to make two major decisions that, as Acheson said, "took a step never before taken in [US] history."[32] The first, in 1949, was to end an almost two-hundred-year-old isolationist tradition and become part of an entangling foreign alliance, NATO; the second was to reverse a key World War II policy by formally deciding in 1950 to rearm West Germany. This latter decision ran up against strong French opposition, which succeeded in getting the initiative for German rearmament handed to the French, who introduced the Pleven Plan for an integrated European army and used it as a tool to arm the Germans without arming Germany. The Pleven Plan metamorphosed into the ill-fated EDC. The EDC was based on the principle of supranationality and, despite strong support from the Eisenhower administration to the exclusion of all other alternatives, failed, leaving only one alternative that was successfully brought to conclusion by the British.[33]

Several months later, on 9 May 1955, exactly ten years after the armed forces of Germany's Third Reich surrendered unconditionally and ended World War II in Europe, the black, red, and gold flag of the Federal Republic of Germany (FRG) was raised at the Supreme Headquarters Allied Powers Europe (SHAPE) in Rocquencourt, France, alongside those of the fourteen other members of the North Atlantic Treaty Organization (NATO), most of whom had been Germany's enemies just ten years earlier.[34] Six months later, on 12 November 1955, the two hundredth

10   birthday of General Gerhard von Scharnhorst, Prussian reformer and father of the German general staff, the first 101 German soldiers—2 generals, 18 lieutenant colonels, 30 majors, 40 captains and naval lieutenants, 5 first lieutenants, 5 sergeants first class, and 1 master sergeant—received their appointments to the new German armed forces (Bundeswehr) in Bonn's Ermekeilkaserne from newly appointed Defense Minister Theodor Blank.[35]

How this reversal of policy came about is the topic of this book. Starting with the total disarmament of Germany and continuing to the entry of the new Federal Republic of Germany into NATO, the following chapters describe the paths taken by the US State Department and Defense to reach a common goal.

Chapter 1 tells the story of Operation Eclipse, the Allied plan to completely disarm, demobilize, and demilitarize the German nation, first enunciated in the 1941 Atlantic Charter. This plan stemmed from the beliefs that militarism was ingrained in the German soul and that this had made Hitler's rise to power inevitable. It was further believed that only by uprooting this militarism could Germany ever be a productive and peaceful neighbor in Europe. Thus, the total demilitarization of Germany, a goal never before imposed on any other nation, became a major undertaking that required the development of agreed-upon guidance, policy directives, manpower, and time.

Chapter 2 describes and analyzes the State Department's approach to the rearmament of Germany, its approach to European efforts to find security in the Dunkirk and Brussels treaties and, in 1949, its approach to the Washington Treaty that created NATO. The relationship between John J. McCloy and Colonel Henry Byroade and the development of an American plan for a European army is brought to light before arriving at the crisis year of 1950, the Korean War, and a detailed explanation of Acheson's "conversion" and demand to arm the Germans in September 1950.

Chapter 3 mirrors chapter 2, highlighting the military's approach to the "German Question," the thinking within the joint and army staffs on making use of German manpower, and the efforts of the Department of Defense to convince the government that the Germans should be armed. This chapter also discusses the problems with and evolution of different plans to defend Western Europe between 1946 and 1949, the Defense Department's analysis of Europe's defense needs, and the initial weakness of the NATO organization. It concludes with the impact of the Korean War on the rearmament question and the JCS's response to President Truman's letter containing eight questions, the answers to which would help him decide the issue of German rearmament.

Chapter 4 brings the paths taken by state and defense together, presents their joint answer to President Truman's eight questions, and segues to the 12 September 1950 tripartite meeting and the demand to rearm Germany that led to the development of the French Pleven Plan (which soon became the EDC) and the problems that confronted it. This chapter also addresses the Eisenhower administration's plans and attempts to save the EDC from rejection by France and its inability to come up with an alternative.

Chapter 5 continues the narration to the defeat of EDC and the US quandary over what to do next in light of the administration's belief that there was no alternative to EDC. It concludes this history with the solution to the "German problem" found and implemented through the efforts of the British foreign minister, Sir Anthony Eden, who brought West Germany into NATO and opened the way to create a German military force.

The epilogue that follows addresses the activities undertaken and obstacles faced by the three US military services during the EDC phase (as they prepared to train what would become the new West German Bundeswehr) until the FRG's admission to NATO in 1955.

Seven appendices follow that provide additional information on the European Advisory Commission (EAC), a list of the Eclipse memoranda and other directives relating to German disarmament, the Himmerod Conference, an essay on Acheson and the "Single Package," and the "Great Debate" over the power of the president to send troops overseas.

The evidence presented in this book calls for a revision of certain conventional views about West German rearmament and the beginnings of the Cold War. First, once the decision was made to change standing US national policy and arm the Germans, the US government lost effective control of the process when it voluntarily ceded leadership of the implementation of German rearmament to France. Second, despite the efforts of two US administrations, neither pleas nor threats were able to save the EDC from defeat. Third, the United States' total commitment (at the highest levels of the US administration) to German rearmament within the EDC precluded consideration of an alternative. Lastly, when a solution

12   to the German rearmament problem was found following the defeat of the EDC, the United States found itself pledging an open-ended troop commitment on the European continent, a pledge that remains in force today, albeit somewhat diminished from what it was prior to the fall of the Berlin Wall in 1989.

1

Operation Eclipse

The idea to disarm, demobilize, and demilitarize Germany was first enunciated in the Atlantic Charter of 14 August 1941, and began to take concrete form in May of 1943 when the Combined Chiefs of Staff to the Supreme Allied Commander (designate; COSSAC), under Lieutenant General Sir Frederick E. Morgan, were charged by the Combined Chiefs of Staff (CCS) to plan, among other things, for the occupation of Germany in the event of a sudden German collapse.[1]

This plan, originally called Operation Rankin and then Operation Talisman before it became Operation Eclipse, was two years in the making, and this chapter, which relates its history, also serves to establish a starting point from which to view the underlying theme of this book—the rearming of the Federal Republic of Germany—and the problems encountered by the United States as a result of reversing a long-standing policy to keep the Germans disarmed for decades. This chapter also speaks to the lack of government guidance given to US military forces as they prepared to occupy Germany and, to a lesser extent, the belated and misguided plans and preparations the government had for the occupation without a full understanding of what the occupation would entail.

The total demilitarization of Germany became a major undertaking requiring the development of agreed-upon guidance, policy directives, manpower, and time. Plans were developed at various levels and in various agencies on both sides of the Atlantic, which were embroiled in interdepartmental rivalries and tensions. Furthermore, they had also been left to act in the absence of authoritative guidance and, in the case of the United States, presidential decisiveness. During the Roosevelt administration, for example, decision-making was unstructured and interdepartmental

14 coordination was both informal and haphazard. Additionally, the State Department had lost the president's confidence and its influence waned while the military assumed considerable prestige.[2]

Two months later, in July 1943, the British War Cabinet revised its 1942 organization to create a posthostilities subcommittee under COSSAC to tackle the question of how Germany was to be treated after victory was achieved. The purpose of this new committee was "confined to the consideration of drafts for instruments to conclude hostilities and to enforce compliance with armistice or surrender terms."[3] It assigned Colonel T. N. Grazebrook to head the subcommittee and tasked it to "prepare drafts of documents . . . required in connection with the formal suspension of hostilities . . . and to submit plans for the enforcement of such instruments by armistice and disarmament commissions."[4]

In December 1943, a British government report entitled *Occupation of Germany* outlined the cases for and against total occupation and asked whether it was necessary. The report specified that one of the United Nations' (UN) objectives upon cessation of hostilities should be the "rapid and total disarmament of Germany and the breakup of the German military machine." It made the case that the situation that existed following World War I should not again be tolerated and that sufficient armed forces should be distributed throughout Germany to prevent the delay in and difficulty enforcing the terms of surrender in the Versailles Treaty. The point was further made that the sooner Germany was disarmed, the sooner the work of reconstruction could begin. The authors believed it would take two years after the war ended to complete the total disarmament of Germany and the destruction of its armaments industries.

To ensure that the post–World War I scenario would not be repeated, the British proposed that eleven divisions of land forces, seven regiments of armored cars plus the necessary nondivisional units—a total of 310,000 personnel—supervise the first two years of the posthostilities period. To back this force up, twenty-eight air force squadrons, to include light and fighter-bombers as well as reconnaissance aircraft, would be needed.[5] The assumptions made in the report show the level of distrust the British had for Germany, as well as British fears that a resurgent Germany would somehow find a way to circumvent the disarmament regime that would be imposed upon it.

The British also believed that once the Allies entered Germany they would find a significant amount of civil disorder as well as large numbers of German troops who would need to be disarmed, hence the need for the large number of ground forces. The report also indicates that the presence of a large Allied air force as well as occasional mass formation flights would have a considerable effect on German morale by reminding the Germans that they had been defeated.[6]

It was not until 1944, however, that the broader concepts of occupation began to be reflected in Allied planning. With the establishment of Supreme Headquarters Allied Expeditionary Force (SHAEF) under General Dwight D. Eisenhower in January 1944, the disarmament and demilitarization issue became the responsibility of the deputy chief of staff for operations (G-3), Major General Harold R. Bull (US), and, following the cessation of hostilities, the deputy chief of staff for civil affairs (G-5, Civil Affairs Division), Lieutenant General A. E. Grasset (UK).[7] What little direction SHAEF could get came from the US War Department, the British War Office, and the joint European Advisory Commission (EAC) established by the Moscow Conference of Foreign Ministers in October 1943.[8] It was, however, in the posthostilities subcommittee under Colonel Grazebrook, now part of SHAEF's Operations Division (G-3), that many of the most important demilitarization staff studies and memoranda were developed.

Among the various agencies responsible for formulating presurrender and postwar policy for Germany, those in Washington were slowest to recognize the need for postwar planning and most severely plagued by serious divisions and fundamental differences in outlook. The Working Security Committee (WSC), composed of war, navy, and state department representatives, was created in December 1943, but agreement on the function of the committee was never really reached. In addition, the perspectives of the state and war departments regarding the tasks to be performed by Allied military forces during the occupation were greatly at odds with one another and began long before the war in Europe ended. In fact, until 1948, the State Department maintained liaison with the War Department on German issues through an "Occupied Areas" office, as it did not have a German division.[9]

As an example, when the EAC held its first meeting in January 1944, three months after it was formed, Ambassador John G. Winant, the US representative, had yet to receive any guidance from Washington concerning the main task of the meeting (i.e., preparing surrender terms for Germany). Furthermore, according to Winant's biographer, the ambassador received only one policy directive with authoritative clearances between March and October 1944. During this period, Winant sent his political advisor, George F. Kennan, to Washington to seek guidance, to no avail, and in July 1944, Winant's military advisor, Brigadier General Cornelius W. Wickersham, also personally appealed to the WSC for policy guidance with little apparent success. Washington's failure to provide guidance was also felt by Eisenhower, who, following the entry of US combat forces into Germany in September 1944, urgently requested guidance from Washington regarding the control and occupation of Germany.[10] The infighting within the WSC precluded any effective communication or coordination until early March 1944.[11]

It appears that the multiplicity of agencies, both military and civilian, in the United States and Great Britain made the posthostilities planning process thorough and extremely broad in its coverage, but also overly bureaucratic, cumbersome and, to some degree, duplicative. From the end of the war in Europe until the USSR walked out of the Allied Control Council (ACC) in 1948, the disarmament and demilitarization process was increasingly encumbered by political obstacles that left many tasks unresolved. Thus, as will be seen, it was left to SHAEF to formulate the plans that would permit Eisenhower to carry out the tasks required to disarm German soldiers, disband and demobilize Germany's armed forces, dispose of German war matériel, and begin the process of demilitarizing Germany.

Initial Thoughts on Disarming Germany

In late November 1943, using the initial posthostilities plan Operation Rankin Case C,[12] COSSAC drafted an initial study that provided suggestions for the composition of the disarmament detachments that would supervise the process to be effected by the German High Command (Oberkommando des Heeres, or OKH). This was, of course, predicated on the belief that German troops remained subject to the discipline of the OKH. The proposed disarmament detachments were to be small and consist only of the personnel needed to communicate the orders of the Allied High Command and supervise their observance. A follow-up study highlighted several areas of concern, such as the guarding of dumps and the responsibility for disarming the German Air Force (Luftwaffe) and Navy (Kriegsmarine). It was also brought up that as the naval ports and facilities were on land, creating points of contact with land forces, they should not be the unilateral responsibility of the Admiralty.[13]

On 23 December 1943, the first full draft of COSSAC's disarmament study was forwarded to general staff officers (GSOs 1) for review. Its objective outlined the steps to be taken by the supreme commander to enforce disarmament of the German Army in his area of responsibility (AOR) between the time of the envisioned armistice and the transfer of responsibility to a disarmament commission. The scope of this paper covered German forces outside Germany, German forces in transit over the frontiers of Germany, and German forces in Germany. Contrary to the initial study, it stated that naval disarmament was an Admiralty responsibility and thus would not be considered in the paper.[14]

The draft disarmament study also indicated that the posthostilities subcommittee was drafting a paper on the composition and functions of a European disarmament commission for consideration by the COSSAC and, upon approval by the British government, submission to the EAC. That said, the study postulated that the supreme commander, Allied Forces (SCAF) would be responsible for the complete disarmament of the German armed forces until the transfer of responsibility to the disarmament commission took place—a period expected to be approximately two months. It absolved the SCAF of any responsibility for the disbanding of the German armed forces or the dismantling and destruction of German fortifications and similar works.

Among the several main considerations in this paper was the admonition that disarmament was to be immediate and that no German should be allowed to enter Germany bearing arms. Citing the circumstances that followed World War I, the paper stated that "after the last war it was possible for the Germans to pretend that the German Army had never been beaten in the field because it returned to Germany still bearing its arms. This is another mistake which must not be repeated."[15] It also reminded its readers that the German Army had been able to hinder the effectiveness of the Military Control Commission after the last war, which was why total disarmament needed to be carried out immediately after the armistice, without exceptions. By 1 January 1944, the second draft of this study had grown in size and detail, adding sections for action by the air commander in chief as well as ground and air force commanders.

An unofficial assessment of this disarmament issue by the land forces subcommittee estimated that the British alone would need to provide 270 officers and 1,300 other ranks to man the necessary disarmament detachments, both fixed and mobile. Aside from the security of dumps, depots, and stores of war matériel, two key concerns were that it would prove difficult for Allied forces to enter Germany fast enough to ensure the rapid disarmament of the German forces already inside Germany, and that their ability to supervise the expected millions of disarmed German soldiers found in barracks and camps both inside and outside Germany would

18   be insufficient.[16] That said, the British appear to have believed that creating new staff for disarmament at this time was a waste of already scarce manpower. Instead, it was decided that a number of personnel from the Staff Duties Section would form the nucleus of a disarmament staff until Rankin C conditions were obtained. Colonel Grazebrook was named to undertake this task.[17]

German evasions of the terms of the Versailles Treaty and their protestations that the war had not been lost were themes repeated both in Washington and London. According to the terms of the World War I armistice, the Germans were required to evacuate German-occupied territories on the Western Front within two weeks. Any troops remaining in these areas were to be interned or taken as prisoners of war (POWs). Allied forces were to occupy the left bank of the Rhine within a month, and a neutral zone was to be established on the right bank. In terms of military equipment, the Germans were to turn over to the Allies 5,000 artillery pieces, 30,000 machine guns, 3,000 trench mortars, 2,000 aircraft, 5,000 locomotives, 150,000 railway wagons, 5,000 trucks and its entire submarine fleet. The majority of Germany's surface naval fleet was interned; the remainder was to be disbanded.[18]

A memo by a prominent German lawyer who had fled to the United States and joined the US Army, prepared for Major General John H. Hilldring, chief of the newly formed Civil Affairs Division in the War Department, and written from personal knowledge, stated that when the armistice was signed in 1918, it was signed "at Compiegne at a time when the German armies were holding in Russia, Turkey, the Balkans, Belgium and France. The German soldier did not realize he was defeated. . . . After the proclamation of the Armistice the German troops going back through France and Belgium gave the appearance of well-organized fighting units. They had observed good marching discipline, and were fully equipped with rifles, machine guns and cannons. Their flags were flying and their bands were playing."[19]

On 14 January 1944, Major General C. A. West (UK), deputy chief of staff (G-3), highlighted in a COSSAC memo the fact that there was a complete lack of UN policy to help deal with problems arising from Operation Rankin. General West specifically addressed the issue of armistice terms and disarmament, stating that there had been considerable guidance from British sources but that they dealt exclusively with long-term policy after the initial occupation of Germany. It was essential now, he wrote, that papers on all these problems be prepared with some urgency. This would allow the SCAF to lay down policy for the first ninety days following the armistice. He then outlined ten issue areas that needed addressing to include armistice terms and disarmament, and assigned both G-3 and G-4 (Logistics) divisions the responsibility for developing these papers. He also addressed both the navy and air staffs and invited them to nominate officers to work on issues of interest to them.[20]

By 25 January, the draft COSSAC disarmament paper had become a SHAEF paper and been sent to SHAEF's head planners, indicating that significant amendments from the previous meeting had been incorporated and that unless controversial points arose during the coordination process there would be no further meetings on that paper. Among the various changes incorporated was a war establishment / table of organization (WE/TO) for the disarmament mission that now included manning for separate US and British units.[21]

The paper was released under the signature of Colonel Grazebrook, then Deputy Chief Staff Duties Section (G-3). The fifteen-page paper contained four appendices and a map. Extremely detailed, it included suggested sizes and compositions for mobile missions as well as disarmament detachments to be set up in German military districts (*Wehrkreisen*), and outlined the responsibilities of SHAEF and the German commanders who were to be used to implement disarmament under Allied supervision. In April, the study, now titled *Primary Disarmament of the German Armed Forces*, was forwarded to the SHAEF chief of staff, General Walter Bedell Smith, for approval. The cover letter stated that the total personnel requirement for the necessary disarmament missions would be 272 officers and 165 enlisted men and other ranks. This study, which was the second of four such studies, was approved on 29 April 1944 and issued as PS-SHAEF (44)10.[22]

There was one aspect of this study to which the British Foreign Office objected. The offending paragraphs stated that German forces would be used to guard German arms and supply depots in liberated territories to prevent them from being raided by Allied nations. The Foreign Office suggested that Allied governments would be offended to learn that after their liberation from the Germans, German troops were being retained on their territory to do a job the Allies could do. Furthermore, the Foreign Office believed the Allies would be none too pleased that Germans were needed to protect the dumps from Allied nations. The Foreign Office expressed its hope that these paragraphs would be thoroughly reconsidered.[23]

Several days later, the Allied naval staff sent a memo to the Admiralty asking for guidance on naval objectives that still needed to be occupied

20 and on additional naval operations that were to be carried out. It suggested that naval disarmament requirements could be met by including naval representation in the disarmament missions then being prepared by SHAEF. The memo also included an enclosure with a timetable establishing when various ports were to be occupied under the present plan as well as under an accelerated, modified plan. The timetable indicated that none of the German ports could be occupied sooner than seventeen days after the armistice was signed.[24]

In early February, the War Office asked SHAEF for estimates of manpower needs for the control and disarmament commission. The War Office said that the bulk of the requested technical personnel would come at the expense of the 21st Army Group and forces in the United Kingdom that were needed for reinforcement or maintenance, and asked that requirements be kept as small as possible until the war was over.[25]

Responsibilities of the Supreme Commander

Concurrent with the planning taking place in SHAEF during 1944, questions concerning the postsurrender responsibilities of the supreme commander continued to be raised. In May, General Eisenhower received his first directive on military government in Germany. Known as CCS 551, *Directive for Military Government in Germany Prior to Defeat or Surrender*, the directive vested in him supreme legislative, executive, and judicial powers but contained nothing regarding disarmament or demilitarization.[26] The receipt of CCS 551, and its guidance for military government in those areas of Germany captured by the Allies before the war was terminated made the lack of definitive guidance regarding Eisenhower's responsibilities following Germany's surrender even more urgent. Accordingly, and shortly before planning for Operation Talisman began, two additional documents, a staff study (titled *Preparations for the Armistice and Post Hostilities Middle Period*) and a memorandum (titled *Short Term Post-Hostilities Responsibilities and Planning*), addressed the responsibilities of the supreme commander and his powers during the "middle" or "military period."[27]

The key feature of the staff study was its recommendation that the German Supreme Command of the Armed Forces (Oberkommando der Wehrmacht, or OKW) should be used to impose the will of the Allies upon a defeated Germany. Acknowledging that the EAC was still working on the Instrument of Surrender and that directives to complement the surrender document were still required from CCS, the study went on to consider the kinds of problems the supreme commander would confront during the middle period before an Allied control authority was established. These issues included control of the OKW, which was expected to remain in existence to ensure the terms of surrender were met; the disposal of enemy war matériel and captured arms; the destruction of enemy fortifications; the disbandment of the German armed forces, including their discipline, provisions, and use as labor before being demobilized; and lastly, the disposal of the German secret police, the Gestapo, and the denazification of those police forces that would be retained to impose law and order.[28]

The memorandum, written by General Bull, reflected the contents of a memo written by Colonel Grazebrook one month earlier. General Bull bemoaned the still-confused state of postwar planning and preparation and the fact that the CCS had yet to send any guidance relating to the supreme commander's responsibilities. Many different bodies, he continued, primarily in the United Kingdom, were studying the problem but there was no real coordination between them or within SHAEF, despite the great deal of planning that had been carried out by the various divisions.

Attached to Bull's memorandum was a second memorandum, designed to be sent to the CCS by Eisenhower, outlining actions that needed to be taken by SHAEF to provide Eisenhower with the necessary special staffs he would require to initiate plans for the immediate postsurrender period. Most importantly, it recommended that the SHAEF planning staff be placed at the disposal of the EAC for "consultation and exploratory work."[29] The attached memorandum recognized that it was not possible to predict when Germany would surrender but that, though the EAC was working on establishing the necessary postdefeat machinery to be set up in Germany (and Austria), it was likely the actual surrender could come about before the Allies had agreed on what to do. Therefore, the memorandum continued, it stood to reason that Eisenhower, as the supreme commander, needed to be prepared to initiate the occupation and control of Germany immediately following the cessation of hostilities, and that his responsibilities in that respect would continue for some indeterminate period.

The second memorandum also highlighted the fact that the British Chiefs of Staff had already established the Control Commission Military Staff (CCMS) and that extensive planning had been accomplished on behalf of the British Chiefs of Staff. It also recognized that the British Foreign Office and other ministries had established various working committees but that apart from the work done by military staffs of each nation in the EAC and that already done within SHAEF, General Eisenhower was unaware of any comparable posthostilities planning by either the Soviet Union or the United States.

The memorandum ended with a series of conclusions and recommendations regarding General Eisenhower's need to cope with the fact that there might not be enough time before the war ended for the EAC to complete its work or to select and train the specialist staffs he needed for the occupation. These specialist staffs needed to be assembled to fit the final British and US organization for control in Germany.

The recommendations included steps to ensure that SHAEF would have the necessary US and British personnel to implement the planning and man the executive staff, as well as sufficient authority to approve directives to these staffs and subordinate field commanders to occupy and seize administrative and political control of West Germany and disarm the German forces in Western Europe.[30] The memorandum was never sent because a cable arrived from the CCS that gave "the Supreme Commander the responsibility to act for a period after the signing of the Armistice."[31]

At approximately the same time, and for the reason outlined in Bull's memorandum, Eisenhower requested the establishment of the nucleus of an American control council to prepare for the postsurrender period. In a memo hand-carried to the JCS by General Wickersham, Eisenhower cited the existence of the British Control Council element while bemoaning the lack of any parallel US or Soviet group in the United Kingdom aside from those assigned to the EAC. He also indicated that he was not aware of any such planning staffs in either the United States or the Soviet Union.

Eisenhower related further that SHAEF had begun a great deal of posthostility planning and that American and British specialist personnel had been earmarked for training. A basic manual for military government had also been drafted based on previously received presurrender guidance. The problem, however, was the lack of top-down planning: nothing had been done to provide senior leadership for Allied control staffs, policy guidance, or key personnel. The stage had now been reached, Eisenhower continued, where the appointment of a nuclear group had become an urgent necessity. Eisenhower then recommended that immediate appointments be made for deputies to the yet-to-be-named chiefs of the control council, for a US equivalent of the British element in the Disarmament, Demobilization, and Demilitarization Group, and for key personnel in the Military Government Group.[32]

On 4 August, the JCS approved Eisenhower's requests and agreed that US personnel should be so assigned. The JCS further concurred on the appointment of a general officer to be the acting deputy to the chief US representative to the control council and named Wickersham, still the US military representative to Ambassador Winant on the EAC, to fill the position. Ten days later, the JCS authorized the assignment of 289 officers, 32 warrant officers, and 356 enlisted personnel—some of whom were to come from the European theater as well as the war and navy departments—to the US element Eisenhower had requested.[33]

What is interesting and underscores the lack of coordination between the EAC, the JCS, and SHAEF is that eight months earlier, in mid-December 1943, Major General Ray W. Barker (US), deputy chief of COSSAC, had written to Major General Hilldring to ask about the status of the plan for German disarmament following the cessation of hostilities. He reminded Hilldring that the EAC had been tasked with creating the Terms of Surrender, of which disarmament was an important element. Given the broad guidance that was expected from the EAC, Barker wrote that a number of questions—some which would have political as well as military and technical ramifications—would arise and that answers would need to be found. Barker suggested coordinating the US-British position on these issues in order to have a common position upon which to base discussions in the EAC, formulate Allied policies, and prepare operational plans to implement EAC decisions. To this end, he suggested that the United States send a cadre of knowledgeable officers, headed by an officer of "suitable background and attainment," to London to join with a similar group created by the British War Office. Barker closed by requesting that this cadre come with an agenda and firm guidance from both the War Department and the Department of State.[34]

While no record of General Hilldring's response to Barker has been found, Hilldring obviously took the opportunity to fill what appeared to be an organizational vacuum and advance the interests of his Civil Affairs Division. He drafted and forwarded to the JCS a proposal that, in effect, duplicated General Barker's suggestion to develop a cadre to deal with disarmament issues and even included several of Barker's paragraphs verbatim as justification. Hilldring's proposal stated at the outset that no agency had been designated to prepare policy recommendations for the JCS covering problems arising from this issue. Hilldring concluded that an agency was required to oversee the development of said policies for JCS approval and transmission to the US delegate on the EAC. However, instead of recommending that a cadre of qualified officers be sent to London, as Barker had suggested, Hilldring recommended that his Civil Affairs Division become that new agency, stating that the creation of a new entity, such as the proposed disarmament committee, was "unnecessary and undesirable."[35] Hilldring sent a copy of his proposal to General Wickersham in London, apparently in reply to a letter from Wickersham that addressed the same topic.[36] Based upon Eisenhower's memoranda to the CCS and the JCS, it appears that nothing became of Hilldring's proposal.

The failure to provide guidance to Eisenhower, however, remained unresolved as late as fall 1944.[37] In mid–October 1944, Grazebrook submitted a number of papers to SHAEF's deputy chief of staff outlining the need for a senior officer to be in charge of posthostilities planning, as the EAC had still failed to devise any such policies and the three Allied powers had not come to an agreement on any final policy as of that date. This vacuum meant that the supreme commander would not be afforded the luxury of guidance regarding the occupation of Germany, unless a senior officer was appointed. Grazebrook felt that a senior officer could direct a survey of all the tasks and responsibilities that would face the supreme commander to ensure that the plans, now coming to fruition in SHAEF, represented a sound policy for him to follow under any of the conditions he might face.[38]

Once Grazebrook learned that his memo had been approved, he submitted a second paper with recommendations for executing his proposal, a list of agencies with whom coordination would be essential, and the suggestion that, due to its familiarity with the issues to be confronted, his posthostilities subsection become the staff of the new senior officer or co-coordinator for planning. Grazebrook then appended a list of important papers that had been or were being prepared by SHAEF or outside agencies, as well as a list of matters that required further attention, many of which were incorporated into subsequent studies, occupation directives, and laws.[39]

This planning coordination was undertaken by the deputy chief of staff and the first meeting to coordinate plans and policies was called for 8 November 1944.[40] This initial meeting had far-reaching results in that it highlighted a number of issues that needed review, revision, or initiation, and a progress report issued a few weeks later showed that various SHAEF staffs were rapidly working to resolve these issues.[41]

An April 1944 SHAEF staff study, *Preparation for the Surrender and Post Hostilities Middle Period*, laid out the conditions and defined the responsibilities that would confront General Eisenhower upon the cessation of hostilities in Europe.[42] In terms of the need to disarm and demilitarize German forces on the continent, the study initially envisioned retaining the OKW intact in order to control the German armed forces. While SHAEF was to remain temporarily in Great Britain, it was considered important for propaganda and psychological reasons to locate US and British officers at the OKW headquarters to establish appropriate control and to transmit necessary directives from SHAEF to the German military.

Additionally, the OKW was to remain responsible for the provisioning, maintenance, and housing of the German forces under its command. The study further stated that the terms of surrender would prohibit all forms of military training and that demobilization might be delayed for a considerable time as there might be a need to use the German forces for labor, either in Germany or in the liberated countries.

In early July 1944, SHAEF notified the naval, air force, and major SHAEF staffs that a CCS message gave the supreme commander the responsibility to act for an indeterminate period of time after Germany surrendered. The addressees were told that, as a result, SHAEF now had to decide on the scope and limitations of that power. Two appendices were attached to the notice. The first was a draft that outlined the basis for planning Operation Talisman, which only covered the movement of Allied forces into the liberated countries and Germany and not what was required in order to enforce the terms of surrender. This latter issue was covered in the second appendix, *Outline of Post-Hostilities Functions*, which was meant to cover the period between the surrender of Germany and the assumption of responsibility for Germany by the Allied Control Commission (ACC).

The several objectives for the postsurrender occupation of Germany, as stated in this appendix, were derived from an EAC document of 31 May 1944 and were as follows: to complete the disarmament of Germany and destroy the German war machine, convince the German people they had suffered a total military defeat, destroy the National Socialist Party and system, and prevent German militarism and National Socialism from going underground. In addition, the objectives directed the Allies to lay the foundation for the rule of law in Germany, and to encourage individual and collective responsibility in the German population.[43]

According to this latter appendix, the documents and proclamations being drafted by the EAC lacked the detail necessary to issue the required orders to the Germans pertaining to the occupation and the German

26   Armed Forces. It was determined that SHAEF would therefore have to prepare these orders. The appendix also addressed the fact that as the disarmament of German forces was an essential prerequisite of occupation, SHAEF would also have to provide special disarmament personnel with the technical knowledge to assist in the disarmament and control of German bases and supply depots. In this vein, the outline recommended that planning be restricted only to the "immediate disposal" of surrendered war matériel and that the control of Germany's armaments industry was not considered a priority.

The appendix also addressed the issue of the control of German forces, which it considered essential. It suggested that control staffs placed at various German military headquarters would suffice and that the provision of previously trained personnel would also fall upon SHAEF but that they could be found in the several existing SHAEF headquarters and staffs.

The SHAEF staff erroneously assumed that the demobilization and disbandment of German forces would *not* take place during this period and thus should not be included in this postsurrender planning document without further instructions. As will be seen below, within six weeks of Germany's surrender, members of the German armed forces, with the exception of those cited as "war criminals," security suspects, or members of the Schutzstaffel (the infamous SS), were being disbanded and demobilized.

Lastly, to provide guidance to subordinate commanders, the appendix recommended that a postsurrender handbook be prepared to obviate the necessity of preparing and issuing innumerable additional directives.[44]

Operation Rankin/Talisman/Eclipse

The complaint that the military planners were left without policy by their governments was the most prominent complaint in papers relating to planning for the occupation. The fact that SHAEF had to undertake these coordination meetings underscores this lack of guidance, and the reports written as a result further illuminate the extremely broad and complex nature of the problems the SHAEF staff was forced to solve on their own. A clear example of this lack of guidance is voiced by Morgan in the transmittal letter to Operation Rankin, in which he addressed "the essential difficulty in planning operations before the clear establishment of the political policy whence those operations derive their necessity."[45]

When COSSAC, under the direction of General Morgan, was established following the Casablanca Conference in early 1943, it was charged with three tasks by the British Chiefs of Staff. The first and third tasks were pure combat operations: plan deceptive operations to keep German divisions in Western Europe, thereby relieving the pressure on the Soviet Union, and plan for the invasion of the continent (i.e., what became Operation Overlord).[46] Behind this directive was the idea, based on experience derived from the end of World War I, that Germany might suddenly collapse. It was also supported by naïve and wishful thinking that stemmed from recent German defeats in North Africa and Stalingrad and the planned Allied invasion of Sicily. The idea that Germany would simply "disintegrate" was voiced by Morgan. In the directive for the plan that began on 22 May 1943 and was given the code name Rankin, Morgan said that the expected German "disintegration" would not necessarily take the form of a complete collapse but could be a partial withdrawal from occupied territory or the result of an Allied breakthrough.[47]

This belief in a German disintegration was still held by Morgan in the summer of 1943 and by the Joint Intelligence Committee (JIC) following its review of the German situation, as is reflected in the Rankin plan published in August of that year:

> The general situation as it exists today must appear to the German military leaders as verging on the desperate. . . . They are now faced with a serious situation on the Russian front and with the urgent problem of stopping the breach developing in Italy and the Balkans. Their U-boat campaign has met with a serious set-back. Finally, the ever-increasing Allied air offensive, to which there is no serious likelihood of a reply being possible, must be making the planning of the production increasingly difficult and must be causing serious doubts as to how long the home front can stand up to the combined strain of Allied bombing, the blockade, and military reverses.[48]

Planning for the occupation and demilitarization of Germany was a complex matter. Planners were asked to envision the situation as it would be when the time came. Thus planners were given an "intellectual exercise of unusual difficulty," one much broader than what military planners are normally given.[49] In other words, since the plan they were asked to develop would cover the period following Germany's surrender, Germany's defeat was not the objective. Instead, the plan would have to cover a myriad of problems ranging from displaced persons and Allied

28   POWs to the disposal of captured German war matériel, the disbandment of the German Armed Forces, and the destruction of Germany's
industrial warmaking potential.[50]

Planning for Operation Rankin continued slowly despite the fact that
the first Quebec conference provided no guidance to COSSAC regarding posthostilities planning. It did, however, provide support for a continued planning effort.[51] On 23 August 1943, the plan, which contained
three scenarios that were envisioned as signaling the end of hostilities, was
approved by COSSAC. The first scenario, named Rankin Case A, simply foresaw a rapid collapse or substantial weakening of German strength
and morale, allowing Allied forces to land on the continent earlier than
planned. The second scenario, Rankin Case B, saw a German pullback
to its prewar borders, also allowing Allied forces an early entry on the
continent. Rankin Case C, the third and final contingency, foresaw an
unconditional surrender, thereby allowing an unopposed Allied entry into
Germany with a force of approximately twenty-five divisions. It was the
only case that had anything to do with the occupation of Germany and
therefore became the primary plan.[52]

Rankin Case C did not, however, consider much beyond the immediate disarmament of the German armed forces. The plan only provided
guidance for stationing troops in certain strategic areas, not all the locations that eventually came under SHAEF's purview. It did not address
what to do with German military forces once they were disarmed or
how to treat German police or paramilitary forces. Furthermore, it failed
to address how Allied forces would take up their positions with sufficient
speed to disarm the German troops before they were able to retreat into
Germany. In addition, it also failed to address the question of Germany's
military-industrial complex, due in part to the lack of comprehensive
postwar planning at the most senior levels of government.[53]

Nonetheless, with support for continued planning from the Quebec
Conference, General Morgan gave priority to Rankin Case C and a final
draft was prepared in October 1943 and issued as a planning directive to
both the British 21st and American 1st Army groups. A revision of the
plan covered occupation areas deep in Germany and included Berlin. It
also specified the involvement of US forces. There remained, however, no
additional guidance regarding the disarming of German forces. Operation
Rankin—whose target date was set for 1 January—never went into effect. Despite the great effort and time that went into its planning, Rankin
continued to be based on what proved to be false assumptions. As late as

July 1944, the senior officer of the British CCMS stated his opinion that "the German surrender probably would take place with our forces still well outside the German frontier" and that planning in the CCMS was being conducted on that basis.[54] Rankin's significance according to Mc-Creedy, however, was that it began a "process of thinking and preparing for postconflict operations that would continue through the rest of the war."[55]

This process of "thinking and preparing" was supported by General West, who underscored the importance of not waiting for policy to be laid down by the Allied powers. It was essential, he wrote in January 1944, "that [they] . . . prepare now, as a matter of urgency, papers on all these problems" (armistice terms, disarmament, and the disposal of captured war matériel among other issues).[56] Thus, as D-Day approached, there was an explosion of planning activity and as early as April 1944, two postconflict staff studies were underway and the subjects listed by General West as needing urgent attention eventually became Operation Eclipse memoranda or administrative memoranda.[57] Thinking shifted from anticipation of the sudden military collapse envisioned by Rankin to the realization that the war would only be brought to an end by military operations.

Following a directive to all chiefs in the G-3 division from General Bull, a weekly progress report covering the activities they had completed or taken under study during the previous week began to arrive. On 26 April, the posthostilities planners indicated that two papers—*Primary Disarmament of German Forces* and *Preparation for the Armistice and Post-Hostilities (Military) Period*—had been approved by the chief of staff. Another report, issued on 31 May, stated that Operation Rankin C, continental operations, had been redesignated Operation Talisman.[58]

By mid-June, Colonel Grazebrook's posthostilities subsection appeared to be fully engaged on several drafts dealing with the control and disposal of German forces, and on 9 July, planning for Operation Talisman formally began.[59] The objectives of Talisman were, inter alia, to disarm the Germans in the West to prevent a resurgence of hostilities and to occupy strategic areas on the continent to enforce the terms of surrender, which was to be accomplished in three stages. A supplement to the outline plan concluded that the supreme commander's first three responsibilities would be (1) disarming the German forces, (2) disposing of surrendered war materials in the short term, and (3) controlling the German forces through subordinate headquarters but not through the OKW.[60]

The plan encompassed a very narrow view of occupation and thus rejected responsibility for control of the German munitions industries, the

30   disposal of enemy war matériel, and the disbandment of German forces.[61]
The planning directive condensed the scope of the operation and made
several technical changes to the three stages of the operation. Additional
functions and tasks were also added, including the partial demobilization
of the German armed forces for use as labor. The directive also defined
Talisman as "plans and preparations for operations in Europe (excluding
Norway and the Channel Islands) in the event of German surrender. Operations in Europe will include the liberated countries until their indigenous governments are firmly established and in complete and independent
control, and will include Germany until it is taken over by the Tripartite
Military Government."[62]

    The Talisman outline plan was distributed as a planning directive on
13 August 1944 and had a number of significant changes, including the
assignment of responsibilities to the major commands. It also redefined
surrender as a "formal surrender signed by properly constituted German
authorities, or the capitulation of the major portion of the German forces
opposing the Allied Expeditionary Force."[63] In this latter case, the supreme
commander would designate a date, to be known as A–Day, signifying the
beginning of Talisman. Thus, the plan allowed more flexibility in that it
could be implemented not only upon Germany's official surrender, but at
the discretion of the supreme commander should a significant portion of
Germany's forces surrender. In addition, the definition of German forces
was expanded to include both paramilitary forces and the police, and a
distinction was made between primary and complete disarmament and
control of German forces.[64]

    On 16 August 1944, Lieutenant General Omar Bradley, commander
of the 12th Army Group, and Field Marshal Bernard Montgomery, commander of the 21st Army Group, were directed to initiate plans and preparations in the event of a German surrender, which was not expected
before 1 September 1944.[65] The main objectives of this operation were
to (1) completely disarm and control all German forces within SCAEF's
area of responsibility, (2) enforce the terms of surrender, and (3) establish
law and order.

    To this end, both army groups were expected to plan and execute
the operation in their AOR and to collaborate closely with one another.
Appendices to the outline plan provided the estimated number of troops
available to both commands between 1 August 1944 and 1 January 1945 as
well as the number of troops required. General Bradley was informed that
his army group would have a large surplus of forces that might be required

by the British 21st Army Group. One week later, both commanders were given drafts of the *Directive for Military Government of Germany* for their concurrence.

In early September, however, Lieutenant General Smith, SHAEF's chief of staff, sent a letter to the chiefs of staff of the commander in chief of the Allied Naval Expeditionary Forces (ANCXF), the senior air officer of the Allied Expeditionary Air Forces (AEAF), and key SHAEF staffs stating that as Allied forces would soon be entering Germany and thus facing Talisman conditions, it was essential that army groups and air forces receive early guidance. He therefore requested that the memoranda for which they were responsible be prepared for distribution as soon as possible, even if incomplete. Several days later, Colonel Grazebrook was authorized to issue several memoranda on a provisional basis.[66]

Operation Talisman planning increased the size of the force required to thirty-nine and two-thirds divisions. A revised Talisman outline plan, distributed in October 1944, delineated zones of occupation as decided on by the second Quebec conference.[67] On 30 October, the 21st Army Group notified Supreme Headquarters that a captured German document indicated that the code name Talisman was compromised, so on 11 November, the new code name Eclipse was substituted and planning continued under the new name.[68]

Eclipse was different than its predecessors in that its objectives were broadened to encompass not only the primary disarmament and control of the German forces, but paramilitary organizations and the police as well. It specified, for example, that operations in Europe included "operations in Germany until control there is taken over from the Supreme Commander by the Tripartite Military Government or by US and British Commanders" while retaining the definition of surrender from Talisman.[69] It further explained that operations would most likely take place in two phases. The first would involve advancing to secure "especially important strategic areas deep within Germany, including Berlin" and the second would, in part, involve deploying forces to secure additional strategic areas and "carry out the disarmament and disposal of enemy forces in Germany."[70]

The plan provided guidance to the several Allied army groups and air forces as to their respective responsibilities in both phases, among which were the primary disarmament and masking of enemy forces in contact with Allied forces; the flanking of the Allied axis of advance; the controlled concentration of enemy forces in areas selected by the Allies; the

32   arrest and detention of individuals on the black list; and the seizure and control of German war matériel. Eclipse accepted that it was unlikely that the Nazi regime would be overthrown by internal forces and postulated that there would be neither a collapse of the German armed forces nor unconditional surrender until Germany had suffered "a further major defeat" that would enable the Allies to penetrate the homeland. The plan briefly outlined conditions expected in Germany following its collapse and indicated that while there might be some resistance and sabotage, these instances would be isolated. The possibility of civil war, however, was not discounted.[71]

Between 28 September and 13 December 1944, progress reports indicated that a study entitled *Disposal of the German Military Caste* had been circulated to planners and that Memo 9 (army disarmament) and the *Operation 'Eclipse' Appreciation and Outline Plan* had been approved and issued. They also reported that the handbook had been approved by the chief of staff and was in publication.[72] Also in preparation was the first draft of a memo suggesting priorities for the destruction of war structures in Germany and the first draft of Eclipse Memo 17 (disbandment of the German armed forces). In addition, the final draft of Memo 10 (air force disarmament) had been approved by the planning staff. Nonetheless, and despite General Smith's request, of the total seventeen Eclipse memoranda, only ten had been issued by late January 1945.

The Eclipse Memoranda

Operation Eclipse was spelled out in the *Appreciation and Outline Plan* and in seventeen memoranda, five of which speak directly to the issues of disarming, demobilizing, and disbanding the German armed forces.[73]

Eclipse Memorandum No. 1, "Instrument of Surrender, Surrender Order and Sanctions," was issued in November 1944 but revised in April 1945. It was a lengthy, detailed memorandum that contained a short series of opening paragraphs that laid out what would take place in the event of (1) a formal surrender, with or without an EAC-agreed Instrument of Surrender (in which case special orders to the German High Command had been prepared by SHAEF and were appended to the memo as Appendix A), or (2) no formal surrender, and the sanctions that would be imposed if resistance to either form of surrender were encountered.[74]

The main elements of this memorandum were included in five additional appendices:

Appendix B: Supreme Commander Special Orders to the German
High Command (OKW) of common concern to all three services or the direct concern of OKW only.

Appendix C: Special Orders to the German High Command (OKH)
relating to Land Forces.

Appendix D: Special Orders to the German High Command
(OKM) relating to Naval Forces.

Appendix E: Special Orders to the German High Command (OKL)
relating to Air Forces.

Appendix F: Measures which may be taken to enforce the terms of
surrender or in the event of no surrender to compel the enemy
to comply with the Laws of War.

Part I of Appendix B was quite all-inclusive and held the OKW responsible for carrying out the orders of the Allied representatives and for
ensuring that the commanding officers of all units of the German armed
forces and their subordinates were notified that they would be held personally responsible for carrying out orders of the supreme commander in
their areas of responsibility. It also established timelines for when the Allies
were to be given information regarding the locations of the German High
Command and all its departments and branches, as well as the locations
of all experimental or research facilities, underground installations of all
kinds, and missile launching sites.

Part II of this appendix was devoted to the control, maintenance and
disarmament of the armed forces and made the OKW responsible for its
immediate and total disarmament. It provided initial guidance regarding
the maintenance and guarding of war matériel, specifying that none was
to be destroyed without prior orders from the Allied representatives, that
all land minefields were to be clearly marked, and that mines and obstacles
on roads, railroads, waterways, and ports were to be removed immediately.
It also ordered the removal and destruction of all booby traps, demolition
charges, and concealed explosives.[75] The remaining parts dealt with Allied
POWs and civilian internees, telecommunications, merchant shipping and
ports, and so on and contained four annexes, one of which was a list of war
matériel to be withdrawn from the Germans while a second contained a
list of war matériel to be retained.

The first parts of appendices C through E mirrored Part I of Appendix
B by requiring each individual German armed service to provide information as to their order of battle and the locations of their units, weapon

34 systems, ships, and so on within a specific period of time. Part II followed a similar pattern, specific to each particular service. For example, the naval appendix stated that all ships and submarines at sea were to report their positions and head for the nearest German or Allied port, breech blocks were to be removed from all guns, and all torpedo tubes were to be unloaded. Aircraft were to be grounded and immobilized by methods described in the air force appendix and removed from runways, and their guns were to be unloaded and bombs removed. German field and home armies' armaments were to be placed in dumps as directed by appropriate Allied representatives and various classes of war matériel (armored vehicles, artillery, small arms, ammunition, etc.) were to be laid out in stacks or parks within each dump. All other war matériel (in factories, dumps, depots, etc.) was to be maintained but remain where it was located. War matériel in transit, in the absence of orders to the contrary, would be allowed to proceed to its destination, where it would then be placed in dumps or depots.

Of the five appendices to this memorandum, only three were relevant to all German commanders, requiring them to immediately inventory all war matériel of any kind in any location within their area of responsibility. These lists were to be prepared in quadruplicate and completed within two months following the cessation of hostilities. Standardized forms were attached to the memorandum to be used for the inventory. Lastly, German authorities were responsible for handing over and delivering in good condition any war matériel that was requested by the Allies and would remain responsible until such matériel had been accepted by the Allied representatives.

Eclipse Memorandum No. 9, "Primary Disarmament of German Land Forces," Eclipse Memorandum No. 10, "Primary Disarmament of German Air Forces," and Eclipse Memorandum No. 11, "Primary Disarmament of German Naval Forces," dealt specifically with the three individual services and were, for the most part, quite similar. Memorandum No. 9 was, however, the most comprehensive of the three. It began by defining war matériel as "materiel intended for war on land, at sea, or in the air," which included:

    a.   All arms, ammunition, explosives, military equipment, stores and supplies and other implement of war of all kinds.

    b.   All naval vessels of all classes, surface and submarines, auxiliary naval craft, all merchant shipping whether afloat, under repair or construction, built or building.

   c. All aircraft of all kinds, aviation and anti-aircraft equipment and devices.

   d. All military installations and establishments including air fields, seaplane bases, ports and naval depots, storage bases, permanent and temporary land and coast fortifications, fortresses and other fortified areas, together with plans and drawings of all such fortifications, installations and establishments.[76]

It continued by outlining the objectives of primary disarmament, which were to prevent a continuance or renewal of hostilities, to safeguard the deployment of the Allied Expeditionary Force during Operation Eclipse, and thereafter to facilitate the establishment of law and order in the supreme commander's AOR.

Although this memorandum addressed the primary disarmament of German land forces, it also delineated the responsibilities of the Allied ground forces in the disarmament process by defining what made up the German land forces. Thus, the Hermann Göring Parachute Panzer Corps and German Air Force field divisions, parachute formations, and other similar Luftwaffe units attached to the German Army became an Allied ground force responsibility. Similarly, the disarmament of German naval forces ashore, Luftwaffe and naval flak organizations, and the Nazi party Flieger Korps were also determined to be Allied ground force responsibilities.

Of particular interest is the guidance given that where it was not possible to provide Allied forces to guard and control dumps containing enemy war matériel, control would be maintained by German forces under the close supervision of the Allied commander in whose AOR the enemy war matériel was located. In fact, the memorandum specified that "the fullest possible use will be made of the existing German military machine, and orders will be issued through the recognized German channels of command wherever they survive the process of occupation."[77]

In line with Eclipse Memorandum No. 1, the maintenance, classification, and inventory of enemy war matériel were made German responsibilities under strict Allied supervision. Lists of enemy war matériel that had to be surrendered and lists of matériel that would be retained so that German forces could carry out orders given to them, including limited numbers and types of weapons (e.g., rifles and pistols), were provided in two appendices.

Similarly, Eclipse Memorandum No. 10 set out plans and policies for the primary disarmament of the Luftwaffe. For this task, the memorandum specifically named the commanders of the Ninth Air Force (US) and the Second Tactical Air Force (UK). This memorandum also defined what formations, units, and personnel were included in the Luftwaffe and followed Memorandum No. 9 in allocating primary disarmament responsibility for some Luftwaffe units to Allied ground forces.

This memorandum further delegated the exercise of the air commanders' responsibilities to the US Army Air Force (USAAF) and Royal Air Force (RAF) air disarmament staffs and, given that the tactical situation on the ground did not reflect the final zones of occupation, guidance was provided regarding the coordination and operational control of the national disarmament staffs while operating in another national Allied commander's AOR (e.g., RAF units operating in Ninth Air Force areas, etc.). The memorandum also referenced Eclipse Memorandum No. 1, Administrative Memorandum No. 5, and the occupation handbook regarding the disposition of captured enemy war matériel and "common use" items.[78]

Similar to Eclipse Memorandum No. 9, the air forces' plan recognized the possibility that sufficient Allied forces personnel might not be available to guard every Luftwaffe establishment to effect direct control over war matériel. Thus, German Air Force commanders were to be held responsible to ensure Allied orders regarding such materiel and its inventory were followed.

The memorandum expected that USAAF and RAF air disarmament staffs would be in position behind advancing Allied forces and thus ensure that Luftwaffe units located within the area of advance were properly disarmed. It also specified that a "Reconnaissance Party" provided by both the US and British control councils would be sent to the Air Ministry and that other elements would go to various Luftwaffe headquarters to compel compliance with the terms of surrender, if required. Specific tasks of these units were set out in an appendix to the memorandum and two other attachments contained organizational diagrams of the respective US and RAF disarmament organizations.

The third memorandum of this group, Eclipse Memorandum No. 11 covering naval disarmament, was the briefest, at only two pages.[79] It accepted the responsibility for disarming all German warships and merchant vessels, delegating the actual exercise of that responsibility to US, British, and Allied naval officers-in-charge in the areas under their control in accordance with instructions laid out in the SHAEF *Military Occupation*

Handbook. In addition, it followed the line of responsibility for disarming naval forces ashore found in Eclipse Memorandum No. 9.

Section III of Eclipse Memorandum No. 9 addressed naval demolition and stated that the demolition of naval defenses in Germany, which included submarine pens, fortifications, and underground storages, to name a few, would most likely not take place during the supreme commander's period of responsibility. Such demolitions, it indicated, would be carried out as part of a long-term policy by the ACC.

The last key disarmament memorandum, Eclipse Memorandum No. 17, "Disbandment of German Armed Forces," was put into operation on 9 May 1945, the day after Germany surrendered.[80] This memorandum laid down the policies by which army group commanders were to carry out the disbandment of the German armed forces. Like many of the other memos, this memo began by stipulating that it was impossible to forecast conditions in Germany when the war ended. It therefore posited several assumptions upon which the plan was based, the essence of which was that Allied forces would have penetrated deep into Germany by the time hostilities ended and that those German forces not already in POW camps would have been moved into containment areas under the control of their own officers working under close Allied supervision.

Additional assumptions were that those Germans eligible for discharge would be released with as little delay as possible to avoid large-scale desertions. Furthermore, it was believed that it would take as many as six months before the occupation armies were fully deployed in their respective zones.

While various memoranda and documents dealing with the anticipated surrender maintained that the German military machine was needed to effect the terms of surrender and control the surrendered German forces, the plans of Eclipse Memorandum No. 17 were designed not to utilize German machinery in the discharge process if it could be avoided.[81] The discharge of captured and surrendered German forces would begin when directed by the supreme commander but would first be subject to the manpower needs of the Allied forces to assist in the occupation and to the manpower needs of the governments of Allied or liberated territories for purposes of reconstruction.

The remainder of the memorandum outlined very specific principles and responsibilities regarding the discharge process, including a very detailed set of statistical procedures by which members of the German armed forces were to be documented and prioritized for discharge. These

38   procedures included the transfer of personnel who had been recruited in a different zone of occupation, non-German personnel, stragglers, deserters, and members of the German National Militia (Volksturm). Part II of this memorandum dealt specifically with the discharge of members of the Waffen SS and paramilitary organizations.

Shortly after this memorandum was issued, General Barker, now assistant chief of staff (G-1, Personnel Division) for SHAEF, wrote General Morgan, SHAEF's assistant chief of staff, that the memo lacked both a "clear definition of the object to be obtained" and "practical guidance to the recipients." With regard to the first omission, General Barker wrote that he would have a paper prepared that would provide a foreword or opening statement to explain the purpose of the disbandment procedure. Regarding the second issue, Barker felt that disbandment had been more than adequately covered in the occupation handbook and that the Eclipse memo was merely an extension of the handbook.[82]

Barker's memo also stated that he did not believe SHAEF would be confronted with a shortage of guards as there were, on the US side alone, sixty divisions in the field.[83] He also felt that the surrendered German forces would not have to be heavily guarded, believing that "from the German point of view, the advantages of obeying orders . . . under this plan, exceeded the disadvantages."[84]

That said, Barker did think that the memo offered a "systematic and efficient procedure" for implementing the disbandment under any of the various conditions that might arise. Furthermore, he added, the statistical and documentation procedures had been thoroughly considered by commanders and appeared to meet the needs of the zone commanders and SHAEF. The only difficulty with the documentation issue, he concluded, was the vastness of its scope.

Despite promulgation of the *Appreciation and Outline Plan for Operation Eclipse* in November of 1944, Memorandum No. 10 (air force disarmament) had not been completed or issued as of 31 January 1945. On 1 February, Lieutenant General Morgan directed that all memoranda that had not yet been issued be completed and that those issued be revised or amended by 10 February.[85] These memoranda were subsequently completed and approved on 10 March 1945 and disseminated to the appropriate commands for action.[86] The first four months of 1945 saw accelerated progress in the development and issuance of additional Eclipse memos and directives, including memorandum nos. 10, 11, and 17, and the *Interim Directive for Occupation of Germany*.[87]

Demobilizing and Disbanding the German Armed Forces

More than a year before the final surrender of Germany, SHAEF's G-3 (Operations Division) gave a great deal of thought to the manner in which members of the German armed forces were to be demobilized. Many issues, such as what to do with non-German members of the German armed forces, where to send Germans for demobilization (particularly those who had been recruited in what was to become the Soviet zone of occupation), what demobilization papers would be needed and what form would they take, and other more mundane details, such as what pensions or gratuities would be provided and what articles of clothing and personal equipment would they be allowed to retain, all required decisions.[88]

For example, on 15 July 1944, a draft directive titled *Disposition of German Armed Forces Subsequent to Surrender* that covered all these issues and more was submitted by the planning committee of the US advisor to the EAC for consideration and for forwarding to the Department of State and the secretariat of the JCS. Among other things, the draft ordered the three Allied commanders in chief to implement the surrender terms and made them responsible for the demobilization and disbandment of German forces in their respective zones and theaters of operation, and it directed the dissolution of the OKW and the service commands at the earliest possible date, but authorized temporary retention of portions of those organizations in order to effect the controlled administration of the German armed forces during the demobilization and disbandment.

It further authorized the commanders in chief to keep and use disarmed German forces or POWs as required to accomplish tasks deemed necessary, such as the destruction of fortifications, rehabilitation projects, and safeguarding surrendered German armaments and equipment. In addition (and in line with the ultimate objective of totally demilitarizing Germany), the commanders in chief were directed to impress upon the German people the complete defeat of the German armed forces. Accordingly, demobilized German personnel would be allowed to return home with only their approved personal effects and enough money and supplies to make the journey. Under no circumstances were returnees to be allowed to return home in military formation or with bands playing or flags flying as had been the case following the armistice that ended World War I.

Other paragraphs of the draft directive dealt with the return of German units outside Germany's 31 December 1937 borders and non–German personnel in the German armed forces. Lastly, commanders in chief were cautioned to refer to as yet unwritten guidance for instructions on the

40 treatment of war criminals before disposing of German personnel or POWs.

This draft, circulated as US Directive No. 15 and EAC(45)1, underwent several amendments and changes but was never approved, so SHAEF was never provided with official guidance on this issue. On 6 December 1945, more than a year later, and months after the war had ended and long after most disarmed German forces and POWs had been demobilized, the ACC issued Control Council Directive 18, "For Disbandment and Dissolution of the German Armed Forces," which contained the same basic guidance as the US draft.[89]

In mid-1944, a key assumption of another draft study outlining the planning process for the disbandment of the German armed forces was that the bulk of these forces in the West would be outside Germany's 1937 borders. Other assumptions were that some surrendered German forces would be used for labor in the liberated areas and that some arrangement would have to be made with the USSR to transfer surrendered personnel to and from the Soviet zone. What was decided at that time, however, was that disbandment during the middle period would be solely based upon the need for labor with priority given to medical personnel, agricultural workers, and workers in certain essential industries. The draft also included details as to what articles of clothing would be issued to disbanded German armed forces members based on their rank (whether their clothing had been issued or paid for by the individual) and the availability of their own clothing. Pay, initially set at 60 Reichmarks for officers and 30 Reichmarks for other ranks, was later modified to 80 and 40 Reichmarks respectively. Food allowances were also specified in this study.[90]

On 28 November 1944, the SHAEF posthostilities planning staff produced yet another study, which essentially recommended that with the exception of certain categories of personnel, all surrendered German armed forces personnel should be discharged and sent home as soon as possible. It portrayed the elaborate and bureaucratic procedures that were being developed and the need for labor as the primary criterion delaying discharge for as long as eight months. It stated further that the large numbers of POWs, estimated at two and a half million, would exceed the Allies' ability to control.[91]

Along with discussions of the disbandment of the German armed forces and demilitarization of Germany in general that will be discussed below, the issue of what to do with German general officers, especially the German General Staff Corps, collectively known as the "military caste,"

was a major issue. On 24 September 1944, Colonel Grazebrook disseminated a staff study for comment on "The Disposal of the German Military Caste." The staff study indicated that one of the primary objects of
defeating Germany was to effect Germany's "complete demilitarization
and eradicate her traditional militarism." It continued that although plans
had been made to disarm and disband the military and destroy its warmaking potential, these plans were superficial: Germany's militaristic spirit
and military caste of highly trained, professional officers remained, and
they held not only the ability to rebuild the Wehrmacht but "the burning
desire" to do so. [92]

The study continued, explaining that although the Versailles Treaty
had forbidden the reestablishment of the great German General Staff, it
had nonetheless been resurrected in other forms. Grazebrook expressed
his fear that while the surreptitious methods used in the 1920s would most
likely not succeed in the 1940s, he was convinced that other methods
would be found unless steps were taken to prevent that from happening.
As long as qualified officers remained in Germany, they would remain a
source of danger. This danger could be prevented by the complete destruction or removal from Germany of the best brains of the military caste. [93]

Grazebrook's study mentioned that there were no organizations parallel to the General Staff Corps in either the German Navy or Air Force, nor
were there equivalents to General Staff Corps officers among the German
officer corps in general. The study specified that German generals should
not be allowed to retain any of their power or be allowed to continue
in office in any capacity. The study recommended that these officers be
detained after their surrender and permanently exiled from Germany in
order to render them "impotent." [94]

Because of the nature of the problem, which went well beyond the
supreme commander's level and was a tripartite matter, SHAEF stated that
all it could do was recommend to CCS that a long-term policy statement
be prepared. [95] A second draft of the study, apparently written on 12 November and designed to reach conclusions that would be incorporated in
an attached cable to be sent to CCS, included policies suggested by both
US and British authorities but also highlighted discrepancies between the
two. The US *Draft Directive to the Supreme Commander Regarding Military
Government of Germany Following the Cessation of Organized Resistance* that
the JCS had given the CCS for consideration stated the following: "All
General Staff Corps officers who are not taken into custody as prisoners
of war should therefore be arrested and held pending receipt of further

42   instructions as to their disposition. You will receive further instructions as to how to deal with other members of the German Officer Corps." A similar British directive submitted to the EAC made no specific mention of the German officer corps or General Staff: "You will be guided in the general disposal of forces under German Command by the following considerations: (1) All sections of the OKW, OKH, OKM, OKL and staffs which are not required for essential administrative control purposes will be detained under guard or disbanded as you may direct as early as practicable."[96]

The five-page staff study, which incorporated many of Grazebrook's earlier statements, underscored the importance of the problem by referring to the abundant historical examples of how the "German Armed Forces reduced by peace treaties to apparent impotence, reemerged in an astonishingly brief period as an effective and potentially dangerous organization."[97] Thus, the objective (the total defeat of Germany), the study continued, was to "prevent a recurrence of this disastrous cycle by effecting the *complete and permanent demilitarization* of Germany."[98]

The study then divided the military caste into three categories: generals, the General Staff Corps, and the professional officer corps. After a brief section on the generals that maintained that generals who surrendered should not be allowed to retain any vestige of authority or continue in office in any capacity, the General Staff Corps received the greatest censure. Defined as the "high priesthood of the German cult of war," the General Staff Corps was cited as "the repository of expert knowledge resulting from exhaustive study and experience, and who sought to perpetuate the teaching of von Clausewitz."[99] The study warned that unless drastic steps were taken, the General Staff Corps would plan and develop a future Wehrmacht, going even so far as to state that "the only fully successful method [of preventing the rebuilding of the General Staff Corps] would be the *extermination* of the military caste," and that if this was not acceptable, some form of permanent control over all members of the General Staff Corps was essential.[100]

The remainder of the study dealt with the need to detain these officers and when that detention should occur. It also advised that a number of German commanders and staff officers would be required to assist in the administration and disbandment of the German armed forces and that close supervision was needed. The study also cautioned that the detention of all potentially dangerous officers was needed to demonstrate Allied determination to stamp out German militarism.

A few days after the study was distributed, Chief Operations A Subsection Colonel C. R. Kutz forwarded his comments on this second staff study. He concluded that segregating or eliminating the German General Staff Corps would be, at best, a temporary expedient as long as German military writings remained. He also felt that their physical extermination would only make martyrs out of them and give General Staff Corps officers even greater prestige. Kutz recommended that a way be found to discredit them in the eyes of the German people and that after their discharge, they be kept under strict surveillance and required to report periodically to Allied authorities. He also recommended that SHAEF's Psychological Warfare Division study the measures that could be used to discredit General Staff Corps officers.

A draft cable was attached to this second staff study requesting guidance from the CCS regarding the ultimate disposition of German General Staff Corps officers and general officers "now being arrested" as none of the existing guidance provided an answer to that question. The draft cable suggested that "drastic steps" be taken and actually included the recommended "physical extinction" of these officers. If that was unacceptable, the draft continued, permanent exile or life imprisonment was to be considered. A policy decision was requested as soon as possible in order to coordinate plans and put them into action. Although this solution was not accepted in the long run, the staff study, signed by Major General E. W. D. Strong, assistant chief of staff (G–2, Intelligence Division), recommended approval.[101] Toward the end of December, however, General Morgan disapproved the several recommendations regarding this issue, stating that though it had not yet been approved, the JCS directive would provide sufficient guidance.[102]

While the final method for disposing of senior German commanders and staff officers had not been determined, guidance provided by SHAEF, which also included Eclipse Memorandum No. 7 and the *Handbook Governing Policy and Procedure for the Military Occupation of Germany*, specified that both active duty and retired General Staff Corps officers were to be arrested, not to punish them but to prevent them from making plans or preparations for future wars and to ensure that their ability to mount subversive activities against the Allies was reduced to a minimum. Additional guidance signed by the SHAEF chief of staff, Lieutenant General Walter Bedell Smith, indicated that they were to be segregated completely in special internment camps. Similarly, general officers not needed to administer and control German military personnel awaiting disbandment were to be deprived of all authority, not permitted to wear decorations or

44   other symbols of military achievement, and be sent to regular concentration areas.[103] They were not to be discharged without authorization from Supreme Headquarters.[104] British officers in particular were convinced that General Staff officers were no good and would do everything possible to retain their power, re-create the General Staff Corps, go underground, plan new wars, and so on. As late as March 1945, the 21st Army Group wanted them to be registered and placed under counterintelligence supervision after their discharge.[105]

The Disarmament School

In early 1944, while the planning for Operation Rankin C was underway and in anticipation of the need to implement those plans, Colonel Grazebrook wrote a memo outlining the need for cadres trained for the disarmament mission as well as a draft syllabus for that training.[106] Grazebrook's suggestions were seen as a good idea by most, although the question of who would ultimately be responsible for the training and where it would be given was left unanswered at that time. Regarding the several suggestions regarding syllabus topics, Colonel Grazebrook was reminded that there were still a number of officers around who had been involved in disarmament matters in the last war and that he would be well-served by having them give "a few informal talks to the cadres."[107]

A month later, on 9 May, the Civil Affairs section of the British War Office indicated that they were prepared to run a disarmament course and, if so directed by either SHAEF or CCMS, could do it with three weeks' notice.[108] After much discussion with headquarters, the European Theater of Operations, US Army (ETOUSA), and the British (to find a suitable location), the disarmament school was established in London with a staff of twenty under the direction of Lieutenant Colonel Frank Kowalski Jr.[109]

Grazebrook's memo, now SHAEF/21540/1/Ops, "Training of Disarmament Missions," proceeded on the assumption that trained disarmament cadres would be authorized before the cessation of hostilities.[110] It suggested a four-stage course of training that would include an introductory course in which students would obtain background information, a period of study covering both general and specific problems they would face, a discussion period in which to exchange ideas and formulate policies, and lastly a period in which the newly trained cadres would, in turn, train the remaining personnel of the disarmament missions and detachments. The memo further recommended that SHAEF (G-3) be responsible for the training and that it commence as soon as possible. An appendix to the memo contained a syllabus of introductory courses that contained eleven topics ranging from the background of the terms of surrender to the plan for the occupation and control of Germany, the German evasion of disarmament clauses of the Treaty of Versailles, the various military, police, paramilitary, and armaments organizations, plans for the control and disposal of German forces and surrendered war matériel, and the imposition of sanctions and reprisals.[111]

On 24 August, Grazebrook learned that General Wickersham had received a reply to a letter Grazebrook had sent him in mid-July to forward to ETOUSA regarding the provision and training of disarmament staffs required for the US zone. The reply stated that ETOUSA had assumed responsibility for training these staffs and prepared a directive ordering the theater commanders to provide the necessary personnel and proceed with training. A detailed list of the numbers, ranks, and qualifications needed by US officers for the various disarmament staffs was also attached.[112] This directive to theater commanders was sent on 27 September 1944 and expanded on 29 October 1944.

Thus, in early October 1944, the commanding general of the communications zone (ComZ) was directed to earmark US personnel for cadres for disarmament and control staffs and to conduct a training course for them.[113] The first course started on 30 October and lasted for three weeks. According to School Memorandum No. 3, the three-week course, comprising approximately 130 hours of instruction, was divided into five phases covering six subject areas: organization for disarmament and control in Germany, policy and plans, German political organization, organization of the German armed forces, German industrial organization, and German supply and communication.[114] The planned student capacity was 160 but more could be accommodated if sent by the army groups. Upon successful completion of the course, those officers attending were to be earmarked for duty with disarmament and control staffs upon cessation of hostilities. A second function of the school was to provide reference manuals to assist disarmament and control staffs in accomplishing their mission.

The first phase, "General Background Subjects," took approximately one-third of the total class time, half of which was presented during the first week and the remainder divided equally between the second and third weeks of the course. The second phase, approximately twenty hours in duration, provided technical training for the students in accordance with their branch or duty assignment and special instruction for the executives and logistics officers. This training also took place during the last

46   two weeks of instruction and included staff studies that each student had to solve on an individual basis.

Phase three consisted of lectures by British and American officers that were given throughout the course. Speakers were obtained from the armed forces division of the US Group Control Commission (US Group CC), US Strategic Air Forces in Europe, US Naval Forces in Europe, and the British CCMS. During the first course given there were a total of twenty-six lectures while the second running of the course contained sixty-five lectures.[115]

Phase four consisted of end-of-the-day "controlled" discussions in lieu of question-and-answer periods after each lecture or presentation. These discussions were led by a member of the school staff and the instructors of the previous day, and went over material presented the previous day. They were also used to underscore points made by the guest speakers.

Phase five took approximately one-fourth of the instruction time and was devoted to the development of staff studies by groups of students according to their duty assignments. It was believed that in this manner, the students would become familiar with sources of information and establish contacts with other groups with whom they would eventually need to establish working relationships.

In mid-September, staff-level discussions indicated that a second running of the disarmament course was needed. The discussions initially concerned training operations and logistics officers but they eventually expanded to include a limited number of key officers involved in the disarmament and demobilization process, some of whom would be retained and assigned to the US Group CC.[116] On 29 October, a letter was sent to the commander of ETOUSA by SHAEF's adjutant general, Brigadier General T. J. Davis, informing him of this necessity and requesting that action be taken to conduct a second course of instruction.

This second, and last, running of the course, which began on 26 November 1944, also ran for three weeks and saw a major expansion of the syllabus and a realignment of the subject matter into five key topics: organization for disarmament and demobilization in Germany, general policy and plans, disarmament and demobilization, Germany under the Nazis, and German armed forces. Air force and navy requirements were handled by their respective services and resulted in the attendance of fifteen naval and twenty air force officers.

In late December, Colonel William Whipple, chief of the SHAEF Logistics Plans Branch, wrote to SHAEF's assistant chief of staff (G-4) to inform him that the second running of the disarmament school would end on 30 December and that present plans called for it to be disbanded. Whipple continued that a study undertaken by Colonel Karl F. Hausauer, chief of the Logistics Plans Branch, Post-Hostilities Section, and the 12th Army Group's operations and logistics staffs saw a need for a third course. The 12th Army Group wanted to permanently augment their staffs with officers trained in disarming enemy armed forces and disposing of enemy war matériel, possibly train French officers of the 6th Army Group, and provide an orientation course for the 15th Army Group officers responsible for Eclipse planning and planning for the occupation of the Rhineland.[117]

However, Brigadier General R. G. Moses, assistant chief of staff (G-4) for the 12th Army Group, wrote SHAEF that he could not at that time justify diverting additional officers for training. He recommended that the present school be discontinued, with the possibility of investigating the establishment a school on the continent when the tactical situation eased (US forces were heavily engaged in the Battle of the Bulge at that time).[118]

Aftermath

Germany surrendered on 8 May 1945 (VE Day) and less than a month later, on 5 June, the ACC assumed responsibility for Germany, relieving Eisenhower of his disarmament responsibilities. At 0001 hours, 14 July 1945, SHAEF was dissolved and its US elements became part of US Forces European Theater (USFET) under Eisenhower, who became commander in chief of the US Forces of Occupation in Germany and the US representative on the ACC for Germany.[119]

The plans laid out by SHAEF and contained in the Eclipse memoranda to disarm, disband, and demobilize German forces were put into operation following VE Day. By late June, just over six million German troops had surrendered and between 15 May and 6 July, six disbandment directives were issued, giving the army groups authority to discharge both POWs and "disarmed German troops"[120] in groups according to age, sex, nationality, occupation, area of residence, and so on—except for those considered war criminals, security suspects, or certain members and ranks of the SS.[121]

Much remained to be done, especially regarding the disposal of enemy war matériel and the destruction and demilitarization of German fortifications and war industries. For the most part, however, these issues were recognized early on as long-term problems to be handled by the ACC. In February 1945, for example, Brigadier W. E. van Cutsem addressed a

48   meeting of the Standing Committee on War Materiel and suggested that it needed to differentiate between disarming Germany and preventing Germany from rearming. The disposal of Germany's war industries fell under the rearming issue, which was a long-term matter best handled at a later time when there might be a clear economic policy.[122]

Disarming the German forces was relatively easy: most simply dropped their weapons, raised their arms, and surrendered. According to a trip report written by Lieutenant Colonel A. F. S. MacKenzie, assistant G-1 in SHAEF's German Affairs Division, following his visit to the headquarters and units of the US 3rd Army, the disbandment process as directed by Eclipse Memo No. 17 was working relatively well. MacKenzie concluded that "Eclipse Memo 17, as written is essentially sound, operationally, and should be continued in effect 'as is.'" He found, however, that although 3rd Army was not complying with the spirit of Eclipse Memo 17, its operating units appeared to be and that Germans were being discharged at a rate of 25,000–30,000 per day. The report highlighted several administrative and procedural problems but stated that as of 8 June, the 3rd Army had discharged approximately 550,000 Germans.[123]

As van Cutsem stated, the remainder of the demilitarization program, which was primarily directed at preventing the remilitarization of Germany, was more involved and took longer. However, Allied forces were given little to no guidance regarding the destruction of enemy fortifications other than it was to be accomplished during the occupation period. It was not until the end of July 1945 that orders to destroy German fortifications and defensive works were issued by USFET with a completion date of 31 January 1946.

Even more remained to be done regarding the disposal of enemy war matériel, the destruction and demilitarization of German fortifications and war industries, and especially the eradication of militarism from the German psyche. The memoranda prepared for Operation Eclipse had begun that process and showed the way for its completion. By mid-1946, more than eight million prisoners had been discharged and two years later, in early 1948, the ACC reported to the Council of Foreign Ministers that the western occupation zones of Germany had been effectively disarmed and demilitarized as of mid-1947.[124] This notwithstanding, negotiations within the quadripartite commission over establishing a disarmament commission, which began in earnest in July 1946 and continued into February 1948, remained partially unresolved.[125] Ironically, while this thoroughly invasive inspection proposal to ensure that a German military potential could never be re-created was being pushed forward by the western Allies, the US Army staff was beginning to draft its first studies on rearming the western part of the soon-to-be-divided Germany.

2 The Diplomatic Path to 12 September 1950

Heinrich August Winkler wrote that the successful Allied invasions and aerial bombardments that took place during World War II brought Germany to its knees. The bombs, the expulsions, and the internal collapse changed German society far more than the first ten years of the Reich had.[1] Still, despite the advent of the Cold War and the increasing hostility of the Soviet Union, the United States (and the State Department in particular) was slow to recognize the significant transformation that had taken place among the war-weary Germans in the western zone and continued to view them with distrust.

Nonetheless, US policy toward Western Europe underwent a major alteration beginning in early 1949. It was a change that precluded the United States from returning to its prewar isolationism and pushed it, by necessity, into a deep and lasting involvement in Western Europe. It resulted, furthermore, in vigorous debates within the Department of State and between it and the Department of Defense over the direction of US–West European and West German policy. This change, in the middle of President Truman's second term, caused several senior State Department officials (including Secretary of State Acheson) to revise their long-held opposition to German rearmament, leading the United States to reverse its European policy completely and formally demand on 12 September 1950 that West Germany be armed.

Throughout this period, the "German problem" remained at the forefront of US policy deliberations regarding Western Europe. The Department of State's position regarding the possibility of German rearmament was contained in the answer to a question posed by the Foreign Assistance Correlation Committee in June 1949. When asked "What will be the relationship of Germany . . . to the problem of increasing the defensive military strength of the Western European countries?" the State Department responded thus: "The United States Government does not envisage that Germany will be in a position to undertake coopera-tive military efforts with other Western European Governments, as *we are fully committed to the complete and absolute disarmament and demilitar-ization of Germany.* She will not have military forces of her own. She will not have industrial capacity for the production of armaments."[2] In Europe, however, the question of German rearmament was on the table during the formation of the Brussels Treaty Organization in 1948 and influenced decisions regarding the duration of the occupation and the need to keep US forces in Germany. Nonetheless, the focus of the De-partment of State remained on West Germany's political and economic integration and continued disarmament.

Beginning in 1946, relations with the Soviet Union began to dete-riorate and the United States increasingly saw the Soviet Union as a real military threat to both European and US security.[3] These perceptions, for-tified by Stalin's election speech of 9 February 1946 and by George Ken-nan's "Long Telegram" two weeks later, as well as Soviet actions in Iran and toward Turkey, led, in part, to the Truman Doctrine in March 1947, the merging of the US and British zones of occupation in May, and the initia-tion of the European Recovery Program (the Marshall Plan) in June of that year.[4] This perception of the Soviet threat was voiced in mid-February 1947 by John D. Hickerson, the deputy director of the Office of European Affairs, in a memo written to his boss, H. Freeman Matthews. Hickerson wrote that Soviet actions in foreign affairs left them "no alternative other than to assume that the USSR [had] aggressive intentions." Hickerson stated further that the United States must be determined to resist that ag-gression by force of arms if necessary because "there could be no deals or arrangements" with the USSR.[5]

By early 1948, the Communist-led coup d'état in Czechoslovakia deepened the perception that the Soviet Union was bent on dominat-ing Europe.[6] Following discussions between Great Britain and the United States in which the British sought US participation in an Atlantic defense pact, the British were given to understand that they and the West European nations would first have to organize themselves. Britain's foreign secretary, Ernest Bevin, took the lead and on 17 March 1948 the Brussels Treaty was signed by the United Kingdom, France, Belgium, the Netherlands, and Luxembourg. While outwardly directed against a resurgent Germany,

52   the possibility of German participation in the pact was supported by all the signatories except France.[7] Three days later, on 20 March, the Soviet military delegation to the ACC in Berlin walked out, and on 1 April, the Soviets initiated restrictions on travel to Berlin followed in mid-June by a total blockade of the city that lasted until 12 May 1949. The blockade and resulting Berlin crisis ended any thought or desire for accommodating the Soviet Union.[8]

In early 1949, Truman transferred responsibility for German policy from the US Army to the Department of State.[9] The United States also departed from its age-old policy of nonentanglement and became a major force behind the creation of the North Atlantic Treaty Organization (NATO), joining with the five Brussels Treaty nations, Canada, Denmark, Iceland, Portugal, Italy, and Norway, in a defensive alliance designed to deter Soviet aggression but also to contain, if necessary, a resurgent and expansionist Germany.[10] The major policy of keeping Germany disarmed and demilitarized still remained front and center, but the State Department's focus shifted to ending the occupation, returning some degree of sovereignty to Western Germany, and tying it closely to the other West European states in some form of federal entity or union.[11] The unexpected outbreak of war on the Korean Peninsula on 25 June 1950, however, resulted in a major reversal of US policy, which would strain relations between the United States and its European allies, especially the French, and would lead to West German rearmament.

US Thinking on Disarmament

Memories of German troops marching home following the 1918 armistice and of the expansion of the Wehrmacht following Germany's withdrawal from the Geneva Disarmament Conference in October 1933 led to a decision that the mistakes made in the armistice agreement and Treaty of Versailles would not be repeated.[12] Even before World War II ended, it became the seemingly unalterable policy of the United States that Germany would be completely and totally disarmed and demilitarized following its surrender. This policy was made very clear on numerous occasions following the war, the last of which ironically came only weeks before Acheson presented the US demand that West Germany be armed to the foreign ministers of Great Britain and France on 12 September 1950.[13]

Perhaps the first and most definitive enunciation of US policy toward the defeated Germany came at the 1946 Council of Foreign Ministers meeting in Paris on 30 April when Secretary of State James F. Byrnes

presented the text of a draft treaty on the disarmament and demilitariza-   53
tion of Germany. In the preamble, which indirectly referred to the *Declaration Regarding the Defeat of Germany* of 5 June 1945, the four Allied Powers "declared their intention to effect the total disarmament and demobilization of Germany" and promised that this total disarmament and demilitarization would "be enforced as long as the peace and security of the world may require."[14]

The body of the draft treaty reflected and expanded upon that declaration by stating that all German forces "shall be and shall remain completely disarmed, demobilized and disbanded" and it specifically included the German General Staff Corps. The final article, Article V, specified that this proposed treaty was to remain in force for a period of twenty-five years and be renewable, if deemed necessary. It was meant to be incorporated in a future peace treaty with Germany, thereby making it the law of the land and binding Germany to it.[15]

Byrnes subsequently addressed keeping Germany disarmed and demilitarized for a generation in an address delivered in Stuttgart, Germany, on 6 September and again in a speech he gave to the American Club in Paris in October.[16] In that latter speech, he repeatedly cited the proposed draft treaty and stressed that there should be no doubt as to American foreign policy toward Germany. He emphasized the US government's firm opposition to any revival of German militarism and proposed that the occupation of Germany not end until a German government accepted the disarmament and demilitarization clauses of the Four-Power Treaty he had proposed. Byrnes then underscored the need to maintain "limited but adequate Allied armed forces" to ensure compliance, and suggested the use of Allied bombers "from France, Britain, the United States or the Soviet Union" to enforce immediate compliance should the German government fail to do so. While the United States initially proposed to continue the disarmament and demilitarization of Germany for forty years after the peace settlement, Byrnes asked only that the Allies agree to keep Germany disarmed and demilitarized for at least a generation. This, he indicated, would assuage the fears of France and the other European nations as Germany rebuilt its powerful industrial economy.[17]

Byrnes's replacement as secretary of state, retired US Army general George C. Marshall, also proposed Brynes's treaty in Moscow in 1947. Although it was rejected by the USSR on both occasions, US policy remained unchanged. This continuity is evident in the summary of the

54   February–March 1948 London Tripartite Conference, which refers to several agreements made by the Allies that the occupation of Germany and the prohibition on the German armed forces and general staff would continue for a long time. Further, it was agreed that the military governors should continue to exercise control pertaining to disarmament and demilitarization, and that a working party should be established to decide which industries should remain prohibited and set production levels for those that were no longer prohibited. The summary also stated that a military security board would be established in the western zones of Germany whose function would be to cover the entire spectrum of disarmament and demilitarization. The summary concluded that even after the occupation ended, Germany would not be allowed to become a military threat and that an inspection mechanism should be created to ensure that it remained disarmed and demilitarized.[18]

By 1947, the United States had decided it had to move forward on Germany without agreement from the USSR. The idea then developed in higher policymaking circles that Western Europe should develop a political personality of its own and that Western Germany could be integrated into that community, which might in time develop into a third force able to stand up to the Soviets without direct US involvement.[19] It was believed that so integrated, West German freedom of action would be sufficiently constrained and no longer pose a threat.[20] In discussions regarding what became the Brussels Treaty Organization and its relation to Germany, Hickerson told Lord Inverchapel that the US envisioned the creation of a European organization capable of standing up to both the United States and USSR.

President Truman and his advisors were ambivalent about the emergence of Soviet power. On the one hand, they saw a need for cooperation; on the other hand, they saw that Soviet actions could endanger US security. These officials did not fear a Soviet attack on the United States—at the time, the Soviet Union lacked both long-range strategic bombers and atomic weapons. What were causes for concern were the increase in Communist party membership in some nations of Western Europe such as France and Italy and the possible takeover of key Western industrial power centers, which would end US hopes for Western Europe's political and economic integration and the continuation of democratic forms of government.[21] Soviet actions in Berlin and Czechoslovakia led Robert Lovett, then undersecretary of state, to opine that "all the Russians [needed] to get to the Channel were shoes."[22]

Western Europe's Search for Security—The Dunkirk and Brussels Treaties

As the gulf between East and West became both wider and sharper, West Europeans began to acquire a 'European' consciousness.[23] What was initially a political struggle, however, increasingly came to be seen in military terms. The military situation in Europe by this time was not what it had been at war's end.[24] Several proposals and discussions between Europe's leading statesmen had taken place during the war concerning Europe's future and the possibilities of some form of Western European Union (WEU).[25] One of the key topics was how to contain a resurgent Germany in the future and the 1947 Franco-British Dunkirk Treaty was an attempt to do just that.

Among the studies and proposals regarding Europe's postwar future was a study by Sir Nigel Ronald, an undersecretary in the Foreign Office, written in 1945. Ronald suggested that a Franco-British alliance, to include Belgium, the Netherlands, Luxembourg, Denmark, Norway, and Spain, would be the keystone of a European defense system. He believed this system would both contain Germany and protect the smaller Allies from falling under Soviet influence.[26] The British Foreign Office was skeptical because it felt that without US assistance, defense against the Soviet Union was unrealistic. Alfred Duff Cooper, British ambassador to France, however, contended that US interference would prevent the United Kingdom from achieving a position of equality between the two new superpowers. A federation of western European seaboard states plus the major Mediterranean powers could become "an alliance so mighty that no power on earth would ... dare to challenge it."[27]

The Anglo-French alliance idea was not followed up, however. Churchill did not believe that France—or any other West European country—would be of value to British security. Current Franco-British relations, moreover, were less than ideal. French and British troops had narrowly avoided a clash in Syria, and Charles DeGaulle, chairman of the provisional government of France, incensed over his wartime treatment by the Allies, was demanding the resolution of several Franco-German border disputes before discussions about an alliance could take place.[28]

The 1946 election of a Socialist caretaker government in France under Léon Blum allowed much Franco-British hostility to be put aside and on New Year's Day 1946, Blum wrote Foreign Minister Bevin that he was willing to sign a Franco-British treaty. The problems that exercised DeGaulle remained, but Blum assured Bevin that they would not present a barrier. Accordingly, negotiations on a fifty-year treaty began that month.[29]

56   When this treaty, the Dunkirk Treaty, was signed on 4 March 1947, it became the first specifically European postwar security arrangement. Although designed specifically to prevent the reoccurrence of German aggression, it also became the first of several attempts to develop both an Anglo–Western European defense group and a North Atlantic security system.[30]

The collapse of the London foreign ministers meeting in December 1947 gave Bevin the necessary incentive to launch his plans for a western union. The London conference broke down over the question of reparations and the Allied refusal to acquiesce to Soviet demands. It was the last attempt to obtain a major East-West agreement on Germany.[31] On 17 December, Bevin spoke in turn to French foreign minister Georges Bidault, Secretary of State George Marshall, and Norman Robertson, the Canadian high commissioner in London. The gist of these conversations was that the time had come to create "some sort of federation" in Western Europe.[32]

The first step toward such an arrangement would involve Britain and France signing bilateral treaties—modeled after the Dunkirk Treaty—with Belgium, Luxembourg, and the Netherlands. Bevin publicly outlined his plan in a speech to the House of Commons on 22 January 1948, saying that Britain could no longer stand outside Europe nor could it "be diverted, by threats, propaganda, or fifth column methods, from [its] aim of uniting by trade, social, cultural and all other contacts those nations of Europe...who [were] ready and able to cooperate."[33]

Bevin was also clearly attempting to get the United States to commit to the defense of Europe. Without an American security guarantee, the British were not sure they could make the Western Union work. Until the union was successful, however, the United States would not discuss participation.[34]

The Benelux countries also put pressure on the United Kingdom.[35] They did not like the Dunkirk model because they believed it was directed solely against Germany and did not reflect current realities. This view was strongly advocated by Paul-Henri Spaak, the Belgian foreign minister, who also urged that the collective arrangement be economic, cultural, and social as well as military.[36] Paris, however, held to the Dunkirk model because of French sensitivity concerning Germany. Any pact directed against the Soviets that did not deal with the possibility of a rearmed Germany was unacceptable to France, a view Britain also shared.[37] In fact, France had previously approached the United States and asked, in light of the fact that the treaty on German demilitarization was dead, whether the United States would be interested in entering a three-power treaty that contained similar stipulations.[38]

On 24 February 1948, a Soviet-backed coup d'état toppled the Beneš government in Czechoslovakia. This event sent a shiver of fear throughout Western European governments, magnified by the weakened state of the almost totally demobilized Allied forces. The coup prompted France to take a much broader view of European security and Britain now also accepted the need for a multilateral pact. Bevin was convinced that the Soviet Union was preparing to extend its grip over the rest of Europe; there were fears of a coup in Italy and the Soviets were pressuring Finland and Norway to sign treaties of friendship and mutual assistance.[39] As a result, on 4 March, negotiations between Great Britain, France, Belgium, the Netherlands, and Luxembourg began in earnest and on 17 March, in an atmosphere of pessimism and crisis, the Brussels Treaty was signed.[40]

The Brussels Treaty Organization (BTO) was more than a response to the apparent Soviet threat. It contained a consultative council, a permanent commission, and a permanent military committee comprised of the five defense ministers, meeting as the Western Union Military Committee. It was envisioned by Bevin as a basis for the organization of all of Western Europe, and as a vehicle to convince the United States that Europe could stand on its own. The immediate US response was a speech by President Truman supporting the new European organization as well as a request to Congress to complete its action on the Marshall Plan. Unknown to the Europeans, however, studies were initiated within both the Department of Defense and the National Security Council to determine how best to support the Western Union, including whether to associate with it at all (see chapter 3, this book).[41]

The French government, however, remained unsatisfied with the US response to the Brussels Pact. In May, France's ambassador to the United States, Henri Bonnet, told Theodore Achilles of the State Department's Bureau of European Affairs that Europe was disappointed that the United States had not acted faster in support of the Brussels Treaty. Achilles said that the United States had made it abundantly clear that the Brussels Treaty countries needed to first formulate and carry out their own plans for an integrated defense before asking the United States for help. Bonnet's response was that United States needed to understand the "French psychological difficulties" and need for reassurance on security in general. Achilles replied that France needed to understand US psychology as well,

58 and gave the following US response to the Europeans: "You made a start, but it's still a small start. Put some military 'bones' on that Treaty, preferably some collective ones."[42]

The existence of the BTO as a viable, independent entity was short-lived, however.[43] Concerned by events in Czechoslovakia and the Berlin Blockade, which followed in June 1948, the five Brussels Treaty members joined the United States, Canada, and five other West European nations (Norway, Denmark, Iceland, Portugal, and Italy) to sign the Washington Treaty on 4 April 1949, creating NATO. Two defense organizations—one spanning the Atlantic and the other containing the germ of a future integrated Europe—now existed in Western Europe where a year earlier there had been none.

Beginning in Truman's second term as president, US foreign policy fell into the hands of a small group of individuals, later known collectively as the wise men.[44] Two of them, Acheson and John J. McCloy, the US high commissioner for Germany, played extremely important roles. A third, lesser-known individual, Henry A. Byroade, a US Army colonel on loan to the Department of State as the director of the Office of German Affairs, was just as instrumental to developing the State Department's German policy during this very volatile period. The fact that Byroade, as an army officer, could discuss key German issues informally with Pentagon staff officers during a period when Secretary of Defense Louis Johnson, a foe of Acheson's, forbade Joint Chief of Staff (JCS) staffers to speak to the State Department without his express permission, proved to be of crucial importance.[45]

Published State Department Policy Planning Staff (PPS) papers shed little additional light on State Department thinking about German rearmament and those that do appear to duplicate thoughts in JCS documents.[46] For example, in March 1948, the PPS recommended that the Western Union should be encouraged to "include eventually ... Germany ... and to deepen its cooperation in all aspects foreseen in its charter ... as well as military." Both George F. Kennan, then head of the PPS, and Hickerson opposed the focus on Germany, conceding, however, that it must eventually "have its place" in that union. Both felt that the union should become more than just a defensive entity, at which point there would be no question of US support.[47]

In June of that year, another PPS paper concluded that the United States should undertake the Washington Conversations (prelude to the NATO treaty) as requested by Bevin and Bidault (then foreign minister).

It was also noted that the Department of State should explore with the
Western Union the problem of increasing the security of several European countries through integration or some form of association with the
BTO, to include a recommendation that "when circumstances permitted,"
the adherence of Germany (or the western zones) be explored. France's
minister in Washington, Armand Bérard, had cautioned earlier in February, however, that his government believed that any German participation
in European security measures meant the reestablishment of a German
army, which his government would not favor unless the British were full
participants.[48]

During this same period, Bevin had conveyed his thoughts to the
State Department on an Atlantic defense system and the future inclusion of Germany "without whom no Western system can be complete."
In State Department discussions with or about the Western Union, the
issue of Western Germany often arose, but the State Department's position remained constant: Germany's participation in Europe's defense was
premature. In addition, the United States remained adamant that it could
not and would not offer any security guarantees.[49]

Rumors of Remilitarization

Throughout 1948, the Department of State and its ambassadors in Western Europe reiterated that the fundamental US policy objective toward
Germany was "to insure that Germany [did] not again menace the peace
of the world and [that it made] a vital contribution to the economic rehabilitation and political security of Europe." Specifically, "disarmament,
demilitarization and reduction and lasting control over Germany's capacity to make war, including security against renewed German or other aggression" were some of the several major US policies that would be sought
through a closer US–West European association.[50] On 31 December 1948,
an article in the *New York Herald Tribune* by Marguerite Higgens stated
that the United States, Britain, and France had appointed a "three-man
Military Security Board which [would] send inspection teams throughout
West Germany to insure continued disarmament." The three appointees
were Major General James P. Hodges (US), Major General Victor J. E.
Westropp (UK), and General Etienne Paskiewicz (France).[51]

US-Soviet and US–West European diplomatic encounters in this period, however, raised press speculation about German rearmament. For
example, on 21 February 1948, a *New York Times* article reported that the
French foreign ministry learned the United States had dropped the Byrnes

60   treaty objective of keeping Germany disarmed for forty years. The article stated further that an assumption being "freely discussed in some quarters" was that the Soviets would "enlist German rearmament in its service," leading to the idea that the United States had better not remain committed "to keeping Germany down in the matter of armaments."[52] Although rumors continued, the topic of German rearmament dropped from the American public's view for the most part until late 1949 when it picked up again following the formation of the FRG.

Toward the end of 1948, the consulates in Frankfurt, Stuttgart, and Bremen were reporting on additional rumors and active discussions among West Germans regarding plans to remilitarize Germany. In November, a report from the consulate in Bremen mentioned that rumors pertaining to the creation of a strong police force as the nucleus for a future Germany army had begun to circulate.[53] In December, the consulates in Frankfurt and Stuttgart were reporting on statements made by (former Nazi) Lieutenant General Franz Halder, who had been until 1942 the Wehrmacht's chief of general staff, Dr. Rudolph Vogel, a member of the Land Executive Committee of the Christian Democratic Union (CDU), and Eugen Kogon, publisher of the *Frankfurter Heft* and a prominent person in Württemberg-Baden, calling for the rearmament of West Germany. Dr. Vogel's articles, several of which appeared in the *Schwäbische Post*, were allegedly inspired by a 24 October article written by Walter Lippman in the *New York Herald Tribune*.[54]

In essence, the German discussions were in favor of a voluntary German contribution to an Allied force in the event of an East German or Soviet attack. These rumors and discussions were abetted by rumors stemming from Moscow and East Berlin that the British were not only recruiting Germans and putting them in British uniforms, but that they were forming German artillery, cavalry, and engineer units as well as establishing special flying and armored schools. While these discussions appear to have run their course by January 1949, one effect was to force the West German political parties to take positions on this issue, which they did by rejecting it.[55]

As 1949 unfolded, the issue of arming West Germany remained unsettled, particularly in France. On 3 January, for example, Bérard was given instructions from Paris to query the State Department about information the French had received that the United States was contemplating the establishment of a German Army. The French government, he was told to say, would view such a step with "extreme seriousness." Samuel Reber

of the European Division replied that the position of the US government
regarding the demilitarization and disarmament of Germany, which had
been set forth repeatedly, had not changed, nor was there any intention to
change that policy.[56]

Then, in mid-January, Secretary of the Army Kenneth Royall wrote
President Truman strongly recommending that all nonmilitary functions of
the occupation be taken over by the Department of State and that a high
commissioner for Germany be appointed. This shift had originally been
proposed in early 1948 but the Berlin Blockade and fears what it might
lead to found everyone in agreement that the army should continue its total
control of West Germany. Royall went on to say that the problems now
being confronted in the administration of Germany were primarily political
and economic and, as a result, problems that arose between the army and
the Department of State were often difficult to reconcile.[57] Subsequent interdepartmental correspondence within the State Department on the role
of the high commissioner recommended that its responsibilities be taken on
simultaneously with the establishment of the new West German government. Former World War II assistant secretary of war and president of the
World Bank John J. McCloy was first put forward as the appointee for high
commissioner in this correspondence, and the suggestion was made that the
office of high commissioner be occupied no earlier than 1 July.[58]

Two months later, in March 1949, the Department of State undertook
a review of its Germany policy and reaffirmed that the primary interest
of the United States with respect to Germany was to guard against any
renewal of German aggression. Regardless of what form Germany would
take in the foreseeable future—divided or whole—an essential element
of US \policy had to be security. It was therefore in the interest of the
United States "to prevent the Germans, or any part of them, from developing military forces until any security threat inherent in them is obviated
by European union or other collective safeguards against aggression." The
review stated further that the United States would look with favor upon
the creation of such a union but that it could only assist in whatever initiative the Europeans themselves took. This latter statement was significant
because it reflected the core of what would become Chancellor Konrad
Adenauer's key policy issue (i.e., that the inclusion of West Germany in
such an undertaking must be as an equal).[59]

A major problem at that time, however, was that despite the desire to integrate Germany into Europe, there was no body—no European union—within which Germany could be integrated. As one State

Department official put it, "Plainly, Germany cannot be fitted into the European community in a satisfactory manner until there is an adequate framework of general European union into which Germany can be absorbed. The other countries cannot be expected to cope with the problem of Germany until there is a closer relationship among them than the existing one."[60]

That same month, however, a policy paper written by Kennan indicated that there was still considerable belief among US policy elites that even the advent of a West German government would not solve the "problem of Germany." The new West German government, the paper stated, would become "the spokesman of a resentful and defiant nationalism," and the "dominant force in Germany [would] become one not oriented to the integration of Germany into Europe but the re-emergence of that unilateral German strength which has proven so impossible for Western Europe to digest in the past. A Western German government will thus be neither friendly nor frank nor trustworthy from the standpoint of the western occupiers."[61] For his part, Kennan only wanted a provisional German administration, leaving the ultimate authority over security and other matters in the hands of the three high commissioners. The US ambassador to the United Kingdom, Lewis Douglas, appears to have believed, like Kennan, that once a West German government was established, US freedom of action would be gone.[62]

Thus, by 1949, the United States was forced to recognize that until a decision was made on Germany it would be necessary, both for its own and Germany's security, to maintain occupation forces in the West German zones until the peace of Europe was secured. The Department of State, however, recognized that as the German people, or a large part of them, might become part of a structure of free European nations, their contribution to the armed security would be a rational expectation. This was further emphasized on the eve of the signing of the NATO treaty during a meeting between Truman, the secretaries of state and defense, and the foreign ministers of the NATO nations.

The purpose of this meeting was to outline a policy toward both Germany and the USSR that would focus on orienting Germany to the West by encouraging economic revival, accelerating the development of democratic institutions, and combating Soviet subversion. The United States had come to believe that the earlier proposals for the disarmament and demilitarization of Germany, such as those first enunciated by former Secretary of State Byrnes and then by his successor, Marshall, no longer

corresponded to the current situation. Other means to provide security
against a revival of German aggression had to be found. Therefore, this
policy did not plan for the continued enforcement of security controls
(e.g., prohibition of key industries or armed forces). The overall goal was
to make Germany a full-fledged partner in an increasingly unified Western Europe and combine "any future German armed forces into a unified
Western defense."[63]

Two momentous events took place in 1949 that changed the face of
European security. The first took place on 4 April when the United States
ended 162 years of steering clear "of permanent alliances with any portion
of the foreign world"[64] by signing the North Atlantic Treaty along with
eleven West European nations and Canada, committing itself to participating in the security of Western Europe.[65] The second event took place
on 23 May when the three merged zones of occupied West Germany
became the FRG, albeit with limited sovereignty. Although military government ended and the military governors were replaced with civilian
high commissioners, the occupation status remained and certain powers
were reserved by the Allies. Chief among them was to guarantee security
against a revival of German military power and to ensure that all agreed
disarmament and demilitarization measures remained in force. To this end,
the Military Security Board was created.[66]

These events, particularly the US entry into NATO, caused the State
Department to again reiterate its position on Germany and to dissemble
somewhat regarding the stationing of US troops in Europe. During Senate
hearings on the NATO Treaty, Secretary of State Acheson was asked by
Senator Bourke Hickenlooper (R–IA) whether Article 3 of the NATO
Treaty meant that the United States would be expected to send "substantial numbers of troops" to Europe as a "more or less permanent contribution." Acheson replied by saying that the answer was "a clear and absolute
'No.'" While Acheson had not intended to deceive—he subsequently recognized his answer was "deplorably wrong"—it was clear that the United
States had committed itself to a permanent presence in Europe, and although the troop numbers at the time were relatively small, they were to
increase rapidly over the next several years.[67]

According to a joint Department of State and Department of Army
memorandum to the president on German policy, the United States,
France, and the United Kingdom were involved in a process of enabling
West Germany to participate in the West European economic program
and become self-supporting. Germany's economic and industrial potential,

64 however, led the United States to recognize that were Germany to be taken over by a hostile power for purposes of aggression, it would pose a danger to the security of the United States and Germany's neighbors.

The memorandum concluded that the economic and industrial recovery of West Germany and its neighbors, which included a "satisfactory military posture" in those nations, would diminish the possibility of aggression throughout all of Europe, including Germany. Nonetheless, security considerations had to be taken into account and for that reason, the United States recommitted its occupation forces until the peace of Europe was established.[68]

In this same memorandum, the United States further recognized that as Germany became firmly embedded in a free European structure, a German military contribution to the security of that structure would be possible, but only if the other free nations of Europe deemed it necessary. That said, in talking points prepared for Acheson, dated 17 May 1949, just six days before West Germany became the FRG, Acheson was advised to reply to questions regarding German entry into NATO with the following: "No consideration has been given to the inclusion of Western Germany for a number of reasons. These include the fact that Western Germany is under the military occupation of several North Atlantic countries, that it has no government, that all Germany will presumably one day be reunited, and that the German people have yet to prove their attachment to the principles of the North Atlantic Treaty."[69]

One month later, on 21 June, the Foreign Assistance Correlation Committee was told that although US policy was fully committed to the complete and absolute disarmament and demilitarization of Germany, "Germany [was and could] to an increasing extent contribute to the general economic strength of the Western European Countries, which is the essential foundation of military strength."[70] This answer allowed Germany to export matériel that could be used by other countries for the production of armaments.

The birth of NATO and the Federal Republic inevitably led to discussions about the role West Germany would play in the defense of Western Europe. For example, in July, the US Embassy in The Hague reported on the contents of a memo presented to the Consultative Council of the Brussels Treaty Powers at Luxembourg by Netherlands foreign minister Dirk Stikker. Stikker's memo essentially stated that West Germany should be integrated as closely as possible but warned that such integration carried a risk. If allowed to remain independent, the FRG could turn to the East and upset the existing balance; therefore Stikker concluded that the

occupation needed to continue until Western Europe was stronger than 65
at present, both politically and militarily, that the FRG was not to have an
armed force, and that it would not be allowed to manufacture war matériel. Many council members believed that West Germany should be at least
an associate member (because of its lack of full sovereignty) but in the end,
no action was taken.[71]

On 10 October, an office memorandum was sent to Assistant Secretary of State for European Affairs George W. Perkins in which the author,
Wayne G. Jackson, a State Department officer, wrote that he had learned
from an unnamed individual who would be speaking with the president
on 11 October that US military authorities in Germany were in favor
of the "prompt rearmament of Germany," and that twenty-five divisions
was the goal. This individual understood further that the Department of
Defense, specifically Army Chief of Staff J. Lawton Collins, was in favor of
arming the Germans.[72]

Perkins subsequently wrote Acheson a memorandum the following
day stating that these rumors of German rearmament were "much exaggerated and substantially without foundation." Perkins went on to write
that it was "true that Pentagon thinking [envisaged] use of German manpower in the defense of Western Europe at some time in the future." It
was not true, however, that the prompt rearmament of Germany, the raising of twenty-five divisions, or the inclusion of Germany in either the
Military Assistance Program (MAP) or NATO was being considered or
favored. Perkins concluded, "We have no reason whatever to believe, and
compelling reasons not to believe, that the military are acting in anyway in
this field without our knowledge."[73] Nonetheless, high-ranking military
officers were, in fact, making statements that led many to believe that the
United States favored German rearmament of some type.[74]

Many newspaper articles and editorials, both in the United States and
Europe, dealt with this issue throughout the remainder of the year. The
gist of these articles was simply that even with NATO, there was a significant force imbalance between the military forces of the Allies and those
of the Soviet Union. Furthermore, with French troops fighting in Indochina and the belief that US occupation forces would be unable to hold
off a Soviet attack until additional forces from the West were able to join
the battle, the rearming of West Germany seemed inevitable.[75] Adenauer
also expressed growing concern about the creation of paramilitary police
forces in the Soviet zone, the so-called kasernierte Bereitschaftspolizei (the
"barracked" riot or readiness police).[76]

Despite denials by Perkins, Schuman, and Acheson of any interest in rearming Germany, a cable from Paris reveals that French deputies continued to speculate about German rearmament and felt that is was coming "nearer and nearer."[77] Schuman's denial came in the form of a statement made by him before the French National Assembly on 24 November in which he said that it was a "a strange paradox" that despite confirmation by the Allies that the demilitarization of Germany would be completed, the idea of a rearmed Germany had "been able to spring up and persist in spite of the denials and in spite of all that is being done to the contrary." Schuman concluded with a pledge, apparently given to him by Adenauer: "The Federal Government asserts its firm determination to maintain the demilitarization of the federal territory and to endeavor, by all means in its power, to prevent the reconstitution of armed forces of any nature whatsoever. To this effect the Federal Government will cooperate fully with the High commission and in the activity of the Military Security Board."[78]

The US position was further muddled by Secretary of Defense Johnson and JCS Chairman Bradley, who, upon arriving in France for a NATO Defense Ministers meeting and despite initially emphasizing that the US had no intention of ever rearming Germany and that there was no hedging or dodging about the American position on that point, subsequently stated that German rearmament was not favored "at this time."[79]

In November, Acheson went to Europe himself and met with Adenauer, then the new West German chancellor. During his discussions with Adenauer on 13 November, Acheson told him that from his talks in Paris, he felt that French public opinion was ready for cooperation with West Germany and that France's premier, Robert Schuman, had the full backing of his cabinet regarding policy on Germany. As the discussion moved to the legal problems of ending the state of war with Germany, Adenauer stated that "[the German government] had no interest in the rearmament of the German nation . . . . It was just too dangerous to provide Germany with arms at this stage."[80]

Several days later, Acheson was asked whether Adenauer had addressed the establishment of a small German army of five divisions as reported in the New York Times. The president was asked the same question at a press conference the following day. Both Acheson and President Truman emphatically denied that report, calling it one of several rumors on this issue.[81]

Some members of Congress, however, appear to have felt differently. While in Berlin in late November, a four-man congressional study mission of the House Foreign Affairs Committee, led by Representative Joseph

Pfeiffer (D-NY) and including representatives Jacob K. Javits (R-NY), 67
Thomas S. Gordon (D-IL), and Clement J. Zablocki (D-WI), stated that
they would recommend including West Germany in the Western Union.
The group also advised against the early withdrawal of occupation forces,
and Pfeiffer said that he was in favor of eventual German rearmament but
within the context of a United States of Europe. Of the four representatives, only Javits stated his opposition to German rearmament "under
any circumstances." On their return, Javits said the mission's report would
"condemn rearmament whether of German soldiers to be used under
German or Allied command."[82]

In this atmosphere of ambiguity, speculation continued, and on 1 December, the French ambassador Henri Bonnet met with Acheson to state
that the "persistent rumors" of German rearmament were upsetting public
opinion in Europe and particularly in France. They were, he continued,
interfering with the main task of integrating Germany into the European
scene, as rearmament was not part of that integration. Acheson replied that
the State Department would continue to do everything it could to stop
the rumors. Several days later, the State Department transmitted a cable to
certain American diplomatic officers telling them to respond to any possible queries regarding the November foreign ministers meeting in Paris
that there were "no rpt no agreements, discussions or conversations of any
kind re: authorization Ger armed forces or any modification existing disarmament and demilitarization agreements and regs pertaining to Ger."[83]

Two days later, on 3 December, Adenauer gave an interview to John P.
Leacacos of the *Cleveland Plain Dealer* that, according to Adenauer's autobiography, was garbled when it appeared in the United States and caused
"great excitement in the world press."[84] In the interview, Adenauer reiterated his opposition to rearmament and stated that the presence of the
occupying powers put the FRG under the protection of NATO: "Since
the western powers have disarmed Germany, it is their duty by morals
and under international law to care for the security of Germany."[85] When
asked about a German contribution to the defense of Western Europe,
Adenauer responded first that the government would not allow the recruitment of Germans into other military services as that would be the
same as "buying a people to have mercenaries."[86] He then opened Pan-
dora's box when he told Leacacos that "Germany should contribute to the
defense of Europe in a European Army under command of higher European headquarters at which time it will not only be urgent but necessary
for the United States military aid program to be extended to Germany."[87]

68   More interesting is what Adenauer said off the record. According to Leacacos, Adenauer then said that the Germans were the only people who could stop the Russians. "However," Adenauer continued, "with the passage of time, the trained soldiers from general to private are forgetting their military skills. Therefore, if the Allies wait too long before they begin training a German army, it may be too late to be of immediate use to defend Germany against Russia."[88]

On 8 December, Adenauer had a discussion with the three high commissioners in which he stated that his recent statements regarding German rearmament were made to allay fears in Germany that were caused by a number of issues. The recent NATO meeting in Paris, he said, had given no information on how Germany might be defended in the case of Russian aggression. Press rumors indicated that two alternatives had been discussed: a European defense on the Rhine and a defense on the Elbe. In addition, Adenauer said that he had evidence that an army was being created in East Germany and that it was no longer possible to believe that these troops were mere police formations.[89]

The Allies, Adenauer said, were duty bound to maintain the security of the Federal Republic. He believed that any defense on the Rhine was a hollow phrase, as Germany was living under a serious permanent threat, and that unless the Soviet Union was stopped where it was, Western Europe would be finished. Adenauer then asked that the western Allies make a declaration to the effect that West German territory would be defended against an attack and that his views be reported to their governments, which was agreed. It was further agreed that all should refrain from public statements on this issue; it was a matter for "no comment."[90]

Adenauer agreed but stated that these remarks should be directed to the press, as they were the chief cause of the trouble. Nonetheless, two days later, on 10 December, the *Washington Post* reported that in his fourth statement in a week, Adenauer "virtually demanded" that German armed forces be included in any West European army. The *Washington Post* article relayed that while he was mindful of the memories of those countries invaded by Germany twice in the past twenty-five years, Adenauer asked them to consider "which is the greater danger—the Russian threat to the Western world or a German military contingent to operate with forces of the other Western nations?" Adenauer also held that "the Germans should be represented in a European striking force with rights similar to those granted other European nations." This time, however, Adenauer did not include the phrase "if the Allies insist."[91]

As 1949 came to a close the issue of German rearmament was what
Hansen Baldwin called "one of the 'hottest issues' in a world-wide cata-
log of hot issues."[92] The State Department was well aware that NATO's
military leaders had decided that a realistic defense of Europe needed a
significant increase in the number of available forces (i.e., the addition
of West German troops). It was not that the Department of State was unequivocally against arming the Germans, but rather that the department
believed that arming West Germany would have significant domestic and
foreign political repercussions that could undermine the entire structure
of Western defense and the reconciliation process that was US Department of State policy. There was also the fear that arming Western Germany
would end any hopes of reuniting the two Germanys.

Additionally, Acheson seriously believed that the key to integration
was in French hands, that only France could take decisive leadership in
integrating West Germany into Western Europe. This led to the US policy
that France should play the key role in European integration, that France
needed to first be built up and stabilized, and that France should be allowed
to determine the speed of Germany's integration into the West. This policy set the stage for the United States' abdication of leadership. It relegated
the United States to the sidelines and to the role of onlooker when arming
the Federal Republic became a reality. The French government, however,
remained "absolutely" opposed to German participation in NATO.[93] To
the Department of State, these and other factors outweighed any military
advantages that might accrue as the result of remilitarization, thus they
continued to deflect and even misinform somewhat on this issue.[94]

In what appears to have sealed the Department of State's position
on German rearmament, the three high commissioners sitting in council
on 15 and 16 December approved and signed a law on the elimination
of militarism that replaced the obsolete provisions of the ACC and the
Office of the Military Government, United States (OMGUS). The new
law provided a single text that prohibited the "teaching of principles and
theory of war and related activities; manufacture, possession, and distribution of articles and devices which may be used for militaristic activities,
unless authorized by the Council" as well as "organizations of a military
or Nazi character."[95]

1950: Year of Crisis, Year of Decision

1950 was the year that the state and defense departments finally agreed in
principle on the basic issue of arming the Federal Republic of Germany.[96]

70   It was also the year that the United States was confronted with the unexpected invasion of South Korea by North Korea. Seen in many quarters as the prelude to war in Europe, the Korean conflict left the Europeans fearful that the United States would overreact to the Communist provocation. They also saw the similarities between the situation in Korea and that in Western Europe.[97] Despite the attack in Korea, State Department policymakers maintained their focus on Western Europe but fought a losing battle against German rearmament.

Perhaps partially because of Adenauer's December 1949 interview in the *Cleveland Plain Dealer*, controversial press statements, rumors, and press reports about possible German rearmament continued into the New Year. In mid-January, for example, Drew Middleton reported in the *New York Times* that Adenauer was being advised by a group of German generals that in the event of rearmament, Germany would need one German infantry division by June 1950 and an additional German armored corps by 1951.[98]

On 20 January, the US deputy high commissioner, General George P. Hays, sent a cable to Acheson containing a statement by High Commissioner McCloy regarding a story in the *New York Herald Tribune*. The story,, attributed to a spokesman for the West German chancellor, alleged that former German generals had been asked by the Allies for their recommendations regarding the defense of West Germany. The story, according to McCloy, was without foundation and distorted facts all out of proportion. There had been no requests from any American authorities to former Wehrmacht generals, nor had there been any change in the oft-repeated government policy that Germany would not be allowed to re-create armed forces or rearm.[99]

The following month, Averell Harriman wrote Acheson following a luncheon with Winston Churchill of Churchill's stated belief that "we [the Allies] are neither agreeing to protect [Germany] nor are we permitting them to defend themselves." Churchill felt that German manpower and industrial production should be used at "the appropriate time to strengthen an integrated Western European defense force ... a new sort of SHAEF, to which the Germans could contribute as part of the whole but without a rounded military force of their own." He implied, however, that none of these things could be done without US participation.[100] On 16 March, Churchill addressed the House of Commons, telling them that the "long western European front against the Soviet Union ... could not be successfully defended without the 'active aid' of Western Germany."[101] The

Foreign Office quickly distanced itself from Churchill and assured Britain's
continental allies and France that it did not favor German rearmament.

In early April 1949, Drew Middleton reported that the West Germans
would be asking the Allied foreign ministers for some declaration of their
intent to defend Germany when they met in London in May. While Middleton's German sources said they were not asking for immediate rearmament, they did want to know when and at what strength they would be
allowed to rearm. Their main concern was the growth of the East German
Volkspolizei (people's police), which they felt posed a grave political danger to West Germany. There was, they said, no German force in the Federal
Republic capable of dealing with the Volkspolizei and they wanted to have
some form of constabulary to maintain internal security. The occupation
powers should not be the ones to police Western Germany, the sources
said, as that would allow the Communists to claim that the Federal Government was kept in power by "foreign troops against the popular will."[102]

This view was echoed later in the month by Kennan. In voicing his
disagreement with a paper on German defense, Kennan wrote in a letter to Mr. Lewis that it was "unrealistic to expect a demilitarized West
German state to have stability unless there is an efficient federal constabulary . . . to balance off the East German police forces." Kennan went
even further, stating his belief that the paramilitary units being developed
in East Germany should be approximately matched "man for man and
weapon for weapon." It did make a difference who defended West Germany, he continued, as there was "nothing the Russians [wanted] more
than to see [Allied] forces become engaged in fighting Germans, while
they [sat] on the sidelines and [made] political capital out of it."[103]

Kennan was unequivocal in his opposition to German rearmament
or assurances of defense, as he believed that as long as West Germany was
occupied, an attack against it would be an attack on the Western occupation forces. There was time, Kennan wrote, to talk about West Germany's
future security when the end of the occupation became imminent. He
was also opposed to German entry into NATO. Using Iceland, Italy, and
Denmark as examples, Kennan felt it unsound to ask substantially demilitarized countries to enter into arrangements that implied mutual military
obligations, which would be the case if West Germany was admitted.[104]

One day after Kennan delivered his paper, McCloy sent a cable to
Byroade informing him that he, McCloy, had decided the US approach
to Germany was unrealistic: "We have attempted to improve on Versailles
by absolutely forbidding Germany to rearm."[105] McCloy felt that this

restriction, which made sense in the context of postwar cooperation, was no longer valid in the now-divided world. Real security for Western Europe, he continued, would only occur by adding Germany as a full partner. Although he also felt that pressing for German rearmament now was premature and that it might be a while before it became urgent, the issue, he stated quite presciently, "may well rise from our need rather than German demand."[106]

At approximately the same time, according to a *New York Times* article by Drew Middleton, a directive was circulated to all European command force headquarters to draft plans for a "logistical development based on a further five-year occupation" of West Germany. Middleton interpreted this as a response to Germany's request for a security guarantee, which meant that while there would be no troop increase, one could assume that the progressive takeover by German civilians of the army's administrative duties would allow a "corresponding increase in the ratio of combat to non-combat soldiers in the theater." As he had no way of knowing that McCloy was slowly changing his mind regarding German rearmament and defense needs, Middleton saw the extended occupation as an explanation of McCloy's recent, unequivocal statements rejecting German rearmament.[107]

Despite increased discussions regarding German rearmament—even former German generals were producing papers on German participation in a European-Atlantic armed force complete with active and passive air defense—the Military Security Board promulgated a law, to remain in effect for two years, designed to prevent German rearmament and ensure its industrial demilitarization.[108] This law, announced on 8 May 1949, the fifth anniversary of Germany's defeat, limited German industry in four ways: it prohibited or limited the quantity of certain types of products, capped the capacity of certain types of industrial production, required Military Security Board approval for certain industrial activities, and provided for the surveillance of industrial production facilities and equipment affecting the security field.[109]

In early June, NSC 71 was issued and contained extracts of three statements by the JCS regarding German remilitarization. While the second of the three advocated the "appropriate and early rearming of Western Germany," the last extract dealt specifically with the creation of a five-thousand-person federal police force in Germany. This force was to be recommended by the three high commissioners and called the "Republican Guard." The extract included this statement: "Joint Chiefs of Staff

strongly urge that the Foreign Ministers approve this recommendation, 73
since such a force could well be the initial step in the eventual rearming
of Germany."[110]

NSC 71 drew the immediate attention of President Truman, who sent
a memo to Acheson telling him that he had read NSC 71 and that it
was "decidedly militaristic" and, in his opinion, not realistic under present conditions. He told Acheson that he desired to discuss it with him on
Monday, 19 June.[111] Colonel Byroade coordinated within the European
Division and prepared a long, impassioned paper for Acheson to use at the
National Security Council, where he was to address both rearming and
the police issue. In his cover letter to Acheson, Byroade said that McCloy
told him that he now had direct evidence that the British representative in Germany had instigated the letter Adenauer had sent to the High
Commission requesting twenty-five thousand federal police.[112] Byroade
recommended that a message be sent to Ambassador Douglas in London
to speak "quite frankly" with Bevin, as these tactics could rapidly destroy
the effectiveness of the High Commission. Byroade then suggested that
the United States adopt an earlier French proposal to (1) strengthen the
police situation by creating within the West German *Länder* (states) additional units with more effective weapons and greater mobility and (2) to
define a procedure whereby the chancellor could call upon those units.[113]

In the paper, Byroade wrote that the meeting in London of the three
foreign ministers and the meetings in the North Atlantic Council (NAC)
made it clear that the rearmament of Germany and its inclusion in NATO
were premature "to the point where profitable discussion cannot yet be
held on this subject." The paper continued that the next eighteen months
would be crucial in shaping Germany's development, and that neither
the German people nor their elected leaders wanted to see a German
armed force. World conditions, Byroade wrote, could cause this position
to change but the advantages of not adding German forces to those of the
West far outweighed the risks. An abrupt reversal of this policy, he continued, could undermine Allied unity and without unity, there would be
no strength.

Additionally, Byroade wrote that Germany could not continue to pay
its share of occupation costs (currently 22 percent of its budget) and contribute to the military defense. Thus, it would be necessary to look at other
nonmilitary ways that Germany could contribute to the strength of the
West and the reconstruction of Europe. He addressed the possibility of
using German manpower in a balanced North Atlantic force, a concept

that, if successful, could provide a framework within which limited German rearmament might be possible. In his opinion, however, that framework had not been worked out sufficiently to solve the existing obstacles.

Byroade added a note of caution, saying that although Germany was predominantly anti-Communist and outraged by past Soviet behavior, the outrage was not such that they could not be tempted to make a deal with the East. Thus, it would not add true strength to the West to create a strong Germany military force whose loyalty could not be counted on with "reasonable" certainty.

The paper concluded by agreeing that the current German police force needed strengthening but questioned whether, given Germany's history with a centralized police force, additional and specially trained forces should be created in the German states that could be called upon by the federal government. He indicated that this question, which had not yet been decided, was really of no interest to the Department of Defense and that a federal force would require a constitutional change. This question was before the High Commissioners and, he added, was not considered a step in the initial phase of the rearmament of Western Germany.

The issue of a West German federal police force took yet another turn a few days earlier. On 13 June, McCloy cabled Acheson to inform him that Graf Gerhard von Schwerin, a former German general and unofficial military advisor to Chancellor Adenauer, had gone in April to England on a trip to discuss German remilitarization with certain British officials and ministers of Parliament, including Sir Ivone Kirpatrick, the soon-to-be British high commissioner for Germany, among others.[114] Schwerin, according to the cable, was told that while the official British position was against rearmament, the majority opinion in Britain was now in favor of it and that the United States "would present no great problem and could 'be brought into line quickly.'" McCloy stated that, based on Schwerin's admissions regarding his England trip and other information, it was "becoming increasingly evident that the UK was utilizing pressure for the creation of a German police force as a first step toward the remilitarization of Germany." McCloy further surmised that Adenauer may have been complicit, although both the United States and the French had taken Adenauer's request for a federal police force at face value and not as a Trojan horse for a future German army. McCloy concluded with his impression that the United States was not prepared to agree to remilitarization and that the suggestion would be premature until a stronger democratic Germany emerged. He then requested the department's views on the police question.[115]

On the same day that he read NSC 71, President Truman wrote Acheson that he had received a telegram from McCloy regarding the rearming
of Germany. Truman ventured that it seemed to him that "the British were
doing everything to break up western European unity [by advocating]
the rearmament of Germany." Truman cautioned against making the same
mistake that was made after World War I, when Germany was allowed to
maintain one hundred thousand soldiers who became the foundation for
"the greatest war machine that ever came forth in European history." He
then told Acheson that McCloy should be called home and that he, Acheson, McCloy, and the secretary of defense should discuss the proper approach to a police force in Germany, one that could maintain order locally
but not be allowed to develop into "a training ground for a military machine that [could] combine with Russia and ruin the rest of the world."[116]

Toward the end of June, Acheson responded to McCloy's earlier cable
with a cable of his own condemning the British ploy and the instigation of
Adenauer's letter requesting a twenty-five-thousand-person federal police
force. He agreed with McCloy's position and conclusions and included
for McCloy a copy of Byroade's paper. Acheson concluded by stating that
in regard to Adenauer's request, the United States was not prepared to see
the creation of a large, centralized barracks police. A small force of five
hundred to two thousand men under federal control for the Bonn enclave
was acceptable but beyond that widespread disorder could be dealt with by
an adequately built-up and strengthened state police. This should suffice to
meet Adenauer's plea without creating a danger to democracy inherent in
a centralized German police force.[117]

McCloy responded urging Acheson to seek a common understanding among the three Allied governments regarding German remilitarization and to make a comprehensive pronouncement that was more than a
"mere reaffirmation that we do not intend to rearm Germany."[118] Acheson
agreed but wanted to wait until the NSC had an opportunity to discuss
the issue. McCloy also told Acheson that Adenauer had told him about
Schwerin's trip to the United Kingdom and that a source close to depart-
ing British deputy high commissioner General Robertson had told Mc-
Cloy that Robertson had urged Adenauer to request twenty-five thousand
police and that the British would support that requst.[119]

NSC 68, Korea, and the "Single Package"

As noted above, Truman, supported by Congress and Secretary of Defense
Johnson, had severely curtailed defense spending and hoped to cut it even

more. He found it cheaper to increase the atomic inventory than increase the size of the armed forces. Acheson discretely opposed the president on this issue by using the strategic review of Truman's H-bomb decision to make the case for increased defense spending.[120]

The Soviet detonation of an atomic bomb brought up the issues of what was needed to continue the policy of containment, whether the Soviets had the ability to develop a thermonuclear bomb, and whether the United States should itself move forward with the development of a thermonuclear weapon—the hydrogen bomb. When Truman was told that the Soviets did have the necessary technical capability, he ordered the NSC to reexamine US national security objectives. The result of that reexamination was NSC 68.[121]

Formal responsibility for drafting NSC 68 belonged to a joint State-Defense review group of eleven, with Paul Nitze, Acheson's close associate, as chairman. It was written in February and March 1950. The JCS supported NSC 68 and their position effectively forced Secretary of Defense Johnson to sign on as well.[122] NSC 68 took the view that the \ Soviets were evil incarnate, driven by a fanatical belief system that they wanted to impose on the entire world. This desire to dominate Europe would endanger US security, but not everyone saw the situation as so dire, including the president and Soviet experts Charles 'Skip' Bohlen and George Kennan. Many thought there were other, more economical means of confronting the threat. The Korean War changed all that.

Acheson's major concern was that a nuclear-armed Soviet Union would overwhelm NATO's under-armed conventional forces. Thus, the three main objectives of NSC 68 were to bolster US conventional capabilities, to strengthen the strategic nuclear force, and to assist America's allies, especially in Europe, with improving their military posture. These objectives were initiated when President Truman approved NSC 68 on 30 September. Ironically, the issue of German rearmament was not considered in NSC 68. Instead, it considered separate agreements with Japan, West Germany, and Austria to use their "energies and resources" in support of the free world.

As a result of NSC 68, the overall defense and international affairs budget climbed from $17.7 billion in fiscal year 1950 to $52.6 billion in fiscal year 1953, with the rearmament of West Germany included in the programs authorized by these funds.[123]

North Korean forces crossed the 38th parallel separating North and South Korea on 25 June 1950, attacking both South Korean and US forces.

The focus of US foreign policy remained on Europe, neither Byroade or   77
Acheson saw the attack as sufficient cause to change policy on Germany,
fearing that any change would have a negative effect on the French.[124]
However, the situation and the tenor of discussions regarding German
rearmament would shortly change.

For many Europeans, and Germans in particular, the parallel between
Germany and Korea was unmistakable: both were divided into two states,
one Western-oriented and the other Communist-oriented. Additionally,
the nature of the police buildup in East Germany, specifically the kasserni-
erte Volkspolizei and Bereitshaftspolizei, which were more like an army,
made the possibility of aggression from the East more likely. These factors
combined with heightened fears within the Truman administration regarding possible Soviet aggression in Europe to produce a consensus that
West Germany needed to be armed.[125]

President Truman claimed that the Communist attack on South
Korea made it clear beyond a reasonable doubt that Communism had
passed from "the use of subversion to conquer independent nations and
[would] now use armed invasion and war." Secretary of Defense Johnson
echoed Truman, saying the attack was "undeniable proof" that international Communism was "willing to resort to armed aggression . . . even at
the resultant risk of starting a third world war." Even John Foster Dulles
wrote in the *New York Times Magazine* that the attack "may invalidate the
assumption that the Soviet Union would not risk war for several years to
come." For a short time, Western Europe shared these assessments of Soviet
intentions.[126]

With the outbreak of the Korean War, McCloy began to change his
mind regarding German rearmament, and on 14 July he sent an "Eyes
Only" cable to Acheson and Byroade describing a talk Sir Ivone had had
with Adenauer, which he had then reported to McCloy and French high
commissioner André François-Poncet. Adenauer, according to Sir Ivone,
had again expressed his concerns over the question of security for the
Federal Republic in light of Korea and the lack of concrete preparations
by the Allies in Europe. Adenauer acknowledged that the creation of a
German army was out of the question but argued that some arrangement
had to be made in case of an attack by the Volkspolizei.

Sir Ivone felt that the Germans needed to know that the Allies were
doing all they could to protect them and said that, at a minimum, an "effective German auxiliary," was needed—whether federal or state police
was immaterial—to control refugees and to keep order while Allied forces

78   prepared for an attack. McCloy implied that he was skeptical of Sir Ivone's concern, thinking that it might be a way for him to again press the British interest in creating a federal German police force using Korea as a "gambit." McCloy felt, however, that continued bad news from Korea could disturb the general equanimity of the population.

In separate inserts in his cable, McCloy added that Poncet subsequently told him that German service troops with Allied armies should be trained and in an emergency be a "means for Germans to fight with us," and also that he had seen Adenauer and been told much of what Adenauer had told Sir Ivone. McCloy believed there was a lack of sufficient emergency planning regarding the use of Germans and that in his judgment, "it [was] necessary to advise the Germans that at some point [the Allies] would permit them to fight shoulder to shoulder with [them] when the need should arise." He then put forth his belief that those Germans who wished to should be permitted to enlist in the US Army, something he had already told General Thomas T. Handy, commander in chief of the US European Command (CINCEUCOM), who was, as he understood, about to request permission to do just that. McCloy concluded that "it would be to [the Allies'] advantage to start planning for the use of German manpower along the line suggested above and subject to the conditions stated above" and requested guidance on the issue "as soon as possible."[127]

Based on the perception that Germany first needed to be brought into the Western camp economically and politically, State Department policy had been to keep the FRG disarmed and demilitarized for decades. Ironically, this policy did not reflect a consensus within the department. While there were many in the Department of State who felt that arming the FRG would provoke the Soviets into attacking before armed German forces could be fielded, others, including Secretary of State Acheson, believed that if anything would provoke the Soviets, it would be the continued weakness of the Allied military position. Many other senior State Department officers were slowly changing their minds and favoring the rearmament of Germany, Averell Harriman among them.[128] Regardless, an office memorandum written by John Hay of Public Affairs to Geoffrey W. Lewis, deputy director of the Office of German Affairs, stated that the US government's consistent policy has been that Germany should not be rearmed. It referred to the 23 May formal note by the American, British, and French governments to the Soviet government regarding the remilitarization of the East German police by citing that in every agreement, the United States had been "committed unequivocally to the principle that Germany will be demilitarized, that her

military forces will be completely and finally abolished, and that no revival
of German military activities will be allowed." The memo referred to press
statements made by the secretary on 7 and 16 June that referred to this protest note and ended by stating that there had been no change to the State
Department's position on that subject.[129]

In mid-July, McCloy again cabled Byroade stating that if the United
States did not find the means to allow Germany to fight in an emergency,
the United States would lose West Germany politically and militarily
without hope of getting it back. If there was a real war, McCloy continued,
the United States would lose a valuable reserve of manpower—a reserve
the Russians would certainly use against the United States. McCloy concluded that given the situation regarding Korea, it was time to consider the
radical changes needed for German participation in Europe's defense.[130]

Acheson, who had the benefit of his own and the State Department's
"great deal of thinking" on this subject, met with the president at the end
of July. This meeting marks what many have called Acheson's conversion.
Acheson felt that the NSC was asking the president to decide if West
Germany should be rearmed, and only after he approved would methods
for executing the decision be looked into. Acheson felt this was the wrong
approach. The question, Acheson said, was no longer whether Germany
should be rearmed but "how this could be done without disrupting anything else [the United States was] doing and without putting Germany
into a position to act as a balance of power in Europe."[131]

Acheson then suggested the idea of a European or Atlantic defense
force as a mechanism by which a Western German military contribution could be integrated into the defense of Europe without the creation
of a German national army, ministry of defense, or General Staff Corps.
Truman gave his approval and directed Acheson to proceed along those
lines.[132] Acheson himself said that his conversion to German participation
in European defense was quick: "If there was to be any defense at all, it had
to be based on a forward strategy. Germany's role must [be] primary."[133]

Acheson's conversion may not have been as sudden as he said or it
appears. As early as 1949, Acheson had decided that US policy had to be
one of "situations of strength."[134] He had been thinking about rearming
Germany privately but disavowing it in public. Acheson realized that the
need for a "forward strategy"—a defense line as far east as possible—made
it imperative that Germany be involved militarily.[135] Months later, while
at the Paris Foreign Minister's Conference in November 1949, Acheson
told Bevin and Schuman that the United States' hope was to make these

80   former enemies (Japan and Germany) willing and strong supporters of the free world structure. Acheson believed that "Germany should be welcomed into Western Europe, not kept in limbo outside as had been the case after the war of 1914–1918."[136]

The idea of a European defense force had been germinating in the minds of McCloy and Byroade as well, and had been discussed in a State Department position paper prepared for the London Tripartite Conference in May. But it was during the first week in August that these ideas began to jell and come to fruition. On 3 August, McCloy sent Byroade a cable in which he offered a number of conclusions, namely that the problem of the defense of Western Europe could not be solved merely by strengthening Western Europe's national armies, particularly because France lacked both the capacity and will to build an army capable of bearing the brunt of West European defense. McCloy continued that he was absolutely opposed to re-creating any German national army "now or in the foreseeable future." He recognized, however, that an effective defense of Western Europe required a real contribution of German resources and men. He concluded that the time was ripe for the creation of a genuine European army that would give the French hope of an effective defense without the risk of a German national army.[137]

Byroade responded the following day, telling McCloy that his cable had "filled in the missing portions" of a paper he, Byroade, had drafted the day before on the formation of a European army. Byroade's plan described a highly integrated European army with as much an international character as possible. It was an attempt to apply the Schuman Plan concept to the military field, allowing for a German contribution without a German national army. It was an effort to create, as the French wanted, a "German army that would be weaker than the French, yet also stronger than the Russians."[138] Byroade's paper became the State Department's official position and was forwarded to the Defense Department for concurrence and to satisfy the president's directive that the two departments reach a common position. The most politically significant portion of the paper was the statement that if the United States would participate, conditions appeared favorable for creating a truly effective European defense force that could assimilate a direct contribution by Germany, but that this would require from Germany "the voluntary surrender of a degree of sovereignty in the most vital of all elements of sovereignty, i.e., the security field."[139]

Yet again, the department's official pronouncements, as well as some of its internal communications, continued to blur the issue. Just the day before Byroade's response to McCloy, a summary of telegrams pertaining to Germany informed the secretary of state that Charles Spofford, the US representative to the North Atlantic Council of Deputies, had been told that when speaking to other NATO representatives, he should tell them that given the current world situation, the United States felt that the required defense effort could not be met without the contribution of Germany's productive capacity to turn out noncombat equipment. Spofford was instructed to make it clear that this proposal did not reflect "any change in the basic U.S. position on German rearmament."[140]

Just over a week later, at the 11 August Council of Europe meeting, Churchill called for the creation of a European army that included German participation. Anticipating questions on the US reaction to this resolution, both Byroade and James Webb recommended diplomatic responses for the secretary of state and the president, respectively, though neither of the recommended responses mentioned the official US position of no German rearmament. Instead, it was recommended that both men disavow any detailed knowledge of the scope of German participation in Churchill's proposal and say that the US government could not usefully comment on it.[141]

As will be seen in chapter 3, the Department of Defense had been working since early 1948 on arming West Germany and had been in constant contact with the Department of State, especially since early August, regarding when and how to arm the Federal Republic. Although the positions of the two departments were not that far apart, there were several significant differences that needed to be ironed out and clarified, specifically the JCS position that the German contribution be a national army in NATO. Thus, on 26 August, and in light of the upcoming meeting between Acheson and the foreign ministers of Great Britain and France on 12 September that was to be followed by a meeting of the NAC, President Truman sent each secretary an identical letter that contained eight key questions. He requested that both departments work together to answer these questions and develop recommendations for his decision by 1 September.

The most significant questions asked essentially whether the United States was prepared to[142]

- commit additional forces to the defense of Europe;
- support the concept of a European defense force, including Germans, on anything other than a national basis;

- look forward to the eventuality of a supreme commander for that force;
- support the creation of a combined staff for that supreme commander;
- consider full US participation in a European defense force (i.e., accept responsibility for having an American supreme commander); and
- consider other ways in which the United States could invigorate NATO.

On 30 August, Acheson, Byroade, Paul Nitze, and Perkins met with General Omar Bradley, then chairman of the JCS, to discuss the JCS response to Truman's questions, and according to a memorandum of that meeting prepared by Byroade, there did not appear to be any major disagreements.[143]

As an aside, the day before, on 29 August, Adenauer had sent a memorandum to McCloy in which he pointed out that events in the "Far East" and belief in the ability of the West to counter Soviet moves in Western Europe had been badly shaken to "an alarming extent and had led to a dangerous lethargy among Germans."[144] Adenauer again pointed out the weakness of the Federal Republic police vis-à-vis the East German Volkspolizei and wrote that he had repeatedly requested that Allied occupation forces be reinforced as the defense of the FRG was in their hands. Lastly, and perhaps most importantly, Adenauer stated that the FRG was prepared to contribute a German contingent should an international European army be formed. "This shows unambiguously," he wrote, "that the Federal Chancellor rejects the remilitarization of Germany as a separate national military force."[145]

Adenauer sent a second, undated aide memoir to Allen Dulles, who forwarded it on 8 September to his brother, John Foster Dulles, who forwarded it to Byroade on 11 September. The aide memoir reiterated Adenauer's position that the events in Korea had caused a serious loss of confidence within the FRG and that to save the psychological situation there, the occupying forces needed to be significantly reinforced with at least two to four armored divisions. To fully thwart a Soviet attack, however, at least twelve armored divisions sent to Germany's eastern border would be required. "Only when this is done," wrote Adenauer, "will it be possible to recruit troops in Germany and to place German industry at the service of Western defense."[146]

Acheson relates in his memoir that the state and defense departments
debated the issue for two weeks before a compromise was reached, which
he then carried to the Tripartite Meeting in New York. The compromise,
also known as the 'single package,' contained several key elements and
was intended to be offered to the Allies on a take-it-or-leave-it basis. The
'package,' approved by Truman just a few days earlier, offered to increase
US forces in Europe by approximately six divisions, eight tactical air
groups, and appropriate naval forces, and promised US participation, along
with the United Kingdom and all the other NATO armies, in a combined
European defense force with an international staff and a supreme commander. However, this was to be contingent on the Allies boosting the capabilities (and size) of their forces and accepting the inclusion of German
detachments that would be added at the division level without a German
general staff.[147]

One purpose of the single package was to convince the Europeans
that the United States would be there to defend them, not liberate them.
Acheson may have been thinking of an interview given by French premier
Henri Queuille to the *New York Times* at the time the NATO Treaty was
signed in March 1949. Queuille said that the Allies knew that if Western
Europe were occupied America would again come to liberate them. "But
the process would be terrible," Queuille had said. "The next time you
would probably be liberating a corpse."[148]

Acheson later called the single package a "mistake" and claimed he
was forced into accepting it by the military. Acheson, however, was not
a person to be easily cowed nor one who would subscribe to a position
he did not approve.[149] If the package as presented to Bevin and Schuman
was a mistake, it may have been because of the manner in which it was
presented (i.e., not so much that it mandated the arming of the Federal
Republic but that it was presented as an all-or-nothing demand).[150] This
presentation set the stage for the long, drawn-out four-and-a-half-year
battle to put Germans back in uniform.

The determination of the United States to keep Germany disarmed
and demilitarized had come face to face with political reality. Some officials within the State Department had already begun to see the situation
in a different light, some before the outbreak of hostilities on the Korean
peninsula, others afterward. Of interest, however, and not addressed elsewhere to any great extent, is the fact that it was McCloy and Byroade, two
State Department officers, who first developed a definitive plan to arm
West Germany within a European defense force, not the French. Aside

84   from an unfavorable review from the JCS, nothing was ever done with this plan. Despite the repeated urging by the JCS and the secretary of defense to arm West Germany by bringing it rapidly into NATO, Acheson decided that the process had to be led by the French. As a result, and despite having a US plan for an integrated European defense force, Acheson let the French assume leadership. What he did not expect was for them to present a plan that was unworkable from the start.[151] This begs the question of whether the following four years, during which the Pleven Plan, the precursor to the European Defence Community, was offered as the solution, would have ended differently had Acheson made the McCloy-Byroade plan a part of the single package and not ceded the initiative to France.

Additionally, while the argument has been made that the United States remained the leader of the Alliance, when it came to the actual process of how to arm the FRG and under what conditions, the US government became an onlooker, relegated to the sidelines.[152] As will be seen, nothing that either the Truman administration or later the Eisenhower administration did, from accepting and blindly supporting the Plevin Plan, providing repeated assurances of maintaining an adequate troop presence in Europe as long as needed, and even threatening France with a cutoff of aid funds, induced France to ratify the EDC Treaty—a plan of French making—and accept German rearmament.

3 The Military Path to 12 September 1950

Official histories of the Office of the Secretary of Defense, Joint Chiefs of Staff (JCS), and even the individual military services addressing this period are brief by design, highlighting only the major issues or major points of an issue or strategy debate. Nonmilitary historians addressed this period and the military problems that confronted the United States during the early Cold War period in a similar fashion. While they addressed the issue of German rearmament, they failed to delve into depth or detail sufficient to understand the decision-making process or explain the specific motives of the JCS and the manner in which it dealt with the Department of State. This chapter presents a much more complete and nuanced picture of the period by bringing the contents of plans, memos, cables, and other correspondence of the JCS, the Joint Strategic Planning Committee (JSPC), and other involved military agencies to light. It will also delineate clearly the unchanging position of the Department of Defense on the question of German rearmament and the variance with the policy being followed at the time.

Simply put, the Department of Defense wanted the formation of a national West German army while the Department of State, as seen in chapter 2, wanted armed German units in an integrated European army. The difference was a question that Carl von Clausewitz addressed and answered over one hundred years earlier: whether a unified federal (national) army or separate armies in an alliance is more effective. For Clausewitz, as for the Department of Defense, the answer was the national army.[1]

When the war in Europe ended in May 1945, there were sixty-one US divisions, (approximately 915,000 men) in the Allied force under Eisenhower.[2] The Japanese surrender just four months later and public pressure led President Truman and Congress to bring the troops rapidly home from Europe.[3] Less than one year later, on 1 January 1946, after a much faster than expected demobilization that forced Eisenhower to complain to Congress, there were only 622,000 US troops assigned to the European Theater, a number that was estimated to be reduced to 307,000 by 1 July 1946.[4]

By 1947, just one year later, only 12 under-strength divisions, primarily trained and equipped for occupation duties, remained of the 97 US Army ground divisions that had been active at the end of the war, and only two were in Germany.[5] At the same time, according to intelligence estimates used by the Joint War Planning Committee (JWPC), the USSR had retained 50 divisions in their zones of Germany and Austria, 20 divisions in Poland, 20 divisions in Hungary and Yugoslavia, and a further 152 divisions in reserve in the Soviet Union along with a number of frontline aircraft. The JWPC also estimated that an additional 61 divisions belonging to Soviet satellite countries in Europe would also be available. Freely admitting Soviet superiority, the JWPC concluded that the USSR could, in the event of war, overrun Europe and reach the English Channel in its initial drive. Under those circumstances, they saw no other alternative but to have US forces withdraw from the continent as rapidly as possible.[6]

There was little if any thought within the US military establishment in the immediate years following the end of World War II about rearming Germany. The US army of occupation was deeply involved in carrying out the disarmament, demobilization, and demilitarization directives of the ACC. The War Department, however, which became the Department of Defense following the National Security Act of 1947, was slowly recognizing a growing military threat in its erstwhile World War II ally, the Soviet Union. This threat took on greater urgency following the 1948 Czech coup and the Berlin Blockade later that year, forcing the JCS to think seriously about the defense of Western Europe.[7] Outnumbered in manpower and associated with relatively weak allies who were still recovering from the ravages of the war, the Pentagon sought a solution that would utilize the manpower and fighting experience that recently defeated Germany could provide. Therefore, to better understand why the US military so quickly reconsidered rearming the recently disarmed Germans, it is imperative to gain an understanding of the military situation as seen by the newly organized JCS in the early postwar years.

When the war ended, a new team occupied the War Department. Aside from their responsibilities for demobilizing the army, they were also made responsible for occupation policy, which, according to John J. McCloy, resulted in chaos. There was little planning or coordination, so friction ensued between the War Department, the State Department, and senior military officers in the field, which was exacerbated by feuds between the services over roles and missions. President Truman was not immune to problems either, as he faced domestic strife, inflationary pressures, and congressional and public demands to bring the troops home.[8]

Furthermore, according to Leffler, Truman's administration was in disarray. The beginning of the Cold War found the president's advisors bickering among themselves, legislators antagonized, and officials in Washington unable to establish foreign policy goals or choose between domestic and international priorities.[9]

Prior to 1947, strategic planning consisted primarily of studies of specific areas or problems. For example, Soviet actions in 1946 in Iran and subsequently Turkey, combined with Stalin's speech of 9 February and George Kennan's subsequent analysis of it, led the JCS to fear the loss of the Mediterranean and contend that the Soviet Union constituted "the greatest threat to the United States in the foreseeable future." In mid-April, a JCS analysis concluded that the Soviets could conquer most, if not all, of Western Europe.[10]

Following passage of the National Security Act in July 1947, the newly reorganized JCS was made responsible for war planning. The earliest plans, which were prepared without political guidance (as none was given), assumed the United States would use nuclear weapons.[11] As Lawrence Freedman writes, however, the JCS had determined as early as 1946 that the use of nuclear weapons might not be decisive. Victory would require the "actual capture and occupation of the enemy homeland."[12] Furthermore, US demobilization had been such that the few atomic bombs possessed by the United States would do little if anything to compensate for the lack of troops on the ground.[13] Nonetheless, for a number of technical and strategic reasons (e.g., the development of the B-36 long-range strategic bomber, which lessened dependence on overseas bases), the US military came to believe that strategic bombing with nuclear weapons could be decisive.

These ideas were embodied in the first plan, code-named Broiler, which was approved in December 1947. Broiler was a plan for the initial stages of war, beginning anytime within the next three years. Its aim was to secure the United Kingdom and the Cairo-Suez area by launching a strategic air attack against the USSR. That said, the force disparity between the United States and the USSR forced planners to accept the loss of both Western Europe and the Middle East. Given the requirements and time it would take to mobilize, it was believed that an offensive to retake the continent would not be possible for at least ten months after D-Day.[14]

Broiler, however, elicited doubts among members of the JCS regarding its reliance on atomic weapons. Admiral William D. Leahy, chairman of the JCS, and especially Admiral Louis Denfeld, the chief of naval operations, saw Broiler as a complete surrender of all of Western Europe's manpower, resources, and industrial capacity to the Soviets, which they could then use against the United States. Denfeld believed a more realistic strategy would have the United States align itself with the West European powers to defend along the Rhine. He felt that together with the Western Union, the military arm of the newly created Brussels Treaty Organization, and additional US forces, it would be possible to hold part of Western Europe.[15]

In April 1948, US, British, and Canadian planning officers developed and approved an outline emergency war plan (EWP)—an abbreviated version of Broiler—code-named Halfmoon, which included a larger list of nations allied against the USSR that was to be the basis for each nation to develop parallel plans. Halfmoon, approved in May 1948 as a global war plan, was focused on securing or regaining Middle East oil. Its major flaw (which was recognized even then) was its failure to provide assistance to Western Europe. Again, the shortage of forces left the planners no alternative. Only the United Kingdom, which was to act as a platform for US strategic air forces, was to be defended. No serious effort would be made to hold Western Europe and Allied occupation forces were to withdraw to the Rhine, hold as long as possible, then withdraw to French and Italian ports for evacuation. Sufficient mobilization to retake the lost territories was expected to take approximately twelve months.[16]

To facilitate future planning, Eisenhower, who had been recalled from retirement by President Truman to be the acting chief of the JCS and special advisor to the president, issued a policy memorandum on 25 February 1949 setting forth wartime objectives for Europe. A portion of the guidance stated: "The security of the United States requires . . . the holding of a line containing the West European complex preferably no farther west than the Rhine." Eisenhower, however, recognized that the forces available, including those from members of the Western Union, were insufficient to hold the Rhine, so he called for plans to hold a "substantial bridgehead" in Western Europe and to provide for a "return" at the earliest possible moment.[17]

This new plan, designated Offtackle, was approved on 8 December 1949. It was the first plan based on political guidance as well as the first that directed the defense of Western Europe. Both Halfmoon and Offtackle reflected the doubts of the army and the navy about the efficacy of an "atomic blitz" and also their belief that slowing a Soviet advance in Europe had to be an objective. Offtackle also eliminated the Middle East as a US priority.[18] Despite the creation of NATO in 1949, US and Allied forces remained numerically insufficient to hold the Rhine or maintain a bridgehead north of the Pyrenees. Withdrawal and return, possibly only twenty-four months after D-Day, most likely from North Africa, remained the only possible alternative.[19]

Marc Trachtenberg writes that even before the Soviets acquired the atomic bomb in August 1949, it had become clear that a buildup of conventional capability was required. General Omar Bradley, then army chief of staff, stated that a strategy of first abandoning then liberating Western Europe would produce impotent and disillusioned allies who, in the event of war, could not be counted on: "We cannot count on friends in Western Europe if our strategy in the event of war dictates that we shall first abandon them to the enemy with a promise of later liberation."[20]

Although what lay behind these thoughts was only voiced loud and clear several years later, it was becoming evident to some that if war was to be fought on German soil, Germany had to be defended as an ally because it would need to contribute to its own defense. A German contribution, however, required a significant change in West Germany's status. The rationale was that Germany's willingness to provide troops in her own defense would be a test of her commitment to the West. As early as 1947, Clay had remarked that "in the event of another war, the Germans probably would be the only continental people upon whom [the US] could rely."[21]

Predating these thoughts was a report by the Joint Strategic Survey Committee (JSSC) on 29 April 1947 and a staff study drafted for the JSPC in March 1948, which addressed the issue of West German resources. Paragraph six of the enclosure to the appendix of the JSSC report said the following: "Potentially, the strongest military power in this area [Western Europe] is Germany. Without German aid the remaining countries of Western Europe could scarcely be expected to withstand the armies of our ideological opponents until the United States could mobilize and place in the field sufficient armed forces to achieve their defeat. With a revived Germany fighting on the side of the Western Allies this would be a possibility."[22]

The JSPC study also stated that German "resources in manpower should be put to building forces to fill the military vacuum in Western Europe." It further recommended that staff conversations be undertaken with European Allies to determine the military uses to which West Germans might be put. Finally, the study concluded that the current EWP had to be changed to indicate a preparedness to fight and contain a Soviet attack on a line east of Denmark, West Germany, and Italy.[23] Ironically, this recommendation unknowingly supported the Western Union's 1948 objective to fight as far east as possible in Germany, an objective the JSSC had thought unrealistic.

Knowing that the United States could not assist the West Europeans, the JSSC simply did not believe that the European nations could "do other than simply delay Soviet encroachment" without Germany, even after years of intensive preparation. The JSSC stated that the United States would use offensive air and naval operations with ground support, including atomic warfare, "designed to secure the offensive initiative and bring about, at the earliest possible date, the capitulation of the enemy."[24] Even so, a return to Western Europe was only expected to be feasible after twenty-four months, when the necessary forces (totaling forty-one US divisions and sixty-three tactical air groups) would invade, World War II style, from England and North Africa.

In a December 1947 study looking at the military and security implications of a possible Soviet proposal for the early withdrawal of occupation forces, the army chief of staff recommended that the following wording be inserted: "The German people have the potential of ultimately providing effective resistance to forceful expansion into Western Europe. If they should be permitted to develop their military potential by the Western Allies, they are the people most likely to provide such resistance unless the United States abandons them to Soviet domination before a German government is set up which is capable of effectively resisting Soviet penetration."[25]

The study was based on the already accepted assessment that the Soviets would occupy Western Europe to the English Channel in the west and to the Pyrenees in the south before the United States could act effectively. The basic thrust of the army chief's memo was that Germany's potential could only be realized by a radical change in the Allied position regarding the disarming and demilitarization of Germany. Thus, by the end of 1947, thoughts regarding Germany and its relation to European defense were advancing slowly but surely in American military circles.

During the April–May 1948 period, a series of papers from the JSPC concerning the United States' involvement in Western Europe were sent to the JCS. One such report, like the previously mentioned staff study, recommended the EWP be revised to say that US forces would "fight and delay" as cleverly as possible and not deliberately evacuate.[26] It further assumed that if there were no war by 1953, US and Allied forces would be able to stop the Soviets from advancing west of the Rhine. In accepting the ability of the Soviets to "conquer and substantially occupy" the whole of Western Europe within six months, the report concluded that in order not to lose Western Europe to Communism, the United States had to show the Allies a determination to fight shoulder to shoulder with them, but still only commit to ensuring the integrity of Western Europe west of the Rhine. A British report of conversations with the JCS stated that while the United Kingdom planned no withdrawal from the Rhine, the United States foresaw ultimate withdrawal to the Pyrenees, where it planned to retain a foothold on the continent.[27]

This report also addressed the use of West German resources, including manpower, contingent on their political reliability, the degree to which their use in preparation might provoke the USSR, and most importantly, the attitude of other West European countries (notably the French) toward a possible resurgence of German military power. This report was followed immediately by another document cautioning that as the EWP did not envision the introduction of additional US forces on the European continent for the defense of France or the Benelux nations, these plans were not to be discussed with them. The document went on to say in so many words that this policy would avoid lowering the morale of those nations, who could best help by vigorously defending their own territory.[28]

A third document stemming from a planners conference in May 1948 revealed that the British contingent to the conference had proposed that General Clay (then Commander in Chief, US Forces of Occupation Germany, and Military Governor of the American zone of occupation) be authorized to participate in planning discussions for the evacuation of Allied forces from Germany, Austria, Trieste, and other locations. One of the more important assumptions in the document, one that had direct consequences on US military thinking later on, was that in a conventional war (i.e., one without nuclear weapons), the Western Powers could not put up any great resistance to a Soviet advance, so a protracted war would ensue that would "so destroy Western Europe that recovery might be impossible."[29]

This posed an almost insolvable dilemma. To withdraw, after pledging to remain, would be to give Western Europe to the Soviets. Using nuclear weapons in an attempt to forestall an invasion would destroy Germany at the very least, while not using them would most likely also result in the destruction and loss of Western Europe, given the weak conventional forces available.[30]

Cooperation with the Western Union

On 19 March 1948, two days after the Brussels Treaty Organization was formed, a staff study initiated by General Albert C. Wedemeyer, the army's director of plans and operations, was sent to the JCS and General Bradley. The study suggested overall political and military means to be employed by the United States regarding Western Europe in order to check and ultimately reverse the expansion of Soviet communism. Written after the Czech coup, it highlighted several risks to be avoided and strongly urged the creation of a military European recovery program (i.e., a "military Marshall Plan") to coordinate efforts.[31]

Wedemeyer's paper emphasized the need to change the strategic concept based on reconquering Europe after Soviet occupation. As translated in the JCS paper derived from Wedemeyer's study, the United States could no longer act as though Europe must first be conquered and occupied by the Soviets, denuding the United States of allies, before a policy for victory could be adopted. Halfmoon, the current emergency war plan that called for the "immediate and frantic" evacuation of US occupation troops, had to be changed. The United States, it continued, must be prepared to fight with its allies in Europe against any odds.

Paragraph 15 of the JCS version of Wedemeyer's paper, which quoted his study verbatim and mirrored the March 1948 JSPC study cited above, read: "Any use to which German resources [are put], including resources in manpower, should be put [to use] *militarily* in building forces to fill the military vacuum in Western Europe," though it added the caveat that this "should be determined only after consultation with other peoples of Western Europe and then in light of their recommendations." The JCS draft was entitled "Coordination of U.S. West European Military Resources to Counter Soviet Communism" and concluded that no choice existed "but to provide Western Europe, within our capabilities, every assistance, including both economic and military assistance, which may be required to counter the Soviet threat."[32]

In April 1948, a National Security Council (NSC) paper, NSC 9, proposed that the United States establish a relationship with the recently formed Brussels Treaty Organization (but not as a member). In addition, the US government was to ascertain the views of the Brussels Treaty members "regarding the conclusion of a Collective Defense Agreement for the North Atlantic Area," and until such a time as a defense agreement was signed, declare that an armed attack against any of the organizations' signatories would be an armed attack against the United States.[33] The JCS, however, was not too happy with NSC 9. They felt that military commitments should only be taken after commensurate increases in appropriations and military potential had been made, as well as authorization for necessary civilian and industrial readiness. There was yet another mention of a German contribution in April when Admiral Denfeld recommended a change to the draft of NSC 9/1, which would add a new paragraph that would allow, when circumstances permitted, other countries such as Germany to be invited to adhere to the Five-Power Treaty and the Defense Agreement. NSC 9/1 was replaced at the request of the State Department by NSC 9/2, which had a somewhat different thrust.[34] The JCS, however, reinserted Denfeld's words and the newer version was approved by the NSC and forwarded to the secretary of defense on 19 May 1948. NSC 9/2 concluded that the president was prepared to authorize US participation in the London five-power military talks on a nonmember basis.

A few weeks later, Secretary of the Army Kenneth Royall told the NSC, most likely in reference to NSC 9/1, that any agreement with the Western Union regarding European defense should leave the possibility of German accession open. The NSC, however, in line with President Truman's thoughts, found the question of German participation in Europe's defense premature.[35] Nonetheless, on 23 June, Undersecretary of State Robert A. Lovett wrote Secretary of Defense James Forrestal that the provision of NSC 9/2 for the United States to associate itself with the Brussels Treaty should be carried out and requested that he be informed who was being sent and how soon.

A further revision to NSC 9/2, NSC 9/3, acknowledged the Vandenberg Resolution, which outlined the support of the senate for US association with regional and other collective arrangements (i.e., the Brussels Treaty Organization) that affected national security. NSC 9/3 was otherwise identical to NSC 9/2.[36] NSC 9/3 was approved by the president on 2 July 1948 and one week later, on 8 July, Major General Lyman L. Lemnitzer was selected to lead the US delegation to the military arm of the Brussels Treaty Organization, the Western Union Military Committee.[37] The small group led by Lemnitzer was to participate on a nonmembership

94   basis to discuss military plans and draw up a tentative, coordinated supply plan.[38] It was not until 15 July, however, that the United States received a formal invitation from the chairman of the Brussels Treaty Permanent Commission, Gladwyn Jebb, to send American military experts to participate in the work of the Western Union Military Committee.[39]

    The French took credit for initiating the invitation. According to Jefferson Caffery, the US ambassador in Paris, he had been shown in strict confidence the draft of a document on French views concerning the security problems of the Western democracies that was to be sent to Foreign Minister George Bidault once it had been cleared by Prime Minister Robert Schuman and Minister of National Defense Pierre-Henri Teitgen. The key elements of the draft were that France saw Germany as an *eventual* threat and saw the Soviet Union as an *actual* threat, but one whose intentions were unclear and difficult to define. It was this threat and Western Europe's current weakness that led France to believe that cooperation with the United States was imperative, hence the invitation to participate as observers. In return, however, France wanted to be admitted to the US-UK military commission.[40]

    At about the same time, Wedemeyer, now deputy chief of staff for plans and combat operations, travelled to Europe to appraise the situation created by the Berlin Blockade. He sent a cable to Undersecretary of the Army Kenneth Draper telling him of a meeting with Teitgen, armed forces inspector general de Lattre de Tassigny, and the chiefs of staff of the army and the air force, generals Revers and Lecheres. Most significant from that meeting was Teitgen's acknowledgment that there was "no purely German danger" at the time and that France was ready to accept the American view that the only real present danger was the Soviet Union.[41]

    Teitgen went on to say that the defense of Europe, which would be fought in Germany as far east as possible, required sixty divisions, twenty-five to thirty of which France was prepared to provide in two years, if given heavy matériel from outside. In addition, Teitgen warned that unless the United States guaranteed assistance, the French people, sensing defeat, would turn to Communism and the "internal battle" would be lost.[42] As the French government had ordered a stand on the Rhine until the last man, he asked what the United States would do.

    A few weeks later, Wedemeyer cabled Bradley and Major General Ray Maddocks, director of the army's plans and operations division, with an appraisal of European personnel and their thoughts. Wedemeyer repeated that the French had definitely decided to fight as far east of the Rhine as possible and that Field Marshal Montgomery had told him the French planned on raising forty-five divisions if appropriate equipment could be made available.

Wedemeyer also reported that Montgomery had told him the British had been ordered to fight east of the Rhine or to use the Rhine as an obstacle; no retreat was allowed, nor could there be a retreat to a peripheral strategy—the Rhine had to be held. As the Allies grew stronger, the defensive line would move further to the east. Montgomery also felt that the five-nation Western Union should immediately appoint a British officer as supreme commander but that should war occur, the supreme commander should be an American.[43] The JCS agreed that a defense of the Rhine required a supreme commander and if the Western Union wanted an American officer for that position, it would be General Clay.[44] A few days later, Lemnitzer recommended that the US delegation to the Western Union remain as the association was both necessary and highly desirable. The US presence, he said, had had a notably good effect on and a great ability to influence planning.[45]

In mid-August, the American and British chiefs of staff reached an agreement that due to the plethora of additional duties imposed on Clay as the US military governor in West Germany, he could not serve as the supreme commander for Western Europe. It was therefore suggested that the supreme commander be a French officer supplied with an integrated staff. The two chiefs of staff also agreed to appoint an Allied commander in chief for Western Europe and suggested Field Marshal Montgomery, Field Marshal Alexander, or French general Juin.[46]

During the last few days of August, senior officers from the Department of Defense—the secretary of defense, the JCS, and senior civilian officials—met in Newport, Rhode Island. While the discussions ranged wide over a number of issues pertaining to the services, it focused at one point on the appointment of a supreme allied commander for Europe. Secretary of Defense Forrestal felt that appointing Eisenhower would be a clear reminder to the USSR of the consequences of going to war and that it was probably the only way to avoid war. Wedemeyer, however, countered that Eisenhower's appointment would compel the United States to send additional forces to Europe and mentioned that the current US war plan focused on the Middle East. Wedemeyer also volunteered that under the current conditions, the United States would be unable to fight a successful war in Europe for a period of one year to eighteen months.[47]

Toward the end of September, Lovett sent an aide memo to the French advising them that on 16 July, the JCS had authorized Clay to participate in the formation of a joint planning staff for the purpose of planning coordinated operations for the withdrawal to and defense of the Rhine.[48] The three Allied commanders in chief, however, were already engaged in that planning process in Wiesbaden, Germany. At about the same time, the JCS notified the Western Union combined chiefs of staff that the Western Union would not have any control over US strategic air forces, as they would report directly to the JCS.[49] From the tenor of the exchanges between the JCS and the US delegation to the Western Union, it appears that the United States had no real problem giving operational control of US forces to the Western Union in the event of war. What the JCS wanted, however, was evidence of completed operational plans so that a timely decision could be made at government level.[50]

At the first meeting of the newly established Western Union Chiefs of Staff Committee in early October, Air Marshal Arthur Tedder, the Western Union's chief of staff, privately told General A. Franklin Kibler, who had replaced Lemnitzer as head of the US delegation, that contrary to previous assertions, all available British army forces would be sent to the Middle East at the outbreak of war and not to Europe. Kibler apparently responded by telling Tedder that before the United States could make any commitment to the defense of Western Europe, it needed to be assured that the Western Union had a sound defense plan and that they were doing the maximum to help themselves and each other improve their capabilities.[51]

In November, the United States was also invited to participate in the Western Union's Committee on Equipment and Armament. Both invitations—to participate in the Chiefs of Staff Committee and the Equipment and Armament Committee—were approved and Kibler was named to the Chiefs of Staff Committee. Nonetheless, the United States remained adamant that participation in all these committees would be on a nonmember basis, as the United States would not join the Western Union.[52] Kibler recommended to the JCS that when important US policy decisions or announcements affecting the Western Union were made, a high-ranking JCS officer should be present at the Western Union Chiefs of Staff meetings.[53]

Also in the fall of 1948, an army-initiated study set out a number of basic and additional assumptions, most of which were almost utopian, that nonetheless were used to determine whether or not the defense of Western Europe could be a successful undertaking. The basic assumptions put forth were that (1) it was cheaper and more effective for the security of the

United States to give the West Europeans the capability to defend themselves; (2) if attacked, the West European nations would defend themselves
to the utmost; and (3) that a program of rearming Western Europe would
be initiated no later than 1 January 1949.[54]

The additional assumptions put forth were that (1) the defense
of Western Europe was possible if a strong rearmament program was initiated by the West European nations with US aid; (2) the West European
nations included the United Kingdom, France, Belgium, Luxembourg, the
Netherlands, Italy, Switzerland, Spain, Portugal, West Germany, and Austria
(Denmark, Norway, and Sweden were considered "possible" but for the
most part viewed as a separate category); (3) West European nations would
develop an organization that would be able to coordinate and utilize their
combined strengths; (4) the European Recovery (Marshall) Plan would
continue to a successful conclusion; and (5) that the combined productive
efforts of Western Europe and the United States would provide enough
armament to make defense practical and effective.

The study assumed that the Soviet Union and its allies would attack
without warning, that they would have sufficient stockpiles of matériel to
conduct operations for nine months, and that military operations would
be conducted primarily on land and with conventional weapons until at
least 1955. Lastly, the study's assumptions about the Allied forces were (1)
that the Allies would use the atomic bomb; (2) that the Western Union
would have already agreed on weapons and equipment standardization;
(3) that each nation would have pooled its existing production capability
and would contribute its fair share; (4) that US equipment requirements
would be based on a force of twenty-five divisions plus reserves; and (5)
that equipping and rearming would not prohibitively affect the civilian
economies of either the West European nations or the United States. The
study stated that it was purely an army study but nevertheless also made
the assumption that sufficient air support would exist to ensure at least
tactical air equality.

To defend Western Europe, it was determined that the most practical and advantageous defense line, which would run from the North
Sea to the Adriatic, would be to the west and south of the line from the
Rhine River to Lake Constance to the high Alps to the Piave River—
a total distance of 887 miles. To defend this line against an enemy that
was assumed to have a force 50 divisions strong on D-Day, reinforced
with an additional 50 divisions by D+30, an Allied force of 78 divisions—57 in the northern group of armies and 21 in the Alps group of

98   armies—would be needed.[55] The study looked at manpower both under
arms and total (male population between 15 and 49 years of age) available to achieve this force. The numbers provided in the study indicate
that as of 1 August 1948 there were 2.4 million men already under arms
(the equivalent of 61½ divisions), excluding West Germany, but that they
lacked mobility, signal communications, antiaircraft artillery, and ammunition. When total available manpower was addressed, it was found that
there were 59.7 million men between 15 and 49 available, 19.8 million
of whom were already trained reserves (9.6 million men and 4.0 million
reserves were German).

From the above, the study concluded that there was no shortage of
manpower or trained reserves and that the defense of Western Europe
along the Rhine-Alps line could be effective. It also concluded that, given
the initial assumptions, the Allies could field sixty divisions by 1 October
1948 and build up to a grand total of ninety-six divisions by 1 January
1953. The cost of this buildup to the United States in surplus military
stocks, including processing, handling, and transport, was estimated to total
$14 billion.[56]

The dreary outlook for the defense of Western Europe continued to
be the main theme in November as well, when the JSPC sent a memo to
General Gruenther confirming the findings of an earlier Western Union
Chiefs of Staff Committee report indicating that as West Germany would
not be in any position to assist in checking a Soviet advance for many years,
there was no question of holding West Germany with the forces available.
Allied forces would have to withdraw to assist in the defense of the Rhine.
The defense of Italy and Trieste was not contemplated. The line to be held
was the Ijssel-Rhine-Franco-Italian border on the Mediterranean.

The JSPC memo essentially agreed with the Western Union report
but felt that the ability to hold the Rhine for any length of time was ques-
tionable and that the key aim should be to deploy forces in such a manner as to delay the Soviet Union for as long as possible. A few days later, a
joint US-British intelligence report on Soviet intentions and capabilities
stated that the West Germans could neither be relied upon nor expected
to provide military support, as they continued to harbor some hostility
against the West. Maps accompanying the report showed Soviet forces on
the English Channel in the vicinity of Amsterdam in D+10 and at the
Franco-Spanish border at D+60.[57]

As 1948 drew to a close, the secretary of the army travelled to Germany, Austria, and Trieste. In a paper titled "Things to Do on Trip," a series

of notes indicated that he was to discuss with Clay rearming Germans in the west zone, a centralized West German police force, Kennan's study on the withdrawal to the perimeters of the occupation zones, and relocating US supply depots to ports in France.[58]

Distrust of Germany was again made manifest when a military security board, stemming from the May 1948 London Conference that reaffirmed the disarmament of Germany, was appointed on 10 December to "ensure observance of clearly-worded laws regarding disarmament and demilitarization" and to ensure that "the development of general activity in Germany, the purpose of which is economic and political recovery, is not deflected from its peaceful aims, and does not create significant war potentials." The board was composed of a commission of three general officers, one from each of the Allied occupying powers (France, the United Kingdom, and the United States) representing the respective military governors, a committee of deputies, and three divisions: military, industrial, and scientific research. Within each division, national elements of each of the three powers were represented and tasked with working in a coordinated manner to ensure compliance, make recommendations, and report any violations.[59]

At the same time (and as indicated in chapter 2, this book), rumors of German rearmament began circulating in the German and foreign presses. As a result of earlier discussions between Secretary of the Army Royall, Secretary of Defense Forrestal, and General Clay, a staff study was initiated in the army's plans and operations division or policy branch on the subject of a German police force for the western zones that recommended the establishment of a centralized police force. Undersecretary of the Army Draper wrote Clay asking for his thoughts. Assistant Secretary of the Army Tracy Voorhees cautioned that any indication that the Allies were "forming the nucleus of a German army" had to be avoided. Secretary Royall, however, overruled the conclusions.[60]

The year 1949 was a watershed year for the United States and the US military establishment. As mentioned in chapter 2, on 4 April 1949, after a long series of negotiations with the Western Union member nations, Canada, and five other West European governments, the United States became one of twelve signatories to the North Atlantic Treaty.[61] Five months later, in September, the Federal Republic of Germany came into being and the question of Germany's military potential now became an explicit Cold War issue. *Le Monde*, a French newspaper, commented that "the rearming of Germany is contained in the Atlantic Pact like the yolk in an egg."[62]

NATO in its formative year was, according to Paul Nitze, "a North American political commitment to the defense of Europe rather than a framework for a military organization."[63] Although functional, the initial NATO organization was cumbersome and diffuse. Each member nations' forces were assigned tasks for which they appeared best suited in one or several regional planning groups. There was, however, no command organization.[64]

Furthermore, Allied response to Soviet military strength was hesitant and restrained. The West European Allies refused to divert funds from rebuilding and economic programs to build up their militaries. In February, for example, General Clarence Huebner, commander in chief of the US European Command (CINCEUCOM), discussed the need for a defense organization inside the NATO organization. He pointed out that in the ten months since the Brussels Treaty Organization had been in existence, it had been impossible for the members to reach any agreement on the contribution of forces for the defense of Western Europe. Not only that, they had refused to guarantee that they would even provide forces on any particular date in the future. Huebner stated that as a result, US occupation forces, which represented an insignificant number of the total forces needed and available, took on an exaggerated place in the planning process and thinking of the Western Union. The British, for example, refused to give an estimate of their force contribution until they were assured that the continental countries would put up sufficient forces to make a defense of the Rhine possible.[65]

Adding to this problem, the US Congress was slow to appropriate funds to assist the Allies. As of April 1950, for example, only $42 million of the promised $1.3 billion Military Development Assistance Plan (MDAP) had been spent. US strategy, which also became NATO strategy, continued to be one of liberation following a Soviet attack, and evacuation to a line behind the Pyrenees remained the ground forces' only option. It was hoped, however, that with the few US troops available acting as a trip wire, US nuclear capability would deter the Soviets from attacking at all.[66] As of 1 July 1949, those 'few' occupation troops in Germany amounted to one and two-thirds divisions and 175 aircraft.[67]

This weakness was further underscored when, during discussions between the JCS and the British chief of staff in August 1949, the JCS stated that the United States could either support the Cairo-Suez area or keep a toe-hold in Europe on the Rhine, but not both. Once NATO became effective, however, the JCS indicated that holding farther east might be a

possibility. If that was not possible, the United States would be prepared to
return to Europe as soon as possible.[68] It should be noted that Offtackle,
the operable EWP at that time, conceded most of West Europe to the
Soviets and focused on securing the United Kingdom and protecting the
Mediterranean littoral while looking to French Morocco as the initial assembly point for US forces. Bradley, then chairman of the JCS, told Air
Marshal Lord Tedder that it would take three months for the United States
to get forces to the Rhine, but that they would do so only if it was evident
that the Rhine could be held. Otherwise, US forces would go elsewhere
and hold the enemy at the Pyrenees. The JCS still believed it would take
twenty-four months after the beginning of the war to be ready to attempt
to defeat Soviet forces on the European continent. [69]

All in all, there was little talk of defending Western Europe, much
less West Germany until late 1949. In fact, and as will be seen below, it
was only after the outbreak of the Korean War in 1950 that plans for
the defense of Western Europe were developed by NATO. Furthermore,
since West Germany was not considered part of the North Atlantic Treaty
area, there was no obligation on the part of either NATO or the Western
Union to defend it.[70]

1950: Year of Decision

In mid-January 1950, a lengthy background study titled "U.S. Policy Respecting the Disarmament and Demilitarization of the Federal German
Republic" was used by the army's G-3 Plans Division, International Branch
to answer a broad spectrum of questions. The questions covered German
participation in the defense of Western Europe, Soviet use of armed forces
being created in East Germany, West German political reliability, the psychological effects of German rearmament on other West European countries, and the ability of the Allies to control German rearmament.[71]

The answers proved that providing German troops in a war against
the USSR offered several advantages, not least among which was their
singular experience of being the only West Europeans to have fought
against the Soviets. Because they would be fighting to protect their own
soil and as 'comrades-in-arms' with the Western powers rather than as a
defeated nation, it was believed that their fighting qualities would not
be exceeded by any other West European force. It was also determined
that unless industrial restrictions were lifted, Germany would not be in
a position to contribute what would be necessary for a reconstituted
armed force.

The study went on to say that over seven million German men were considered fit for military service and that given the training many underwent in the Wehrmacht, they would be fit for military service after a relatively short period of refresher training. In addition, the study found the German male to be "temperamentally well-suited for military service" with a fighting ability "judged to be among the highest in the world," making him without equal in Western Europe.[72]

The disadvantages were, first and foremost, the belief that a remilitarized Germany would be a provocation to the Soviet Union and that it would end any possible Franco-German rapprochement. The study also expressed the belief that, considering Germany's past history, any permission to rearm would see the Germans rearming rapidly (either secretly or overtly) and to the fullest extent the international community would allow. The study concluded that once the armed strength of the West European powers was rebuilt, then and only then could some form of German defense participation be considered.

There was also a favorable consensus in the study regarding German reliability, with respect to both the armed forces and the state.[73] The study acknowledged that with the establishment of a German armed force, the government would insist that its status as a defeated enemy nation end, and that there would most likely be demands for a peace treaty and full sovereignty. It also noted that the government could possibly threaten to align itself with the USSR if its demands were not met, but the study's authors doubted that these threats would be carried out given that West Germany's leaders were considered traitors by the Soviets and that the West Germans were strongly opposed to Communism and hated and feared the Soviets.

The study concluded that (1) given the expected political repercussions in the European countries, France in particular, it was not yet time to consider rearming Germany; (2) long-range strategic plans should, however, consider a part for German armed forces in the defense of Western Europe; and (3) accordingly, "careful political and psychological preparations should be put into motion to make the execution of this program palatable to the peoples [of Western Europe]."[74]

It appears that by this time, the State Department was beginning to acknowledge the Pentagon's deep concern for and interest in rearming West Germany. In early April, Lieutenant Colonel Daley of the G-3 International Branch wrote a staff study called "Possible Contributions by Germany to Her Own Security" for informal distribution to the JSSC, the Office of the Secretary of the Army, Office of the Secretary of Defense,

Office of Military Affairs, Operations Division, Joint War Plans Branch,
and Colonel Byroade at the State Department.

The study cited all the limitations posed by the United States and
Allies on the creation of a German armed force and a centralized police
force or gendarmerie. It cited Senate bill SB-2269, which, if it had passed,
would have authorized up to ten thousand aliens (Germans) to enlist in
the US armed forces. It also cited West Germany's monetary contribution
to support the occupying powers, which was in the region of $600–$700
million, more than the total defense budgets of some of the West European
nations. Colonel Daley concluded that a decision needed to be made on
whether Germany was to be armed or not.[75]

In mid-April 1950, in preparation for the tripartite meeting in London the following month, the Department of State had, as part of the nor-
mal coordination process between departments, given the JCS a number
of papers for review. It was noted by the JSSC in a memo to the director of
the JCS that there was no mention in those papers of German rearmament
as an element of US policy.[76] A few days later, army G-2 (intelligence)
commented on an army general staff study with the recommendation that
a paragraph in the general summary be rewritten to remove an implicit
tone of criticism. The suggested rewrite was:

> It is well to reexamine the political basis for United States
> policy of disarmament. The present United States Policy Direc-
> tive for Mr. McCloy is to insure that "the country (Germany)
> will not be a threat to the independence of other nations or the
> peace of the world." The basis for this policy would appear to
> be invalid. In order to attempt to avert a possible (but un-
> proven) long-term threat to the peace of the world (a rearmed
> Germany) the Western Powers are denying themselves mate-
> rial help in off-setting a definite known present threat – Soviet
> Russia. Recognizing the political difficulties which must be
> overcome in order to profit by a German contribution to the
> security of Western Europe, the goal would appear to be an
> armed Germany. With such a decision, steps should be taken
> toward the objective of a major German contribution to the
> Security of Western Europe.[77]

On 2 May, the JCS made their first unequivocal statement regarding
German rearmament. In a memo to the secretary of defense regarding the

104   draft of a Department of State paper titled "The Problem of Germany," the JCS stated that it was

> firmly of the opinion that, from a military point of view, *the appropriate and early rearming of Western Germany is of fundamental importance to the defense of Western Europe against the USSR.* In order to insure that the energy and resources of the German people become a source of constructive strength to the free world rather than again becoming a menace, either independently or with the USSR primarily, the present disarmament and demilitarization policy with respect to Western Germany should be changed. The Western Germans should, as soon as possible, be given real and substantial opportunity to participate in Western European and North Atlantic regional arrangements.[78]

The state paper, originally McCloy's paper (State FM D A-2/3b), had been forwarded to the JCS for comment and concurrence in preparation for the May Foreign Ministers Conference in London. JCS concurred but recommended the incorporation of several previously expressed JCS views on German rearmament and export controls.[79] State had refused to incorporate those views in an earlier paper ("Protest to Soviet Union Concerning East German Militarized Police") because it felt these views should have first been discussed in the NSC. The JCS felt that even though reiterating its views would not alter the State Department's position, it was necessary and appropriate to repeat them for the record, which they did in a memo to the army chief of staff.[80]

On 8 June, at the request of the secretary of defense, the views of the JCS on the subject of "United States Policy toward Germany" were made known in NSC 71. In this document, the JCS repeated comments they had made in late April 1950 underscoring their belief that US disarmament policy prevented Germany from contributing to the strength of the North Atlantic community. While the JCS comments focused on Germany's economic strength, pointing out its value to the West and the importance of denying it to the USSR, it stressed that before progress could be made toward developing Western Germany into a valuable asset to the Western European and North Atlantic communities, France needed to be prevailed upon to agree to modify the overly restrictive controls on German industry.

NSC 71 repeated the 2 May JCS statement regarding the early rearming of Western Germany and included the recommendation that

> the United States adopt the following policy:
> Bring about recognition by the Western European nations,
> particularly France, of the necessity of changing the present dis-
> armament and demilitarization policy with respect to Western
> Germany so that Western Germany can contribute effectively
> to the security of Western Europe.
> It is recognized that the political and psychological in psy-
> chological obstacles in Western Europe will have to be over-
> come if the present Allied policy is changed. Pressure should be
> brought on France to insure that unilateral action by France,
> such as that recently taken by France regarding the Saar Basin,
> is not repeated but that France be persuaded to recognize that
> the USSR is a greater menace to the independence of France
> than is Germany.[81]

NSC 71 concluded with the JCS again strongly urging the foreign
ministers of the three Allied powers to approve the recommendation of
the three high commissioners and authorize West Germany to have a
five-thousand-person federal police force.

At the end of June, most likely in reaction to the North Korean attack on South Korea that had taken place five days earlier, Bradley sent
a memorandum to Rear Admiral Arthur C. Davis, director of the JCS, in
which he wrote that he had been thinking for some time about creating
a study on the rearming of West Germany: "If our Chiefs feel that steps
should be taken toward the rearming of Western Germany, I believe we
should make a specific recommendation to the President to this effect."
Bradley felt it was unrealistic to continue talking about building up the
defense of Western Europe "without facing up to this subject of at least
partially rearming Western Germany."[82]

The Department of State responded to the JCS's comments in NSC
71 in the first week of July. Their lengthy response appeared to reflect
the personal anti-rearmament biases of George Kennan and others in
the State Department at the time and ignored the Defense Department's
oft-repeated statement that it believed "the appropriate and early rearming of Western Germany [was] of fundamental importance to the defense of Western Europe."[83] The State Department's response significantly

downplayed the JCS's statement: "It is understood that the Joint Chiefs of Staff are not pressing for the immediate rearmament of Western Germany, but rather recognizing the political conditions, are urging that steps be taken to create conditions in Europe under which agreement could be obtained from all concerned on this question."[84]

The State Department's response went on to say that all (i.e., the US, French, and British governments) agreed Germany had to be quickly brought into a close and firm association with the West, but it had to be done in such a way as to ensure its commitment to the West. The response continued that the London tripartite and recent North Atlantic Council (NAC) meetings concluded that Germany's rearmament and inclusion in NATO was "premature to the point where profitable discussion cannot yet be held." It also stated that the majority of Germans did not want an armed force and that they did not feel their government was truly representative. More time was needed, it continued, to "develop democratic tendencies on the part of the German people and a more responsive form of government." It cautioned that arming the Germans would reverse the progress made by France and that the Germans, already contributing 22 percent of their budget to cover occupation costs, could hardly contribute more.[85]

It briefly addressed the possibility of Germany producing non-ordnance items for NATO forces and implied that a rearmed Germany "could not yet be counted on with reasonable certainty." Lastly, the response stated that after building up strength in the West, and before seeking to rearm Germany, the Allies should "probably wish to make a further effort to reunify Germany."[86]

Three days later, after reviewing both NSC 71 and 71/1, the secretary of the army wrote the secretary of defense that in light of the possible worldwide implications of the Korean situation, the United States "should avail itself of at least a part of the industrial and military manpower potential of Western Germany ... through controlled rearmament." He recommended that the Secretary of Defense take that position in NSC discussions and that the NSC staff prepare papers to that effect, including dissenting views. His proposal also mentioned the controlled rearmament of Japan and the need to firmly control the export of strategic items to the Soviet-controlled areas.[87]

Later that month, General Thomas Handy, who had replaced Huebner as CINCEUCOM, wrote a letter to General Collins, the army chief of staff, describing a conversation he had had with McCloy a few days earlier in which the subject of German rearmament came up. McCloy told Handy that in a conversation he'd had with Chancellor Adenauer, Adenauer stated that in case of war, the West Germans should have some form of organization that could assist in the defense of their country. He spoke in terms of a defensive force of approximately 250,000 men in ten divisions and indicated that the East Germans did not have that problem as they in fact had an army in the form of their Bereitschaftspolizei.[88]

Handy continued that he told McCloy he had given much thought to the subject of the "successful defense of Western Europe" and had come to the conclusion that it would be "extremely difficult, if not impossible, without German assistance." His studies had brought him to the same goal as the chancellor. Handy pointed out the JCS position had been made in a number of papers but had not been accepted by the NSC. While McCloy stated he could not support the rearmament of Germany at this time, he suggested a three-phased approach that would gradually bring the Allies to the same point:[89]

1. Phase one, an additional ten thousand German industrial police be recruited
2. Phase two, institute military training in all industrial police units, to include training as a cadre for Germany military organizations
3. Phase three, the eventual organization of a West German armed force

Handy explained in the letter that he had taken steps to increase the German industrial police by ten thousand, with funds coming from the German mark budget to which the chancellor had agreed. Plans for organizing, training, and housing the additional industrial police were progressing rapidly, though some steps were being taken covertly. Handy included a brief description of the EUCOM labor service and industrial police units and functions as an attachment to the letter and promised to keep General Collins informed.[90]

In a follow-up note that same day, Handy told Collins he had received a series of telegrams between McCloy and Byroade that emphasized McCloy's belief that the Germans should be allowed to enlist in the US armed forces. Handy continued that McCloy also wrote that once the ten thousand industrial police were absorbed, a further increase should be sought. Handy said it appeared that McCloy's thinking regarding German rearmament was changing, as he wrote, "While my view is that we should

108   make no plans to permit Germans to fight with us if an emergency arose, we should make no commitment in this regard unless we have the equipment and the means to enable them to effectively do so."[91]

Ironically, Byroade also forwarded the three cables to Collins on 20 July, asking him in an accompanying letter if he would designate an appropriate person in the Pentagon with whom he could talk about these cables. Byroade indicated that he was somewhat confused by them and felt that McCloy also did not yet have a clear concept on forming and rearming a German army, but appeared to have very definite views about enlisting Germans in the US armed forces. Byroade said that if that were feasible, it might be an option for using Germans in the defense of Western Europe without making the political decision to create a German armed force.[92]

On the same July day that Byroade wrote Collins, the JSSC sent a lengthy report on the rearmament of Germany to the JCS for passage to the Secretary of Defense. The report went to great lengths to counter the State Department's response in NSC 71/1 and put forward the case for the necessity of rearming West Germany. The report indicated that despite the military aid the United States had already provided and continued to provide Western Europe, the lack of the West European nations' military strength invited both subversion and attack by the USSR. The report argued that a certain amount of military strength must be available at the outset of any conflict and that this strength must relate to the defensive position to be held. Current forces in Western Europe were too small and neither the United States nor the United Kingdom were in a position to do more in the early stages of a war. The mobilization plans of the other West European countries were such that they could not mobilize in time to prevent being overrun by the USSR.[93]

The report continued that even by 1954, when war might occur according to NATO plans, the planned strength of Alliance forces would still be insufficient without the addition of German forces. It pointed out that the agreed-upon line of defense—the Ijssel-Rhine River—afforded no defense to Denmark or to one-third of the Netherlands, and that it sacrificed the industrial complex of the Ruhr while permitting the physical unification of Germany under the Soviets. The promise that occupation forces could protect West Germany was illusory without "substantial German military participation."[94]

It accepted that a risk could be incurred if the rearmament of Western Germany was not controlled, but stated that there would be no threat to West European unity, as had been alleged in NSC 71/1, because "all of the military leaders of the Western European nations [had] expressed themselves privately in favor of controlled rearmament of Western Germany." Although there was much more, the report concluded by recommending that regarding the rearming of Germany, the president should be advised that a successful defense of Western Europe against Soviet attack was not then possible nor was it likely to be possible by 1954 unless a rearmed Germany participated. It endorsed the US government immediately pressing for a controlled rearmament of and the organization of an adequate federal police force for West Germany as the initial phase of its rearmament program, and cautioned that if West Germany was not rearmed, the JCS would need to revise their war plans to account for the fact that the United States would have to rely on political measures rather than military measures for the protection of Western Europe against invasion.[95]

The last week of July saw additional action regarding attempts to obtain a positive decision on German rearmament. General Charles Bolte, assistant chief of staff G-3 (operations), wrote General Alfred M. Gruenther, Eisenhower's chief of staff, about a discussion between General Cortland Schuyler, chief of the plans and policy group for the army general staff, and Byroade. Bolte told Gruenther that Byroade had indicated that a number of State Department officers, particularly W. Averell Harriman, believed a decision to rearm Western Germany should be made, and that Secretary of State Acheson was undecided but could conceivably be convinced to make this decision in the near future. Bolte went on to say that Byroade felt that those opposed to German rearmament, including himself, would be forced to accept it if the international situation continued to deteriorate. Byroade said that the State Department did not want to decide, because rearming would mean "a resurgence of the military clique in Germany and the virtual abandonment of the hope for eventual development of a truly democratic government for West Germany."[96]

Byroade also confirmed that the State Department had given full approval to Handy's proposal to increase the industrial police by ten thousand and that they would attempt to obtain French and British concurrence on this matter. Bolte implied that it would be best to give Acheson more time to make up his mind before pushing too hard in the NSC for a decision on the German issue. If Acheson could get NSC support, Bolte surmised, it would be much easier to get presidential approval.[97]

JCS 2124/9 was revised based on some of the objections and comments made by the army chief of staff but without changing the thrust of the argument, and the last paragraph, containing recommendations for advising the president, read

a. The early rearmament of Western Germany, seen in the light of the new United States program of increased military assistance for the countries of Western Europe, could contribute decisively to a successful defense of Western Europe. Without Western German forces, it will not be possible to hold the Ruhr which is vital to Western Europe;

b. The United States Government should immediately press for a controlled rearmament of Western Germany and for the organization of an adequate federal police force for Western Germany as the initial phase of its rearmament program; and

c. The question at this time is not one of whether we should risk the success of our political objectives vis-à-vis Western Germany, but rather whether or not we can afford to jeopardize the security of the United States by not utilizing all of the forces that are available to us.[98]

On 1 August, Bolte sent a letter with an attached staff study to Gruenther informing him that the army G-3 staff had given the matter of a controlled rearmament of West Germany a great deal of study and concluded that "the only practical way ... would be to provide for the entrance of Western Germany into the North Atlantic Treaty Organization ... to permit her to furnish her pro rata share of ground forces as her contribution to the collective security ... of Western Europe." The memorandum continued that the objective was to establish an approved position within the NSC in order to conduct talks with the French and British. It recommended that the attached staff study become the official Department of the Army position, that Gruenther discuss this matter with Averill Harriman and others at the State Department and even provide them with a copy of the staff study, and that G-3 be prepared to use the staff study to make the necessary changes to JCS 2124/11 ("The Problem of Germany").[99]

Military staff studies are usually written in four sections: the problem, assumptions, discussion, and conclusions. What is of interest is that this particular staff study saw the problem as one of determining the best method for providing a controlled rearmament of West Germany and assumed, for the purpose of the study, that the departments of state and defense were both in "entire agreement" that West Germany had to be rearmed, which, of course, was not the case. After a wide-ranging discussion, it decided that various recommendations (enlistment of German aliens in the US Army or the utilization of German "service troops" as a first step toward German rearmament) should not be accepted. Nor should any other alternative method, such as the establishment of a European Army outside NATO or the Western Union defense organization or the absorption of German units into British, French, or any other West European army be concurred with. It added that the Department of Defense should no longer press for the establishment of a federal West German police force because such a force was unpalatable to the Department of State and no longer necessary since agreement had been reached on rearmament. The Department of Defense should instead exert all its efforts toward obtaining authorization for a controlled rearmament of West Germany.

The study also wanted the Department of Defense to immediately press for West Germany's entrance into NATO, and stated that only after consultation with the governments of Great Britain and France should there be a decision on the number of divisions to be furnished by West Germany and the exact nature of the controls to be placed on its rearmament. It suggested, however, that for planning purposes, fifteen or twenty divisions should be provided.[100]

Several days later, on 5 August, a conference was held at the State Department with Byroade representing the Office of German Affairs, and Lieutenant Colonel V. P. Mock and Major J. G. K. Miller representing the Department of the Army's G-3 Division. Byroade, who had read the 1 August staff study, stated that the army had misunderstood the Department of State's position regarding German rearmament. He clarified that the Department of State was opposed to it unless there was a "proper political formula and organizational framework" that would be acceptable to the European powers, particularly France, and would not jeopardize German internal political objectives. Byroade informed the conference that public opinion polls taken in West Germany showed that the Germans were opposed to a German army but would accept service in a European army. He argued that the army proposal appeared to be for the rearmament of a German national army, indicating that the views of the Department of State and the Department of Defense were far apart.[101]

Byroade then presented the outline of an idea he was working on regarding a European army.[102] Both Lieutenant Colonel Mock and Major Miller replied that Byroade's plan was nothing more than the present

Western Union organization expanded to include the United States and Western Germany. They also said it was unrealistic to continue NATO and the Western Union with their complicated structures and the great amount of equipment being provided to both by the United States under MDAP, and then add yet another separate European army that would also need equipment from the United States.

Both sides however agreed that something had to be done to provide a combined command structure and that the division was the largest German unit that should be permitted under a rearmament program. The conference concluded with Byroade speaking about the security problem and the psychological nature of the problem. If it were leaked that the United States was contemplating the use of German manpower, he argued, it would confirm to the Germans that the United States considered them "cannon fodder." Additionally, a leak of plans to supply Germany might discourage French participation in NATO. Lastly, he believed that the first step required foreign minister–level talks on the political aspects of his plan and that if agreement was reached, the French should take the lead.

On 9 August, General Handy again wrote General Collins, telling him that plans "for the organization, housing, employment, and training of the 10,000 additional industrial police [were] well along." One thousand had already been recruited and when he was queried regarding the issuance of arms to industrial police units, he answered only that the industrial police were being reorganized and issued small arms to make them more efficient. He wrote that discussions with McCloy on this matter continued but that he disagreed with parts of a paper prepared by the office of the high commissioner that had been discussed at a conference in Frankfurt. Specifically, General Handy questioned the accuracy of statements regarding German unwillingness to support a German army and disagreed with statements that it was undesirable or politically unfeasible to create national German armed forces "at this time." Handy did not disagree with McCloy and the State Department's belief that German rearmament could only happen within the context of a European army or another integrating approach that would make it politically feasible; he just said, "I do feel that the use of German manpower, resources, and productive capacity is a prime necessity for the successful defense of Western Europe." [103]

After the two G-3 representatives reported to General Bolte on their meeting with Byroade on 5 August, Bolte drafted a memo to Gruenther on 10 August briefly summarizing the meeting and the State Department's insistence on Germany's integration in a European Army. Bolte wrote that Byroade had informed the G-3 representatives that this position had been endorsed by ambassadors Bruce (in Paris) and Douglas (in London), and of course, High Commissioner McCloy. Bolte stated that, in his opinion, the Department of State's proposal would "reduce the military sovereignty status of the European countries to the level of Germany," which was at odds with G-3's intention to "raise Germany's status to that of the other countries and accept her, subject to controls, into NATO and Western Union arrangements." Nationalism, which the Department of State appeared to fear, was the foundation of the defense efforts of the Western Union and NATO. Bolte's memo then recommended that the JCS forward its views on German rearmament to the secretary of defense, indicating that revisions to JCS 2124/11 were being forwarded separately, and that Gruenther brief the JCS on the elements of Byroade's proposal, which was attached to the memo.[104]

That same day, Schuyler met with Byroade and his assistant, Colonel Gerhardt, to discuss German rearmament and the differences between the positions of the departments of state and defense. According to the memo written of this meeting, Schuyler explained to Byroade how NATO worked and planned, and that Byroade's idea of having one American commander in charge of both field forces and economic issues was inappropriate. Schuyler explained a number of other issues that, ultimately, caused Byroade to change his mind and agree that German forces could, in fact, be integrated into NATO, provided an American was made commander of these NATO forces.[105]

Byroade showed Schuyler a 'memorandum for the record' from the secretary of defense showing that the president had given his general approval to the idea of German military units in some form of army for the defense of Western Europe and stating that the secretary of state would be presenting a paper to the NSC on that subject. Byroade finished by saying that he would be drafting that paper but that he would coordinate fully with G-3. Nonetheless, he specified that the paper would stipulate that any German units created needed to be integrated into a European force that would have an American commander.[106]

The above-mentioned staff study, the JCS's repeated position given in NSC 71, and continued army insistence that West Germany had to be armed and integrated into NATO through a program of controlled armament supervised by NATO apparently convinced Secretary of Defense Johnson. On 14 August, he concluded that due to "present developments in the international situation" (i.e., Korea), the rearming of Germany was necessary to the defense of Western Europe.[107] Johnson's position undoubtedly led to the revisions of the JCS paper on the German problem that inextricably linked the security of the United States with that of Western Europe and became the Defense Department's response to the State Department paper on establishing a European defense force.

This paper, sent by Undersecretary of State H. Freeman Matthews to the secretary of defense, stated that it was the desire of the Department of State to reach an early agreement on the subject of the European Defense Force in order to present it to the president by the beginning of the following week for the upcoming September meeting between Acheson and the foreign ministers of Great Britain and France.[108]

The Department of State paper began with a long "Estimate of the Situation," which described the inability of Western Europe to defend itself and the failure of United Nations forces, including US forces, to staunch the North Korean aggression. These issues caused the West Europeans to "contemplate their own fate" and, despite trust in an eventually mobilized America, fall hopeless and despondent at the thought of another occupation. It recognized that the need for some form of German contribution to the defense of Western Europe was apparent but stated that the Department of State still strongly opposed the creation of German national forces, a view supported by the US ambassadors in Western Europe and by France, "who [was] assuming more and more the position of leadership on the Continent."[109]

The paper continued that if the United States was willing "to accept the responsibility of full participation in the European defense effort ... [that the United States] believed conditions may now be favorable ... for creating a really effective European Defense Force which could assimilate a direct contribution by Germany in a manner acceptable to all concerned." It then restated what Bolte had said earlier to Gruenther: "This involves in practice the voluntary surrender of a degree of sovereignty in the most vital elements of sovereignty, i.e., the security field." The State Department paper assumed that given an international commander with "real authority," the European nations would accept this and that this surrender of sovereignty would be a driving force toward increased European unification.[110]

The paper went on to describe the basic elements involved in forming a European defense force: government direction; command and general staff direction; organization of field forces; production, procurement, and supply; and individual national security organizations (except that

Germany would have no general staff; instead, there would be a federal   115
ministry to organize the recruitment of German national units and act as
a service and procurement agency).

The paper concluded that the United States should accept this force
and that a chief of staff for Western Europe should be appointed to prepare
for the appointment of a supreme commander, much like the COSSAC
organization of World War II. It recommended a centralized direction of
procurement and production, that the supreme commander be an American, and that this matter be discussed as a matter of urgency with the
European nations concerned.

JCS's response was to recommend that its memo, included in an earlier version of its "Problem of Germany" paper (JCS 2124/11), be submitted to the Secretary of Defense with some minor revisions. The key
revision, which clearly stated the Defense Department's position, was in
paragraph 8:

> It is realized that the Western Allies have taken and are tak-
> ing steps toward the re-admission of Germany as a member
> of Western society. *The Joint Chiefs of Staff would urge, however,*
> *that the United States insist upon participation of Western Germany*
> *in the North Atlantic Treaty arrangements.* This participation is a
> logical and necessary step in the implementation of German
> rearmament and the establishment of German forces as a factor
> in NATO planning. The integration of German forces into
> NATO would contribute materially to the ultimate success
> of the political and economic measures being undertaken to
> join Western Germany firmly with the West. Furthermore, this
> indication that Western Germany was being accepted as an in-
> tegral and coequal member of the Western community should
> generate in the German people an instinctive will to fight in
> the defense of that community.[111]

It should be noted that in recommending the early rearmament of
Germany in JCS 2124/11, the JCS was again unequivocally saying, "The
question at this time is not one of whether we should risk the success
of our political objectives vis-à-vis Western Germany, but rather whether
or not we can afford to jeopardize the security of the United States and
of Western Europe by not utilizing all of the forces that can be made available to us."[112]

JCS Response to President Truman's Letter

As related in chapter 2, on 26 August, President Truman sent each secretary a letter that contained eight key questions that he requested both departments work together on to develop recommendations for his decision regarding German rearmament. On 28 August, G-3 responded to the army chief of staff with general answers to be used as a basis for discussion, but requested that final answers be deferred until the JSSC had completed its study of the questions. Briefly, a synopsis of G-3's recommendations were:[113]

1. Agree to the principal of committing additional US forces to the defense of Europe [though no valid capability existed to do so until June 1951].

2. Strongly recommend German participation in the defense of Europe but the State Department's concept of a unified European defense force is unrealistic. The only practical method to defend Western Europe is to strengthen NATO and integrate Germany therein.

3. Favor a supreme commander, but only in time of war. A COSSAC-type headquarters is all that is needed now.

4. Favor a Combined Chief of Staff (CCS) organization. See answer 3.

5. No comment on supporting a European war production board. It is a question for the munitions board to answer.

6. Favor full US participation in European defense organs with an American as head of COSSAC and an eventual US supreme commander in time of war.

7. Favor transforming the Standing Group into a Combined Chiefs of Staff organization.

8. Invigorate NATO, in favor of the immediate integration of Germany and Spain into NATO.

On 1 September, the JSPC drafted a memo for the secretary of defense in which it acknowledged that the initial response to the president's questions was only an outline position for the Defense Department to adopt.[114] It then offered comments to the "Conclusions" of the Department of State's paper to flesh out the outline. In addition to the general answers provided for the president's questions, which were expanded, the memo stated emphatically that the United States should not accept the

European Defense Force concept and repeated that this concept reduced the military sovereignty of the European nations to Germany's level, which was counter to JCS's proposal to raise Germany's status to that of the other West European countries. It again reiterated that the Department of Defense believed, contrary to the Department of State, that the controlled rearmament of Germany under NATO would not bring about the creation of a German Defense Ministry, a general staff, or a war industry that would terrorize Europe.

In an appendix to the memo, the JSPC laid out a plan for the development of what it called German Security Forces. It opened by stating that "the active and effective integration of the people of Western Germany into the defense of Western Europe would add materially to the assurance that Europe [could] be held against a Soviet invasion." It repeated yet again that the United States could not afford to jeopardize its security and that of Western Europe by not utilizing all of the forces that could be made available. Furthermore, it reiterated the US position that NATO was "the appropriate framework for promoting the integrated defense of the North Atlantic Treaty area," and that the United States should participate fully in all of NATO's defense agencies. The appendix continued that at the appropriate time, there should be a NATO supreme commander, that the Military Production and Supply Board should be strengthened, and that the United States was prepared to accept responsibility for its chairmanship. Most prophetically, it also stated that a strengthened NATO made a separate Western Union organization superfluous and that it should be absorbed into NATO at an appropriate time.[115]

On 2 September, a page was added to the appendix that outlined the program for West German Security Forces. This additional page contained the recommendation that US and Allied policy regarding Western Germany be changed, stating that it would offer the following: "(a) The immediate provision of adequate security forces for Western Germany, including police forces adequate to counter the threat from the East German indigenous forces; and, (b) The initial steps toward entry of Germany into NATO at the earliest practicable time." It allowed for the creation of a German training command under a German officer, possibly titled "Inspector General, German Security Forces," and recommended the initial organization of two to four infantry divisions, subsequently growing to a total of ten to fifteen. It specified that weapons and supplies would come, in part, from other NATO countries while deficiencies and heavy equipment would come from the US Military Assistance Program.[116]

Lastly, the addendum outlined controls to be placed on the German forces, to wit: no air force or navy; German forces in Germany would be proportionally smaller than French forces in France; the largest German unit would be the division which, following training, would be allocated to each of the Allied forces in Germany; German industry would produce only light transportation and equipment (heavy equipment, such as tanks and heavy weapons, would come from other sources); the highest rank for German commanders would be at the division level; and lastly, there would be no German General Staff Corps.[117]

Following discussions in the Joint Staff and the individual service staffs, the chief of naval operations recommended that two significant changes be made to the appendix. The first was that West Germany be allowed to have a tactical air force and limited naval forces, such as those required for harbor defense and coastal patrol activities. The second was that German divisions, once trained, be deployed as directed by the NATO standing group and that advanced training be accomplished under appropriate Allied force commanders.[118] As will be seen in chapter 4, these recommendations were approved.

From the earliest days of the Cold War, the Department of Defense, while mindful of US policies meant to keep Germany disarmed, recognized the need to join forces with the United States' West European allies to establish a line of defense in western Europe, and also that this would be impossible without West German participation. In particular, it recognized and valued the additional combat power German troops and combat experience would bring to the defense of Western Europe. To that end, the various Department of Defense organs spent a great deal of time and effort attempting to provide the president with the best military advice possible while still respecting the constraints imposed upon them. Even so, they never wavered in their belief that a national German army within NATO was the best solution to the "German question."

4

From EDF to EDC to NATO

Acheson's presentation of the US demand to rearm West Germany on 12 September 1950 initiated a chain of events that led to the French-inspired Pleven Plan and the European Defence Community (EDC) concept ostensibly designed to integrate West Germany into a European defense force. Once the French were allowed to take the lead, the United States made itself an onlooker, sitting on the sidelines, unable to direct the course of the initiative it had created. Over the next four years, the EDC concept became US policy. The Department of Defense attempted to support it but never abandoned its advocacy of West Germany in NATO. Nonetheless, the Truman and later Eisenhower administrations clung to EDC as the only way to integrate a West German military contribution to the defense of Europe.

The final joint State-Army response to President Truman's eight questions was signed by Acheson and Secretary of Defense Johnson on 8 September and forwarded to the president that same day.[1] As part of the answer to the first question (whether the United States was prepared to send additional forces to Europe), Johnson recommended that additional troops be committed at the earliest possible date and estimated that the overall strength of US forces in Europe should be "about 4 infantry divisions and the equivalent of 1½ armored divisions, 8 tactical air groups, and appropriate naval forces," but added that "the U.S. should make it clear that it [was] now squarely up to the signatories of the North Atlantic Treaty to provide the balance of the forces required for the initial defense."[2] The following day, President Truman made public his decision to reinforce Europe "based on the sincere expectation that [American] efforts [would] be met with similar action on their part."[3]

Acheson wrote in his memoir that the departments of state and defense debated the rearmament issue for two weeks before a compromise was reached, which he then carried to the Tripartite Meeting in New York. This compromise, also known as the single package, was meant to be offered to the Allies on a take-it-or-leave-it basis and contained several key elements: in addition to increased US forces in Europe, it offered US participation with the United Kingdom and all the other NATO armies in a combined European defense force, an international staff, and a supreme commander. The offer, however, was contingent on the Allies boosting the capabilities (and sizes) of their forces and accepting the inclusion of German contingents that would be added at the division level but without a German General Staff.[4]

The September Tripartite Meeting of the "big three" (Acheson, Schuman, and Bevin), at which the US position on the rearmament of West Germany was presented, and the NATO Foreign Ministers Meeting that followed have been examined by a number of scholars. So too have the negotiations over the French alternative, the Pleven Plan, and its successor, the EDC.[5] While it is not the intent here to repeat what has already been so well covered, I must add that the single package, also dubbed "the bomb at the Waldorf" by the French, was neither a "bomb" nor the surprise Schuman claimed. If anything, it was most likely a misunderstanding by both Schuman and Bevin. While the issue of arming West Germany was not on the meeting agenda, both Foreign Ministers had been informed days beforehand of Acheson's thoughts.

Ten days earlier, on 2 September, Acheson had sent Ambassador Bruce in Paris and Ambassador Douglas in London an eyes-only cable instructing them to "call urgently" on the French and British Foreign Ministers and tell them that the US government had been closely following European suggestions to create a unified European defense force and that if created, there would have to be a provision to establish a supreme commander. "In this event," Acheson wrote, "it should be necessary to integrate into such a Force German units in a controlled status without thereby creating a German National Army."[6] Acheson wrote further that the US government believed that for this to be effective, additional US troops might be required. He added that the US Government believed these suggestions were important and that he proposed to raise them at the September tripartite. Furthermore, he specifically asked that Schuman and Bevin be told that US participation in the defense of Europe would involve greater commitments than the United States had previously been willing to consider and that such commitments would be dependent on Europeans willingness to make greater efforts to increase their existing forces.[7]

In addition, on 6 September, Bevin sent Acheson a personal message, the substance of which was also communicated to French prime minster René Pleven, relaying that the British chiefs of staff had concluded that the West European nations could not "build up the necessary strength to assure the defence of the territories of N.A.T. [North Atlantic Treaty] Powers without the participation of Germany."[8] Bevin wrote further that His Majesty's Government was not prepared to agree to the re-creation of a German army, although the incorporation of German contingents in the Western defense forces, should the United States or France wish to discuss it, would not be excluded. He believed, however, that the German government would find it impossible to remilitarize on the scale recommended by the British chiefs of staff and thus felt it best to first create the 150,000-man federal police force that Chancellor Adenauer had asked for on 17 August.[9]

Bevin's message also included a number of pros and cons, including the statement that the Germans would have "a regrettable, if understandable, malicious satisfaction that the western Allies who [had] so effectively disarmed Germany should now stand in need of German assistance." He summed up his thoughts by stating that the Alliance was caught up in a vicious circle: "The French will not agree to any form of German re-armament until France is strong. But France will not make the effort to be strong unless there is a real prospect of assuring Western defence, which in turn cannot be done without a measure of German rearmament."[10]

Acheson evidently believed his proposal would be taken positively: On 8 September, four days before the foreign ministers met, the State Department drafted an optimistic communiqué, which stated that

> the Ministers are fully aware of the natural desire of the German people to participate in the defense of their homeland in case of necessity. The Ministers have accordingly discussed the association of Germany in an improved organization for European defense, in which the United States would play a full role. This matter will continue to be studied and will be the subject of discussions with the Governments of the German Federal Republic . . . as well as the other free European governments. The German people can be assured that they will be permitted to join in the defense of Germany as part of the common defense of the common freedom of Western Europe.[11]

One can only conclude that the issue of West German participation in the defense of Europe was now on the table and an expected topic of discussion at the upcoming tripartite and NATO foreign ministers meeting, and that both the British and the French knew it.

The September 1950 Tripartite Meeting

The minutes of the opening meeting on 12 September indicate only that Acheson stated that it was unreasonable to attempt to defend all of Germany without getting assistance from the Germans, and that the United States preferred to see German units serve in a European defense force rather than create a German police force. No mention was made of what that European defense force should look like—an example of which McCloy and Byroade had so painfully worked out—only the US preference that there be one. Schuman appeared to agree, stating that it would be illogical to defend Western Europe, including Germany, without contributions from Germany. His opposition initially stemmed from his belief that due to the scarcity of resources available for defense, they needed to first be distributed to the NATO countries, and that when a "minimum level" was reached and the combined staff and supreme commander had been appointed, only then might France consider the German matter. While it was expected that France would be difficult, it was not expected that France would refuse to even consider German rearmament "in principle," which is exactly what it did. This setback and subsequent attempts by new secretary of defense George Marshall to relax the US proposal did not sit well with the JCS. In hindsight, it is clear that the Pentagon was looking at a strategic military problem while the European allies were looking at a political German problem.[12]

Bevin's response was to voice concern that such a plan would put the Germans in a "bargaining position," which would make the situation very difficult. He believed the Germans would not go along and thought it better to give the Germans what they asked for rather than asking them for something. Bevin again voiced his fear of a German resurgence but allowed that the United Kingdom would have the best people available examine the matter.[13]

Following the first day's afternoon session, Acheson met privately and separately with both Bevin and Schuman but each discussion was primarily about the president's statement that the United States would participate in creating forces in Europe for its defense, unity of command, and financial and supply matters. Both Bevin and Schuman agreed to strengthen

West Germany's police, but Schuman insisted that the police could not be allowed to become a German army. The result of that meeting was both parties agreeing to ask the high commissioners to formulate views on the integration of German contingents in a European force and to instruct the NATO defense ministers to submit an approved medium-term defense plan for 1954 and plans for force composition and distribution for 1951 and 1952.[14]

On the morning of 14 September, Acheson, who had been sending cables to the president on a daily basis during the meetings, confessed that he didn't think Bevin and Schuman had "yet grasped [the proposal's] full significance and implications." He mentioned that while Bevin did not support the US position on using German forces, he did not oppose it. Schuman, on the other hand, "expressed the very strong and firm opposition of his government" to the idea of creating "purely German units." Acheson indicated the three would again meet privately in an attempt to find some formula that the French could accept.[15]

The minutes from 14 September, however, repeat much from earlier meetings: the identified need for German forces to enable the defense of Western Europe as far east as possible, Bevin's response that he could not yet give an answer, and Schuman's reply that it was a question of manpower versus matériel and that adding German manpower would give the Russians cause to go to war. Acheson countered that it would take time to increase production and even longer for Germany to begin to draft soldiers. He said that Russia was currently deterred by the US atomic arsenal but that this would not always be the case, which was where the danger lay, not in the creation of German forces. Acheson then asked Schuman and Bevin for a decision on German participation but said that the decision would not have to be put into effect for some time.

Bevin again responded that he wanted to give an answer but could not, and even though McCloy had relayed that Adenauer wanted German forces to participate,[16] Schuman again replied that the French public opinion would not accept a rearmed Germany until France was armed. He did say, however, that he had asked his government for a "conditional decision" and expected an answer by 18 September.[17]

On 15 September, Acheson wrote that in the meetings of the previous two days, the other foreign ministers had "persistently failed to come to grips with the central problem of the defense of Europe." Acheson had pointed out in a private meeting with Bevin and Schuman and the three high commissioners that the president had brought about "a complete revolution in American foreign policy" and that the steps to put substantial US forces in Europe and place them in an integrated force, to agree to a command structure, and so on were "unprecedented steps in U.S. history." He complained that it was clear that the British and French were prepared to accept what the United States offered but not prepared to accept what the United States asked—they "flatly refused in any way the question of German participation."[18]

That same day, Acheson addressed the fifth session of the NATO foreign ministers meeting and spoke quite eloquently and specifically about what the United States desired. He immediately put aside the question of German police, saying that while it was necessary in whatever form it might take, it was an internal security issue and not the kind of force that would oppose the East German Bereitschaften or a Soviet invasion. He then addressed the German military issue, stating, again very unequivocally, that he did not mean a German national army. German units, he said, would be incorporated in and under the command of the force for the defense of Europe. He hoped the units would be small so that they could be combined with English, French, or Canadian units, and reassured the others that the ordnance should be produced outside Germany to preclude any capacity for independent action. He explained further that each German unit would be equipped in such a manner that its equipment would be of little use unless it remained part of the European defense force.[19]

Acheson then addressed the time factor, emphasizing the fact that Germany had no governmental structure or legal basis at the present to deal with the military question. By the time the necessary changes to West Germany's constitution, the Basic Law, were made, a list of men of military age created, trained, and so on, at least two years would have passed. In order to develop Western European strength in time, it was necessary to act soon. He also countered arguments that creating German units would interfere with equipping members of NATO, explaining that it would take anywhere from eighteen months to two years to produce that equipment in volume and that there would be no diversion of equipment. Lastly, he said that NATO should not use fear of provoking Russia as a reason not to build military strength, because military weakness was what might actually bring on an attack.[20]

The following day, 16 September, a member of the army staff wrote Admiral Robbins, the US military advisor to Acheson, that General Schuyler believed the JCS felt quite strongly that "we" (the army) should stand for acceptance of the full US concept, particularly the acceptance of German participation. The army felt a limited delay of a week, should the foreign ministers reach an impasse, was acceptable before they reconsidered the issue. They also found a month's delay acceptable but desired a showdown at the defense ministers meeting in October. The army was willing to accept an even greater delay but insisted that German integration take place and that it not be deferred too long.[21]

While the three foreign ministers and the remainder of the NATO foreign and defense ministers discussed the pros and cons of arming West Germany, the Defense Department continued to move forward in the expectation that West Germany would, in fact, be armed. On 19 September, for example, General Bolte cabled General Handy: "In view of the imminence of possible decision by Foreign Ministers and North Atlantic Council authorizing creation of a West German security force, believe we should accelerate planning for such forces."[22] Two days later, General Bradley sent two memos to Marshall. In the first, the JCS recognized that it would take time before German divisions could be formed but maintained that the ultimate objective should be kept in mind during negotiations. Bradley also recommended that a program leading to some security forces in Germany be started immediately.[23] The second memo stated: "Our eventual objective must be, without creating a German national army, to obtain a German contribution to a European defense force equivalent of about 10–15 divisions, with certain safeguards, including: (1) No aviation, (2) Limitations on armament production, (3) No national German General Staff."[24]

The following day, Byroade sent a memo to Spofford at NATO, telling him that the United States should take the position that the US plan already contained safeguards to prevent the creation of an independent German force that could be misused by the German government. However, within those safeguards, Germany had to be incorporated in a way that gave it substantial equality.[25]

Byroade's memo contained additional safeguards that had not been previously discussed (e.g., a limit on the number of German divisions). US thinking, he said, was that the German contribution should not exceed one-fifth the total force (about twelve to fifteen divisions), which was less than the current number of French divisions. Additionally, to facilitate additional safeguards, Byroade suggested that Germany should[26]

1. be restricted to a ground force role without either air or naval forces, or offensive equipment, even in "the long distant future";

2. utilize only the best of the present German senior officers and begin training a new officer corps over which the Allies could retain significant influence as soon as possible;

3. allow a required Federal Ministry to perform necessary administrative and logistical functions, normally performed by G-1 (personnel) and G-4 (logistics; less major items) staffs, but very little G-2 (intelligence) and no G-3 (operations) functions; and

4. continue to prohibit and restrict industries in Germany and use the Military Security Board to enforce certain demilitarization controls, thus maintaining those fundamental controls that would prevent future German aggression.

On 23 September, Ambassador Bruce sent a cable to Acheson suggesting that Acheson approach both Schuman and French defense minister Jules Moch and request that Schuman offer a French suggestion on how to best utilize German troops, similar to the way the French had offered a plan regarding the pooling of European coal and steel. Bruce further suggested that Acheson tell both French ministers that leadership in this matter should come from France.[27]

On 26 September, the North Atlantic Council (NAC) issued the final communiqué of the September meeting, which was intentionally vague and reflected the impasse brought about by French fear and intransigence. The communiqué read, in part, "The utilization of German manpower and resources was discussed . . . . The Council was in agreement that Germany should be enabled to contribute to the build-up of the defense of Western Europe and, noting that the occupying powers were studying the matter, requested the Defense Committee to make recommendations at the earliest possible date as to the methods by which Germany could most usefully make its contribution."[28]

Two days later, in a separate and unrelated twist, Bolte received a memo from his G-3 Division informing him that none of the available fiscal year 1951 Mutual Defense Assistance Program (MDAP) funds allocated for equipment could be used to fund a possible rearming of Germany.[29]

As a result of the impasse in the NAC, Marshall decided to have the Defense Department immediately begin drafting a unilateral US proposal on Germany to present to the NATO Defense Committee during its October meeting, using the joint State-Defense position of 8 September as a foundation.[30] One week later, Byroade wrote Acheson that he had heard from Paul Nitze that Marshall was not happy with the paper. Marshall, according to Byroade, felt the paper should "deal with a series of steps which would automatically lead to the desired end result instead of defining the end result as an objective to be agreed."[31] Byroade believed that the approach taken in the paper was the correct one, but Marshall obviously wanted a different approach.

According to Byroade, the Bureau of German Affairs believed that the key issue before the NATO defense ministers regarding Germany was "to record and reach agreement to the principles on which the French failed to agree to in New York" (i.e., to include German units in a European defense force). In other words, it was of little value to move slowly on Germany, as Marshall wanted (i.e., moving through the steps to first get approval for German companies, then battalions, then regiments, and finally divisions), if there was no agreement on whether Germany should be allowed to participate to begin with. Byroade concluded that all that was needed from the NATO defense ministers was agreement on a list of safeguards they considered appropriate.[32]

Acheson then spoke with Robert A. Lovett, the new deputy secretary of defense, the following day and noted, "Lovett agreed that the U.S. should not back off its position but keep the heat on France. If France refuses, it should be up to them to come up with a new proposal. The U.S. should insist on a solution to the German participation question as it is essential to the whole plan."[33]

At about the same time, several US Senators were also voicing their thoughts regarding German participation in the defense of Europe. On 4 October, Senator Willis Smith (D-NC) visited Major General Kohler, director of the Joint American Military Advisory Group to Europe, and told him that he considered arming Germany essential.[34] A few weeks earlier, on 22 September, Senator Tom Connally (D-TX), chairman of the Senate Foreign Relations Committee, spoke in the Senate regarding Germany:

> We must acknowledge the right and indeed the duty of the
> Germans to contribute not only to their own defense but to
> the defense of Western Europe as well. It is time that provision
> is made for the inclusion of German units in the integrated
> European army toward which we are working.
>
> Now I understand fully and sympathize thoroughly with
> the natural reaction of the French people to anything that looks
> like German rearmament. The sound of Nazi hobnails goose
> stepping down the boulevards of Paris is too fresh in their

memory for them to have any other reaction. But they must be convinced that what is sought does not involve the creation of a German army. What is sought is the creation of a European army. What is sought is the use of German troop units in an integrated European force under a supreme allied commander. With this sort of arrangement French people will have an iron-clad guaranty that a German army, under a German general staff, will never again menace France's eastern borders.[35]

On 11 October, a high-level meeting between state and defense officials took place that included Acheson, Marshall, Lovett, and Ambassador Bruce, as well as members of the Office of European Affairs and the JCS. During the meeting, Acheson provided Marshall with a copy of a cable sent by McCloy that contained a number of recommendations on how to proceed with the French on the issue of German rearmament.[36] Acheson then stated that there was merit to allowing the French to take the lead on European unity, which included military unity.[37] He also suggested that Marshall stand firm and make no concessions to the French regarding German units in the European Defense Force (EDF), and gave Marshall a copy of a message Bevin had sent to Schuman that supported the position that, given French opposition, it was up to the French to make a counter-proposal.[38]

Over the next several days, both General Handy and the JCS drafted papers that contained recommendations and proposals regarding the organization, training, and equipping of German forces. In a three-part cable to General Collins, Handy underscored the inability of his command to logistically support any police, civil defense, or labor service programs with his resources. He referred to a September 1950 EUCOM study on the organization of the West German army and outlined his command's position on it. Essentially, Handy felt that responsibility for the creation of the army should be given to the West German government and that training and operational control should be the responsibility of the supreme command. He further recommended that equipment for German units be furnished and maintained by the German government, augmented as necessary by other sources. Lastly, he recommended the German contingent be initially composed of 250,000 men organized into ten divisions, including supporting troops and tactical aviation. Of these ten divisions, three infantry divisions should be placed in the British zone, three in the French zone, and two infantry and two armored divisions in the American zone. These units would be organized similar to US divisions, have the necessary lines of communication support to give them sustained combat capability, and be furnished with major equipment items by Allied nations.[39]

The EUCOM study was followed by a report from the JSPC for the secretary of defense to use at the upcoming NATO defense ministers meeting. Among the report's enclosures was a memo for the secretary of defense that contained what may have been the first threat made by the United States against France to reexamine its options should agreement on German participation not happen. Most significantly, paragraph 4.f. stated that if the NATO defense and military committees could not come to agreement on the "immediate initiation of the organization of German military units within the integrated force for the defense of Western Europe . . . the U.S. course of action for the conduct of a war against the USSR . . . should be reexamined."[40]

The Pleven Plan

On 24 October, Prime Minister Pleven submitted a plan for "the creation of a European army linked to the political institutions of a united Europe."[41] It is obvious from a memo Bradley wrote to Marshall that he (Bradley) was somewhat confused as to what the French intended. Bradley pointed out that regarding the size of units, the French definition, depending on who one spoke with, was contradictory.[42] In one instance they spoke of divisions but in another suggested they would not consent to German divisions.[43] The proposal also specified that the supreme commander would be placed under the European minister of defense and not NATO, and furthermore, that the European minister of defense would receive guidance from a council composed of ministers from the participating countries and thus act as an intermediary between the European community and NATO. The bottom line, Bradley wrote, was that the position of European minister of defense cut across almost all NATO lines and would make NATO inoperable.[44] Eisenhower called it as "cockeyed an idea as a dope fiend could have figured out."[45]

Defense Minister Moch formally presented the French plan to the NATO Defense Committee on 28 October.[46] The Pleven Plan took Acheson and the State Department completely by surprise. They had expected a Schuman Plan–like proposal, similar to the one created for the European coal and steel community but for military collaboration. Instead, what they saw was a plan that would rearm the Germans without rearming Germany and turn German soldiers into cannon fodder.[47]

130   The French refused to discuss any proposal other than theirs. The gap between the French and the US positions was such that the Defense Committee was left with no other option than to submit the German question to both the Military Committee and the Council of Deputies to study the issue and report back. At the Defense Committee meeting on 31 October, Marshall made it clear that no decision could be made on the next two agenda items—the creation of an integrated force in Europe and the establishment of a Supreme Headquarters Allied Powers Europe (SHAPE), and the reorganization of NATO—without agreement on the scale and nature of German participation. The threat of the United States withdrawing its contribution caused the ministers to agree to a recess to allow the French to reexamine the issue.[48]

On 8 November, Chancellor Adenauer addressed the Bundestag during a foreign policy debate and made the following declaration regarding the French plan:

> The Federal Republic considers the Pleven Plan a valuable contribution to the integration of Europe which is one of the pre-eminent aims of the Federal Government. The Federal Government considers, however, that the present international tension requires an earlier solution than would be possible through the implementation of the Pleven Plan. It is of the opinion that a general settlement might come about through negotiations with the Soviet Union. These negotiations can only be successful, however, if the Soviet Russian threat is faced by a defensive front of Western powers which is at least as strong as that of the Soviet Union. The Federal Government is of the opinion that the Federal Republic of Germany must be prepared to make an appropriate contribution to the building up of this defensive front, should such be requested by the western powers in order to secure its existence, the freedom of its population, and the further existence of western cultural ideals. Prerequisites for such a contribution are Germany's full equality of rights within this defensive front side by side with the other participating powers and further, that this defensive front be strong enough to make any Russian aggression impossible.[49]

In mid-November, the army's G-4 reported that for logistical planning purposes, the MDAP stockpile for Austria could be considered a source of equipment for early delivery to Germany. Bolte then cabled Handy, informing him that the JCS had an allocation of $200 million from the fiscal year 1951 supplemental MDAP appropriation for grant aid for West German rearmament and equipment, to be stockpiled in the United States and EUCOM until the creation of German armed forces was approved. These funds would also be used to train a minimum of four West German divisions, though politics kept German units no larger than Regimental Combat Teams (RCTs).[50]

At the same time, the State Department was also clarifying its position. State Department summaries of telegrams, copies of which were sent to President Truman, indicated on 10 November that the State Department had informed its missions in the North Atlantic Treaty countries that most members of the NATO Defense Committee believed that the Pleven Plan was militarily unsound and impossible to realize politically, and that it failed to solve the problem of how to rapidly build a European defense system.[51] The State Department also informed its missions that the United States believed that any compromise solution would have to meet three criteria: the plan had to be militarily sound, agreed to by all the NATO members and West Germany, and immediately implementable.

On 20 November, the State Department provided guidance to Spofford at NATO regarding the size of German units to be contributed, the early appointment of a supreme commander, and the timing of steps for creating a defense force. Regarding the unit size, state's guidance was that Spofford should make it very clear that the minimal acceptable size for German units was the division but that during a transitional period, smaller units could be considered, provided it was understood that they would be assembled into divisions for effective use by the supreme commander as soon as he determined it to be necessary.[52]

The first week in December saw a flurry of activity at both the defense and state departments, much of it regarding US-French disagreement on the size of German units and whether the United States would approve appointment of a supreme commander before the size issue was settled. A teleconference on this issue took place on 3 December between Spofford, members of the State Department, the Office of the Secretary of Defense, the Department of the Army, and the NATO Standing Group. Spofford reported that as a result of negotiations and a proposal he had made (to which the French had agreed), there was a reasonable chance for US-French agreement that week.[53]

That same day, the JCS was asked for their views on a State Department paper stemming from discussions between the president and Prime Minister Clement Attlee of Great Britain on the subject of European defense arrangements, including German participation. The essence of the paper was that the world situation would not allow further delay and that the lack of an agreement on German participation was resulting in a deteriorating situation in Germany.

The point was made that if agreement with France could be reached on the participation of German units in a European defense, the United States could immediately proceed, without waiting for German acceptance, with the appointment of a supreme commander and the creation of an integrated force for the defense of Europe. The State Department paper also stated that German participation warranted a change in the relationship between the Allies and the German government through the relaxation of occupation controls (a statement the State Department felt the British would concur with but not the French).[54] Nonetheless, the State Department believed the United States should support the French efforts to consolidate the continent as a possible solution to both European defense and the German problem.

The JCS did not object to the State Department paper but they believed there should be no new US military commitments of any nature made to the French in Indochina or Europe other than aid until the Korean emergency was resolved. They were also greatly concerned about the politico-military solidarity of the NATO countries but said that if the early appointment of a supreme commander would improve the situation materially, they would "consider" such an appointment. Lastly, they emphasized that the need for the early utilization of Germany's war potential and for increased effective forces in being to achieve a "tangible measure of increased defense capabilities in Europe" was imperative.[55]

A few days later, President Truman met with Prime Minister Attlee. When the discussion turned to Western Europe, Marshall was asked to speak. Marshall stated that many in Congress felt the US position on European unity and rearmament was impractical and that they wanted assurances that the plan for the defense of Western Europe had a reasonable chance of success. Without such assurance, he maintained, there would be no further appropriations for European rearmament. Without French cooperation and a real assurance of a German build up, Marshall insisted, any further conversations "would get nowhere." Acheson interjected that he thought the appointment of a supreme commander would help and

General Bradley underscored the need to assure Congress that both European rearmament and the plan to defend Western Europe would be efficient.[56]

Before that meeting took place, Acheson had called Lovett and told him that there would be a "row with the British on the views that [he and Lovett were] discussing with the French to encourage them to solve the problem." Acheson asked Lovett for clarification on the JCS's statement that they would be "prepared to consider [appointment of a supreme commander] when the North Atlantic treaty organization reached agreement on German rearmament," expected by the end of the week. Acheson then said he would take the JCS paper to the meeting with Attlee and tell him that if the French agreed, he was authorized to agree to the appointment of a supreme commander. [57]

The following day, 7 December, Bolte wrote Collins that there had been several important developments since his last memo. The French had indicated that NATO should not proceed with the "actual" rearmament of Germany until an attempt had been made to reach a negotiated settlement with the USSR. Bolte also wrote of press reports where the French had agreed to the participation of German units of RCT size in an integrated force under a supreme commander.[58]

The very next day, Bolte sent another memo to Collins with a summary of a teleconference held with Spofford that day. Spofford reported that the French had accepted and the NATO deputies had approved the US version of the NATO report, which read: "The size of the German formations to be constituted should not under present conditions exceed that of a regimental combat team or brigade groups. *However*, when these regimental combat team or brigade groups are formed and trained, the question of the manner in which they should be used must be determined in the light of conditions at the time, due weight being given to the views of the Supreme Commander."[59]

The summary also included concerns of the French representative Hervé Alphand that German RCTs not be combined together or placed under control of the German government during the interim period. The French feared that German divisions could be formed clandestinely or that the RCTs would be unrestrained under direct German government control. The NATO deputies agreed that this issue should be referred to the Military Committee.

The NAC met again in Brussels on 18 and 19 December to approve, among other things, German participation in the defense of Western Europe,

134   and to request the appointment of a supreme commander. Previously, on 15 December, Lovett had called Acheson to advise him of a conversation he had held with Eisenhower the day before. Among the issues discussed was Eisenhower's appointment as supreme commander, which was a foregone conclusion. Eisenhower suggested that instead of offering the appointment to any particular individual, the Europeans be asked to invite the US government to select an individual and then ask those governments if that individual was acceptable.[60] The NAC did, in fact, make such a request, and at its sixth session on 18 December it approved a resolution that Eisenhower be appointed supreme commander. It then sent a recommendation to President Truman that he appoint Eisenhower to the position. The president's formal reply was that he was in agreement with the view of the NAC that Eisenhower's "experience and talents [made] him uniquely qualified to assume the important responsibilities of this position."[61]

Always in the background, however, was the Soviet threat, its impact on US readiness and German rearmament. In briefing notes prepared for the president at the 11 December NSC meeting, it was suggested that the president ask Bradley to discuss US military position vis-à-vis the USSR and probable development during the initial stages were a general war to occur in the near future. The notes suggested the United States should not gamble that the USSR was bluffing and should prepare for total war in the near future. It could be avoided, however, if the United States acted with unity, determination, and wisdom. The United States should do all it could to avoid war with the USSR without sacrificing self-respect or endangering US survival. The United States should prepare for full mobilization and meet the 1954 defense targets as rapidly as possible. Lastly, in light of the Soviet declaration that it would not tolerate German rearmament, US efforts to organize and train West German units should be done with the greatest of care.[62]

In the last week of 1950, the Central Intelligence Agency (CIA) issued a National Intelligence Estimate (NIE) on probable Soviet reactions to arming West Germany.[63] The CIA indicated in this short, two-page estimate that a rearmament of Western Germany as then contemplated (i.e., creation of defensive forces) would not be considered by the USSR as menacing their security. It continued, however, that the USSR was unlikely to believe that the process would stop short of complete remilitarization once started. The Soviets recognized, however, that a remilitarization program would take time and thus, their immediate objective would be to hinder and delay its progress and to exploit the disagreements that existed over it within Western

Europe to weaken the cohesion of the Alliance, prevent its strengthening,
and seek to bring about German unification on Soviet terms.

The USSR had already expressed its concern in notes sent to the Western powers calling for a meeting of the Council of Foreign Ministers as well as separate notes to the British and the French.[64] The NIE also indicated that the Soviets might increase their forces in East Germany and their satellites and suggest to all that German remilitarization would result in German aggression. The NIE also submitted that if Soviet diplomacy and propaganda failed to halt German rearmament, the USSR might adopt more drastic measures that could involve the risk of war; in other words, if West Germany was rearmed, the USSR could use that to justify an increase in Soviet forces in East Germany and the satellites. The NIE concluded that the Soviets would most likely exhaust all practical means of preventing German rearmament and suggested that if the USSR became convinced that complete German rearmament, as well as NATO rearmament and political solidarity between West Germany and the Western powers, could not be stopped, the USSR would seriously consider going to war.

Despite having reached agreement on German participation in principle (the Pleven Plan), the actual recruitment and building of cadres for the FRG's contribution was placed in limbo.[65] Neither blandishment from the United States nor the Truman administration's subsequent acceptance of EDC and the European Army concept as the only way to put West Germans in uniform moved the French. In addition, aside from high level talks with the Germans, the French insisted that there be no official military to military talks with the Germans until the EDC Treaty was ratified. This created a number of program delays and problems with US military planning that will be discussed in the epilogue.

At this juncture, it should be noted that General Eisenhower was initially skeptical of the EDC—he had said that he did not want any "reluctant Hessians" in his army.[66] In June 1951, however, after a lunch with Jean Monnet that had been arranged by McCloy, Eisenhower "embraced" the concept of a "United States of Europe" and gave his support to the EDC.[67] One month later, in July, he sent a personal message to both Marshall and Acheson in which he said he was

> convinced the time has come when we must all press for the
> earliest implementation of the Eur Army concept. Bruce,
> McCloy, and I are in full agreement that implementation of the

> Eur army concept despite the many complicated details which will have to be worked out, offers the best and earliest possible chance for a solution to the problem of (a) obtaining the necessary [defense] contribution from West [Germany]....
>
> Having become convinced that the establishment of an Eur army will be a major constructive step, I now propose to support it in every possible way.[68]

Later that month, on 22 July, Eisenhower met with a visiting subcommittee of the Senate Foreign Relations Committee at SHAPE and told them the following: "When I came over here I disliked the whole idea of a European Army, and I had enough troubles without it. However ... I made up my mind to go into the thing with both feet.... I realize that a lot of my professional associates are going to think that I am crazy. But ... joining Europe together is the key to this whole thing."[69]

In giving its support to the EDC, the United States placed four conditions on the emerging organization. They were (1) that the EDC must create administrative arrangements that would allow it to participate in the defense of Europe, (2) the European Army would be under SACEUR's command, (3) the lengthy negotiations establishing EDC and its superstructure would not impede the build-up of German units, and (4) the EDC's administrative machinery was not to interfere with NATO.[70]

This decision, enunciated in NSC 115, put the German rearmament question squarely in the context of a broader European policy. As a result, US basic goals remained the same but had a sounder basis. The question, however, was whether the US commitment to EDC had put the United States in the "hands of the French."[71]

Building a New German Military

Discussions between the three Allied high commissioners and the West German government on constructing the German contribution began in early January 1951. One of the first questions asked by the German delegation was what they were expected to contribute by the end of 1951. The Allied High Commission had agreed on 100,000 men as an interim measure but the army's G-3 Plans Division recommended a stronger program and proposed a figure of 195,000.[72] This number was based on several things: the German desire for equality; the Allied wish to secure the maximum effective German contribution; the fact that there was equipment in the Austrian MDAP stockpile sufficient to equip four divisions; and the $200 million from the supplemental fiscal year 1951 MDAP funds that had been recommended by the JCS for the German rearmament program. The memo justifying these numbers also contained Allied safeguards: all German units were to be under SHAPE's control; total German land formation would not exceed one-fifth of the total of Allied land formations; German formations would not exceed RCT size until authorized by NATO; and German units would not be developed at the expense of other forces.[73]

Over and above the safeguards described above, the Joint Report of the North Atlantic Council Deputies and the Military Committee to the NATO Defense Committee, approved on 18 December 1950, continued to reflect a fear of Germany, with over a dozen additional militarily significant limitations placed on Germany, including limiting the mission of its future air force to air defense and ground unit support and the types of naval craft its navy could have, as well as prohibiting it from contributing complete armored formations. It further proscribed Germany from supervising its own officer recruitment and training and limited German planning, operations, and intelligence staffs to tactical units only.

Other limitations barred German industry from producing heavy military equipment, military aircraft and naval vessels other than minor defensive craft, and atomic, biological, or chemical weapons. Research and development was also restricted by requirements laid down by the NATO Military Committee and allowed only under Allied supervision.[74]

One month later, on 18 January 1951, McCloy responded to the German size recommendations with an additional set of questions:[75]

- What was total strength of the German forces to be created by end 1952?
- Whether the allies could train 15 percent of the German contribution with the equipment available within 3 months beginning 15 Sep 1951?
- What proportion of the 15 percent could be trained by British, French or US forces? (Germany preferred that the United States train its nuclei).
- Would equipment for 50 percent of the German force contribution be available by the end 1951 and the remainder by 1 April 1952?
- Which US schools were available to train selected Germans?

The JCS response provided only a recommendation for the end 1952 strength of German forces, justifying its limited response by the fact that the military aspects of German participation were up to NATO in accordance with the Medium Term Force Goals. As to the questions related to training, the JCS felt that as West Germany had not yet agreed to nor accepted the invitation to contribute forces, it was premature to discuss those issues.

Nonetheless, the force strength recommendation made by the JCS for forwarding to the US representative on the NATO Standing Group was as follows:[76]

Total Army: 440,000
Ground Combat: 247,000
    30 RCTs (187,000)
    3 AAA Brigades (15,000)
    Combat Support (40,000–45,000)
Ground Service: 107,500
    Technical Service Support (100,000)
    Administrative Service Support (7,500)
Overhead and Mobilization Base: 85,000
    Administrative Operations (35,000)
    Trainees, Transients, Patients (50,000)

Total Navy: 10,000

Total Air Force: 45,000 (10 fighter wings with 3 squadrons each)
    Ground personnel (43,000)
    Pilots (2,000)

The JCS added a caveat to these figures, stating that while they were considered suitable for ongoing negotiations, the JCS could give no positive assurance that there would be sufficient armament and equipment produced by the NATO countries or German industry to justify creation of those forces in 1952. The phased buildup, the caveat continued, had to be adjusted to plans allocating equipment to the Allies that would only be known over the next several years.[77]

Throughout 1952, the State Department, with assistance from the Defense Department, was involved in discussions on various financial and other requirements of the EDC, as well as cajoling the various European nations regarding the timing of the ratification of the EDC Treaty.[78] On the more military level, planning for the arrival of German troops continued and discussions regarding the creation of a Military Assistance Advisory Group (MAAG) for Germany began.[79] On 22 February, the NAC reaffirmed the urgency of the defense of Western Europe and the early establishment of the EDF, including a German contribution of the size and nature recommended by the NATO Military Committee.[80] In March, the secretary of defense assigned an officer from his office to be his representative to the Paris EDC–high commissioners–SHAPE discussions assessing the validity of the cost estimates of the German contingent to EDC. An air force officer from the US Air Forces in Europe (USAFE) was also assigned to assist him. The United States sought to begin furnishing training equipment in phase with the German buildup beginning in 1953.[81]

One issue that continued to plague US attempts to speed up the process of obtaining German soldiers was funding for the creation of a German military. It had already been determined that German forces could not come into being until the EDC Treaty was ratified. Once that was done, before the United States could provide military assistance to that country, US law required that Germany's eligibility to receive military assistance be certified. Accordingly, in early July the Secretary of Defense requested that the JCS provide a military determination of German eligibility (i.e., advise whether the FRG was "of direct importance to the defense of the North Atlantic Area" and whether its increased ability to defend itself was "important to the preservation of the peace and security of the North Atlantic area, and to the security of the United States"). It also asked the JCS to counsel whether the grant of military assistance to the FRG would strengthen US security.[82]

Along those lines, in mid-July, the JCS recommended that the secretary of defense hold in abeyance any consideration for the organization of a MAAG-Germany until the EDC came into force and Germany's requirements were determined. The JCS also recommended that until that occurred, the commander in chief, Europe (CINCEUR) should be charged with planning activities related to the MDAP as it applied to German units created for the EDC.[83] This planning was to be coordinated with the Embassy Paris Observer's Group.[84]

Toward the end of September, the continued mistrust of Germany on the part of the French was evident during discussions held with Theodor Blank, West Germany's future defense minister, and General Hans Speidel regarding end-item delivery schedules. One of the problems Blank was

140   confronting was the question of German troop deployment. He knew, he said, how many barracks he already had and, based on the planned German contribution to the EDC, how many he would need to build. What he didn't know was where to build them. The French, he related, believed that it would be dangerous to provide Germany with that information as they believed the Germans would then start working sub rosa.[85]

This mistrust, as well as a concern over rising German nationalism, was not confined to the French. In a two-part letter to Paul Nitze, John Ferguson, deputy director of the Policy Planning Staff, wrote about discussions he had had on Germany with George Kennan, former army undersecretary and current US ambassador to NATO, William Draper, Walter J. Donnelly, who had replaced McCloy as US high commissioner, and David Bruce in London. According to Ferguson, Donnelly said that France would not be able to control Germany in the EDC as it could in NATO. The problem of German membership in NATO was not yet urgent but it would arise after the EDC Treaty was ratified. He feared that West Germany's membership in the EDC was simply an attempt to get the Allies to help it regain East Germany. Kennan was even more fearful: He felt that if the West Germany was admitted to NATO, a civil war would ensue.[86]

On 18 November, just a few weeks after Eisenhower was elected President of the United States, he was invited to a meeting with Truman and Acheson to "establish the framework for full understanding of our problems and our purposes in the interim until January 20."[87] Truman saw two problems regarding European defense. The first dealt with the need for a meeting with the North Atlantic Council to discuss the military programs of the NATO members whose proposed force contributions far exceeded their economic capabilities.[88]

The second problem was the problem of EDC Treaty ratification. The United States, Truman said, had hoped the treaty would be ratified by the end of 1952 or even January or February 1953 at the latest. But after the French attack on the treaties, a recent "unwise" press conference by Schuman, and the defeat in the German Bundestag of a motion to take up the treaties on 26 November, there was a real crisis in West European collaboration. France and Germany were "jockeying" to see who should act first and neither was willing to do anything until the new Eisenhower administration came in.[89] It was serious in respect to the defense of Western Europe but could also initiate a reaction against the continuation of the occupation and postpone implementing the treaty with Germany.[90]

One week before Eisenhower's inauguration, Deputy US High Commissioner Samuel Reber sent a cable to the secretary of state describing the impact of these delays in the ratification process. Doubts that the treaty would ever be ratified were slowing down planning on German forces and military production. The EDC Interim Commission (EDC-IC) had not made progress developing organization and procedures, nor had it been possible to develop a German utilization plan, develop policies on production and procurement in Germany, or begin contracting for infrastructure and equipment. The one piece of good news was that within the Military Security Board, both the French and the British agreed to allow the US member to unilaterally approve German requests for increased capacity in shipbuilding, synthetic oil, synthetic rubber, and precision bearings, if necessary. Reber concluded that despite continued criticism from the German Social Democratic Party (SPD), the Adenauer government's western orientation would not change and that West European progress and recognition of Germany's role would only increase German integration.[91]

The Eisenhower Administration Takes Over

On 14 January 1953, just a week before the inauguration, Vice Admiral A. C. Davis, deputy US representative to the NATO Standing Group, sent a memorandum to the JCS stating that the NAC had recognized that "the defense of Europe, including Western Germany, as far to the east as possible will require a German contribution in terms of effective military units." He continued that ending the occupation would be the simplest and quickest way to accomplish this and bring the Federal Republic directly into NATO. Despite recognizing that this was politically unacceptable to France, the NATO Council found the EDF, as part of an integrated NATO Defense Force, acceptable as long as it did not delay a German contribution.[92]

Admiral Davis continued, "It is now, however, two years since this method of providing for German participation ... was initiated and it is obvious ... that there will be further and probably prolonged delay in ratification of an European Defence Community treaty." He urged the JCS to consider, as a matter of priority, "the increasingly urgent status of the problem with a view to the possible advisability of developing and recommending alternative action leading to German participation as soon as possible."[93]

When Eisenhower came into office in January 1953, his administration totally accepted the support given to EDC by the Truman administration.

Eisenhower had been converted from skeptic to strong supporter of EDC when he was SACEUR and by the time he became president, according to Ruane, he became a "zealous proselytizer. That said, EDC's greatest champion was John Foster Dulles, Eisenhower's secretary of state."[94] President Eisenhower believed that Europe could not be defended without Germany in the EDC, that the EDC would become the military component of NATO, that it would end Franco-German enmity, and that it would allow the United States to reconfigure its defense strategies and priorities, ultimately reducing the defense budget and bringing American troops back home.[95]

Eisenhower was also convinced that the requirements for a strong economy and those for national security programs had to be balanced. Thus, his administration introduced a new defense policy, called the "New Look," that was designed to reduce defense expenditures to a level that could be sustained "for the long haul." A key component of the New Look was reliance on nuclear weapons and the armed forces were authorized to plan for their use as needed. Aside from the emphasis on strategic air power, the intent of the new policy was to curtail the army's intent to submit large manpower and matériel requirements that would prepare the army for another world war.[96]

Shortly after his inauguration, Eisenhower, now an avid proponent of European integration, sent his new secretary of state, John Foster Dulles, and Harold Stassen, the director of the Mutual Security Agency, to Europe to observe and listen. Before he left, however, Dulles spoke on national television about the purpose of his and Stassen's trip. He made a point of telling viewers that the United States had made a major $40 billion investment in Europe and that "if it appeared that there were no chance of getting effective unity, and if in particular France, Germany and England should go their separate ways, then certainly it would be necessary to give a little rethinking to America's own foreign policy in relation to Western Europe."[97] While there, Dulles met with the leader of the German SPD, Erich Ollenhauer, and stated that the United States would not accept a German national army under any conditions. It was his belief that the establishment of such an army would lead to another Franco-German war, a position that was incomprehensible to the SPD leaders. Dulles left the impression that the United States had "completely closed the door" to any alternative to the existing European defense plans.[98]

Several weeks later, army chief of staff General Collins and Chief of Naval Operations Admiral William Fechteler responded to the JCS

concerning Vice Admiral Davis's memorandum about a possible alternative to EDC. Collins's lengthy response was thorough and critical. He
began by stating that he did not consider it appropriate for the JCS to
offer gratuitous and premature recommendations and comments on this
complex problem to the Secretary of Defense. While he agreed that no
new course of action should be recommended, Collins stated that Germany's membership in NATO was the most desirable alternative if the EDC
Treaty was not ratified. Collins acknowledged that this method was unacceptable to France and posited other possible alternatives. He also restated
JCS's position of October 1950, in which the chiefs had declared that in
the event that a German contribution was not possible, the United States
should reexamine its contribution to the defense of Western Europe. He
did not believe that this would necessarily lead to a "peripheral strategy,"
but did say that there had been no analysis made of possible US courses of
action should German rearmament not be allowed and that now was the
time to undertake such an analysis.[99]

Fechteler's response consisted primarily of modifications to what was
a follow-on report by the JSSC and a reply to Davis. He too felt that if
the most desirable arrangement could not be had, alternatives should be
explored to avoid an "all or nothing" situation. He also opposed a target
date of 1 July 1953 for ratification of the EDC Treaty and beginning of
the German buildup as proposed by the JSSC. It was unreasonable, he
wrote, to expect ratification and buildup by any specific target date. His
rationale was that if the date was not met, the project would be abandoned,
and that if German membership in NATO was unobtainable, the United
States should undertake action to rearm Germany by other means.[100] Both
Collins and Fechteler recommended that the JCS take no action regarding
alternatives to EDC until requested by the secretary of defense.

On 3 March 1953, Leon W. Fuller, deputy director of the Office of
German Political Affairs and member of the Policy Planning Staff, circulated a paper he had written titled "An Alternate U.S. Course of Action
Respecting EDC and a German Settlement." Among the points raised in
the paper, Fuller highlighted his beliefs that the chance of the EDC being
ratified by mid-1953 was less than even, that France still saw Germany,
not Russia, as the enemy, and that German participation in EDC was only
incidentally to augment the strength of European defense. He also wrote
that the EDC would be ratified only as a result of US pressure and that the
merger of national sovereignty that the EDC demanded was something
that neither the United States nor the United Kingdom would agree to.[101]

Fuller argued that EDC was a means to an end, not the end itself. The United States, he wrote, had yet to explain how EDC would lead to German unity or peace, even though the new Eisenhower administration was even more explicitly committed to EDC than its predecessor, such that the failure of EDC would force alteration of US military strategy in a manner "highly adverse" to US security and political interests in Europe. He contended that ratification could actually intensify the cleavage of Germany and launch the United States irretrievably into a power struggle with the USSR. Lastly, he wrote that France and Germany believed that an effort should first be made to achieve a settlement with the USSR or come to a showdown.[102]

Fuller concluded with a ten-step course of action to be taken by the United States in which it was necessary for the EDC to be ratified in order to impress upon France and Germany that failure would possibly fatally weaken the West in any political trial of strength with the USSR.

On 6 March, the JSSC forwarded to the JCS yet another revision of the "Problem of Germany" report. This revision contained virtually all the recommendations made by Collins and Fechteler and an appendix, a memorandum for the secretary of defense, that outlined the JCS's rather pessimistic view of the situation. While repeating that German membership in NATO was preferable to EDC, it accepted the fact that France would never accept Germany as a full-fledged member in the Alliance. The JCS stated that no other alternatives would be as effective but that they had to be examined. However, the absence of full participation in the common defense effort from France and Germany meant that the concept of forward defense might have to be abandoned, possibly leading to a peripheral defense strategy, "with all of its grave military disadvantages."[103]

Presenting their position, as all JCS papers did, from the "military point of view," the JCS addressed the delays in arming the Germans, stating that there should already have been a substantial German contribution. The military appreciation for years 1954–55 indicated it would be a dangerous period and, considering the time required to create, organize, equip, and train German forces, a protracted delay in ratification of the EDC Treaty could have serious military consequences. Furthermore, if EDC was abandoned and German NATO membership vetoed, the United States needed to take vigorous action to rearm Germany within the framework of other suitable political arrangements.

The appendix closed by stating that given the State Department's awareness of the urgency of the situation and its efforts to bring about

EDC ratification, the JCS would exert no further pressure. The JCS also indicated, however, that if called upon to comment, they would be prepared to express their views on the German rearmament issue to include the degree to which they would support limits on additional military aid or other military concessions to France to further induce her participation in EDC.

Toward the middle of March, most likely after the above memorandum had been sent to the secretary of defense, the JCS sent a brief reply to Admiral Davis. In it, the JCS opined that without a substantial German contribution, the defense of Western Europe would be shallow, expensive, and probably ineffective. Nonetheless, how Germany was to be rearmed was a political matter to be determined by the political elements of the government. Regardless of how it was to be accomplished, the speedy creation of effective German combat units and maximum use of Germany's productive capacity were definite and urgent military requirements.[104]

While the idea of putting pressure on France to ratify EDC by limiting the amount of military aid given to it floated around the defense and state departments, Eisenhower threw out another possible inducement at an NSC meeting on 25 March. During the discussion, Secretary of State Dulles painted a rather bleak picture of what might happen in Europe if the EDC, which he saw as the last chance for European unity along lines desired by the United States, "went down the drain."[105] The FRG, he believed, would unilaterally assume a larger measure of sovereignty with US and British support, engendering irreconcilable French hostility. Nonetheless, Dulles indicated that he and other US officials would explore, together with the French, ways to reduce the strain imposed on France by its involvement in Indochina. It was beyond France's capabilities, Dulles explained, to shoulder the load imposed by its European commitments as well as those in Southeast Asia.[106]

Eisenhower then inquired whether the JCS might find it of value to examine the possibility of offering the French a preeminent command position in Europe. Given that military prestige was very important to the French, he suggested that they might be offered either the Central European Command or even General Matthew B. Ridgway's job as SACEUR. Dulles agreed that such an offer would offset France's fear that the EDC meant loss of French identity and leadership on the continent. Dulles then turned to General Bradley, asking whether the JCS could proffer an opinion within the next two days. Bradley said it could but ventured that the question was more political than military and that the State Department

146   should consider the political implications as well as the degree of opposition the United States would encounter from the other European states. The president's proposal and his desire that state and defense explore its feasibility were noted.[107]

As these discussions continued to circulate within both defense and state, on 7 April 1953 Frank C. Nash, the assistant secretary of defense for international security affairs provided Adenauer with a summary of budgetary action the United States had taken to provide the FRG with certain items of major military equipment. The summary, subsequently known as the 'Nash Commitment,' did not, however, provide an itemized list of equipment to be allocated or indicate the size of the program. The statement contained, in part, the following:[108]

> Taking into account the equipment availabilities for and requirements of the EDC countries as a whole . . . the United States has made budgetary provisions . . . to provide to the [EDC] the major equipment required . . . for the first six German groupements and twenty-four German air squadrons, on a basis comparable to that used in providing equipment to the other EDC countries. This equipment will include:
>
> a.   For Army Contingents:
>   In general, only those items having a primary military application, such as tanks, combat vehicles, field artillery, anti-aircraft artillery, mortars, machine guns, ammunition, and basic signal and engineering equipment, including components and spare parts.
> b.   For Air Force Contingents:
>   Fighter-bomber aircraft, tactical reconnaissance aircraft, primary and jet training aircraft, ground handling equipment, maintenance training units and related equipment, electronics maintenance training units and related equipment, electronics and communications equipment, machine guns, bombs, rockets, and miscellaneous ammunition.

The statement contained other, general information regarding ongoing negotiations for the return of certain confiscated naval vessels, conditions under which the equipment would be delivered, and the need to complete arrangement regarding plans for the build-up of German forces in order that

delivery plans could be formulated. It also stated that more detailed information would be available once the EDC Treaty had been ratified.[109]

A Question of Alternatives to EDC?

Several months earlier, Leon Fuller had written, "The new [Eisenhower] Administration is even more explicitly committed to EDC than its predecessor."[110] In a letter to General Gruenther in February 1953, Eisenhower wrote that his commitment to Europe was "continuous, intense and sympathetic."[111] He believed that West Germany (tied closely to the West) and Atlantic security were inseparable. The EDC promised that integration and strength. According to Stephen E. Ambrose, Eisenhower even dreamed about German unification and a major German contribution to the EDC. The EDC also meant security for the world and on a more domestic note, a smaller defense budget, a smaller American defense establishment, and lower taxes for the American people.[112]

This was made evident in a nationally televised speech Eisenhower gave on 16 April in which he said, "It [the free world] knows that the defense of Western Europe imperatively demands the unity of purpose and action made possible by [NATO], embracing the European Defense Community. It knows that Western Germany deserves to be a free and equal partner in this community."[113] The following day, John Ausland of the Bureau of German Affairs wrote his colleague Coburn Kidd that Eisenhower's speech "added up" to the US belief that German unification "should be achieved within the framework of a broad European community based on the west European community" and only through membership in the EDC.[114] This idea was further clarified by Eisenhower in a personal letter to Winston Churchill in which the president wrote: "another subject of vital interest to us both . . . is the need, in Europe, for uniform progress on the Common Defense Plan and for greater political and economic unity."[115]

There is evidence, however, that growing dissatisfaction with the slow pace of EDC discussions led to talk of alternatives within the State Department, specifically between the Bureau of German Affairs and the Policy Planning Staff. The Bureau of German Affairs, for example, saw five possible alternatives to EDC while the Policy Planning Staff saw only three. Each saw German national forces as one possible alternative. NATO was the preferred alternative for the Bureau of German Affairs but only a "possibly" preferred course in the Policy Planning Staff's eyes. The Bureau of German Affairs, however, saw no real "practical" alternative to EDC. The

148 Policy Planning Staff proposed to temporarily give up the effort to get a German defense contribution if EDC failed and recommended opening a new set of negotiations to obtain "some acceptable arrangement" serving the same purpose as EDC.[116]

In early July, Adenauer wrote Dulles suggesting that a four-power conference on the German question meet in the fall. A week later, a meeting between Dulles, acting British foreign secretary the Marquess of Salisbury, and Georges Bidault, the French foreign minister, took place in which the three governments concurred with Adenauer and proposed an early autumn meeting with the USSR. The possibility of a four-power meeting led the NSC Planning Board to develop an updated position paper with respect to Germany. This led to a Department of Defense position paper to place against a State Department position paper in the NSC.[117]

On 30 July, the JCS responded to a request from the Secretary of Defense to examine the draft Department of Defense paper. Having learned, however, that the NSC intended to use the State Department's draft as its working document, the JCS elected to discuss only the "fundamental security considerations" involved rather than addressing the Department of Defense draft, and recommended that its comments be used to present the Defense Department's position. That said, the JCS found itself in general accord with the draft and the risks it entailed but feared that pursuing its objective (i.e., negotiating with the USSR over Germany) could lead to prolonging the EDC negotiations, thus delaying the attainment of the German contribution the JCS still considered an urgent requirement. Prolonged negotiations, according to the JCS, would allow the Soviets to progressively increase their nuclear capabilities and possibly use the transition period (the necessary drawdown and redeployment of Allied occupation forces and redesign of NATO defense plans) to launch a general war. It was, therefore, imperative that the United States impress upon its Allies the urgent need to ratify EDC and rapidly integrate German forces into the West's defense efforts.[118]

NSC 160/1, the US position paper approved by Eisenhower on 13 August, restated the existing US position on West Germany. This paper, however, also asserted that while a unified Germany, free of Soviet occupation forces, was essential for an "enduring settlement, both in Germany and in Europe," a free and united Germany oriented to the West would be unacceptable to the Soviet Union, and a "neutralized" Germany, armed or not, would entail sacrifices and risks to the West "incommensurate with any possible gains."[119]

NSC 160/1 also recognized the Department of Defense's fears that possible four-power talks would most likely delay progress toward EDC, but also that French ratification appeared unlikely until such talks were held or blocked by the USSR. It called for the United States to support "with all available means" the creation of the European Community and the ratification of the EDC Treaty as no satisfactory alternative to the EDC had been found. The NSC document also urged the United States to review alternative courses of action should delays be prolonged, including not only the preferred NATO alternative but also bilateral steps with West Germany if this could be done without serious diplomatic repercussions from France.[120]

The delays in ratification also had an effect on West German party politics. In late October, the US high commissioner to the FRG, James Conant, wrote Dulles that due to nationalistic elements in Adenauer's coalition, the chancellor might have been "flirting" with the idea of a national German army in NATO. This was also in part due to France's delay in ratifying the EDC Treaty. Conant was deeply concerned about the possible creation of a national army, though he was aware that some in the Pentagon were in favor of the NATO option, as was the former British high commissioner Sir Ivone Kirkpatrick. Conant suggested that Washington have a serious discussion regarding a German national army and possible alternatives and stated that he personally favored the withdrawal of all but a token of the occupation forces as part of a strategy of peripheral defense, rather than see a German national army evolve.[121]

Two weeks later, Conant wrote an even more pessimistic letter to Dulles, stating that it was clear to him that Adenauer was clearly seeking an alternative to EDC. He accused "some American Army and Naval officers" of making statements to Theodor Blank, and some former German officers of advocating a German-American military alliance and criticizing the French. Conant recommended that Eisenhower send Adenauer a letter affirming that the United States would not support a German national army and that the defense of Europe depended on good Franco-German relations.[122] The following week, on 20 November, Dulles wrote Adenauer at the behest of the president indicating the president's concern about reports that Germany was seeking alternatives to the EDC. Dulles stated unequivocally that the US position with respect to Europe was based "on the imperative necessity of a Franco-German unity as the only foundation of any real strength in Europe," and that it was not based upon a choice of either France or Germany but on both.[123] The United States

150   was convinced that effective Franco-German integration in the military and related fields provided the only adequate security arrangements for Europe. Dulles closed by saying that there was *no alternative* to EDC.

As 1953 came to a close, the frustration experienced by the administration over the continued delay in ratifying the EDC Treaty was clearly visible. On 22 December, Dulles presented "A Report on the North Atlantic Treaty Organization" to the National Press Club. He spoke of Eisenhower's address in London on 3 July 1951 in which Eisenhower spoke of the immense gains unity could bring but also that "the project faces the deadly danger of procrastination." That was two and one-half years ago, Dulles said, and the observation had come to pass.[124] Dulles then mentioned his 14 December address to the NAC, in which he repeated in more forceful terms what he had told the nation earlier in the year: "If, however, the European Defense Community should not become effective, ... there would indeed be grave doubt as to whether Continental Europe could be made a place of safety. That would compel an agonizing reappraisal of basic United States policy."[125]

5

1954–55: EDC Defeated, "German Problem" Solved

The Four-Power Conference took place in Berlin in February 1954. While there, Dulles sent a cable to the State Department advising that should Pleven and General Ely come to the United States to discuss Indochina, EDC should also be included in the conversation. Dulles underscored the support the United States had given France in the United Nations and materially in both Europe and Indochina. The United States had made it clear to the world that France shared in the leadership of the free world alongside the United States and Great Britain. If France rejected the EDC, however, he cabled that it would be impossible for the United States "to maintain [the] fiction [that] France [was] capable of [a] role of leadership in European and world affairs when France, by its very action in killing EDC . . . [would] have demonstrated its incapacity for such leadership."[1]

Despite his and the president's annoyance with the French and their belief that no alternative to EDC was immediately available, Dulles was instructed to provide France with certain assurances in writing. Thus Dulles wrote that the United States had made a number of commitments: to maintain its fair share of the forces needed for the joint defense of the Atlantic area in Europe, including Germany; to regard any action that threatened the integrity or unity of the EDC as a threat to the security of the United States; and to remain part of NATO as long as the solid core of unity the EDC would provide to the European continent existed.[2]

By April, however, despite US assurances and assurances from new French prime minister Joseph Laniel that the debate on the EDC would take place in the National Assembly, the actions of the French Socialist Party and the deteriorating situation in Indochina cast an additional pall

152   on French views of EDC. Thus, in the afternoon of 22 April, Dulles cabled the president that the repudiation of EDC by French Socialist leader Guy Mollet the previous night and the Socialist Party's desire to add additional preconditions to the EDC Treaty were, according to Bidault, a "grave and perhaps mortal blow" to hopes for ratification. Additionally, the virtually hopeless situation in Indochina, for which US support was requested, was such that if Dien Bien Phu fell, France would pull entirely out of Southeast Asia and assume no other commitments.[3] The next evening, Dulles spoke with Laniel who also told him that the loss of Dien Bien Phu would have "a profound effect on EDC, probably destroying [the] possibility of favorable French action."[4] The situation there, Dulles wrote even later that night, was "tragic."[5] Tragic was not an understatement. On 7 May, Dien Bien Phu fell and five weeks later so did the Laniel government. Radical politician Pierre Mendés-France became the new prime minister.[6]

By the latter part of June, a number of issues—continued delays in ratification, Mendés-France's talks of possible changes to the EDC Treaty in order to obtain a majority in the National Assembly in favor of the treaty, the failure of the Four-Power Conference in Berlin, and the Soviet Union's grant of sovereignty to East Germany—led the secretary of defense to ask JCS to make recommendations for alternative measures to obtain German contribution. JCS again concluded that "concurrent agreements to end the German occupation and to accept West Germany as a full-fledged, sovereign partner in NATO would be the most desirable method . . . provided the participation of France or other NATO countries in the common defense effort is not jeopardized thereby."[7]

JCS's response also indicated that they could make no prediction as to when, if ever, France would ratify the EDC Treaty. They concluded further that the FRG would not accept anything less than full sovereignty, and that EDC without France, while technically possible, fell short of what EDC was designed to achieve. As an alternative to full NATO membership, the JCS posited the possibility of an associate member status for the FRG with restrictions on size and force composition not to exceed those it would have had in EDC.

The final JCS recommendation was that to achieve a German contribution, the United States and the United Kingdom should approach France jointly and tell it that in the event that France failed to agree to either EDC or German entry into NATO, the two countries would bilaterally restore sovereignty to the FRG and assist in its rearmament and eventual integration into NATO.

Interestingly, US Air Force chief of staff, General Nathan F. Twining, voiced strong opposition to this approach: "For almost two years, the Western nations have attempted to obtain French . . . consent to European Defense Community, so that a German contribution to the defense of Europe can be obtained. All of their efforts have been fruitless, and in my view, EDC is consequently a dead issue." Twining continued that Germany presented the greatest potential defense against Soviet expansion and that he was so strongly convinced of this that he believed that "the United States must take the risk of adversely affecting friendship with France and perhaps other nations by moving for the immediate rearmament of Germany, Germany's integration as an equal member with all others in NATO, and complete political sovereignty for Germany."[8]

German rearmament, Twining continued, should be accomplished, if possible, by the United States acting jointly with the other NATO nations, or, if that was not possible, jointly with the United Kingdom, and failing that, unilaterally. The United States should inform the other nations of its intentions and give the French a limited time to decide what their policy would be. Twining closed by recommending that the JCS study be returned for restudy and rewriting.[9]

On 25 June, Robert Murphy, deputy undersecretary of state, forwarded to Admiral Arthur W. Radford, the new chairman of the JCS, a copy of a letter that Conant had sent to Livingstone Merchant, assistant secretary of state for European affairs, a week earlier. The letter reflected Conant's pessimism about the French ratifying the EDC Treaty and contained a document that proposed that, in the event the French were unable to bring the EDC to debate before the National Assembly adjourned for the summer, the High Commission's charter be "stretched" to allow a majority two-to-one vote to suffice to grant West Germany sovereignty and allow the recruitment of Germans for military training to proceed. Conant also suggested that this action be publically announced. He opined that it was possible that neither Adenauer nor the British would be satisfied with this proposal as it meant "hanging on to EDC," but felt that if a start could be made recruiting and training these troops as auxiliaries to British and US forces, they would be available if a decision to create a national German army within NATO were made.[10]

On 25 June, the JCS submitted its revised response to the secretary of defense on the EDC alternatives study. It recommended, in order of preference, full NATO membership for West Germany or the independent rearming of West Germany by the United States and the United Kingdom.

154   The JCS further recommended that the United States and the United Kingdom take measures to bring about French ratification of the EDC or an agreement to accept Germany into NATO. If this were not possible, the United States and the United Kingdom should make it clear to France that they would proceed bilaterally to restore German sovereignty, assist Germany in its rearmament efforts, and seek Germany's full integration in NATO. The JCS concluded its response by stating that "if none of these courses of action can be implemented, the United States should then reappraise its basic policy toward Western Europe and its NATO commitments."[11]

Three days later, on 28 June, the United States and the United Kingdom agreed to a secret minute on Germany and the EDC. It reaffirmed the two countries' support for EDC and contained, in essence, Conant's earlier recommendations regarding granting German sovereignty but disregarded his recommendations to arm the FRG. Instead, the minute stated, an agreement would be reached with Adenauer to "defer for the time being the unilateral exercise by Germany of the right to rearmament."[12] The German view, according to Dulles, was that the FRG was perfectly willing to accept the same limitations on its forces as applied to other NATO members but would refuse to be singled out by limitations applicable only to Germany. Adenauer did not favor a separate national army, Dulles said, but he would not accept an inferior military position.[13]

On 13 July, the three service secretaries indicated in a note to all holders of the EDC alternative study that they agreed with the secret minute. However, as the last paragraph addressed the possibility of French rejection of EDC, they requested the views of the State Department in order to begin "appropriate contingency defense planning."[14] One week later, the State Department issued a lengthy position paper that began by reconfirming the US position that EDC was the best means to obtain a German defense contribution and that the primary goal of the United States was to obtain approval of EDC by the French National Assembly before the summer recess.[15]

That said, the paper enunciated the position that in the event of continued delay, a slightly modified version of Conant's proposal be implemented, where the United States and the United Kingdom initiated training of German cadres who would become "potential instructors of future German contingents of the European Defense Force"[16] and attach them to US and British forces in Germany, along with appropriate technical MDAP agreements. This would keep pressure on the French to ratify

EDC and place the Germans on equal footing with all. It would also convince the French that the "agonizing reappraisal" was not a bluff.

The State Department paper continued that if the French rejected EDC, full German membership in NATO would become the best alternative. Failing that, bilateral US-UK rearmament of Germany would be the only other alternative. The paper also stated that aside from being "quick and simple," any proposal for bringing Germany into NATO had to be acceptable to France and could not discriminate against Germany. It recognized that reconciling these conflicting criteria would be a problem, and set out a six-step program to achieve this goal. One step of the program included the consideration of a separate, formal US-UK-French-German security treaty.[17]

On July 27, Congress again reflected its dissatisfaction with the continued delay in ratifying the EDC Treaty. This time the Senate Foreign Relations Committee passed a sense of the Senate resolution informing the president that he should take whatever steps he deemed appropriate and constitutional to restore sovereignty to Germany should he judge this to be desirable and in the national interest.[18]

At the beginning of what proved to be the fateful month of August, the State Department revised its position paper. It was shortened considerably and now included the French in the training of German cadres and in an interim defense agreement, if they were willing. Other sections, including the one on a separate, formal US-UK-French-German security treaty, were deleted and in their place the paper gave a role to the three High Commissioners, emphasizing their ability to function by majority vote to ensure that France could not block through the High Commission any necessary changes to Germany's Basic Law to implement its military contribution.[19]

As the month of August progressed, cables crisscrossed the Atlantic, particularly between Churchill, Eden, Dulles, and even Adenauer. Several relayed to Dulles conversations held between Churchill and Mendés-France while the latter was returning from an EDC signatory conference in Brussels. Mendés-France promised to hold a vote on the EDC by month's end but implied that his cabinet refused to allow it to be a vote of confidence. He repeated his belief that despite his efforts, he would not be able to garner a majority and that EDC would fail in the National Assembly. Ironically, Mendés-France told Churchill and Eden that he was ready to consider German entry into NATO and, as a first step, restore political sovereignty to Germany.[20]

Churchill often mentioned the need to take on the NATO solution in his cables to Dulles but Dulles disagreed, saying that even if it were possible, the NATO solution would confront the same indecision and procrastination. In fact, as late as 24 August, while forwarding to Eisenhower an exchange of messages with Churchill, Dulles indicated that he hoped it was not too late for EDC and cited from a telephone call he had with Ambassador Douglass Dillon in Paris that Dillon, Bruce, and John Hughes still felt there was a "shred of hope" for EDC.[21] In fact, Dillon and Bruce, supported by Assistant Secretary of State Walter Bedell Smith, proposed a last-minute Brussels conference of the EDC signatories, the United States, and the United Kingdom, to be held on 30 August, the same day the National Assembly was scheduled to vote on EDC.[22] They hoped in this way to make one last attempt to pressure France into voting for ratification. Both Churchill and Eden opposed this idea and the matter was dropped.[23] On 30 August 1954, the French National Assembly employed a parliamentary procedure to table the vote on the EDC. EDC was dead.[24]

Despite the fact that the defeat of the EDC had been predicted numerous times by others, the US commitment to it had been such that US policymakers were left without an alternative; they "did not have any constructive proposals to advance."[25] In 1953, for example, the JCS had been directed to "suspend" consideration of alternatives, and even as it became obvious that the EDC would be defeated, some State Department officials, particularly Secretary of State Dulles, refused to accept the possibility that the EDC would not be approved. In fact, State Department opposed discussion of alternatives fearing that would arouse suspicions that the United States had given up on EDC, thus weakening efforts supporting ratification. Eisenhower and Dulles also believed that talk of alternatives would be interpreted thusly.[26] Both President Eisenhower and Dulles continued to seek a way to bring a German contingent into an integrated European Defense Force as a means of controlling the Germans while adding their combat power to the defense of Western Europe.[27]

The NSC, however, continued to debate internally what it and the Secretary of State should do—whether another form of EDC would work and whether it should seek to arm Germany unilaterally or together with the United Kingdom. On 16 September, the NSC Planning Board drafted a paper, "NSC 5433: Immediate US Policy toward Europe." This paper was an attempt to formulate an approach that would assist the United States in reaching its objective of arming the FRG. It began by stating that in view of France's rejection of EDC, the United States was faced with two options: "a. Continuing to pursue its present objectives in Europe by means other than EDC; or b. On the assumption that continued pursuit of all these objectives is no longer feasible, determining what objectives should then be pursued."[28] The paper also laid out a program of action that included restoring sovereignty to the FRG, admitting the FRG to full membership in NATO, and obtaining acceptable safeguards on German rearmament, including being prepared, with appropriate legislative authority and if necessary as a quid pro quo, to commit the United States to maintaining troops in Europe.

Secretary of State Dulles told the NSC that he was convinced the Europeans were more concerned with a replacement for EDC, as it was their problem and not a US problem. He continued that if the Europeans agreed on a substitute for EDC, they would want to know if the United States would cooperate with them as it had on EDC. Dulles also told the NSC that if France shot down the NATO solution, there was no good alternative, and that the United States must not assume it could unilaterally rearm Germany if the French refused to agree.[29]

The Department of Defense, obviously tired of repeated delays, debates, and what appeared to be procrastination on the part of the State Department, sought what it had always sought—the immediate, controlled rearmament of a national West German army that would be integrated directly into NATO with or without French participation. It acknowledged that "failure to obtain French cooperation for a German contribution . . . [would] require a basic change in NATO commitments and structure," but that this should not deter the United States from working out the best possible arrangements with West Germany for the United States' own interests as well as the interests of a free Europe.[30] Secretary of Defense Charles Wilson quite explicitly told the NSC that if the United States had to "buy the French into supporting the program of action, the deal wouldn't be worth anything."[31]

Great Britain Takes the Lead

In early September, the solution to the German problem began to emerge. Although several individuals lay claim to the solution and may, in fact, have contributed to it, true credit goes to British foreign secretary Anthony Eden for taking the lead and implementing it.[32]

Legend has it that Eden came upon the solution while taking a bath one day but it appears that the idea may actually have come from Mendés-France. As Kevin Ruane reveals, the planning for a nonsupranational alternative to EDC began in secret within days of Eden becoming foreign secretary in October 1951 and only ended in May 1955 when it became a reality.[33] According to Ruane, to counter the possibility of a US troop withdrawal, Eden began to contemplate keeping British troops on the continent and on 14 April 1954, a day after signing a formal association agreement with the EDC, he announced to the House of Commons the transfer of four armored divisions of the British Army of the Rhine (BAOR). By the Bermuda Conference in December 1953, Eden and his advisors had concluded that West Germany should be admitted directly to NATO. Eisenhower, however, reaffirmed his commitment to EDC, telling Eden "it's EDC" and it had to be done. The Americans left Bermuda believing they had successfully defeated the British plan to substitute "some NATO plan for EDC."[34]

Ruane also states that Eden's desire to take the lead in this endeavor was partly an attempt to prove to the United States that the European NATO nations had the capacity for self-help. The first step in Eden's plan was to assuage French fears of a future German aggression by admitting the FRG (and Italy) to the enlarged Brussels Treaty Organization and amending the organization's raison d'être to focus on threats from any direction, including Germany. The second step, although not guaranteed, was to admit a sovereign West German national army to NATO on the basis of equality but only after the Bonn government voluntarily accepted certain limitations. Adenauer did, in fact, voluntarily accept the EDC limitations and declare that West Germany would not produce atomic, biological, or chemical weapons, guided missiles, warships over three thousand tons, long-range artillery, or strategic bombers.[35]

Eden's solution, while it lessened the assurance of a revival of German militarism, contained no supranational characteristics, and saw the United Kingdom as a full member "sharing from within instead of buttressing from without." Eden began a tour of the six BTO capitals to seek support for this plan but did not notify the United States until after he had started his tour.[36] By mid-September, Eden had personally brought all the BTO members on board.

Nonetheless, Dulles remained "skeptical" and upset and continued to stand by EDC. The French vote that defeated the EDC caused him to again declare that the vote "[imposed] on the United States the *obligation* to reappraise its foreign policies, particularly those in relation to Europe."[37] He did not approve of Eden's solution because it did not have enough "supranational characteristics" and he considered it only a makeshift solution that needed further examination. He then went to Germany to dissuade Adenauer from accepting Eden's plan but failed, after which he went to London where he met with Eden and warned him that continued US defense participation was doubtful.[38] The United States again stood aside, "defeated and demoralized," realizing that the Europeans did not want an American plan, only American encouragement and assurances.[39]

Neither President Eisenhower nor many in the State Department were as opposed to Eden's plan as Dulles. Undersecretary of State Walter Bedell Smith submitted two proposals: the first was to accept the British plan subject to unilateral assurances from Germany, and the second was to initiate a defense agreement between the United States, the United Kingdom, and West Germany, possibly including Italy and the Brussels Treaty nations but excluding France.[40]

Ruane surmises that due to Dulles's travels, he may not have been aware of the contents of NSC 5443, which was approved by the President and issued as NSC 5433/1.[41] In the revised NSC 5433/1 officials in the State Department recommended the Europeans take the lead in solving the problem. As written, NSC 5433/1 actually supported the Brussels Treaty–NATO sequence of events and omitted any reference to "peripheral defense," which Eden saw as implied by Dulles's "agonizing reappraisal," and which the JCS saw as an alternative only in the event that France refused to accept FRG's entry into NATO.

By the end of September, however, Dulles had come around. Not only did the United States not have an alternative to Eden's plan, Eisenhower's position was that preserving the NATO alliance took precedence over any united Europe plan. By admitting the FRG to NATO, the Eden plan provided the only logical method by which West Germany could be both armed and controlled.

The French balked again at Germany's admission to the London conference but when Eden submitted his alternate plan, the historic commitment of four divisions and a tactical air force to the defense of continental Europe, Mendés-France rejoiced knowing that France would never be left alone with a rearmed Germany. The United States had no choice but to repeat the assurances it had given four years earlier to maintain troops in Europe as long as needed in order to recapture the leadership on the German question. The London and Paris negotiations Eden engineered with the EDC signatories, Italy, Canada, and the United States led to the expansion of the BTO and the creation of the Western European Union (WEU) with West Germany as a member, the end of the occupation of West

160   Germany, and eventually the admission of West Germany to NATO in May 1955.[42]

These actions brought closure to America's most important European policy issue of the period. In the end, there was nothing the United States could do but cooperate, as Dulles had indicated earlier.[43] On 1 February 1955, Eisenhower again provided the assurances the Europeans had been looking for, committing US forces to an open-ended stay on the European continent. Three months later, on 9 May 1955, ten years after World War II in Europe ended, Germany was formally admitted to NATO. The way was now clear for the arming of the Federal Republic of Germany.

Epilogue

The Role of the Three US Military Services

During the long, drawn-out Pleven Plan / EDC period, only NATO member-nations were eligible for the Mutual Defense Assistance Program (MDAP). This meant, of course, that the FRG was excluded. The Defense Department, however, impatient and unwilling to wait on political decisions, began planning a provisional rearmament program for the FRG without its actual participation.[1] Thus, as related in chapter 4, in mid-1952 USCINCEUR was made responsible for planning activities related to the MDAP as it applied to German units created for the EDC.

The real effort from all the services began after the EDC Treaty was signed on 27 May 1952, but each of the three US military services became involved at different times and in different ways. The USAF, for example, was more deeply involved in the creation and development of the Luftwaffe, its sister service in the new West German military (Bundeswehr), and the training of its recruits than the other two US services. However, information on the actual training plans and policies formulated by each of the services remains incomplete and somewhat spotty.[2]

It was not until immediately after the rejection of the EDC Treaty by the French National Assembly that the Department of Defense decided to continue its plans for German rearmament with the British, with or without French cooperation. Thus, on 2 September 1954, Deputy Secretary of Defense Robert B. Anderson directed the JCS to prepare a plan for the Secretary of Defense by 15 October with recommendations for logistical and military assistance to the FRG. Specifically, the request was for recommendations regarding[3]

    a.   the composition of the German forces, including recommendations regarding tables of organization and equipment;

    b.   the training organization and procedures;

    c.   the facilities requirements for German and U.S. forces in Germany, including turn-over to Germans of facilities now being used by U.S. forces;

    d.   the procedures for logistical support; and

    e.   the rate of buildup of the German forces.

USCINCEUR directed the commanders of the three service components in Germany, US Army Europe (USAREUR), US Air Forces Europe (USAFE), and US Naval Forces Germany (NAVFORGER), to prepare appropriate recommendations and to assume that the EDC planning basis of 12 army divisions, 1,326 aircraft, and 300 naval vessels would still be applicable. All three service components met in Paris on 16 September to assist in drawing up a program for US military assistance based on JCS recommendations.[4] There would be no waiting for any specific international political guidance. German forces would be limited to the EDC allocation, US training would cover the Germans from cadre to combat-ready status and be time-phased to match the buildup of the German armed forces, and most significantly, German forces would be developed as a national force—something the Defense Department had wanted from the very beginning. It was also decided that the Defense Department and the individual services should plan to assign sufficient personnel to the Military Assistance and Advisory Group-Germany (MAAG-Germany) to preclude any delay in the buildup of German forces, and that training and rearmament would take place even before a political settlement was agreed if the circumstances warranted.[5]

There were, however, as Acheson had earlier pointed out, several obstacles to overcome before a German armed force could be created. For example, there was neither a German governmental entity nor constitutional authority to raise, command, finance, or man an armed force in the FRG. Chancellor Adenauer was well aware of this problem and requested assistance from US authorities to ensure that as the governmental and constitutional processes unfolded, the new German military would develop in a democratic manner until those entities came about.[6]

Another key obstacle that hindered each of the services from providing training assistance was the inability to disclose classified information to the Germans. US regulations on disclosure handicapped discussions between US planners and their German counterparts throughout the period. Even as late as December 1954, there were only forty-three of the eight hundred or so employees of Amt Blank (also known as Dienststelle Blank, the precursor of the German Defense Ministry) who were cleared for NATO classified information.[7] This absurdity was demonstrated again in early 1955 when German planners gave USAREUR its draft plan, which, according to previous agreements, USAREUR was obligated to classify at the same level the Germans had classified it. In this case, the classification was Top Secret. As a result, USAREUR planners were prohibited from discussing the German plan with its authors. Each service was able to get certain workarounds approved without changing the disclosure regulations, thereby allowing classified information to be released on a strict need-to-know basis. Nonetheless, the development of assistance plans was hampered.[8]

Each of the three service components in Europe were eventually given responsibility for providing training assistance to their German counterpart service. Some had already been involved in planning for the FRG's rearmament as early as 1951.[9] That said, each service played a significantly different role in the rearmament process and US military assistance, training, and organization were viewed in completely different ways by former German Wehrmacht and Luftwaffe officers.

German army divisions had been organized differently than US divisions and their tactical doctrine was also unlike American practice. Former Wehrmacht officers considered US weapons, such as tanks and machine guns, inferior to those the Germans had developed during the war. In addition, they felt that the German army had been the better army in all respects and that the war had only been lost due to the Allies' overwhelming superiority in manpower and matériel. After all, hadn't the US Army used former German generals to write about the war and lessons learned so that the Americans could learn from German experience? For this reason they did not consider themselves a junior partner and therefore saw little need for training or tutelage.

Former Luftwaffe officers, on the other hand, had seen their air force decisively defeated, and recognized that air combat had changed significantly since the war. Furthermore, despite their having flown the first jet aircraft in combat, technology had advanced well beyond where they had been at the end of the war. Additionally, each of the German military experts who had participated in the Himmerod Conference knew that a new Luftwaffe would be dependent upon a technologically superior mentor[10]—the disarmament and dismantling program following the end of the war and the prohibition on any aviation activity had left German

164   aviation knowledge and technology at the level it had been in 1945. Only the United Kingdom and the United States qualified as possible guides.[11] Thus, they were eager to copy what the US Air Force had to offer in the way of organization, equipment, tactics, and training. It was, they believed, the only way to build a modern and sizeable air force.[12]

The US Navy

The role of the US Navy was, perhaps, the easiest and least important. Despite the demilitarization of Germany following World War II, the British Royal Navy had organized a German Minesweeping Service Authority (GM/SA) on 12 July 1945 to clear the Baltic Sea and the North Sea of mines. GM/SA utilized approximately 40 percent of the former Kriegsmarine's mine-sweeping personnel (nearly twenty-seven thousand personnel).[13] In 1947, the GM/SA was disbanded and reestablished as the Minesweeping Group Cuxhaven under the Allied Control Authority, and its personnel were given German Civil Service status. In November 1950, following the September NATO meeting and Acheson's single package presentation, a plan by the commander, US Naval Forces Germany (COMNAVFORGER) was initiated to disband the Cuxhaven group, reclaim its leased minesweepers, and establish three labor service units (LSUs): LSU (A) at COMNAVFORGER headquarters in Heidelberg, LSU (B) at the US Naval Base Bremerhaven, and LSU (C), which reported to the US Navy's Rhine River Patrol and was divided into three flotillas based at Wiesbaden-Schierstein, Karlsruhe, and Mannheim to provide assistance in manning the navy's ships and shore facilities at those locations. All three LSUs benefitted from the transfer of personnel from the Cuxhaven group and were operational by 1 July 1951.[14] Although LSU (B) at Bremerhaven continued its minesweeping duties, advanced training programs for all LSU personnel were established by the US Navy following the German government's ratification of the EDC Treaty in 1953. Instruction in naval weaponry, sonar, navigation, electronics, and engineering were provided under the unspoken assumption that these personnel would be turned over to the German government once Germany's role in EDC was finalized. These efforts had the approval of Amt Blank. The US Navy made classrooms and equipment available to the German LSU personnel and encouraged them to avail themselves of the many courses offered. The navy even went so far as to dry-dock minesweeping boats to allow their crews and additional LSU personnel to obtain the training that was being offered. By 1955, 33 percent of LSU personnel were taking the various courses offered.[15]

Similar to what the army had done in employing former German officers to write histories of the war, the US Navy assembled a Navy Historical Team (NHT) at Bremerhaven to "reconstruct the German perspective of the war at sea." The NHT, however, also evolved into a semicovert "coordinating staff" that examined the organization and needs of a future West German navy. In October 1950, at the request of General Adolf Heusinger, the senior officer in Amt Blank, several officers from the NHT were reassigned to his staff to act as naval specialists at the EDC Conference. Also in October, former admiral Friedrich Ruge joined the Himmerod Conference and brought with him a paper composed by the NHT team, which was incorporated into the final Himmerod Memorandum. Following some minor modifications by Admiral Gerhard Wagner, the head of the NHT, the naval proposal, renamed the Wagner Paper, was adopted as the basis for negotiations at the EDC Conference by Amt Blank.[16]

The first negotiations regarding the creation of a West German navy actually took place between then General Eisenhower and Adenauer in January 1951 at the Bonn Conference. In September 1951, the JCS set, for planning purposes, the strength of the future German navy at 183 active vessels, just three fewer than had been agreed at the EDC Conference. While negotiations over the EDC Treaty ratification continued in 1953, the United States drafted two initiatives to assist the future German navy: the first was to earmark MDAP funds for the new navy and the second was to return over 300 vessels confiscated from Nazi Germany and allocated to the United States by the Tripartite Naval Commission. Many of these returned boats later entered service with the Bundesmarine, as the new navy was called, in 1956. Also, in April 1953, 18 minesweepers were included for delivery as part of the Nash Agreement.[17]

Interestingly, the French, Belgians, Dutch, and Italians saw no need to have an EDC naval component. The Germans, however, insisted on one and Wagner brought the German position to Captain George Anderson of the US Navy, who acted as arbitrator. Anderson supported the German position but recommended a smaller force. Ironically, once this issue was solved and numbers and armaments decided upon, the French naval representative on the EDC Interim Commission (EDC-IC) became a strong supporter of the Germans and worked diligently to support them.[18]

The US Army

In late March, early April 1951, Headquarters European Command (HQ EUCOM) was tasked with supporting a request from Amt Blank for

166   assistance in ensuring that the new German armed forces would be established in a democratic manner. HQ EUCOM tasked the Personnel and Administration Division with developing appropriately written material to fulfill that request. EUCOM specified that the material should not just be a set of recommendations but clear and concise presentations of the subject being treated (i.e., how it came about, why it was applied, and the advantages and disadvantages, if any, to be obtained). All staff divisions were expected to participate.[19]

There does not appear to have been any further contact between the Germans and EUCOM until 1953. As mentioned earlier, the JCS had recommended in July 1952 that final organization for administering a military assistance program for the FRG be deferred until the EDC Treaty came into force. In the interim, the JCS also recommended that to prevent any overt planning activities from jeopardizing the EDC program, all activities should be coordinated with the EDC-IC.[20] As will be seen below, this created major obstacles for both the army and the air force.

In early 1953, former Wehrmacht Colonel Bogislav von Bonin, chief of the planning section in Amt Blank, attempted to establish closer contact with USAREUR. These attempts were denied by HQ EUCOM as being in violation of the JCS policy that all queries of a military nature had to be placed through the EDC-IC. Thus, on 4 May 1953, CINCEUR requested sixty-three additional personnel and authority to establish a Detachment A (Det. A) to facilitate coordination with the EDC-IC. He was told, however, that until the fiscal year 1954 MDAP was approved by Congress, which was expected in July, no personnel allocations could be made.[21]

In June 1953, a joint State–Defense–Foreign Operations Administration message addressed the need to reevaluate military assistance planning. At that point in time, however, USAREUR's role was limited and the command had little knowledge of German plans. Forced to being an "info" copy recipient on correspondence between EUCOM and the Office of the High Commissioner for Germany, USAREUR's planning activities were confined to recommending the use of training areas and providing lists of possible caserns and barracks and depot facilities for release to the Germans. Again, because of concerns about French sensitivities, USAREUR was unable throughout 1953 until the collapse of EDC in August 1954 to develop definitive and all-encompassing plans for assistance to the proposed German EDF contingent.[22]

Several months later, on 20 August, a second CINCEUR request for specialized school-trained personnel was also denied because the EDC

Treaty had still not been ratified. CINCEUR was finally authorized to establish Det. A, but only by using personnel from his own resources.[23] Once formed, Det. A was made responsible for liaising between EDC-IC and HQ EUCOM. The EDC-IC was made up of military, economic, political, and legal committees. Despite its many accomplishments, the military committee (chaired by French general R. M. E. Delaminate) was hindered in its efforts to create a German contingent by so-called political events throughout its existence. In fact, USAREUR considered the EDC-IC to have been a failure, as it was unable to function because of the delays imposed on planning activities by the several French committee members and chairmen that brought assistance planning by US military entities "virtually to a standstill."[24]

In addition, Det. A was further limited in that the assistance it was authorized to provide to the EDC-IC and its working groups pertained only to US forces' organization and procedures. Although some of that information was provided to German members of the commission, Det. A was reluctant to form a closer relationship with the Germans for fear of repercussions from the French. As mentioned above, USAREUR saw the EDC-IC as an obstacle rather than a benefit in providing assistance to the Germans. Every attempt by USAREUR to assist in planning for German contingents had to be cleared by the commission and Det. A was in no position to pressure it into allowing more specific planning out of fear it would jeopardize EDC's future in the French National Assembly. Thus, the EDC made little progress in obtaining a viable West German contribution to the defense of Western Europe.[25] One year later, in the fall of 1953, Det. A was replaced by the Advanced Planning Group in EUCOM's Military Assistance Division.[26]

Throughout the EDC phase, USAREUR expected to be required to initiate a training program for the future West German army but it was not until 15 July 1954 that its capabilities to support such training were delineated. Thus, immediately after the collapse of the EDC in August, USAREUR G-3 Operations Division instructed all staff divisions to begin the development of appropriate plans but to ensure that the amount of assistance offered would not affect USAREUR's combat readiness. Similar to USAFE, USAREUR was concerned that its role in training the German army would expand its mission beyond its capabilities.

As a result, a series of conferences were held in Paris on 18–19 November 1954 between USAREUR and EUCOM. At the third such conference, a compromise was reached based upon congressional action that specified that EUCOM had full authority and responsibility for providing assistance to the German army. The final letter of instruction, issued on 1 December 1954, delegated to USAREUR responsibility for providing German cadre and specialist training and logistical support, as well as certain financial responsibilities.[27]

A few months earlier, in September 1954, the JCS designated the Advanced Planning Group (APG) to act as the single point of contact between EUCOM and the German planners. In this respect and until the FRG regained full sovereignty, APG would represent the military part of the US country team in West Germany. US policy, as it concerned only its military relationship, was to consider the FRG a sovereign nation. The APG would, therefore, function as a proto-MAAG until an actual MAAG-Germany was established. It would continue discussions with German military planners and the EUCOM component command planners, and would arrange direct contact between them. EUCOM planned to man APG with sixty-nine personnel—one-half the strength of the future MAAG—by 31 March 1955. If additional personnel were needed during the actual training phase, they would be acquired from the army and the air force.

The APG's manifold responsibilities included advising the US ambassador to the FRG as needed, coordinating the MDAP for West Germany, and assisting the West German government in preparing requests for aid and training. In this respect, it would screen all assistance requests before forwarding them to USCINCEUR. Its responsibility also extended to preparing deficiency lists and recommending end-item requirements, delivery requirements, and prioritizing the distribution of supplies among the various German units. Last but not least, the APG was responsible for obtaining space in US service schools for German military personnel and for exercising control over US training and technical personnel assigned to German units. Thus, a sound working relationship between the APG and USAREUR became a high priority.[28]

On 2 September 1954, after the collapse of the EDC, USAREUR G-3 distributed to various USAREUR staff divisions and subordinate commands a directive entitled *Planning in USAREUR for Assisting in the Formation of the German Army*.[29] The directive's basic assumption was that the EDC manpower levels for the West German contingent would remain the same, that Amt Blank would become the West German Defense Ministry, and that restrictions on contacts with Amt Blank would be relaxed. It assumed that when requested, USAREUR would provide all practical training assistance to German planners, including mobile training teams and space in USAREUR training schools.

USAREUR's staff divisions responded by submitting their preliminary plans to G-3, which were then incorporated into a staff study. This study, which included a time-phased planning program, was first coordinated with the APG and then sent to the USAREUR chief of staff for approval and for forwarding to HQ EUCOM by 1 February 1955. Due to changes in the German plan following the demise of EDC (i.e., German forces would now be created as a national force), the new plan called for the creation of an army of six infantry and six armored divisions as well as five armored, two mountain, and two airborne brigades. Because the plan's due date of 1 February could not be met, there were several time-consuming conferences between USAREUR and Amt Blank planning staffs to make adjustments, but the lack of lists of available MDAP items precluded determining logistics and maintenance requirements. As a result, USAREUR requested an extension until 1 April, which was approved.[30]

To further complicate matters, however, the new German plan required the United States to provide a total of 284 officers and 1,507 enlisted men to fill the training team complements. This exceeded the EDC training personnel requirement by 16 officers and just over 1,000 enlisted men. Additionally, the Germans wanted to retain the US trainers for a period of six months while US plans foresaw only three months. After the dust settled, the numbers were whittled down considerably and the final total of army trainers that the United States agreed to provide was 222 officers and 680 enlisted men, to be supplied by USAREUR, the APG, and the Department of the Army. In addition, 100 German interpreters were added to those numbers.[31]

Providing training areas for the six army RCTs the FRG would be providing under the EDC concept proved problematic. USAREUR claimed that the three large training areas then in use—Grafenwöhr, Hohenfels, and Wildflecken—were barely sufficient for US and French forces. German utilization could only be on a "space available" basis. German attempts to acquire additional land in Central Army Group's (CENTAG [US]) area proved fruitless due to heavy opposition by the German populace and a lack of support from USAREUR.[32]

In October 1954, the JSPC looked at the issue of training areas and decided that the areas used by US forces in Germany would have to be shared equally. USAREUR was initially opposed but relented somewhat after accepting the fact that combat-ready German divisions would be

170   a major asset to the West's defenses. As long as the training of US forces
        would not be affected, they accepted the reality of the situation. Enter the
        Department of the Army, which, based on previously reached agreements
        (e.g., "Forces Convention and Relations," and the "Convention on Rights
        and Obligations"), stated that the Germans were required to find their
        own training areas. With that, USAREUR reverted to its original position
        and the problem was sent up to SHAPE.[33]

        Following a conference involving SHAPE, LANDCENT (Land
        Forces Central Europe), NORTHAG (Northern Army Group [UK]), and
        CENTAG, a decision was reached that once the FRG became a member
        of NATO, it would be able to utilize all of NATO's training areas within
        and outside West Germany, and that additional training areas should be
        provided by whichever country was best able to do so.[34] Thus USAREUR
        developed plans in February 1955 to allow German forces to use either
        German or USAREUR resources for the first ten months of the planned
        thirty-six-month buildup phase and that USAREUR facilities would be
        on a space available basis for the next two months. As for the remaining
        two years, German planners were unable to provide USAREUR its re-
        quirement as they did not know which areas would be made available or
        released to them. This problem, as well as several others, bounced back and
        forth between USAREUR and SHAPE but no permanent solution was
        found prior to Germany's entry into NATO in May 1955.[35]

        The most intractable planning problem that faced USAREUR was
        that of logistics support for the new German army. The logistics problem
        was, in fact, two problems. The first involved providing support to the US
        training teams deployed to fourteen German training sites and the second
        involved receiving, storing, maintaining, and distributing MDAP items
        destined for the German army.

        In February 1954, the Department of the Army directed USAREUR
        to provide storage facilities for equipment that would be given to the Ger-
        mans. USAREUR, however, lacked sufficient storage west of the Rhine,
        where it would be less vulnerable to attack. USAREUR was then au-
        thorized to store the MDAP materials east of the Rhine and two areas
        were selected, one near Bremerhaven in northern Germany and one near
        Darmstadt in the south. No action was taken, however, as the NASH Plan
        had not begun and the entire future of the EDC was still in question.
        When EDC collapsed, USAREUR was forced to change its plans. It de-
        cided that it wanted the Darmstadt facility for its own use—NATO plans
        were now to hold east of the Rhine rather than fall back to a defensive

position on the west bank—and USAREUR discarded the Bremerhaven area depot as too far away and too vulnerable. Furthermore, the Germans had selected and EUCOM had approved an unused Eberstadt area for their southern depot.[36]

As a partial solution, German civilian storage facilities were contracted for use but only after additional MDAP funds were made available. In addition, EUCOM arranged for matériel stored in the United States to remain there until called for by USAREUR. It was also stipulated that the FRG was not to receive anything until a new MDAP agreement had been negotiated. Despite the above, as late as March 1955, nine weeks before Germany was admitted to NATO, the full extent of the types and amounts of US equipment that was to be furnished to the FRG was still unknown, thereby hindering the completion of USAREUR's plans.[37]

Problems were also encountered hiring German personnel to be trained as assistant instructors and matériel maintenance personnel. Hiring was difficult because of housing shortages at the mostly rural training sites. Additionally, German nationals who were to be hired and integrated into the German army after the EDC Treaty was ratified could not be told what they were being hired to do because of security regulations. In addition, Amt Blank could not guarantee their integration into the army.[38]

In mid-March 1955, USAREUR G-3 submitted a revised draft assistance plan. It was forwarded to HQ EUCOM who forwarded it further to the Department of the Army without comments or recommendations that differed from the original USAREUR draft. The draft, "USAREUR German Army Assistance Plan," was subsequently approved by the Department of the Army in August 1955. Unfortunately, those portions of the draft plan that required German action or agreement in order to be implemented had not been coordinated with the German planners. When the plan was forwarded to the army, it contained a statement that the plan was only a basis for initiating training assistance and that once coordinated with the Germans, ultimate implementation would be affected.

Therefore, on 29 April, a meeting between USAREUR representatives and the APG was held to determine which portions of the plan could be released to the Germans. Finally, on 9 May, the day Germany was admitted to NATO, modified copies of the assistance plan were released to Amt Blank. The Germans were told, however, that the plan was only a draft and did not imply a commitment by the United States.[39] The plan, as approved, envisioned eighteen training teams and two equipment maintenance teams for a total of 910 officers and enlisted personnel. The majority of the personnel were to be in place approximately 1 June 1956 and would be required for five to eight months. The training program was to be phased out by February 1957, assuming actual activation of the German army took place on 1 January 1956. It was also requested that the maximum number of assigned personnel receive German language instruction or refresher training as needed.[40]

Not all of the delays or obstacles faced by the US military planning elements were due to EDC restrictions or US regulations. Amt Blank was also responsible. Theodor Blank, who had been appointed by Adenauer to head the office and who became Germany's first defense minister, was a trade unionist with little knowledge of military matters and a poor manager. Amt Blank was also severely undermanned, given to factional debates between traditionalists and antitraditionalists. As a result, many of the mundane planning issues so important to the creation of a new armed force were either given a low priority or ignored. Furthermore, although the manpower of Amt Blank increased from one hundred military personnel in 1952 to three hundred in 1954, they were simply overwhelmed. There were twenty-eight sections in the Luftwaffe staff, six of which, including the organization, personnel, and communications sections, had no section leader. Additionally, on the eve of rearmament in January 1955, the Luftwaffe admitted it had neither the time nor personnel to prepare its own plans for logistics, basing, and support structure.[41]

The US Air Force

In February 1951, a few months after the arrival of General Lauris Norstad as commander in chief, US Air Forces Europe (CINCUSAFE), USAF War Plans Division formulated the service's first thoughts on German air rearmament.[42] A staff study, sent to USAFE, contained five points:[43]

1. The new German Air Force (GAF) should have a minimum of 750 front-line fighters capable of both air defense and ground support missions;
2. The German Air Force should be equivalent to 10 US fighter wings, organized on self-contained bases with German technical and administrative support;
3. German Air Force personnel should be trained outside of Germany;

4. The German Air Force should be supplied with major equip-
    ment under the same policies as other continental countries,
    with MDAP aid forthcoming as necessary; and

5. 1 January 1954 should be the completion date, with force for-
    mation beginning in November-December 1952.

A revised study was sent to USAFE the following month that assumed
that ten fighter wings would require 65,000–70,000 men and 1,200 pilots
(using a ratio of 1.5 pilots per aircraft).[44] The study held that a sufficient
pool of experienced personnel existed in West Germany who would require only minimal training; that there would be no problem providing
bases for the ten wings; and that of the three aircraft deemed suitable for
the German Air Force—the French Vampire 53, the British Venom, and
the US F-84E Thunderjet—the Venom was considered the best but the
ability of the British to produce sufficient numbers of surplus aircraft was
unknown. USAFE responded in May with a staff study in which it opposed the limit of 750 aircraft. USAFE felt that this number should not be
a ceiling that Germany could not exceed if it were able to obtain equipment from sources other than the United States.[45]

Actual USAF participation in planning for German rearmament,
however, began on 6 April 1951, when USAFE received an invitation
asking that a representative be sent to the eighth meeting of the Allied
High Commissioners and German representatives in Bonn. This Allied
Rearmament Conference (the Bonn Conference) provided Germany a
forum in which to offer their first official proposal for a new air force.
The Germans proposed an air force of approximately 1,900 aircraft with
emphasis placed on the tactical support of ground operations. USAFE
disapproved of this concept and recommended the establishment of an independent air force.[46] General Heusinger, the German representative and
army officer, quantified that the new Luftwaffe would require approximately eighty-eight thousand personnel, three thousand of whom would
be flight personnel. At another meeting several weeks later on 20 April,
Heusinger stated that about nine thousand former Luftwaffe veterans were
living in West Germany and suggested that as many as would volunteer
and qualify should be retrained. Since USAFE was not authorized to consult with the Luftwaffe planners in Bonn, nothing further was done with
this suggestion.[47]

The next significant event took place in November 1951 when former German colonel Eschenauer, chief of the Air Planning Group in Amt

174   Blank, invited USAFE to discuss the reconstruction of airfields, deployment of German air units, and training for future air force personnel. Until then, USAFE had not been aware that such an office existed within Amt Blank. USAFE accepted the invitation and saw the opportunity for full staff participation. Assistant Chief of Staff for Operations Brigadier General Robert F. Tate told Deputy CINCUSAFE Major General Truman H. Landon that the time had come to increase USAFE's efforts to liaise with this agency in Bonn.[48] However, on 8 January 1952, Landon informed Eschenauer at a meeting in Wiesbaden that political complications prevented him from sending an air force liaison officer to Bonn. Nonetheless, Landon authorized the establishment of informal staff-wide contacts between USAFE personnel and the German Air Planning Group as an interim measure in order to develop a coherent plan. However, as no official contact was authorized and no formal plan for the rearmament of Germany had been agreed upon, both sides were urged to be discrete to avoid upsetting the French.[49]

Thus, between January 1952 and the end of March, eight meetings were held and because organization and manpower issues were of primary concern to the Germans, the Manpower Organization Division of the Office of the Assistant Chief of Staff for Operations assumed responsibility for the liaison effort. The discussions covered a wide range of topics, including headquarters organization, intelligence procedures, and ground and air warning operations, and incorporated the involvement of the appropriate USAFE staff agencies. USAFE also provided unclassified guidance materials to the Germans to study and to use as planning aids. By April 1952, however, the lack of authority to disclose classified information to the German planners had become a serious limitation, affecting especially communications and air defense planning.[50]

On 20 May 1952, General Norstad informed air force Chief of Staff General Hoyt S. Vandenberg of the informal meetings and what had been accomplished to date and requested that direct contact between USAFE and the Luftwaffe planners be authorized.[51] Norstad made the argument that formalizing these discussions and designating USAFE as the interim air force agency to administer unilateral MDAP responsibilities would allow USAFE to exert influence over the new Luftwaffe from the very beginning. He also stressed that much time would be saved by giving the German planners the benefit of USAF experience and that the aid would be for rebuilding an air force, unlike the aid being given to other Allied nations. Despite the rationale provided by Norstad, HQ USAF denied his request due to the "current status and sensitivity of negotiations" outside military channels.[52]

The following month, on 21 June 1952, USAFE made another request to establish contact with German representatives on the EDC-IC in conjunction with CINCEUR's request to establish a MAAG-Germany advanced planning group. Landon wrote Norstad that

> this entire problem of assisting the Germans in their planning
> is made more acute by the fact that the Air Planning Group
> constitutes only a very small group in the Defense Ministry, a
> body which is primarily composed of former German army
> officers of relatively greater rank than the air people. In addi-
> tion, the only formal contact the Germans have had with U.S.
> Military Forces has been through the High Commissioner's
> office to his advisors, who are officers from EUCOM. We have
> feared, and in some of our early reports concerning the plans
> being formulated by the Germans have indicated, a possibility
> of subordination of the air arm to ground control to an unde-
> sirable degree.[53]

On 7 July, 1952, Norstad wrote air force Deputy Chief of Staff General Thomas White to urge him to support the USAREUR request. Norstad stressed again the need for a strong USAF liaison with the Germans:

> One of our greatest concerns in this matter has been in seeing
> that the German Air Force, when it is formed, is patterned
> along the lines that will permit its effective use as part of the
> defense forces of the Western Powers rather than see it parceled
> out by direct assignment to ground units for limited objectives.
> We have been disturbed that this might happen unless qualified
> advisors were on hand to work directly with the Germans in
> their early planning.[54]

Recall that at Himmerod, the Germans had decided to build a new air force by copying the logistical and organizational structure of the USAF. They also decided to subordinate Luftwaffe units to the army command but failed to consider an air defense role for the new air force. To USAF planners, this was not only naïve but the "doctrine of a defeated enemy."[55] During World War II, the US Army Air Force (USAAF) units in North

176   Africa had been subordinated to army commanders and the system had been a failure. Subordination, as such, was anathema to USAF tactical thinkers and doctrine. It limited the flexibility of airpower and its ability to operate across a combat theater, using its speed and range to mass at decisive points when needed. The USAF wanted a Luftwaffe equal to the other services, capable of a variety of missions, and fully integrated into NATO's Allied Tactical Air Forces.[56]

In mid-July, a week after Norstad wrote White, Eschenauer was transferred and replaced by Colonel Richard Heuser. Before he departed, Eschenauer requested that Heuser be allowed to visit USAFE and that the informal meetings that had been held with the Germans (forced to cease in early June when the French learned of them) be resumed. Confronted with the problem of reestablishing the informal contacts, HQ USAF decided that although permission to establish formal relationships had been denied, informal meetings had not been prohibited. It appears that the delays in the EDC ratification process gave USAF reason to allow the meetings to continue, but they advised that the meetings should not receive any undue publicity. Thus, on 8 August, 1952, Heuser was invited to visit USAFE and the suspension of the informal meetings ended.[57]

Former Luftwaffe officers were allowed to visit not only USAFE but also US tactical units in West Germany as well. They were provided briefings and presentations on organization, technology, operations, and even given orientation flights on the T-33 jet trainer. Former Luftwaffe ace Colonel Johannes Steinhoff, one of the few former Luftwaffe pilots with jet fighter experience, came away from his orientation flight believing that refresher training would be successful only for the most experienced German pilots and that knowledge of English was absolutely essential.[58] It appears that during this same period, HQ USAF officials began making inquiries regarding the number of pilots the new Luftwaffe would need. They were interested in learning how many former Luftwaffe pilots would require refresher training and more importantly, how many could meet USAF physical and English language requirements.[59]

Also in August, USAF influence scored a major victory. Amt Blank announced that the concept of subordinating Luftwaffe units to the army was being dropped. The future Luftwaffe, it had decided, would be a fully independent service and would be fully integrated with Allied air operations. Nonetheless, the planning effort continued to be hampered by both political and bureaucratic restrictions imposed by the EDC, NATO, and even the Defense Department. In particular, similar to the way USAREUR was being hampered, security regulations precluded the sharing of information necessary to various aspects of air force planning. It was not until December 1953 that the air staff, at the urging of USAFE, granted an exemption and allowed USAFE planners to share classified defense information with accredited German personnel.[60]

With the existence of Det. A in Paris as the single, mandatory channel of contact between USAREUR, the EDC-IC, and the German planners, USAFE was only allowed to officially participate in planning for German rearmament when directed by USCINCEUR or higher authority. Det. A, however, was not manned sufficiently to perform its tasks nor, as mentioned above, was it able to liaise closely with the German planners.[61] USAFE, therefore, again sought a clearly defined responsibility for Luftwaffe planning. Similar to USAREUR's requests to be given significantly more responsibility for the German Army portion of the MAAG when it came into existence, General William H. Tunner, then CINCUSAFE, pointed out that while EUCOM retained overall planning responsibility, it continually turned to USAFE to perform the majority of the planning activity without giving the command any "discretionary and creative" planning responsibility. Thus at the 3 December 1953 EUCOM Commanders-in-Chief Conference, the USAFE presentation stated, "It is clear that USAFE, among U.S. elements, has not only a legitimate interest, but indeed a paramount interest in German Air Force planning and development and logically should have commensurate responsibility. There is no question of our ability to do the job. USAFE has been doing it and, despite deterrents, has produced realistic planning."[62]

USAFE's entreaties and efforts to obtain more specific responsibilities had as little success as USAREUR's. Just a few weeks earlier, however, EUCOM had established a triservice advanced planning group (to form the nucleus of MAAG-Germany) that included five air force officers. The new organization moved to Bonn in August 1954, where it served as the single point of contact between EUCOM headquarters and Amt Blank and its eight-hundred-plus German planners on all military assistance and training matters. The above notwithstanding, USAFE continued to seek authority for German Air Force planning, and its views were presented to EUCOM on 16 September 1954 and again on 11 October 1954. Finally, on 3 December 1954, USCINCEUR defined the specific responsibilities of all three service commands as they applied to German rearmament planning. Those given to USAFE were considerable but significantly less than the command desired.[63]

In June, 1953, Lieutenant Colonel Warren Sands arrived in West Germany with a team from Air Training Command. Sands initiated a joint EUCOM-USAFE German planning group effort to prepare a comprehensive training plan, the object of which was to coordinate personnel training with aircraft delivery and unit activation schedules. The plan was based on the EDC goal for Germany of 1,326 aircraft. The aircraft delivery schedule, as per the MDAP, was 978 combat aircraft and 270 training aircraft within three years of EDC ratification. Based on that, the Sands Plan, otherwise known as the German Flying and Technical Training Program, was completed in early July 1953.[64]

Sands' plan provided refresher training for approximately six hundred pilots, basic flight training for one thousand aviation cadets, and nonflying technical courses. While most of the flight training would be conducted in West Germany, some would take place in the United States. HQ USAF approved the Sands Plan and gave USAFE operational control of the training until MAAG-Germany was established. It also assigned to USAFE responsibility for all aspects of the training program outlined in the Sands report. In September 1953, a decision was made at USAF headquarters to establish the 7330th Training Group—the first of three training groups—which was activated at Fürstenfeldbrück Air Base in southern Germany on 1 November 1953. Two other training bases under consideration, Erding and Landsberg, would not be available until 1955, and a fourth, Kaufbeuren, which was being used by the US Army, would not be transferred until September 1954.[65] Forty-six T-6 propeller and forty-seven T-33 jet trainers were scheduled to arrive shortly after 1 January 1954.[66]

Not long after the 7330th Training Group was activated, its plans division undertook a study of the Sands Plan and found that it needed significant revisions and that there were areas that had not been covered that therefore needed to be addressed. These deficiencies were brought to the attention of USCINCEUR on 19 January 1954 and USAFE's recommendation that it unilaterally refine the plan and select the sites for training the Germans was approved on 2 February.[67] Two days later, on 4 February 1954, the 7330th Training Group and an officer from EUCOM's Advanced Planning Group began work on the *Plan for the Implementation of the Federal Republic German Air Force* (GAFP 55-1), the first draft of which was completed three weeks later.

This large-scale training program would be located at the four bases named above, with Erding serving as the USAFE logistics support base. A full USAF training wing would be created with approximately one thousand US air force personnel and one thousand American and German civilians at each base. The end goal was to train a German cadre in eighteen months, after which the Germans would take over the training and the bases would be turned over to full German control.[68]

Although the program had been approved on the US side, it was realized that the assumptions made regarding the Luftwaffe structure had not been verified by German authorities and would, therefore, require modification. Coordinating with the Germans required authorization to release to them MDAP programming equipment delivery data and a host of other necessary items, including site surveys, information on the redeployment of USAFE units from NATO bases destined for allocation to the Germans, the development of a German Air Force logistical support plan, and a determination of USAF ability to support German training needs in the United States.[69]

On 31 March, HQ USAF informed USAFE that it could not support the large number of training spaces that had been requested in the United States. It then directed USAFE to expand its capability to the maximum in Germany and to assume all, or at least the greater portion of the refresher training that had originally been scheduled for completion in the United States. Based on this and a number of other issues needed to expand USAFE's training capability, USAFE was directed to modify its current training plan (GAFP 55-1) , which was renamed *The German Air Element of the EDC Force* (GAFP 55-2).[70]

The revised training plan contained two new sections. The first was a concept of operations and integration of the German Air Force into the EDC force structure. The second provided for an English-language training course. The revised plan also specified that the buildup period would last four years and even included manning details such as pilot-to-aircraft ratios and training wing locations.[71] It was also designed to produce within the first four years 1,800 pilots (80 percent of the total) and 17,000 technicians (personnel for maintenance, intelligence, communications, etc.).[72]

In June, USAF revised the aircraft delivery schedule but due to a lack of disclosure authority, most of USAFE's plans and programs were done without knowledge of German capabilities to support them. On 1 August 1954, the revised GAFP 55-2 was completed and subsequently approved pending revisions that also required input from the German Air Planning Group. As a result, there were many discrepancies between the USAFE plan and what the German planners had developed based on EDC guidance. To facilitate contact with German planners, EUCOM moved the

180   APG to Bonn on 11 August 1954. On 3 December 1954, GAFP 55-2 was again revised to include a training program that comprised both flying and technical training that had been approved by the Germans.[73] The newly revised plan provided for a refresher course of sixteen months for veteran pilots who could speak some English, while those whose English proficiency was low were required to study English for an additional three months. Aviation cadets were sent to the United States for twenty-two months of training. Following refresher and basic training in the T-6 and T-33 respectively, the new Luftwaffe pilots would enter the tactical aircraft course. Both officers and enlisted personnel would attend technical training courses and noncommissioned officers (NCOs) would be selected from the enlisted trainees based on their academic performance, experience, and leadership abilities.[74] GAFP 55-2 was distributed on 25 August 1954 and endorsed by USCINCEUR, USAF, JCS, and the secretary of defense as the initial US plan to support the German Air Force rearmament program. Five days later, on 30 August, France rejected the EDC Treaty and the differences between it and GAFP 55-2 became moot. GAFP 55-2 would now serve as the basic planning document until a new plan, GAFP 56-1, was completed several years later.[75]

    At the same time that USAFE was dealing with Luftwaffe training issues, the command was also attempting to acquire additional facilities and bases for them. During the 1951 German Rearmament Conference, Heusinger set out a tentative proposal for 25 air bases. The German Air Planning Group also raised this question with CINCUSAFE in the summer of 1952 and again in the early months of 1953. Nothing could be accomplished at the time, however, as no authorization had been received from the EDC agency responsible for determining where future Luftwaffe units would be deployed.

    Finally, in January 1953, SHAPE authorized Allied Air Forces Central Europe (AAFCE) and Allied Forces Central Europe (AFCENT, previously LANDCENT) to begin discussions with the EDC-IC on facilities for both the German Army and the Luftwaffe. AAFCE and the EDC-IC failed to come to an agreement, causing planning for Luftwaffe facilities to fall behind. The result was that several former Luftwaffe bases were earmarked for use by German land forces. USAFE's requests for additional meetings to discuss the issue were denied and in May 1953, COMAAFCE noted that further meetings had been postponed. One month later, however, on 26 June, he asked USAFE for a list of air bases that could be released to the Germans and in late July, the EDC-IC reopened discussions on the allocation of nonoperational facilities.[76]

USAFE and USAREUR representatives met on 6 August 1953 to discuss availability and procedures and decided that army-type installations no longer needed by USAREUR would be offered to USAFE, the German Army, and the Luftwaffe in that order. Air force–type facilities not needed by USAFE would be offered to USAREUR, the Luftwaffe, and the German Army in that order. USAFE declared that surplus space would be available at Neubiberg and Landsberg in September 1954, at Fürstenfeldbrück after December 1955, and Erding after March 1956. All four bases, however, would be reserved for joint USAFE-Luftwaffe use. Aside from the above, no further decisions were made.[77]

The problem of installations was further exacerbated when USAFE's dispersal program to reduce vulnerability increased the command's bases requirements. Thus, in September 1954, USAFE notified USCINCEUR that unless the FRG provided alternate facilities at no expense to the United States, or unless agreement could be reached on joint occupancy, USAFE would be forced to keep for itself all the bases foreseen in the German Air Force program. This problem remained unresolved during this period.[78]

As 1955 dawned, the biggest problem confronting USAFE planners in building the new Luftwaffe was finding qualified personnel. While the new German Army would benefit from thousands of former professional soldiers who had been cleared and carefully screened as politically reliable, a number of them already trained and under arms in the Bundesgrenzschutz (the border police), and fully trained former German Navy officers and NCOs had manned several minesweeper flotillas maintained by the Allies, the Luftwaffe had no one who had been trained in high-performance jet aircraft or current radar systems or electronics.[79] Of the six thousand Luftwaffe pilots who had survived the war, only 160 were available and considered qualified to fly jets when the new Luftwaffe began recruiting in 1955–56.[80] Nonetheless, undeterred by the number of unresolved issues, such as the lack of facilities and training aids, and the long-awaited but still insufficient delineation of its responsibilities, USAFE had a training network in place by the time the FRG was admitted to NATO and given full sovereignty on 5 May 1955. It was fully prepared to play a substantial role in building the new Luftwaffe and to accept the first Luftwaffe volunteers at the beginning of 1956.[81]

182   Despite being beset by internally and externally imposed obstacles and a lack of resources and real responsibility, each of the three US services took on and successfully completed the task of laying the groundwork and preparing to train the nucleus of the new German armed forces, the Bundeswehr. Actual training took place after the time frame covered by this book, the navy being an exception, and although the operational readiness of the Bundeswehr took longer to achieve than initially planned, US military planners had done their job and done it well.[82]

Appendix A

The European Advisory Commission (EAC)

The European Advisory Commission (EAC) was a cre-
ation of the Tripartite Moscow Conference of Foreign Ministers of October 1943. Britain's foreign minister, Anthony Eden, who proposed the
commission, desired it to have a broad scope that would include a wide
range of European problems caused by the war but exclude military operations. The commission was to be consultative only and not have any
executive authority, thus it could only accept issues recommended by the
governments of its members and its decisions required unanimity. One of
its first tasks was to make detailed recommendations regarding the terms
of Germany's surrender and, by implication, the disarmament and demilitarization of the European states at war with the three Allies. The EAC
held its first formal meeting in London on 14 January 1944 with John G.
Winant, US Ambassador to Great Britain, representing the United States,
Sir William Strang of the Foreign Office representing Great Britain, and
the Soviet ambassador to Great Britain, Feodor T. Gousev, representing the
USSR.[1] In early November 1944, the Provisional French Government
was invited to join and its ambassador to London, René Massigli, took his
seat toward the end of the month.[2]

In all, the EAC held twenty formal meetings and issued twelve signed
agreements, of which five pertained to Germany. Of those five, only three
provided broad guidance regarding the demilitarization of Germany.

1. *"The Unconditional Surrender of Germany."* There were two ver-
   sions of this document; the first, which took six months to negotiate, was approved on 25 July 1944, and amended on 1 May
   1945 to allow for France's accession to the EAC and to allow

the French representative to sign it while the second, which contained a paragraph that discussed the dismemberment of Germany, was never shown to the French.[3] On 4 May 1945, just days before Germany's surrender, SHAEF Chief of Staff General Walter Bedell Smith informed Ambassador Winant that SHAEF had no authoritative copy of the surrender instrument nor had the Allied governments delegated to SHAEF the authority to sign that document. Thus neither of the two drafts that had been sent to SHAEF were used. Instead, SHAEF drew up and used a briefer surrender document but, at the urging of Ambassador Winant, revised it to include a paragraph (paragraph 4) that did not preclude the use of a surrender document drawn up by the EAC at a later date.[4] The only mention of disarmament contained in the EAC document was in Article 2(a), which stated that "all armed forces of Germany or under German control . . . equipped with weapons, [would] be completely disarmed."[5] The SHAEF document makes no mention of disarmament at all.[6]

2. *"Declaration Regarding the Defeat of Germany and the Assumption of Supreme Authority with Respect to Germany."* This document was approved on 21 May 1945 and signed by the four powers in Berlin on 5 June 1945. Virtually all of the fifteen articles in this declaration directed the German Armed Forces to undertake certain actions following the cessation of hostilities regarding their weapons and equipment, but only Article 2(a) specifically stated that "all armed forces of Germany or under German control, wherever they [were] situated, including land, air, anti-aircraft and naval forces, the S.S., S.A. and Gestapo, and all other forces of auxiliary organisations equipped with weapons, [would] be completely disarmed, handing over their weapons and equipment to local Allied Commanders or to officers designated by the Allied Representatives."[7]

3. *"Certain Additional Requirements to Be Imposed on Germany."* This document, agreed on 25 July 1945, contained thirteen sections with various additional restrictions that inter alia related to finances, shipping, property, and the abolition of German militaristic organizations. Specifically, Section I, paragraph 1 stated that "all German land, naval and air forces, including the S. S., S. A., S. D. and Gestapo with all their organizations, staffs and institutions, including the General Staff, the Officers' Corps, Reserve

Corps, military schools, war veterans' organizations and all other 185
military and quasi-military organizations, together with all clubs
and associations which serve to keep alive the military tradition in Germany, [should] be completely and finally abolished."[8]
Paragraph 2 continued by prohibiting "all forms of military
training, military propaganda and military activities of whatever
nature . . . as well as the formation of any organization initiated
to further any aspect of military training and the formation of
war veterans' organizations or other groups which might develop military characteristics or which are designed to carry on
the German military tradition."[9] In the same vein, Section V,
paragraph 13, prohibited the "manufacture, production and
construction, and the acquisition from outside Germany, of war
materials" and required that all "research, experiment, development and design directly or indirectly related to war or the production of war material" be placed at the disposal of the Allied
Representatives.[10]

A fourth document, "Control Machinery in Germany," signed on 14
November 1944, provided for the initially tripartite and later quadripartite
control of Germany through the Allied Control Authority (ACA). While
not mentioning disarmament per se, it delineated the composition of the
ACA, mandating the Allied Control Council and Coordinating Committee. It also provided for the Coordinating Committee's subsidiary agencies
whose function was, inter alia, to control and disarm Germany.[11]

The EAC came to the end of its existence with the publication of
the "Communiqué: Report on the Tripartite Conference on Berlin" on
2 August 1945. The communiqué, which also announced the establishment of the Council of Foreign Ministers, noted "with satisfaction that the
Commission had ably discharged its principle tasks" but felt that further
work for the control of Germany fell within the competence of the Allied
Control Council. It therefore recommended that the EAC be dissolved.[12]
The EAC accepted the recommendation as a mandate. Its final report
was dated 10 September 1945, although discussion of it continued into
November.[13]

In his report on the activities of the EAC,[14] Ambassador Winant pointed
out that the support for the commission from the United States had been
uneven, given the difficulties within the government in formulating a unified German policy.[15] Commending the work of the US Joint Advisors to

186   the US representative, he reported that the US Joint Advisors had prepared thirty-six draft directives designed to provide General Eisenhower with agreed policy guidance. Of this total, twenty-four draft directives (seven of which dealt with disarmament issues) and five draft agreements were approved by "appropriate authorities" in Washington for circulation and negotiation in the EAC.[16] Although these directives had been circulated within the EAC, none had reached the point of being negotiated. Winant, however, stated that they had informed and influenced the policies of the other Allied governments and that these draft directives had provided the US Group Control Council its first systematic guidance for preparatory planning. They also were incorporated to a large extent in the "General Directive for Germany."

Appendix B

Operation Eclipse Memoranda

Memo No.[1]	Title and Nature of Document
1.	Instrument of surrender, surrender order and sanctions
4.	Outline Air Plan
5.	Supplies, services and facilities in Germany
6.	Signal communications and RADAR
7.	Intelligence requirements and plan
8.	Care and evacuations of Prisoners of War
9.	Primary Disarmament of German Land Forces
10.	Primary Disarmament of German Air Forces
11.	Primary Disarmament of German Naval Forces
12.	Civil Affairs consideration in Liberated Territories
13.	Civil Affairs consideration in Germany
14.	Control of displaced persons
15.	Psychological Warfare Requirements and plan
16.	Public Relations considerations and plan
17.	Disbandment of German Armed Forces
18.	War criminals and security suspects
19.	Powers and rights over German persons

Appendix C
Eradication of Nazism and Militarism

Representative Sample of Orders, Directives, and Laws Dealing with the Disarmament and Demilitarization of Germany

Part 3, chapter 2 of the *Handbook for Military Government in Germany* dealt with the responsibility of the military government to accomplish the task of destroying German militarism and removing all Nazi and militarist influences from the public, cultural, and economic life of the German people. This was one of the principle objectives of the war and was also mandated by the Potsdam Agreement. In the main, the title pertained to the denazification procedures, which were the responsibility of military government officers assisted by counterintelligence personnel and military commanders. The chapter contained five tables outlining civil and governmental organizations to be abolished (Table A); political officers and civil servants to be dismissed or suspended (Table B); Nazi party, police, paramilitary, and government officers to be interned (Table C); positions in Nazi party organizations and formations considered as disqualifying (Table D); and quasi-governmental positions from which principal officers were to be removed. Demilitarization had, by 1946, been completed in terms of personnel and was still underway in terms of physical plants, such as military installations, industries, and the like.[1]

Military Government Law No. 12: Abolition of Employment Preferences in Favor of Former Members of the German Armed Forces and Others

Military Government Law No. 12, enacted on 1 August 1948, repealed the provisions of German law that required employment preference be given to former members of the German armed forces or other

190   Versorgungsanwärter (those eligible for or receiving a government pension) for government posts or other public positions and conferred upon them preferential treatment in appointment to, remuneration for, or promotion in any government post.[2]

Military Government Law No. 54: Use of Wehrmacht Property
Military Government Law No. 54, enacted on 27 August 1945, returned *all* military property that could be used for agriculture or the settlement of Germans and others to the state in which it was situated.[3]

Military Government Law No. 56: Prohibition of Excessive Concentration of German Economic Power
Military Government Law No. 56, also known as the Decartelization Law, was enacted on 12 February 1947 expressly to "(i) prevent Germany from endangering the safety of her neighbors and again constituting a threat to international peace, [and] (ii) to destroy Germany's potential to wage war."[4]

Military Government Law No. 154: Elimination and Prohibition of Military Training
Military Government Law No. 154, which became effective on 14 July 1945, specified various punishments, including the death penalty, for violation of this law.[5]

Military Government Ordinance No. 1
Military Government Ordinance No. 1, Crimes and Offenses, made, among other crimes, the unlawful possession or control of firearms, ammunition, explosives, or other war matériel a capital offense punishable by death.[6]

Military Government Ordinance No. 4
Military Government Ordinance No. 4, later made part of Military Government Regulation 23-400, prohibited the wearing of German military uniforms.[7]

Allied Control Council Law No. 8: Elimination and Prohibition of Military Training
ACC Law No. 8 had a somewhat controversial beginning. It was initially drafted sometime in 1944—it is referenced in JCS 1124 of 20 October

1944 and in JCS 1103 as well. On 4 November 1944, a recommendation was made to amend paragraph 9 of JCS 1103 to include the prohibition of all forms of parades (e.g., military, political, civilian, sports). It also recommended the prohibition of military music and other German and Nazi anthems as well as the display of German national and Nazi flags and paraphernalia. On 19 February 1945, officers of the Demobilization Branch, Army (Ground) Division conferred and established that such a law was necessary and recommended it be published by Supreme Headquarters Allied Expeditionary Force (SHAEF). The draft was subsequently approved by US Group CC, who also recommended SHAEF approve and promulgate it.[8]

SHAEF's G-5 (Legal Division), however, saw several redundancies in the draft, claiming that much of what was in the draft was either already covered by existing laws and ordinances or would soon be. As a result, G-5 felt that the law was not needed at that time but should be considered again after SHAEF was no longer responsible for Germany. These arguments were rebutted by US Group CC which argued that the provisions of the draft law were covered by existing ordinances only in an "extremely technical sense." US Group CC argued further that this law on the elimination and prohibition of military training was a "fundamental and basic element of Allied long-range policy" and that its contents needed to be presented to the German people in a clear and understandable manner. This argument won the day and the ACC promulgated the law on 30 November 1945 with but few changes to the original version.

Allied Control Council Law 23: Prohibition of Military Construction in Germany

This law, which was enacted on 17 April 1946, prohibited, among other things:[9]

a. The preparation, possession, or even making use of models or plans of any military installation.

b. Planning, designing, fabrication, erection or construction of [a]ny military installation.

c. Planning, designing or erection of any type of civil construction, where any details in the plan, design, erection or construction provide for their possible utilization for war purposes, whether for land, sea, or air.

Penalties for violating this law, depending on the seriousness of the violation, encompassed a wide range of prison terms up to and including the death penalty.

Allied Control Council Law 25: Control of Scientific Research

Enacted on 7 May 1946, this law prohibited all research on a number of subjects that had military applications, outlined in four schedules. This law was supplemented by an OMGUS regulation that refined the requirements of the law and included forms that could be filled out and sent in for approval for conducting scientific research.[10]

Allied Control Council Law 34: Dissolution of the Wehrmacht

Although the Wehrmacht was dissolved by Allied Proclamation No. 2 and Disbandment Directive 9, this law, enacted on 26 August 1946, was seen as necessary to prevent the future reestablishment of the Wehrmacht or any of its organizations by any other name and to declare such any such reconstitution illegal. According to article V of this law, violators could also be subject to the death penalty.[11]

Allied Control Council Law 43: Prohibition of the Manufacture, Import, Export, Transport or Storage of War Materials

This law was enacted on 20 December 1946 to prevent the rearming of Germany. Its very specific provisions included even the production of such materials for the occupation forces, as this would create conflict with ACC Law No. 25 by allowing the Germans to retain a degree of technical know-how regarding the manufacture of weapons of war.[12]

Allied Control Council Law 46: Abolition of the State of Prussia

As it had been determined that the Prussian State had been the bearer of militarism and reaction in Germany from the earliest days, this law was enacted on 25 February 1947 to "assure the further reconstruction of the political life of Germany on a democratic basis."[13]

Allied Control Council Directive 16: Arming of German Police

This directive, published on 6 November 1945, authorized the rearming of the German police for the purpose of maintaining law and order. It prohibited the use of automatic weapons, however, and weapons or ammunition of German manufacture, at least until there were sufficient non-German weapons available. The directive further limited the issuance

of weapons to pistols and handguns, except that rural and frontier police
were allowed to be armed with carbines. No weapon was to be issued to
any unit that had not completed denazification and removed any person
deemed hostile to the military government. Ammunition was strictly limited to ten rounds for municipal police units and twenty rounds for rural
and frontier police units. Police units were to be held strictly accountable
for all weapons issued and all ammunition issued and expended.[14]

Allied Control Council Directive 18: For Disbandment and Dissolution of the German Armed Forces

This directive was issued on 6 December 1945 to specify procedures by
which former members of the Wehrmacht, POWs and non-German
members of the military would be demobilized, discharged, and sent to
their previous homes or repatriated as the case might be.[15]

Allied Control Council Directive 22: Clearance of Minefields and Destruction of Fortifications, Underground Installations and Military Installations in Germany

This directive, published on 6 December 1945, began by stating that its
purpose was to *forever* prevent Germany from using these facilities. All the
facilities listed in the appendix of the directive, except those needed by
the occupation forces or civil population, were to be destroyed completely
in accordance with the given timetable—Priority I within 18 months,
Priority II within another four years—so that all these facilities would
be destroyed within five and a half years from the date the directive was
published. Military zone commanders were given discretion to add to the
list and to destroy any discovered military structures, even if they were not
listed in the appendix.[16]

Allied Control Council Directive 23: Limitation and Demilitarization of Sport in Germany

Issued on 17 December 1945, this directive prohibited all sport activities,
organizations, clubs, and so on, that involved aviation, parachuting, gliding,
fencing, military drill or display, and shooting with firearms.[17]

Allied Control Council Directive 28: Reports on Disposal of German War Material in Germany

Issued 26 April 1946, this directive provided for the expeditious destruction and disposal of captured or surrendered German war matériel located

in Germany. It was amended by ACC Directive No. 46, which set a target date of 1 May 1948.[18]

Allied Control Council Directive 30: Legislation Dealing with the Liquidation of German Military and Nazi Memorials and Museums

Enacted on 13 May 1946 and amended on 12 June 1946, this directive prohibited the "planning, designing, erection, installation, posting or other display" of a wide range of objects, including street signs, statues, and tablets, that would keep German military tradition alive, serve to revive it, or serve to "glorify incidents of war." The same directive prohibited the reopening of military museums and exhibitions. Only monuments erected to the memory of deceased members of military organizations—except paramilitary organizations, the SS, and the Waffen SS—were allowed, as were tombstones that existed or were to be erected in the future as long as they carried no indication of militarism or Nazism.[19]

Allied Control Council Directive 32: Disciplinary Measures against Managing and Administrative Staffs of Educational Institutions, Teaching Staffs, and Students Guilty of Militaristic, Nazi or Anti-Democratic Propaganda

Enacted on 26 June 1946, this directive, as its titled implies, provided for the dismissal or expulsion of such individuals and made them liable to criminal prosecution.[20]

Allied Control Council Directive 39: Liquidation of German War and Industrial Potential

Issued on 2 October 1946, this directive was written to take into consideration those remaining elements of German warmaking potential that had not been covered by previous laws and directives. The principles guiding the implementation of this directive were to destroy completely, declare available for reparations, or leave intact for peacetime economic use (in accordance with certain stipulations).[21]

Appendix D

US-Approved Draft Directives of the US Joint
Advisors to the US Representative to the
European Advisory Commission[1]

1. Disposition of German and German Controlled Naval Craft, Equipment and Facilities, EAC(44)34, 24 November 1944.
2. Disposition of German and German Controlled Aircraft, Aeronautical Equipment and Facilities, EAC(44)37, 24 November 1944.
3. Disposition and Control of the German Police EAC(44)38, 25 November 1944
4. Control and Disposal of Nationals, Armed Forces and Property of Enemy Countries other than Germany, EAC(44)39, 25 November 1944
5. Elimination and Prohibition of Military Training in Germany EAC(44)43, 8 December 1944
6. Disposal of German Armed Forces, EAC(45)1, 1 January 1945
7. Disarmament of the German Armed Forces and Disposal of Enemy Equipment, EAC(45)12, 16 February 1945

Appendix E

The Himmerod Conference and the Bonn Report

The Himmerod Conference

Unbeknownst to the United States, the September 1950 meeting of the NATO Foreign Ministers in New York led Chancellor Adenauer to call a conference of German military experts to meet from 6–9 October 1950 at Cloister Himmerod, near Wittlich, in the Eiffel Mountains to discuss and lay out the form a German contribution to the defense of Western Europe should take. Fifteen former Wehrmacht officers took part: nine from the army (Heer) and three each from the air force (Luftwaffe) and navy (Kreigsmarine). Despite some significant differences, it is interesting that this conference, which dealt with a wide range of military issues (including recruitment, education and training, strategy, and most important, the nature of the military tradition that could be imparted to soldiers serving in a democratic society), arrived independently at a German contribution that roughly paralleled that discussed by the JCS.[1]

The conference concluded that the Federal Republic's contribution by the end of 1952 should consist of an army of 12 armored divisions, to include tanks, artillery and antiaircraft artillery, in 6 corps, for a total of 250,000 men.[2] While manpower numbers were not given, the conference saw a minimum need for a Luftwaffe of six tactical air wings totaling 831 aircraft: 180 reconnaissance planes, 279 fighter-bombers and 372 fighters.[3] Similarly, no manpower figures were given for the naval contingent but the conference underscored the Soviet strength in the Baltic and thus the need for, and numbers of, landing craft, small submarines, torpedo boats and minelayers, naval aircraft (both reconnaissance and fighters), submarine hunters, and minesweepers.[4]

The Bonn Report

In June 1951, army G-3 circulated a paper containing a summary of the High Commissioners–FRG talks (the Bonn Report) that began in January.[5] The summary indicated that the FRG accepted a number of the safeguards proposed by NATO, among which were that its participation would be under NATO, that German air units would be under SACEUR (Himmerod recommendations were that they be under German Army command), that recruitment of Germans would initially be by volunteers followed by conscription, that a German arms industry would be established only as requested by France, that a German defense administration would be civilian and under the control of the Bundestag, and that the end strength of German land formations would not exceed 20 percent of the total available to SACEUR.

The Germans rejected the RCT size limit and insisted that the basic unit for German ground forces be a ten-thousand-man division, preferably armored. Accordingly, they also rejected the prohibition on heavy armored formations. They insisted that there should be a central German Defense Ministry. Consistent with Germany's demand for equality, they rejected Allied control of the future German defense administration as well as supervision of officer recruiting, and the restriction on not having intelligence, plans, or operations functions above the tactical level. Lastly, they rejected the limit on the division being the largest national ground force contribution.

Not too long afterward, General Handy (CINEUCOM) forwarded to the JCS comments of its European representative on the Bonn Report, in which he praised the German approach as realistic and sound. He opined that more desirable results would be obtained if each nation, including Germany, were allowed to contribute forces at corps or even army level. The message approved the establishment of a single German defense ministry and cautioned that the "progressive creation of German military forces must be keyed to the ability of the Allies and the Germans to provide the requisite amounts of arms and equipment."[6]

On 6 August, the JCS submitted its assessment of the Bonn Report. With few exceptions, the JCS considered the German proposals acceptable. The JCS agreed that German ground formations should be of at least division size but disagreed with the German desire to have all divisions armored, as this did not coincide with NATO requirements and was logistically difficult. Regarding the German desire to have corps commands, the JCS waffled somewhat and addressed the possibility of an "international" corps as meeting Germany's requirements. In the end, the JCS indicated that any corps organization should be flexible and allow the SACEUR to deploy all NATO forces as he deemed necessary.[7]

Regarding the Luftwaffe, the JCS accepted the view that matériel procurement provided the greatest obstacle to its organization. They recommended that for planning purposes, the Luftwaffe seek to contribute a total of only 750 aircraft, organized into 10 fighter wings of 3 squadrons each, by the end of 1954. JCS estimated that an eventual minimum Luftwaffe contribution would be in the neighborhood of 1,600–1,800 aircraft. Lastly, JCS concurred with the army staff and CINCUSAREUR that the primary mission should be tactical air support for the German ground forces, a position that was anathema to the US air staff and would be later changed.[8]

On 1 September, G-3 recommended adopting the Bonn Report but did not agree with US Air Force and Navy recommendations to create a deputy inspector general for each of the three German services. G-3's rationale was that "present planning [was] largely for the establishment of Army forces."[9]

On 10 September, the JCS drafted a memo to the Secretary of Defense stating that they had reviewed the Bonn Report and the interim report of the Conference for the Organization of a European Defence Community and noted that while the concept of a European defense force had been accepted by NSC 115, the interim report did not provide for the raising of German forces at the earliest possible date, as required by NSC 115. The JCS then stated that a specific plan to ensure an immediate German contribution was essential and that such a plan should be developed under SACEUR's direction.[10]

Along with those thoughts, the JCS submitted an updated "Force Basis" to be used for planning purposes for the German contribution. This basis specified 10 army divisions, of which 4 would be armored and 6 would be infantry, along with corps and army-type service support units. It allocated 10 fighter-bomber wings (to include tactical reconnaissance aircraft) to the Luftwaffe, and 11,500 personnel and 183 vessels of various types, including minelayers, submarine hunters, torpedo boats, and E-boats, to the navy.[11]

Appendix F

Acheson's "Single Package"

How Acheson's "Single Package" came to be is still a matter of debate. Most scholars take their cue from Acheson's *Present at the Creation*, in which he relates that the State Department and the Defense Department debated the issue for two weeks before a compromise was reached, which he then brought to the tripartite meeting in New York on 12 September. The "package," which had been approved by President Truman just a few days earlier and which the French labeled the "Bombshell at the Waldorf," was intended to be offered to the Allies on a take-it-or-leave-it basis. It contained several key elements: an offer to increase US forces in Europe by approximately 6 divisions, 8 tactical air groups, and appropriate naval forces, and an offer of US participation, along with the United Kingdom and all the other NATO armies, in a combined European defense force, with an international staff and a supreme commander. This offer, however, was dependent upon the Allies boosting the capabilities (and size) of their forces and accepting the inclusion of German contingents that would be added at the division level but without a German General Staff Corps.[1]

Acheson later called the single package a mistake and claimed that he was forced into accepting it by the military, a claim that is supported by many. However, all the available evidence and documentation indicates that by the time the so-called compromise with the military was reached, Acheson had already decided that Germany needed to be armed.[2] "If there was to be any defense at all," he said, "it had to be based on a forward strategy" and Germany's role had to be primary.[3]

Acheson also stated that "the Pentagon needed no persuasion," a fact addressed in chapter 3 of this book.[4] Of particular interest in this respect, however, are David S. McClellan's comments that Acheson may have wanted to avoid a conflict with Bradley, and that the JCS had insisted that the "recommendations must be submitted and accepted as a whole."[5] This claim and other similar statements by McClellan are not supported by the available documentation. On 30 August 1950, Acheson, Byroade, Nitze, and Perkins met with General Bradley to discuss the JCS's response to Truman's eight questions. According to the only memorandum of that meeting, prepared by Byroade, Acheson and Bradley agreed on the army's answers to the president's questions. The memorandum contains no mention of any major disagreement.[6] Furthermore, Trachtenberg and Gehrz and McMahon agree that Acheson was neither a person to be easily cowed nor one who would subscribe to a position he did not approve of.[7] As chapter 3 of this book underscores, had Acheson been forced to accept the JCS position, he would have presented an offer of a German national army in NATO rather than contingents in an integrated European defense force. Beisner writes that Acheson was "fully supportive of the individual contents of the single package."[8] Additionally, he would not have written Ambassador Bruce in Paris that it should be possible to integrate German units without creating a German national army or that he was willing to discuss this at the September meetings.[9]

According to a memorandum of a conversation regarding German rearmament in which Bevin, Acheson, Roddy Barclay, and Lucius Battle took part, Acheson said that if he had to present the matter at the forthcoming meeting of the Defense Ministers, he would "do so as one complete conception pointing out the importance of all parts."[10] Thus, I am convinced, as are Trachtenberg and Gehrz (and I believe the evidence supports this conclusion), that if the package as presented to Bevin and Schuman was a mistake, it was not because it mandated the arming of the Federal Republic but because it was presented as an all-or-nothing demand.[11] It is also possible that the mistake was in not presenting the integrated European army plan worked out by McCoy and Byroade, mentioned in chapter 2 of this book.

Lastly, the alleged "bombshell" was, in fact, no bombshell at all. Recall from chapter 4 the 2 September cable Acheson sent Ambassador Bruce in Paris and Ambassador Douglas in London instructing them to "urgently call" on the French and British foreign ministers, Schuman and Bevin respectively, to inform them of US thinking regarding the creation of a unified defense force in Europe, the appointment of a supreme commander, and the integration of German units in such a force without creating a German national army. Acheson specifically asked that Schuman and Bevin be told the following: "US participation in the defense of Eur and in the direction of such a unified Force would involve greater commitments than we have heretofore been willing to consider. Whether or not we actually make such commitments will depend on whether or not the Europeans are themselves willing to make greater efforts resulting in adequate steps to increase their forces in being."[12] Thus the stage was set for a significant unintentional consequence of the US's German policy— the refusal of France to accept the "arm Germany" portion of the United States' offer and the five-year battle to put Germans back in uniform.

Appendix G
The Great Debate

The single package and the decision to send additional troops to Europe to support the request that the FRG be armed created another unanticipated consequence. This challenge was to the president's power and authority as commander in chief and it came primarily from the Senate. While there was unanimity within the Senate on the need for the United States to check Soviet expansion in Europe, this unanimity did not extend to how that was to be accomplished.[1]

Already incensed over the 'loss' of China to the Communists, the setback in Korea resulting from Chinese entry into the war in November 1950, and the administration's push for a European strategy that included sending additional US troops to mainland Europe, the Senate turned even more against the president and his secretary of state at the introduction of the single package. What became known as "the Great Debate of 1951" actually began in late 1950, but took shape when the 82nd Congress convened in January 1951.[2]

In November 1950, Senator Robert Taft (R-OH) launched an attack on the Truman administration's European policy, calling for a fundamental reexamination of the need to give military and economic aid to Western Europe.[3] Another assault followed in December when former US ambassador Joseph P. Kennedy described Truman's policy as "suicidal" and "politically and morally bankrupt," and called for the withdrawal of US forces from Korea and Berlin. Then, in December, former president Herbert Hoover initiated the main offensive, demanding that the United States send no more men or matériel to Europe until the Europeans turned their territories into an "impregnable fortress."[4]

Hardly had 1951 begun when senators Taft (following a great reelection victory) and Kenneth S. Wherry (R–NE), focused the key argument around the president's authority to send troops to Europe without Congressional approval. To this end, and bolstered by earlier statements by Acheson that neither the NATO Treaty nor the Military Assistance Program (MAP) would commit troops to Europe, Senate Resolution 8, introduced on 16 January, gave the sense of the Senate that no ground troops would be sent to Europe, pending formulation of a congressional policy. President Truman's response was that as commander in chief, he had the authority to send troops anywhere, and that while he was not required to consult with Congress, he was polite and usually always consulted with them.[5]

The debate escalated following the loss of Seoul, the 8th Army's retreat to the Han River in Korea, and a 'Declaration of Policy' signed by 118 House Republicans, which sought a revision of the administration's "tragic" and costly foreign policy. Two Democrat senators, Walter Franklin George (D-GA) and Paul Douglas (D-IL), also joined the chorus calling upon President Truman to obtain congressional approval.[6]

On 1 February, Eisenhower, by then confirmed as Supreme Allied Commander, Europe (SACEUR), spoke to a joint session of Congress of the need for unity regarding the United States and Europe and stated that "someone in achieving that unity [had] to take the leadership," meaning "one nation, not some one individual." He continued that this was the role of the United States and that he believed that "the transfer of certain [American] units should be in direct ratio to what Europe [was] doing."[7] On 22 January, despite Eisenhower's upbeat testimony, Senator Wherry delivered to the Senate Armed Services and the Foreign Relations committees a resolution (S.R. 8) stating that "no ground forces of the United States should be assigned to duty in the European area for the purposes of the North Atlantic Treaty pending the formation of a policy with respect thereto by the Congress."[8]

Two weeks later, on 15 February, Marshall addressed a joint session of the Senate Armed Forces and Foreign Affairs committees and, referring to Eisenhower's earlier testimony, stated that after obtaining express permission from the president, he could inform them that the JCS had recommended to him (and he had recommended to the president, who had approved) that the United States maintain in Europe approximately six divisions of ground forces. As there already were in Europe approximately two divisions on occupation duty, only four more divisions would be sent.[9]

Marshall reminded the committees that what was being done was, in fact, carrying out Congress's earlier instructions regarding the preparation of integrated plans for the defense of the North Atlantic area. Those plans were well advanced, he said, and for General Eisenhower to accomplish his mission it was imperative that he not be denied the freedom of action required by a military commander.[10] Marshall's testimony caused Taft to rethink his position and he agreed to the extent that US troops should not be committed to an international army, that an agreement should first be reached with other NATO countries, and that Congress should approve. Acheson, Marshall, and General Bradley joined forces to oppose this position in a number of hearings that lasted into April.[11]

The debate, however, continued on into April with amendments to S.R. 8 offered, new proposals made, and even a proposal submitted by the administration through senators Tom Connally (D-TX) and Richard Russell (D-GA). In the end, not wanting to force a constitutional showdown, the Senate passed a simpler concurrent resolution, S.R. 99, on 4 April, which approved the designation of Eisenhower as SACEUR as well as the president's actions and the dispatch of four divisions, but qualified it all with a sense of the Senate that the president should consult with Congress and submit semi-annual reports on the implementation of the North Atlantic Treaty.[12]

Notes

Introduction

1. Walter Henry Nelson, *Germany Rearmed* (New York: Simon and Schuster, 1972), 15–16.

2. Heinz Schultz, "The Dilemma of German Rearmament After the Second World War," *Army and Defence Journal* 110, no. 2 (1980): 189. See also the Potsdam Agreement, 1 August 1945, Article II.A.3.(i)(a) through 3.(i)(b)(iii) in *Documents on Germany 1944–1959 and a Chronology of Political Developments Affecting Berlin, 1945–1956* (Washington, DC: Government Printing Office, 1959), http://digicoll.library.wisc.edu/cgi-bin/History/History-idx?id=History.BackgrndDocs.

3. Georg Meyer, "Die Entmilitarisierung in der amerikanischen, britischen und französischen Besatzungszone sowie in der Bundesreublik Deutschland von 1945 bis 1950," in *Entmilitarisierung und Aufrüstung in Mitteleuropa 1945–1956* (Herford, Deu.: E. S. Mittler & Sohn, 1983), 11–14. There is also a large section devoted to taking lessons from history in Richard M. Wellig, "Surrender," in *Germany*, book 4 of *History of the Civil Affairs Division, War Department Special Staff, World War II to March 1946* (unpublished manuscript, Box 2-3.7 AA.Q, Center for Military History Library, Ft. McNair, Washington, DC).

4. Marc Trachtenberg, *History and Strategy* (Princeton: Princeton University Press, 1991), viii. See also: John Lewis Gaddis, *We Now Know: Rethinking Cold War History* (Oxford: Oxford University Press, 1997; Marc Trachtenberg, *A Constructed Peace: The Making of the European Settlement, 1945–1963* (Princeton: Princeton University Press, 1999; Thomas Allan Schwartz, *America's Germany: John J. McCloy and the Federal Republic of Germany* (Cambridge, MA: Harvard University Press, 1991; Melvyn , *A Preponderance of Power: National Security, the Truman Administration, and the Cold War* (Stanford: Stanford University Press, 1992; James McAllister, *No Exit: America and the German Problem, 1943–1954* (Ithaca: Cornell University Press, 2002); Robert Mc-Geehan, *The German Rearmament Question: American Diplomacy and European Defense after World War II* (Urbana: University of Illinois Press, 1971); and David Clay Large, *Germans to the Front: West German Rearmament in the Adenauer Era* (Chapel Hill: University of North Carolina Press, 1996).

5. With the exception of Birtle's *Rearming the Phoenix*, the gap in information about planning by the individual military services has only recently been partially filled by the following: James S. Corum, "American Assistance to the New German Army and Luftwaffe," in *Rearming Germany*, ed. James S. Corum (Leiden, Nld.: Brill, 2011), 93–116; Corum, "Adenauer, Amt Blank, and the Founding of the Bundeswehr, 1950–1956," in Corum, *Rearming Germany*, 29–53; Douglas H. Peifer, "Establishing the Bundesmarine: The Convergence of Central Planning and Pre-existing Maritime Organizations, 1950–1956," in Corum, *Rearming Germany*, 117–41; and Donald A. Carter, *Forging the Shield: The U.S. Army in Europe, 1951–1962* (Washington, DC: Center of Military History, 2015).

6. See, for example, Laurence W. Martin, "The American Decision to Rearm Germany," in *American Civil-Military Decisions: A Book of Case Studies*, ed. Harold Stein (Tuscaloosa: University of Alabama Press, 1963), 646–47. Throughout 1948 and into 1949, rumors concerning German rearmament were rife in Germany, France, and the United States. See Eric Willenz, "Early Discussions Regarding a Defense Contribution in Germany (1948–1950)," RAND Research Memorandum, RM-968, 15 October 1958; Norbert Tönnies, *Der Weg zu den Waffen* (Cologne: Erich Pabel Verlag, 1961), 28–31, 34–46; Drew Middleton, "Europeans Ponder Army for Germany," *New York Times*, 16 November 1949, 1–2; C. G. D. Onslow, "West German Rearmament," *World Politics* 3, no. 4 (July 1951): 451; "Armed Germans," *Washington Post*, 29 November 1949, 12; Joseph Alsop and Stewart Alsop, "Matter of Fact," *Washington Post*, 30 November 1949, 13; "Bradley Expresses Confidence," *New York Times*, 28 November 1949, 7; Drew Middleton, "Berlin Held Part of West's Defense," *New York Times*, 29 November 1949, 7; and Konrad Adenauer, *Memoirs, 1945–53*, trans. Beate Ruhm von Oppen (Chicago: Henry Regnery Company, 1966), 267.

7. Ingo Trauschweizer, *The Cold War U.S. Army: Building Deterrence for Limited War* (Lawrence: University of Kansas Press, 2008), 18 ff; Russell F. Weigley, *History of the United States Army* (New York: Macmillan Publishing Co., Inc., 1967), 501–2; and S. Nelson Drew, ed., *NSC-68: Forging the Strategy of Containment* (Washington, DC: National Defense University, 1994).

8. See, for example, Trachtenberg, *Constructed Peace*, 95.

9. Lawrence Freedman, *The Evolution of Nuclear Strategy*, 3rd ed. (Basingstoke, Eng.: Palgrave Macmillan, 2003), 4.

10. Trachtenberg, *Constructed Peace*, 95–96; and Michael Creswell and Marc Trachtenberg, "France and the German Question, 1945–1955," *Journal of Cold War Studies* 5, no. 3 (Summer 2003): 5–28, especially 19.

11. The one exception is Kenneth O. McCreedy, "Planning the Peace: Operation Eclipse and the Occupation of Germany," *Journal of Military History* 65,

no. 3 (July 2001): 713–39. See for example: Paul Y. Hammond, "Directives for the Occupation of Germany: The Washington Controversy," in Stein, *American Civil-Military Decisions*, 311–464; Martin, "American Decision to Rearm" in Stein, *American Civil-Military Decisions*, 645–65; *The First Year of the Occupation*, 3 vols., Occupation Forces in Europe Series, 1945–46 (Frankfurt-am-Main, Deu.: Germany, Office of the Chief Historian, European Command, 1947); and Earl F. Ziemke, *The U.S. Army in the Occupation of Germany, 1944–1946* (Washington, DC: Center of Military History, 1975).

12. "Statement by the Secretary of State to the North Atlantic Council," *Foreign Relations of the United States, 1952–1954*, vol. 5, *Western European Security*, part 1, ed. William Z. Slany (Washington, DC: Government Printing Office 1952–1954), 463 and editorial note, 468.

13. Wiggershaus, "Western German Military Integration," 376.

14. Mark A. Stoler, "National versus International Security and Civil-Military Relations, January 1944–January 1945," and "Aftermath and Conclusion" in *Allies and Adversaries: The Joint Chiefs of Staff, the Grand Alliance, and the U.S. Strategy in World War II* (Chapel Hill: University of North Carolina Press, 2000). Stoler gives an explanation of the lack of coordination between the State Department and the War Department and the reasons for a lack of postwar planning that resulted. He also describes the change in US views of the Soviet Union from ally to enemy. George F. Kennan describes President Roosevelt's adversity to discussing postwar problems while the war was still ongoing. Kennan, *Memoirs*, vol. 2, *1950–1963* (Boston: Little, Brown and Company, 1972), 417–18. See also McCreedy, "Planning the Peace," 719.

15. Meyer, "Die Entmilitarisierung," 16–17. The board existed until the FRG was admitted to NATO in 1955 and never, during its existence, did the German government speak out against the disarmament regime the board was tasked to enforce.

16. Meyer, "Die Entmilitarisierung," 18–19.

17. Adenauer, *Memoirs, 1945–1953*, 292.

18. John Lewis Gaddis, *Strategies of Containment: A Critical Appraisal of American National Security Policy during the Cold War* (New York: Oxford University Press, 1982); and Leffler, *Preponderance of Power*.

19. In discussions regarding what became the Brussels Treaty Organization and its relation to Germany, John D. Hickerson, director of the Office of European Affairs, told Lord Inverchapel that the United States envisaged the creation of a "third force"—a real European organization capable of saying no to both the United States and the USSR. It was believed that if it was integrated in this way, West Germany's freedom of action would be sufficiently constrained and thus it would

no longer pose a threat. Memorandum of Conversation, Hickerson–Lord Inverchapel, 21 January 1948, RG 59, Central Decimal Files, File 840.00 1945–1949, Box 5643, National Archives and Records Administration (hereafter NARA). See also Thomas Allan Schwartz, "The Case for German Rearmament: Alliance Crisis in the 'Golden Age,'" *Fletcher Forum* 8 (Summer 1984): 297; Trachtenberg, *Constructed Peace*, 62–63; and US Department of State, "PPS/13: Résume of World Situation," in *Foreign Relations of the United States, 1947*, vol. 1, *General: The United Nations* (Washington, DC: Government Printing Office, 1947), 770–77.

20. See, for example: Kevin Ruane, *The Rise and Fall of the European Defense Community: Anglo-American Relations and the Crisis of European Defence, 1950–55* (New York: St. Martin's Press, 2000); Michael Dockrill and John W. Young, *British Foreign Policy, 1945–1956* (New York: St. Martin's Press, 1989); and Saki Dockrill, *Britain's Policy for West German Rearmament 1950–1955* (Cambridge: Cambridge University Press, 1991).

21. The plan to rearm West Germany also contained a promise to send more troops to Europe. This incensed Congress highly because of the lack of consultation so soon after the outbreak of the Korean War and the need to send more troops there. This, and the drafting of NSC-68 led to a three-month debate in early 1951 that led to a bill one could easily call the forerunner to the War Powers Act of 1973. See Birtle, *Rearming the Phoenix*; Norbert Wiggershaus, "The Problem of Western German Military Integration," in Norbert Wiggershaus and Roland Foerster, eds., *The Western Security Community 1948–1950: Common Problems and Conflicting National Interests during the Foundation Phase of the North Atlantic Alliance* (Oxford: Berg Publishers, 1993), 378; and S. Nelson Drew, ed., *NSC-68: Forging the Strategy of Containment* (Washington, DC: National Defense University, 1994), 3. See also appendix G, this book.

22. McGeehan, *German Rearmament Question*, xi.

23. Large, *Germans to the Front*, 31.

24. Vladislav Zubok and Constantin Pleshakov, *Inside the Kremlin's Cold War: From Stalin to Kruschev* (Cambridge, MA: Harvard University Press, 1996), 54, 70; Jen Hoffenaar, Dieter Krüger, and David T. Yabecki, eds., *Blueprints for Battle: Planning for War in Central Europe, 1948–1968* (Lexington: University of Kentucky Press, 2012), 8; and Wiggershaus, "Western German Military Integration," 385–86.

25. Stoler, *Allies and Adversaries*, 211–15; and JSPC 876, 21 April 1948, Report to the Joint Chiefs of Staff on the United States Military Alliance with Nations of Western Europe, RG 218, Geographic Files, 092 Western Europe, Sect. 2. While the documents I reviewed say nothing about the impact of the Soviet nuclear explosion on the rearming of Germany, it represented the loss of the US nuclear monopoly, which would have triggered a major reappraisal of Western

defense strategy. Also, these weapons were not seen as a "pivotal weapon of war" and the city-busting nature of the nuclear weapons of the period made a strong ground-based defense imperative. See, for example: Trachtenberg, *A Constructed Peace,* 96 ff; David A. Rosenberg, "The Origins of Overkill," *International Security* 7, no. 4 (1983): 3–71; Ernest R. May, "The Impact of Nuclear Weapons on European Security 1945–1957," in *The Quest for Stability: Problems of West European Security, 1918–1957,* ed. R. Ahmann, Adolf M. Birke, and Michael Howard (London: Oxford University Press, 1993), 513–32; and Drew, *Strategy of Containment.*

26. It took eight months of tweaking and refining for NSC-68 to win the president's acceptance and endorsement of its 48.2 billion defense budget for fiscal year 1951. Drew, *Strategy of Containment,* 4–5.

27. Leffler, *Preponderance of Power,* 386. Although Leffler's rationale pertains to the arguments made just prior to the September 1950 New York Tripartite Conference, his definition of the differences is just as applicable to this time frame.

28. Some officials in the State Department were against German rearmament. George Kennan, for one, was against rearming Germany as was John J. McCloy who, while accepting the need, thought it was premature. Averell Harriman and Paul Nitze were also against it until the attack in Korea. Kennan, *Memoirs, 1950–1963,* 108, 243; Robert L. Beisner, *Dean Acheson: A Life in the Cold War* (Oxford: Oxford University Press, 2006), 357, 360; Marc Trachtenberg and Christopher Gehrtz, "America, Europe, and German Rearmament, August–September 1950: A Critique of a Myth," in *Between Empire and Alliance: America and Europe during the Cold War,* ed. Marc Trachtenberg (Lanham, MD: Rowman and Littlefield, 2003), 8; Walter Issacson and Evan Thomas, *The Wise Men: Six Friends and the World They Made* (New York: Simon and Schuster, 1986), 517; and Schwartz, *America's Germany,* 129.

29. Army intelligence, however, was of the opinion that the Soviet Union would have no difficulty overrunning Western Europe. Leffler, *Preponderance of Power,* 149.

30. Drew, *Strategy of Containment,* 1–2; and Weigley, *History of the United States Army,* 502. President Truman was committed to a budget ceiling of $15 billion. He had brought Louis Johnson in as secretary of defense to enforce this limit on the services and Johnson cut expenditures below that limit. See also Samuel F. Wells Jr., "Sounding the Tocsin: NSC-68 and the Soviet Threat," *International Security* 4, no. 2 (Autumn 1979): 123–24.

31. Large, *Germans to the Front,* 86.

32. Trachtenberg and Gehrz, "America, Europe, and German Rearmament," 1.

33. For an excellent review of the political aspects of the Pleven Plan, named after French premier René Pleven, and its effects on both France and Germany,

see F. Roy Willis, *France, Germany and the New Europe, 1945–1967*, rev. ed. (Oxford: Oxford University Press, 1968), especially chapters 6–8; and Edward Fursdon, *The European Defence Community, a History* (New York: St. Martin's Press, 1980).

34. Andrew J. Birtle, *Rearming the Phoenix: U.S. Military Assistance to the Federal Republic of Germany* (New York: Garland Publishing Inc., 1991), 201. Throughout this narrative the terms 'Germany,' 'West Germany,' and 'the Federal Republic of Germany' will be used interchangeably.

35. Nelson, *Germany Rearmed*, 21–22; and Donald Abenheim, *Reforging the Iron Cross: The Search for Tradition in the West German Armed Forces* (Princeton: Princeton University Press, 1988), 3. The Ermekeilkaserne was built as an infantry barracks in Bonn in 1883. Following WWII, it became first the German government's Press and Information Office and in 1951, the office of Theodor Blank, West Germany's first minister of defense and thus the first Defense Ministry. As such, it is the birthplace of the Bundeswehr.

Chapter 1: Operation Eclipse

1. McCreedy, "Planning the Peace," 716. The text of the Atlantic charter can be found at http://avalon.law.yale.edu/wwii/atlantic.asp.

2. The preferred British term, "posthostilities period," and the American term "postwar period" are used interchangeably throughout this book. For examples of the interdepartmental rivalries and tensions that existed in Washington, see Philip E. Mosely, "The Occupation of Germany," *Foreign Affairs* 28, no. 4 (July 1950): 584–86; Mosely, "The Dismemberment of Germany," *Foreign Affairs* 28, no. 3 (April 1950): 487–98; Hammond, "Washington Controversy," 311–464; and Leffler, *Preponderance of Power*, 27–28.

3. US Army, European Command, Historical Division, *Planning for the Occupation of Germany*, Occupation Forces in Germany Series, 1945–46 (Frankfurt-am-Main, Deu.: Office of the Chief Historian, European Command, 1947), 29. While COSSAC spoke in terms of "armistice," the American Advisory Committee on Post-War Foreign Policy had been considering the concept of "unconditional surrender" as early as May 1942 and had made this recommendation to President Roosevelt as it pertained to Germany and Japan. In January 1943, at a meeting in the White House, Roosevelt told the Joint Chiefs of Staff (JCS) that the United Nations (UN) were going "to continue until they [reached] Berlin and that their terms would be unconditional surrender." Additionally, while the final communiqué of the Casablanca Conference (14–24 January 1943) did not contain those words, Roosevelt's press conference notes include the following sentence: "The President and the Prime Minister, after a complete survey of the world

war situation, are more than ever determined that peace can come to the world only by a total elimination of German and Japanese war power. This involves the simple formula of placing the objective of this war in terms of an unconditional surrender by Germany, Italy and Japan." US Department of State, *Foreign Relations of the United States: The Conferences at Washington, 1941–1942, and Casablanca, 1943* (Washington, DC: Government Printing Office, 1943), 505–6, 635, 837; Maurice Matloff, *Strategic Planning for Coalition Warfare, 1943–1944* (Washington, DC: Office of the Chief of Military History, 1959), 18, 37–40; and Charles Bohlen, *Witness to History, 1929–1969* (New York: W.W. Norton & Company, 1973), 156–57.

4. C.O.S. (43) 199 (Final), 25 July 1943, RG 331, Records of Allied Operational and Occupation Headquarters, World War II, Entry NM8/2, Box 115, Folder 388 Germany, Early Post Hostility Planning, Vol. 1, National Archives and Records Administration (hereafter NARA), College Park, MD. Colonel Tom Neville Grazebrook, DSO, CBE, instrumental in the development of the Eclipse memoranda, was an officer of the Gloucester Regiment who had seen action as commander of the 6th Inniskilling Fusilliers in North Africa, Sicily, and Italy. He was subsequently promoted to brigadier and served on the secretariat of the Allied Control Commission (ACC). Grazebrook was awarded the US Legion of Merit in November 1945.

5. C.O.S. (43) 311, 12 December 1943, Annex to Report: *Military Occupation of Germany*, 4, 14, Folder COS (43) Papers, Non (O) papers, RG 331, Records of Allied Operational and Occupation Headquarters, World War II, Entry 3, Box 131, NARA. Responsibility for providing occupation forces was assumed to be divided equally among the Allies, the USSR included.

6. Ibid., para. 12.

7. US Army, *Planning for the Occupation*, 30–31. General Eisenhower's position as supreme commander was often indicated in official correspondence by the acronyms SCAF (Supreme Commander, Allied Forces), SCAEF (Supreme Commander, Allied Expeditionary Forces), and SCAP (Supreme Commander, Allied Powers).

8. For a brief overview of the EAC, see appendix A, this book.

9. Stoler, *Allies and Adversaries*, 191, 196. See also Kennan, *1950–1963*, 417–18.

10. It should be emphasized at the outset that despite the delays and difficulties in Washington, its role, as well as that of the EAC, was one of providing broad guidelines for the occupation and subsequent military government of Germany and not specific details regarding disarming the German armed forces. Nonetheless, much of the delay in providing guidance was due to the lack of cooperation between the war and state departments and also between the US and British governments over the role of the Combined Civil Affairs Committee in Washington.

Forrest C. Pogue, *The Supreme Command*, United States Army in World War II, European Theater of Operations Series (Washington, DC: Center of Military History, 1996), 77–78, 339–48.

11. Mosely, "Occupation of Germany," 583–85. See also Bernard Bellush, *He Walked Alone: A Biography of John Gilbert Winant* (The Hague: Mouton, 1968), 197.

12. See the section on Operation Rankin/Talisman /Eclipse later in this chapter.

13. COSSAC/2323/Ops, Subject: 'Rankin' Case C – Disarmament, 26 November 1943, RG 331, Records of Allied Operational and Occupation Headquarters, World War II, Entry NM8/27, Box 92, Folder 388.3-2 GPS Method of Disarmament, NARA.

14. Ibid.

15. Ibid.

16. C.A. 7/BM/30/1 – Disarmament of Germany, undated [but based on the date of the cover letter, this estimate was written on or before 8 January 1944], RG 331, Records of Allied Operational and Occupation Headquarters, World War II, Entry NM8/27, Box 92, COSSAC Disarmament Study, NARA.

17. COSSAC/17235/Ops, Subject: Operation 'Rankin' C, 10 January 1944, RG 331, Records of Allied Operational and Occupation Headquarters, World War II, Entry 27, Box 92, NARA.

18. "The Allies' Armistice Demands," official release by the German government published in the *Kreuz-Zeitung*, 11 November 1918 (World War I Document Archive, Brigham Young University Library). http://wwi.lib.byu.edu/index.php/The_Allies%27_Armistice_Demands.

19. Memo of Capt Oppenheimer for Gen Hilldring, 23 March 1944, Subject: Comments on Mr. Warburg's Proposal re Surrender and Post-Surrender Policy toward Germany, in Wellig, "Surrender," 4.

20. COSSAC/17235/Ops, Subject: Operation 'Rankin' C, 14 January 1944, RG 331, Records of Allied Operational and Occupation Headquarters, World War II, Entry 27, Box 92, NARA.

21. SHAEF/21540/SD, Subject: Disarmament, 25 January 1944, RG 331, Records of Allied Operational and Occupation Headquarters, World War II, Entry NM8/2, Box 115, Folder 388.3, Germany: *Disarmament of German Armed Forces and Disposal of Enemy Equipment (Post Hostilities)*, Vol. 1, NARA. SHAEF was established in mid-January 1944. Manning was as follows: Basic control team would comprise five officers, eighteen other ranks, including signal personnel, a rifle platoon (for security), one 2½-ton truck, six ¼-ton trucks with trailers, and two motorcycles. Control teams at higher headquarters would consist of eight officers, two of whom were to be German speakers, a liaison officer from the other nation, twenty-one other ranks, a rifle platoon, three cooks, a motor pool

noncommissioned officer (NCO), seven jeeps, seven ¼-ton trucks, and two motorcycles. Air component control teams were even larger with twelve officers, twenty-seven other ranks, a Royal Air Force (RAF) regiment or headquarters platoon, six jeeps with trailers, and two motorcycles. Mission control teams had ten officers, twenty-six other ranks, an RAF regiment or headquarters platoon or security detachment, three jeeps with trailers, and two motorcycles, while an air component detachment control team consisted of eight officers, thirty-five other ranks, an RAF regiment or headquarters platoon or security detachment, eight jeeps with trailers, and three motorcycles. All air force intelligence personnel were required to be fluent in German.

22. Ibid.

23. Letter, SA/672/PO2, Subject: Primary Disarmament of German Forces, 3 July 1944, RG 331, Records of Allied Operational and Occupation Headquarters, World War II, Entry NM8/27, Box 92, Folder 388.3-3, Primary Disarmament of German Forces; Training of Disarmament Cadres, NARA.

24. 330/X/09240/1/10, 28 January 1944, RG 331, Records of Allied Operational and Occupation Headquarters, World War II, Entry NM8/2, Box 115, Folder 388.3 Germany, Disarmament of German Armed Forces and Disposal of Enemy Equipment (Post Hostilities), Vol. 1, NARA.

25. SD4/BM/207, 7 February 1944, Subject: Manpower Requirements for Control/Disarmament Commission; and Appendix C, SHAEF/21540/1/SD, 16 February 1944, both in RG 331, Records of Allied Operational and Occupation Headquarters, World War II, Entry NM8/27, Box 92, Folder 388.3-3, Primary Disarmament of German Forces; Training of Disarmament Cadres, NARA. A summary of British Army personnel required lists a total of 383 officers and 2,586 other ranks for the disarmament process.

26. US Army, *Planning for the Occupation*, 47. CCS is the acronym for Combined Chiefs of Staff.

27. PS/SHAEF(44)9, Preparation for the Surrender and Post Hostilities Middle Period, 29 April 1944, RG 331, Records of Allied Operational and Occupation Headquarters, World War II, Entry 1, Box 72, NARA; SHAEF/21542/Plans, 29 April 1944, RG 331, Box 72, NARA; SHAEF/21542/Plans, Short Term Post-Hostilities Responsibilities and Planning, June 1944, RG 331, Box 72, NARA; and US Army, *Planning for the Occupation*, 37–42.

28. Many of these problems were subsequently addressed by papers and directives that eventually appeared as memoranda appended to the Operation Talisman successor, Operation Eclipse.

29. SHAEF/21542/Plans, Short Term Post-Hostilities Responsibilities, June 1944, NARA.

30. Tab A to SHAEF/21542/Plans, Short Term Post-Hostilities Responsibilities, June 1944, NARA. See also US Army, *Planning for the Occupation*, 50–52.

31. US Army, *Planning for the Occupation*, 52.

32. JCS 923, 26 June 1944, Post Hostilities Planning, RG 260, Entry A1/17, Box 38, NARA.

33. JCS 923/3, 4 August 1944, Post Hostilities Planning, RG 260, Entry A1/17, Box 38, NARA; and enclosure to JCS 923/4, 14 August 1944, RG 260, Box 38, NARA.

34. Letter, Barker-Hilldring, 18 December 1943, RG 260, Entry A1/12, Box 12, Folder 134.18, I Directive No. 16 Disarmament German Forces, NARA. The "similar group" mentioned was most likely the British CCMS.

35. Hilldring, *Planning for Disarmament, Demobilization, Demilitarization of Axis Countries upon Defeat*, 2 March 1944, RG 260, Entry A1/12, Box 12, Folder 134.18, I Directive No. 16 Disarmament German Forces, NARA.

36. Hilldring sent it to Wickersham on 2 March 1944. Wickersham was at the time the US military advisor to the US delegate to the EAC. He had been the first commandant of the School for Military Government at the University of Virginia, Charlottesville before becoming the military advisor. In August 1944, he was assigned as acting deputy to the chief, US Group Control Council (US Group CC) and placed in charge of organizing that group. He was replaced in London by Brigadier General Vincent Meyer. Harry L. Coles and Albert K. Weinberg, *Civil Affairs: Soldiers Become Governors*, United States Army in World War II Series (Washington, DC: Office of the Chief of Military History, 1964), 11, 16.

37. Stoler writes that Secretary of War James V. Forrestal was deeply concerned about creating appropriate political military coordination in postwar planning and achieving coordination at the highest policy levels. His attempts, however, and those to reinsert the service secretaries into key roles in political-military affairs, were rebuffed by President Roosevelt. Stoler, *Allies and Adversaries*, 191–96.

38. SHAEF/21540/5/PHP, Subject: Memo on Planning for the Occupation of Germany, 15 October 1944, RG 331, Entry 40, Box 273, Folder 388.3-7 G.S., Planning for Occupation and Control of Germany, NARA; and GCT/388.3-7/ PHP, Subject: Coordination of Planning for the Occupation of Germany, 21 October 1944, RG 331, Box 273, NARA.

39. Appendix 1 and B to SHAEF/21540/5/PHP, Subject: Memo on Planning, 15 October 1944, RG 331, NARA; and GCT-388.3-7, Subject: Coordination of Planning, 21 October 1944, RG 331, NARA.

40. AG 387-1 COS-AGM, 27 October 1944, RG 331, Entry 40, Box 273, Folder 388.3-7 G.S., Planning for Occupation and Control of Germany, NARA;

SHAEF/21540/5/PHP, Subject: Memo on Planning, 15 October 1944, NARA; and GCT 388.3-7 PHP, Subject: Coordination of Planning, 6 November 1944, RG 331, Box 273, NARA.

41. SHAEF 21540/5/PHP, Subject: Memo on Planning, NARA; and GCT/388.3-7/PHP, Subject: Progress Report on Matters Considered at the Deputy Chief of Staff Conference Held on 8 November 1944, 19 November 1944, RG 331, Entry 40, Box 273, NARA.

42. SHAEF/21542/Plans, 29 April 1944, NARA. The middle period is defined as the period between the cessation of hostilities and the assumption of control by the tripartite organization.

43. SHAEF/21542/Plans, Subject: Post-Hostility Planning, 9 July 1944, RG 331, Entry NM8/40, Box 262, File SHAEF/215/GDP-2, Operation 'Eclipse' Directives, NARA. The CCS message referred to was presumably CCS 551.

44. Ibid.

45. US Army, *Planning for the Occupation*, 32.

46. Ibid., 9.

47. McCreedy, "Planning the Peace," 714–16. Rankin was the first plan to deal with the occupation of Germany. US Army, *Planning for the Occupation*, 11.

48. US Army, *Planning for the Occupation*, 10.

49. Ibid., 2

50. Ibid., 3.

51. Ibid., 11. The first of the two Quebec conferences was held in August 1943 and was code-named Quadrant.

52. Ibid., 12

53. Ibid., 12, 15. See also McCreedy, "Planning the Peace," 720n24, 721.

54. US Army, *Planning for the Occupation*, 22, 24–25. See also Operation 'Rankin' – Case C, Joint Plan, 23 November 1943, RG 331, Entry 27, Box 93, NARA. The 1st Army Group was subsequently renamed the 12th Army Group.

55. McCreedy, "Planning the Peace," 720–21.

56. US Army, *Planning for the Occupation*, 36.

57. One of these studies was PS-SHAEF(44)10, Primary disarmament of German Forces, 29 April 1944, RG 331, Entry NM8/27, Folder 388.3-3, GPS, Primary Disarmament of German Forces; Training of Disarmament Mission Cadres, NARA. See also US Army, *Planning for the Occupation*, 36.

58. G-3 Ops Division, Supreme Allied Commander, Staff memo 3, RG 331, Entry NM8/26 Box 80 SHAEF, CoS, Future Plans, Decimal File 1943–45, Folder 18450/2 Planning Progress Report 381-9, NARA.

59. US Army, *Planning for the Occupation*, 58. For the initial directive to start Talisman planning, see SHAEF/21542/Plans, Directive for Post Hostilities Planning,

18 July 1944, File SHAEF/215/GDP-2, Operation ECLIPSE Directives, RG 331, Entry NM8/40, Box 262, NARA.

60. US Army, *Planning for the Occupation*, 60–61. This indicates that the recommendations of the April 1944 SHAEF staff study, *Preparation for the Surrender and Post Hostilities Middle Period*, were not accepted.

61. See the summary of the TALISMAN plan in US Army, *Planning for the Occupation*, 58–62.

62. Ibid., 63.

63. Ibid., 65

64. On 18 April 1945, a cable from General Eisenhower to all SHAEF commands stated that unless there was a formal German surrender, there would be no arbitrary date selected for A-Day to signify a changeover from Operation Overlord. The cable continued that it would be assumed that Operation Eclipse had "begun in those areas of Germany progressively overrun by Allied forces." FWD-19403, 18 April 1945, RG 331, Entry 1, Box 72, NARA.

65. SHAEF/17014/2/Plans, 16 August 1944; and SHAEF/G-5/Ops/604, 23 August 1944, both in RG 331, Entry NM 8/26, Box 75, NARA. The appendices with troop numbers, however, were not found in the file.

66. CGT 381-12/Plans, 5 September 1944, RG 331, Entry NM8/23, Box 80, Folder 18450/2 Planning Progress Report 381-9; SHCGT FWD-14351, 9 September 1944, RG 331, Box 80; and CGT 387.4-6/PHP, 25 January 1945, in RG 331, Box 80.

67. The second Quebec conference, code-named Octagon, was held in September 1944. McCreedy, "Planning the Peace," 722–23.

68. GCT 370-27/Plans, 24 November 1944, RG 331, Entry NM8/23, Box 21, NARA; and US Army, *Planning for the Occupation*, 63–70.

69. Operation Eclipse Appreciation and Outline Plan, Section I, Introduction and Objects, Introduction, para. 2. b., RG 331, Entry NM8/23, Box 22, NARA.

70. Ibid., Section III, para. 22.

71. Ibid., Section II, paras. 13–17.

72. US Army, *Planning for the Occupation*, 70–71; and S-72170, 23 December 1944, RG 331, Entry NM8/26 Box 80, Folder 381-2, SHAEF Weekly Planning Cables, NARA.

73. For a listing of the Eclipse memoranda, see appendix B, this book. Despite the last being number 19, there is no number 2 or 3.

74. Eclipse Memorandum No. 1, "Instrument of Surrender, Surrender Order and Sanctions," Appendix A, RG 331, Entry 2, Box 115, NARA. This appendix contained only general principles that had been agreed upon by the Allies. The actual instrument of surrender was not included for security reasons.

75. Eclipse Memorandum No. 1, Appendix B, Part II, paras. 11–16.

76. Enclosure 2, Ltr, Supreme Hq AEF, AG 381-7 GDS-AGM, 16 May 1945, 'Eclipse' Memorandum No. 9, RG 331, Entry 11, Box 6, NARA.

77. Ibid., para. 19.

78. Administrative Memorandum No. 5 was written originally in April 1944 but revised in January 1945. It governed the disposal of enemy war matériel in the liberated countries and Germany. Administrative Memorandum No. 5, Disposal of Enemy War Materiel and War Structures, RG 331, Entry 27, Box 93, NARA.

79. Eclipse Memorandum No. 11, RG 331, Entry 23, Box 21, NARA.

80. Eclipse Memorandum No. 17, RG 331, Entry 11, Box 6, NARA. See also Cable SHGAP S-87506, 9 May 1945, RG 331, Entry 6, Box 30, NARA, in CALA File Vol. 2 of 3, 387.4/1, Armistice, Control and Disposal of German Armed Forces.

81. Ibid., para. 3.

82. Memorandum to: General Morgan, Subject: Eclipse Memo No. 17 (Disbandment of German Forces), 11 March 1945, RG 331, Entry 2, Box 114, NARA.

83. According to McCreedy, there were sixty-one US divisions in Germany on VE Day. Kenneth McCreedy, *Waging Peace: Operation Eclipse I and II – Some Implications for Future Operations* (Carlisle Barracks, PA: US Army War College, 2004), 5. In early December 1944, an estimate of the forces needed to complete the occupation of Germany after the defeat concluded that there would be no problem. Operation Eclipse was a military operation, therefore all forces would be available as stated. The study, signed by Deputy Acting Chief of Staff (G-3) Major General J. F. M. Whiteley, stated further that it would take ten to eighteen months following Germany's defeat for US forces to be redeployed and by this time, all major tasks requiring a large occupation force would have been completed. Lastly, the study pointed out that the respective governments, not SHAEF, would determine the size of the "ultimate occupying force." CGT/387.4-6/ PHP, 9 December 1944, Staff Study, Subject: Estimate of Forces Required to Complete Occupation Immediately after German Defeat, in Folder File 370 Germany: Allied Force Required for Occupation of Germany, Vol. 1, RG 331, Entry NM8/2, Box 113.

84. SHAEF/17014/2/Plans, 16 August 1944; and SHAEF/G-5/Ops/604, 23 August 1944, both in RG 331, Entry NM 8/26, Box 75, NARA.

85. Memo CGT 381-12/Plans, Subject: 'Eclipse' Plans, 1 February 1945, RG 331, Entry 1, Box 72, Folder 381 Eclipse, Miscellaneous Correspondence, Vol. 1, NARA.

86. Memo, 370.2 (G-4), Subject: 'Eclipse' Policy, Hq. 12th Army Group, 10 March 1945, RG 331, Entry 1, Box 72, Folder 381 Eclipse, Miscellaneous

222

Correspondence, Vol. 1, NARA; and 12th AG 370.2 (G-4), 10 March 1945, Subject: Eclipse Policy, RG 331, Entry 11, Box 7, NARA.

87. CGT/400.93-1/PHP, RG 331, Entry NM8/23, Box 80, Folder 18450/2 Planning Progress Report 381-9, NARA; CGT/387.4-5/PHP, Treatment of Senior German Commanders and Staff Officers, 29 April 1945, Folder Arrest and Disposition of German Military Personalities, File 250.3 GE, Vol. 1, RG 331, Entry 27, Box 92, NARA; CGT/381-9/Plans, RG 331, Box 80, NARA; and the several progress reports in RG 331, Entry NM8/23, Box 80, Folder 18450/2 Planning Progress Report 381-9, NARA.

88. SHAEF 21544/Ops, 6 April 1944, RG 331, 290/7/5/3, Entry 6, Box 30, NARA, in CALA File vol. 1 of 3, 387.4/1 Armistice, Control and Disposal of German Armed Forces.

89. RG 260, Entry A1/12, Box 12, NARA; and RG 260, Entry A1/28-31, Box 643, NARA.

90. GAP 387.4, August 1944, First Draft, Disbandment of the German Armed Forces during the Middle Period, in CALA File Vol. 1 of 3, 387.4/1, Armistice, Control and Disposal of German Armed Forces, RG 331, 290/7/5/3, Entry 6, Box 30, NARA. This draft was sent forward for coordination as GAP 387.4/1 on 19 November 1944. GAP 387.4/1, 22 May 1945 amended the pay. In CALA File Vol. 2 of 3, 387.4/1, Armistice, Control and Disposal of German Armed Forces.

91. SHAEF/21544/PHP, GCT/387.4-5/PHP, 28 November 1944, RG 331, 290/7/5/3, Entry 6, Box 30, NARA; and CALA File Vol. 1 of 3, 387.4/1, Armistice, Control and Disposal of German Armed Forces.

92. SHAEF/21544/PHP, GCT/387.4-5/PHP, 28 November 1944, ; and GCT/387.4-5, Subject: Disposal of the German Military Caste, 24 September 1944, both in RG 331, Entry 27, Box 92, NARA.

93. SHAEF/21544/PHP, GCT/387.4-5, Subject: Disposal of the German Military Caste, 24 September 1944, RG 331, Entry 27, Box 92, NARA.

94. Ibid.

95. SHAEF/21544/PHP, GCT/387.4-5/PHP, 28 November 1944, CGT/387.4-5, Subject: Disposal of German General Staff and the German Officer Corps, September 1944, RG 331, Entry 27, Box 92, NARA.

96. Memo, SHAEF/21544/2/PHP, CGT/388.4-1/PHP, Subject: Disposal of the German Military Caste, November 1944, Attachment (Tab A) to SHAEF/21544/2/PHP, GCT/387.4-1/PHP, Subject: Disposal of the German Military Caste, 25 December 1944, RG 331, Entry 2, Box, 114, NARA.

97. Ibid., para. 4.

98. Ibid., para. 5, emphasis added.

99. Ibid., paras. 6, 9, and 12.

100. Ibid., para. 17, emphasis added. As will be seen later (chapter 5, this book), by the mid-1950s this was no longer a concern for either the British or the Americans. Both services had been working closely with German generals on historical studies and with the shadow defense ministry in preparation for the creation of the new German armed force. Corum, "Founding of the Bundeswehr," in Corum, *Rearming Germany*, 45. It was also a group of German generals and admirals who, with the blessing of Chancellor Adenauer, drafted the *Himmerod Denkschrift* in October 1950, which was the first German paper on how the new German armed force should be structured.

101. GRI/CI/CS/091.711-1 (Germany), 27 April 1945, CALA File vol. 1 of 3, 387.4/1, Armistice, Control and Disposal of German Armed Forces, RG 331, Entry 6, Box 30, NARA.

102. Memo to Chief, Plans Section, Subject: Disposal of the German Military Caste, 14 November 1944, RG 331, Entry 27, Box 92, NARA; and General Morgan's Memo to Assistant Chief of Staff, G-3, Subject: Disposal of the German Military Caste, 27 December 1944, RG 331, Box 92, NARA; and "Extermination had been recommended but subsequently withdrawn by Lt. Colonel John Counsel, Chief, PHP Sub-section," Memo, GCT/388.4-1/PHP, Subject: Disposal of the German Military Caste, 6 May 1945, RG 331, Box 92, NARA.

103. CGT/387.4-5/PHP, Treatment of Senior German Commanders and Staff Officers, 29 April 1945, RG 331, Box 92, NARA

104. Handbook Governing Policy and Procedure for the Military Occupation of Germany, RG 331, Entry 2, Box 113, NARA, para. 129; and Eclipse Memorandum No. 7, RG 331, Box 113, NARA, para. 66.

105. 21st Army Group/209694/30/G(Plans)(1), German General Staff Corps, 5 March 1945, RG 331, Entry 27, Box 92, NARA.

106. SHAEF/21540/1/Ops, Subject: Memorandum on Training of Disarmament Mission, 4 April 1944, RG 331, Entry NM8/27, Box 92, Folder 388.3-3 GPS Primary Disarmament of German "forces," Training of Disarmament Mission Cadres, NARA.

107. SHAEF/1005/1/Log-P, Subject: Training of Disarmament Mission, 14 April 1944, RG 331, Entry NM8/27, Box 92, Folder 388.3-3 GPS Primary Disarmament of German "forces," Training of Disarmament Mission Cadres, NARA.

108. SHAEF/23003/Trg, Subject: Disarmament Course – Facilities, 9 May 1944, RG 331, Entry NM8/27, Box 92, Folder 388.3-3 GPS Primary Disarmament of German "forces," Training of Disarmament Mission Cadres, NARA.

109. Training Memo No. [unnumbered], Training Disarmament and Control Staffs, 8 October 1944, RG 331, Entry NM8/40, Box 273, NARA.

110. SHAEF/21540/1/Ops, Subject: Memorandum on Training, 4 April 1944, NARA.

111. The actual materials for both courses are in RG 498, Entry 672, Records of Headquarters European Theater of Operations, United States Army (World War II) Box 1, NARA. The evasion portion was most likely based on a survey prepared earlier by Brigadier W. E. van Cutsem, chief of the CCMS joint historical research staff that outlined the methods by which the Germans had evaded fulfilling the military, naval, and air clauses of the Treaty of Versailles. Van Cutsem later presented this topic in a lecture to the second running of the disarmament course on 16 November 1944. RG 331, Entry NM 8/23, Box 54.

112. Grazebrook's letter is SHAEF/21540/1/Plans, Subject: Provision of personnel for Post Hostilities Disarmament, 19 July 1944. Brigadier General George S. Eyster's reply is SHAEF/23012/GDP, Subject: Disarmament Staffs, 24 August 1944, both in RG 331, Entry NM8/27, Box 92, Folder 388.3-3 GPS Primary Disarmament of German "forces," Training of Disarmament Mission Cadres, NARA. At that time, General Eyster was Assistant Chief of Staff (G-3) US European theater of Operations.

113. Cable, SHGCT, FWD 16637, 2 October 1944, RG 331, Entry NM8/40, Box 273, NARA.

114. School Memorandum No. 3, Course of Instruction, 29 October 1944, RG 331, Entry NM8/40, Box 273, NARA.

115. Disarmament School (ETOUSA) Lectures and Staff Studies, RG 498, Entry 672, Box 1, NARA.

116. Letter, Colonel F.M. Albrecht, A/Chief, Demobilization Section, U.S. Group C.C., to Colonel Karl F. Hausauer, PHP, G-4 Division, SHAEF, 18 October 1944; AG 353-12 GDS-AGM, Subject: Provision and Training of Cadres for Disarmament and Control Staffs, 27 September 1944; AG 388.3-1 GAP-AGM, Subject: Training for Cadres for Demobilization of German Armed Forces and Para-Military Organizations, 29 October 1944; and AG 388.3-1 GAP-AGM, Subject: Training for Cadres for Demobilization of German Armed Forces and Para-Military Organizations, 25 November 1944, all in RG 331, Entry 40, Box 273, NARA.

117. Memo, SHAEF/241/1/GDP-2, Subject: Disarmament Schools, 22 December 1944, RG 331, Entry NM8/40, Box 273, NARA.

118. Letter, Brigadier General R. G. Moses, ACofS, G-4, 12th Army Group to Major General R. W. Crawford, ACofS, G-4, SHAEF, 4 January 1945, RG 331, Entry NM8/40, Box 273, NARA. As it was, 103 officers completed the first course and 105 the second.

119. Pogue, *Supreme Command*, 512, 514–15.

120. In February 1945, in response to an EAC provision in the draft terms of surrender that would have forced SHAEF to treat all surrendered German troops as POWs and thus impose upon SHAEF a burden that was beyond its ability to carry out (namely providing rations to the surrendered Germans equal to those provided Allied forces), SHAEF stated that they intended to treat all members of the German armed forces captured (either after the cessation of hostilities or after the declaration of Eclipse conditions) as disarmed German troops whose maintenance would then be the responsibility of the German Army under Allied supervision. It was also considered undesirable to provide surrendered German forces with a level of rations that far exceeded that available to the civilian population. This was approved by the War Department in April. SHAEF (G-1) Staff Study, Subject: Status of Members of the GERMAN Armed Forces after the Cessation of Hostilities, 9 February 1945, RG 331, Entry NM8/6, Box 30, NARA; SHAEF Cable, SCAP S-81564, 10 April 1945; and War Department Cable, FACS 198, 25 April 1945, both in RG 331, Box 30, NARA. See also US Army, European Command, Historical Division, *Disarmament and Disbandment of the German Armed Forces*, Occupation Forces in Europe Series, 1945–1946 (Frankfurt-am-Main, Deu.: Office of the Chief Historian, European Command, 1947), 19.

121. Oliver J. Frederickson, *The American Military Occupation of Germany, 1945–1953* (Darmstadt, Deu.: US Army, European Command, Historical Division, 1953), 89–90. See also US Army, *First Year of the Occupation*, vol. 2, 132–34; and US Army, chapter 3 in *Disarmament and Disbandment*, 27–39.

122. HQ/1873(Sec E), WMDD/M/45?5, 9th Meeting of the Standing Committee on War Materiel, 23 February 1945, RG 331, Entry NM8/27, Box 93, NARA.

123. Report of Trip, to: Col. S. Lauben, GSC Chief, German Affairs Division, 9 June 1945, RG 331, Entry NM8/6, Box 30, NARA. Emphasis in original. From the letter it appears that 12th Army Group was not coordinating sufficiently nor providing needed guidance on Eclipse Memo 17 for 3rd Army Group to completely comply with its responsibilities, as those of 3rd Army Group's operating units were different.

124. Several reports to the ACC and from it to the Council of Foreign Ministers and the Tripartite London Conference on the status of German demilitarization were made from 1946 on. See, for example: Velma Hastings Cassidy, comp., "Report of the Military Government, OMGUS, No. 30, Jul 1 – Dec 31, 1947, U.S. Department of State," in *Germany, 1945–1949: The Story in Documents*, European and British Commonwealth Series 9 (Washington, DC: Government Printing Office, 1950), 102; "Present Status of German Demobilization, Report to the London Tripartite Conference, 5 February 1948," RG 260, Entry A2 B1

C3, Box 363, Folder Armed Forces Division, Special Reports on Demilitarization (non-industrial) CFM, NARA; and "Report to the Council of Foreign Minister from the Allied Control Council in Germany, CONL/P(47)11, 24 February 1947 in RG 260, Entry A1/62, Box 799, Folder CONL Report to the CFM on Demilitarization (Feb 47) and Armed Forces Div. Report on Aviation (Feb–Mar 47), NARA.

125. An agreement was reached on providing inspection teams from the Combined Services Directorate to check on the demilitarization of former German armed forces personnel, the liquidation of war matériel, and the destruction of military installations. DOCSECO/P(47)/1, RG 260, Entry A1/1790, Box 16, Folder 2022 Inspection Teams, NARA. See also Extract from the Minutes of the 17th Meeting of DOCS (DOCS/M/48/2), 13 February 1948, RG 260, Box 16, NARA.

Chapter 2: The Diplomatic Path to 12 September 1950

1. Heinrich August Winkler, "Democracy and Dictatorship 1945-1961" in *Germany: The Long Road West*, vol. 2, *1933–1990* (Oxford: Oxford University Press, 2007), 113.

2. RG 59, Central Decimal File, 862.20/6-2149, MAP D-G/8 June 21, 1949, Foreign Assistance Correlation Committee, Hearing Book, Part G, "Germany and MA." Emphasis added.

3. In fact, as early as 1944, there were efforts to reverse US policy toward the Soviets that involved Ambassador Averell Harriman, his counselor George Kennan, and the JCS secretary Brigadier General John Dean. Even Secretary of the Navy James Forrestal concluded that the USSR was becoming a new enemy. Soviet intransigence at the 1944 Dumbarton Oaks Conference and their actions in Poland underscored these views. See Stoler, *Allies and Adversaries*, 211–15.

4. See, for example, US Department of State, "Memorandum by the Consular of the Department of State (Bohlen)," in *Foreign Relations of the United States, 1947*, 1:763–65. There are any number of books that discuss the deterioration of US-Soviet relations and the beginning of the Cold War from a wide variety of perspectives. Chief among them are a series of histories by John Lewis Gaddis: *The United States and the Origins of the Cold War, 1941–1947* (New York: Columbia University Press, 1972); *The Long Peace: Inquiries into the History of the Cold War* (New York: Oxford University Press, 1987); *We Now Know*; and *The Cold War: A New History* (New York: Penguin Press, 2005). See also Daniel Yergin, *Shattered Peace: The Origins of the Cold War and the National Security State* (Boston: Houghton Mifflin, 1977); Louis J. Halle, *The Cold War as History* (New York: Harper & Row, 1967); and Walter LaFeber, *America, Russia, and the Cold War, 1945–1996*, 8th ed. (New York: McGraw-Hill, 1997). For background on the "Long Telegram"

and the subsequent "Sources of Soviet Conduct," see George F. Kennan, *Memoirs*, vol. 1, *1925–1950* (Boston: Little, Brown and Company, 1967). "Sources of Soviet Conduct," otherwise known as the "X-article," can be found in *Foreign Affairs* 25, no. 4 (1947): 566–82. According to Vladislav Zubok and Constantine Pleshakov, Stalin saw the Marshall Plan and an earlier plan to revive the Ruhr as attempts to restore Germany's military-industrial capability and direct it against the USSR. Zubok and Pleshakov, *Kremlin's Cold War*, 5–51.

5. US Department of State, "Memorandum by the Deputy Director of the Office of European Affairs to the Director of the Office of European Affairs," in *Foreign Relations of the United States, 1947*, 1:715–16.

6. See, for example, US Department of State, "Résumé of World Situation," in *Foreign Relations of the United States, 1947*, 1:770–75, which predicted the Communist takeover of Czechoslovakia. More recent studies show that Western estimates of Soviet military strength were wildly exaggerated and that their posture was purely defensive. The Soviet goal, given their own perceived strategic weakness, was to defend and hold the borders established after the war for approximately two days until the second strategic echelon would arrive. Only then would they shift to an offensive posture toward the channel coast. See, for example: Vojtech Mastney, "Imagining War in Europe: Soviet Strategic Planning," in *War Plans and Alliances in the Cold War: Threat Perceptions in the East and West*, ed. Vojtech Mastney, Sven Haltemark, and Andreas Wenger (London: Routledge, 2006), 16; and Matthias Uhl, "Soviet and Warsaw Pact Military Strategy from Stalin to Brzhnev," in Hoffernaar, Krüger, and Zabeki, *Blueprints for Battle*, 34–35.

7. Richard Mayne, *The Recovery of Europe, 1945–1973* (Garden City, NY: Anchor Books, 1973), 187. See John Baylis, "Britain, the Brussels Pact and the Continental Commitment," *International Affairs* (London) 60, no. 4 (Autumn 1980): 626–27. Apparently, one foreign minister remarked that the Russians would be in Paris by August, and the French chief of staff agreed. David Dilks, "The British View of Security: Europe and a Wider World," in *Western Security: The Formative Years: Europe and the Atlantic Defence, 1947–1953*, edited by Olav Riste (New York: Columbia University Press, 1985), 53. See also Memorandum of Conversation (Hickerson-Inverchapel), 21 January 1948, and Memorandum of Conversation Achilles-Bérard, 13 February 1948, both in RG 59, Entry (A1) 1189, Lot 53D44, Box 11, NARA.

8. Jonathan M. House, *A Military History of the Cold War 1944–1962*, Campaigns and Commanders series 34, (Norman: University of Oklahoma Press, 2012), 126.

9. Arnold A. Offner, *Another Such Victory: President Truman and the Cold War, 1945–1953* (Stanford: Stanford University Press, 2002), 427.

10. Lord Ismay, who was the first secretary general of NATO, is reputed to have said that NATO was founded to keep the Americans in, the Russians out, and the Germans down.

11. Contrary to a major theory presented by Christopher Layne (*The Peace of Illusions: American Grand Strategy from 1940 to the Present* [Ithaca: Cornell University Press, 2006]), the idea of a Western European union as a "third force" is prevalent in US policy statements of this period. See, for example, US Department of State, "PPS-23: Review of Current Trends, U.S. Foreign Policy," in *Foreign Relations of the United States, 1948*, vol. 1, *General; The United Nations*, part 2 (Washington, DC: Government Printing Office, 1948), 510–18.

12. Gordon A. Craig, *The Politics of the Prussian Army 1640–1945* (New York: Oxford University Press, 1964), 482.

13. On 5 June 1950, Secretary of State Dean Acheson told the House Committee on Foreign Affairs that the United States "would continue to promote German demilitarization." Earlier, on 1 May, he had told the Senate Foreign Relations Committee that talk about rearming Germany was "very undesirable." Robert J. McMahon, *Dean Acheson and the Creation of an American World Order* (Washington, DC: Potomac Books, 2009), 136. See also the cable from Acheson to John J. McCloy dated 21 June 1950 regarding Count von Schwerin's visit to London and the British belief that the United States could "be brought into line quickly" regarding German rearmament in US Department of State, "The Secretary of State to the Office of the United States High Commissioner for Germany, at Frankfort," in *Foreign Relations of the United States, 1950*, vol. 4, *Central and Eastern Europe; The Soviet Union* (Washington, DC: Government Printing Office, 1950), 689–90.

14. Byrnes was referring to his draft treaty that he hoped would be signed by the four powers. The full title of the declaration mentioned was "Declaration Regarding the Defeat of Germany and the Assumption of Supreme Authority by the Allied Powers, Signed at Berlin, June 5, 1945." It was signed by General Eisenhower, Marshal Georgy Zhukov (USSR), Field Marshal Montgomery (UK), and General de Lattre de Tassigny (France). *Documents on Germany, 1944–1959*, 13–18.

15. US Department of State, "C.F.M. (46) 21: Text of Draft Treaty on the Disarmament and Demilitarization of Germany," in *Foreign Relations of the United States, 1946*, vol. 2, *Council of Foreign Ministers* (Washington, DC: Government Printing Office, 1946), 190–93. See also Hastings Cassidy, *Story in Documents*, 101; and Allied Control Council Law 34 and Allied Control Council Directive 18, in appendix C below.

16. "Restatement of U.S. Policy on Germany," *Department of State Bulletin* 15, no. 376 (September 1946): 496–501.

17. Address of the Honorable James F. Byrnes, Secretary of State of the United States of America, at the American Club, Paris, France, 3 October 1946, Papers of Howard Trivers, State Department File, Germany File, Box 1, Harry S. Truman Presidential Library (hereafter HSTL).

18. Report "Talks on Germany," RG 260, Entry A1/62, Box 799, Folder Armed Forces Division and Military Security Board [a second, more succinct summary was dated 4 November 1948]; and "Talks on Germany," (resumed session) Draft Report on Security (as amended 26 May1948), RG 335, Entry 24, Box 8, Folder 334, Military Security Board. In an earlier July 1947 memorandum prepared by the policy planning staff, the third paragraph stated explicitly the "U.S. determination to keep Germany disarmed and demilitarized (Four-power Pact)" (the parenthetical refers to the draft treaty on the disarmament and demilitarization of Germany). US Department of State, "Memorandum Prepared by the Policy Planning Staff," in *Foreign Relations of the United States, 1947*, vol. 3, *The British Commonwealth; Europe* (Washington, DC: Government Printing Office, 1947), 336. See Allied Control Council Laws 25 and 43, and Allied Control Council directive 39 in appendix C below.

19. Trachtenberg, *A Constructed Peace*, 62–63, 114–15.

20. Memorandum of Conversation, Hickerson-Lord Inverchapel, 21 January 1948, NARA. See also Schwartz, "Case of German Rearmament," 297; Trachtenberg, *A Constructed Peace*, 62–63; and US Department of State, "Résumé of World Situation ," in *Foreign Relations of the United States, 1947*, 1:770. Leffler makes a persuasive case that a third force was not desired by the United States. Leffler, *Preponderance of Power*, 461–62, fn 71. The difference, however, is one of interpretation and whether one includes the word "independent." I would argue, however, that the Truman administration's support of EDC and the even stronger support by the later Eisenhower administration imply support for a third force. The degree to which it would be independent remains open to question and dependent on the political and international circumstances at any particular time.

21. Beisner, *Life in the Cold War*, 128; and Leffler, *Preponderance of Power*, 6–9, 27.

22. Beisner, Life in the Cold War, 128. Other authors, such as David Clay Large, claim the statement was "All the Russians needed to get to the Rhine were shoes." Large, *Germans to the Front*, 33.

23. Robert Schuman, "France and Europe," *Foreign Affairs* 31, no. 3 (April 1953): 350–51.

24. Theodore H. White, *Fire in the Ashes: Europe in Mid-century* (New York: Sloane, 1953), 32–33; and Alan K. Henrikson, "The Creation of the North Atlantic Alliance, 1948–1952," *Naval War College Review* 33, no. 3 (1980): 10–11. At war's end, the United States had 68 divisions and 149 air groups in Europe (3,500,000

soldiers). By March 1946, only 400,000 remained. British forces worldwide went from 4,700,000 to 1,247,000. During the 1948 Czech coup, the Western Allies had fewer than 200,000 troops in 7 poorly organized divisions facing 500,000 Soviet troops in almost 30 divisions.

25. Richard Vaughan, *Twentieth Century Europe: Paths to Unity* (New York: Barnes & Noble Books, 1979), 72.

26. John Baylis, "Britain and the Dunkirk Treaty: The Origins of NATO," *Journal of Strategic Studies* 5, no. 2 (June 1982): 240–41.

27. Ibid., 241–42. See also Sean Greenwood, "Return to Dunkirk: The Origins of the Anglo French Treaty of March 1947," *Journal of Strategic Studies* 6, no. 4 (December 1983): 57.

28. Greenwood, "Return to Dunkirk," 50; and Greenwood, "Ernest Bevin, France and 'Western Union': August 1945–February 1946," *European History Quarterly* 14, no. 3 (July 1984): 321.

29. Baylis, "Britain and the Dunkirk Treaty," 242–43; and Baylis, "Britain, the Brussels Pact and the Continental Commitment," *International Affairs* (London) 60, no. 4 (Autumn 1980): 618.

30. Baylis, "Britain and the Dunkirk Treaty," 236. See also Fursdon, *European Defense Community*, 28–29; and Vaughan, *Paths to Unity*, 72.

31. Timothy Ireland, *Creating the Entangling Alliance: The Origins of the North Atlantic Treaty Organization* (Westport, CT: Greenwood Press, 1981), 55. This gives an excellent account of the political environment leading up to the signing of the Brussels and North Atlantic treaties.

32. Baylis, "The Continental Commitment," 619.

33. "Memorandum by Mr. Bevin for the Cabinet on the First Aim of British Foreign Policy, 4 January 1948, Document No. 7," in *Documents on British Policy Overseas*, series 1, vol. 10, *The Brussels and North Atlantic Treaties, 1947–1949*, edited by Tony Insall and Patrick Salmon (New York: Rutledge, 2015), 15. See also Baylis, "The Continental Commitment," 620–21.

34. Baylis "The Continental Commitment," 622–23. To make matters worse, the British government had not yet committed itself to a continental policy to which several military service chiefs were opposed.

35. Benelux: Belgium, the Netherlands, and Luxembourg.

36. Baylis "The Continental Commitment," 624. See also Mayne, *Recovery of Europe*, 187; and US Department of State, "Memorandum by the Director of the Office of European Affairs (Hickerson) to the Secretary of State," in *Foreign Relations of the United States, 1948*, vol. 3, *Western Europe* (Washington, DC: Government Printing Office, 1948), 6.

37. Baylis "The Continental Commitment," 625.

38. Memorandum of Conversation, M. Bérard , Mr. Achilles, Mr. Wallner, February 13, 1948, Subject: Security Against Germany, RG 59, Box 11, Lot 53D444, NARA.

39. Dilks, "British View of Security," 52; Baylis, "The Continental Commitment," 625–26; and Mayne, *Recovery of Europe*, 187.

40. Mayne, *Recovery of Europe*, 187. On the day the Brussels Treaty was signed, President Truman said the following to a special session of Congress: "I am sure that the determination of the free countries of Europe to protect themselves will be matched by an equal determination on our part to help them do so." Baylis, "The Continental Commitment," 626–27. Dilks describes the depression by relating the remark of one foreign minister that the Russians would be in Paris by August, a statement met with agreement from the French chief of staff. Dilks, "British View of Security," 53.

41. See US Department of State, "(Hickerson) to the Secretary of State," *Foreign Relations of the United States, 1948*, 3:6; and Harry S. Truman, *Memoirs*, vol. 2, *Years of Trial and Hope* (Garden City, NY: Doubleday & Co., 1956), 277–84.

42. Memorandum of Conversation, French Ambassador Bonnet to Achilles, 21 May 1948, RG 59, Box 11, Lot 53D444, NARA; Theodore Achilles, interview by Richard D. McKinzie, 13 November and 18 December 1972, Washington, DC, transcript, HSTL, http://www.trumanlibrary.org/oralhist/achilles.htm; and TS Memorandum of Conversation, Lovett-Baydur, 25 May 1948, RG 59, Box 11, Lot 53D444, NARA, in which Lovett told Turkish ambassador Baydur that security guarantees were "contrary to the tradition of the United States."

43. For an interesting but pessimistic view of the Brussels Treaty, see Lawrence S. Kaplan, "Western Union and European Military Integration 1948–1950—An American Perspective," in Wiggershaus and Foerster, *Western Security Community*, 45–68.

44. Isaacson and Thomas, *Wise Men*.

45. Schwartz, "Case of German Rearmament," 298; and Martin, "American Decision to Rearm," 649.

46. See chapter 3, this book.

47. US Department of State, "Memorandum by the Director of the Policy Planning Staff (Kennan) to the Secretary of State," *Foreign Relations of the United States, 1948*, 3:7–8; and US Department of State, "(Hickerson) to the Secretary of State," in *Foreign Relations of the United States, 1948*, 3:6–7. See also Memorandum for the President, "Security against Germany," 11 February 1948, Papers of Harry S. Truman, President's Secretary's Files: (PSF), Subject File, Box 155, HSTL.

48. "PPS/27, Western Union and Related Problems, 23 March 1948," in *State Department Policy Planning Staff Papers 1947–1949*, ed. Anna Kasten Nelson, vol. 2,

1948 (New York: Garland, 1983), 161–64; "PPS/27/2, The Position of the United States with Respect to Support for Western Union and Other Related Free Countries, 24 June 1948," in Kasten Nelson, *1948*, 171–74; and Memorandum of Conversation, M. Bérard , Mr. Achilles, Mr. Wallner, 13 February 1948, NARA.

49. US Department of State, "Summary of a Memorandum Representing Mr. Bevin's Views on the Formation of a Western Union," in *Foreign Relations of the United States, 1948*, 3:4–6. See also Norbert Wiggershaus, "The Decision for a West German Defense Contribution," in Riste, *Western Security*, 198; and Martin, "American Decision to Rearm," 646–47.

50. US Department of State, "Department of State Policy Statement," in *Foreign Relations of the United States, 1948*, vol. 2, *Germany and Austria* (Washington, DC: Government Printing Office, 1948), 1297–98.

51. Marguerite Higgens, "Board to Insure Disarming of Germany Set Up," *New York Herald Tribune*, 31 December 1948, 1. See also John P. Hodges, "Formula for Peace – Military Security Board," *Information Bulletin*, no. 161 (17 May 1949): 5–6, http://digicoll.library.wisc.edu/cgi-bin/History/History-idx?type=article&did=History.omg1949n161.Hodgesformula&id=History.omg1949n161&isize=M.

52. Pertinax, "Byrnes Arms Pact Reported Dropped," *New York Times*, 21 February 1948, 4.

53. Bremen 639, 8 November 1948, RG 59, Central Decimal File, 1945–1949, File 862.2, Box 6705, NARA.

54. Letter, Stuttgart 492, American Consul General to Secretary of State, 1 December 1948, RG 59, Central Decimal File, 1945–1949, File 862.2, Box 6705, NARA. See also Frankfurt 318, 10 December 1948, RG 59, Central Decimal File, 1945–1949, File 740.00119 Control (Germany), Box 3758, NARA.

55. See Moscow 2515, 2 November 1948; Letter, Stuttgart 492, 1 December 1948; Frankfurt 314, 15 December 1948; Frankfurt 332 and 333, 16 December 1948; and Frankfurt 18, 12 January 1949, all in RG 59, Central Decimal File, 1945–1949, File 862.2, Box 6705, NARA.

56. Memorandum of Conversation, Bérard-Reber, 3 January 1949, RG 59, Central Decimal File, 1945–1949, File 862.2, Box 6705.

57. Letter, Kenneth Royall-President, 17 January 1949, RG 59, Central Decimal File, 1945–1949, File 140.00119 Control (Germany), Box 3760, NARA.

58. See, for example: Letter, Assistant Secretary of State Arthur A. Kimball to Robert Murphy, 22 April 1949, RG 59, Central Decimal File, 1945–1949, File 140.00119 Control (Germany), Box 3772, NARA. On 6 June 1949, President Truman, by Executive Order 10062, established the post of high commissioner and nominated McCloy. RG 59, Central Decimal File, 1945–1949, File 140.00119 Control (Germany), Box 3775, NARA.

59. "United States Policy Concerning Germany" [undated, unsigned paper], RG 59, Central Decimal File, 1945–1949, File 140.00119 Control (Germany), Box 3768, NARA. Between May and September 1949, the FRG came into existence, with limited sovereignty. An occupation statute, drawn up by the United States, Britain, and France, defined the roles and responsibilities of the new government while establishing the right of the Allies, vested in three civilian high commissioners, to keep occupation forces in the country and specifically to control, inter alia, disarmament and demilitarization.

60. Extract from ONSC D-3 in "Statement of the Problem," an attachment to Letter, Ware Adams to Robert Murphy, 18 March 1949, RG 59, Central Decimal Files, File 740.00119 Control (Germany), Box 3768, NARA. This is one of four policy papers written by Adams for Murphy.

61. Policy Paper, 8 March 1949, RG 59, Central Decimal Files, File 740.00119 Control (Germany), Box 3767, NARA.

62. Kennan was, and remained, an outspoken foe of German rearmament. Kennan, *1925–1950*, 446–48.

63. "Memorandum for the President," 31 March 1949, Papers of Harry S. Truman, PSF: Subject File, Box 178, HSTL; and "Memorandum for the President," 11 February 1948, PSF, Subject File 1940–1953, Foreign Affairs File, Box 155, HSTL. See also Memorandum of Conversation, 3 March 1949, RG 59, Memos of Conversation, Folder March–Apr 1949, Lot 53D444, Box 12, NARA.

64. "Washington's Farewell Address (1796)," in *American Historical Documents: 1000–1904*, vol. 43 of *Harvard Classics*, ed. Charles William Elliot (New York: P. F. Collier & Son, 1909), http://www.bartleby.com/43/24.html.

65. The original signatories of the NATO treaty were Belgium, Canada, Denmark, France, Iceland, Italy, Luxembourg, the Netherlands, Norway, Portugal, the United Kingdom, and the United States. *NATO Handbook* (Brussels: NATO Office of Information and Press, 1995), 20–21.

66. See Paper B of US Department of State, "Occupation Statute Defining the Powers to be Retained by the Occupation Authorities," in *Foreign Relations of the United States, 1949*, vol. 3, *Council of Foreign Ministers* (Washington, DC: Government Printing Office, 1949), 179; and the speech given by Secretary of State Dean Acheson to the American Society of Newspaper Editors, 28 April 1949, Papers of Howard Trivers, State Department File, Germany File, Box 1, HSTL. The Military Security Board was established by the London Conference of 1948 and came into being on 10 December 1948. Hodges, "Formula for Peace," 5–6.

67. Senate Committee on Foreign Relations, 81st Congress, 1st Session, Hearings on the North Atlantic Treaty, 26, quoted in Dean Acheson, *Present at the Creation: My Years in the State Department* (New York: Norton, 1969), 375. When

the NATO Treaty was signed, there was only one US infantry division and one division-size, lightly armed constabulary force in West Germany. House, *Military History*, 117. It should be noted that Senator Vandenberg thought the NATO Treaty made it unessential to have substantial US forces on the front lines in Europe. Similarly, General Bradley told Senator McMahon that it was not necessary to have a gun or a man or an airplane on the continent "because of the potential for putting them there later if it is desired." Phil Williams, *The Senate and U.S. Troops in Europe* (New York: St. Martin's Press, 1985), 22–13; and Truman's statement in fn 38 above.

68. "Memorandum for the President," 31 March 1949, HSTL.

69. Records Relating to the North Atlantic Treaty Organization, 1947–1953, RG 59, Records of the Office of European Regional Affairs, Lot File 57 D 271, Box 8 of 10, NARA.

70. MAP D-G/8, 21 June 1949, Foreign Assistance Correlation Committee, Part G - Hearing Book, "Germany and MAP," RG 59, Central Decimal Files, File 862.20, Box 6705, NARA.

71. Hague 275, 12 July 1949, RG 59, Central Decimal File, 1945–1949, File 840.00, Box 5646, NARA.

72. Office Memorandum, Jackson-Perkins, 10 October 1949, RG 59, Central Decimal File, File 862.20, Box 6705, NARA.

73. Memo, Perkins to the Secretary of State, 11 October 1949, RG 59, Box 6705, NARA. A similar memo, "Note on German Rearmament" [no author], 12 October 1949, can be found in HST Papers, PSF: Subject File, 1940–1953, Box 155, HSTL.

74. Press speculation was further fueled by remarks made by generals Omar Bradley and Lucius Clay. Bradley, speaking at an Overseas Press luncheon, stated that not only was a "strong ally needed on the continent," but also that as the Russians had put East Germans in uniform as police, the West Germans might also need "some uniforms," if only to maintain security. US Department of State, "Memorandum of Conversation, by the Assistant Secretary of State for European Affairs (Perkins)," in *Foreign Relations of the United States, 1949*, 3:317–19. Clay's remarks, made at a fundraiser for the Arthritic and Rheumatism Foundation and not carried in the domestic press, spoke of the need for a "composite military force of Western European nations to which Germany could contribute limited forces of a special type." Clay also stated that he hoped such a force could be created if the West European nations integrated but that it was a European and not American problem. US Department of State, "The Secretary of State to the United States High Commissioner for Germany (McCloy)," in *Foreign Relations of the United States, 1949*, 3:340–42. See also Middleton, "Europeans Ponder Army."

75. See, for example: Arthur Krock, "Whether to Rearm Germany or Just Some Germans," *New York Times*, 1 December 1949, 30; and Alsop and Alsop, "Matter of Fact," 13.

76. "Paraphrase of Telegram from U.K. High Commissioner to Foreign Office, London. Dated 9th December," RG 59, Central Decimal File, File 740.00119 Control (Germany), Box 3787. See also Adenauer, *Memoirs, 1945–1953*, 271–74.

77. The French remained suspicious, however. François Sedoux, director of the European Office in the Quai d'Orsay, believed that a rearmed Germany would either provoke the Russians into a preemptive strike or propel the Germans into an unholy alliance with them. He sent instructions to France's missions in Bonn, London, and Washington that firmly stated France's opposition to German rearmament, saying that while France favored German integration into a European structure, it viewed "the reconstitution of a German military force to be beyond discussion." William L. Hitchcock, *France Restored: Cold War Diplomacy and the Quest for Leadership in Europe* (Chapel Hill: University of North Carolina, 1998), 117–18.

78. "Statement Concerning Germany Made by M. Robert Schuman before the National Assembly," attachment to Memorandum of Conversation, Acheson-Bonnet, 1 December 1949, RG 59, Records of the Executive Secretariat (Dean Acheson) , Box 13, Lot 53D444, NARA. See also Harold Callender, "Schuman Defends Policy on Germany," *New York Times*, 25 November 1949, 5.

79. "Bradley Expresses Confidence"; and "The Defense of Europe," *New York Times*, 28 November 1949, 7, 26. See also Harold Callender, "French Skeptical on Bonn Rearming," *New York Times*, 29 November 1949, 5; and "Armed Germans," *Wasshington Post,* 29 November 1949 12.

80. "Review of Discussions which the Secretary of State, Mr. Dean G. Acheson, had in Bonn on Sunday, November 13, 1949, with the Chancellor of the German Federal Republic, Dr. Konrad Adenauer," RG 59, Records of the Executive Secretariat (Dean Acheson), Box 13, Lot 53D444, NARA.

81. US Department of State, "The Secretary of State to the United States High Commissioner for Germany (McCloy)," in *Foreign Relations of the United States, 1949*, 3:340–42. The article in question in the *New York Times* indicated that European staff officers were discussing the difference five German divisions would make to the defense of Western Europe and not a plan for German rearmament. Middleton, "Europeans Ponder Army," 1.

82. "Congressmen Ask West Bid Germans," *New York Times*, 22 November, 1949, 11; and "House Group Bars German Rearming," *New York Times*, 14 December 1949, 19.

83. Memorandum of Conversation, Acheson-Bonnet, 1 December 1949; and unnumbered, outgoing State telegram, 7 December 1949, both in RG 59, Central Decimal Files, File 862.20, Box 6705, NARA.

84. Adenauer, *Memoirs, 1949–1953*, 268.

85. HICOG A-671, 12 December 1949, RG 59, Central Decimal Files, File 862.20, Box 6705, NARA, 3.

86. "German Army Unit is Offered to West," *New York Times,* 4 December 1949, 23; and "West Germans Would Arm if Asked by Allies," *Washington Post* , 6 December 1949, 3.

87. "German Army Unit," 23. See also HICOG A-671, 12 December 1949, NARA, 2.

88. HICOG A671, 12 December 1949, NARA.

89. The statements to which Adenauer referred were those he made to the press following the Leacocos interview in which he reiterated his position against German rearmament in principle and the need for Germany to devote its strength to reconstruction. Adenauer, *Memoirs, 1945–1953*, 268.

90. "Paraphrase of Telegram," 9 December, NARA. As a result of Adenauer's comments, the United States subsequently made an official protest to the Soviet Union regarding the existence of an East German army. On 9 December 1949, however, Byroade wrote Acheson stating that all information available indicated that there was neither an East German army nor a police or paramilitary force that could be considered an army. What did exist in East Germany was a border police (Grenzpolizei) and an alert police (Bereitschaftspolizei) with a combined total of thirty thousand members. Their training was primarily military and they were equipped with light infantry weapons but they had "practically no combat effectiveness." Memorandum, Byroade-Acheson, 9 December 1949, RG 59, Central Decimal Files, File 862.20, Box 6705, NARA.

91. "Adenauer Virtually Demands German Unity in West's Army," *Washington Post*, 10 December 1949, 1.

92. Hanson W. Baldwin, "German Arming Issue," *New York Times*, 29 December 1949, 6.

93. DEPTEL 4013, October 19, 1949, RG 59, Central Decimal File, File 711.40, NARA and Synopsis C, Aug–Dec 1949, Dean G. Acheson Papers, Princeton Seminars File, Box 78, HSTL. Emphasis added.

94. See, for example: "Europeans Ponder Army," 1; "Congressmen Ask West," 11; Alsop and Alsop, "Matter of Fact," 13; and US Department of State, "Memorandum by the Assistant Secretary of State for European Affairs (Perkins) to the Secretary of State," in *Foreign Relations of the United States, 1949*, 3:285.

95. Bonn 66, 17 December 1949, RG 59, Central Decimal File, File 740.00119 Control (Germany), Box 3787, NARA.

96. As will be seen in chapter 3, the JCS had long advocated the rearming of Germany.

97. William Stueck, *Rethinking the Korean War: A New Diplomatic and Strategic History* (Princeton: Princeton University Press, 2002), 220.

98. Drew Middleton, "German Officers List Arms Needs," *New York Times*, 14 January 1950, 1.

99. Frankfurt 602, 20 January 1950, RG 59, Central Decimal Files, File 762A.5, Box 3896, NARA. It is possible that these stories of Americans asking German generals for advice may be referring to those generals who had been recruited by the US Army in 1946 to write the history of the war on the eastern front. Aside from this Operational History (German) Section of the US Army's Historical Division, three other German organizations were involved in rearmament planning but at a later date: Amt Blank, the Gehlen Organization, and the Control Group, the successor to the Historical Division's German Section. Alaric Searle, *Wehrmacht Generals, West German Society, and the Debate on Rearmament, 1949–1959* (Westport, CT: Praeger, 2003), 94–97.

100. Memorandum for the President, 13 March 1950, Dean G. Acheson Papers, Secretary of State File 1945–1972, Memoranda of Conversations File, 1949–1953, Box 66, HSTL.

101. Benjamin Welles, "Britain Rules Out Rearmed Germany," *New York Times*, 18 March 1950, 4.

102. Drew Middleton, "West Germans Ask Assured Defense," *New York Times*, 10 April 1950, 8. About this time, Chancellor Adenauer engaged General Graf Gerhard von Schwerin as his "Advisor for Military and Security Issues." Von Schwerin was a strong advocate for a large national police force that would become the cornerstone of a future German military. Corum, "Founding of the Bundeswehr," 34.

103. Letter to Mr. Lewis (GER), 24 April 1950, RG 59, Central Decimal Files, File 762A.5, Box 3896, NARA. Lewis was Geoffrey W. Lewis, acting director of the Bureau of German Affairs in the State Department.

104. Ibid.

105. US Department of State, "United States High Commissioner to Secretary of State," in *Foreign Relations of the United States, 1950*, 4:633

106. Ibid., 635.

107. Drew Middleton, "U.S. Drafts Plans to Occupy Germany for 5 Years More," *New York Times*, 23 April 1950, 1.

108. "A Memorandum on the Issue of an Active Participation by Western Germany in the Defense of Europe and the Western World," 25 April 1950,

attachment to Memo for: ADPC, 31 May 1950, Subject: Western German Rearmament, RG 59, Central Decimal Files, File 762A.5, Box 3896, NARA. The papers by German generals are most likely from the same individuals and groups mentioned in footnote 99, this chapter. The only other group of former senior German officers that wrote papers on rearmament was the group that met at the Himmerod Abbey in October 1950 (see appendix E, this book).

109. Drew Middleton, "West Imposes Ban on German Arming," *New York Times*, 9 May 1950, 1, 6.

110. NSC 71, A Report to the National Security Council by the Secretary of Defense on United States Policy toward Germany, 8 June 1950, Papers of Harry S. Truman, PSF: Subject File, 1940–1953, National Security Council - Meetings File, Box 180, HSTL.

111. Memorandum for the Secretary of State, 16 June 1950, Papers of Harry S. Truman, PSF: National Security Council–Meetings File, Box 180, HSTL.

112. Frankfurt 5449, 24 June 1950, RG59, Central Decimal Files, File 762A.5, Box 3896, NARA. Part of this cable was sanitized to remove "sensitive information," so the individual speaking to McCloy is not known, but the source told McCloy that it was Robertson (Sir Brian Robertson, the former British High Commissioner for Germany) who had urged the chancellor (Adenauer) to request 25,000 police and that the British would strongly support him.

113. Memorandum for the Secretary of State, 16 June 1950, HSTL. Byroade's paper, a comment by Perkins, and Byroade's cover letter are all attached to Memorandum for Mr. Jessup, 14 June 1950, RG 59, Central Decimal Files, File 762A.5, Box 3896, NARA. Byroade's paper became NSC-71/1, 3 July 1950, RG 273, NSC Policy Papers, Box 9, NARA. According to Spencer Mawby, Adenauer allegedly made the request for twenty-five thousand police on 28 April 1950. Mawby, *Containing Germany: Britain and the Arming of the Federal Republic* (New York: St. Martin's Press, 1999). Ironically, Adenauer does not mention this in his autobiography nor is there any mention of Graf von Schwerin. Adenauer, *Memoirs, 1945–1953*. It should also be noted that both Mawby and Saki Dockrill write that by late 1949, the British had accepted the rearming of Germany but preferred a gendarmerie that would serve as the first step in that direction. Mawby, *Containing Germany*, 28–32; and Dockrill, *Britain's Policy*, 15.

114. Frankfurt 5052, 13 June 1950, and Frankfurt 5453, 25 June 1950, both in RG 59, Central Decimal Files, File 762A.5, Box 3896, NARA

115. Frankfurt 5052, 13 June 1950, NARA.

116. Memorandum for the Secretary of State, 16 June 1950, HSTL.

117. Unnumbered Deptel, 24 June 1950, RG 59, Central Decimal File, File 762A.5, Box 3896, NARA.

118. Frankfort 5449, 24 June 1950, RG 59, Central Decimal File, File 762A.5, Box 3896, NARA.

119. Deptel 3224, 30 June 1950, RG 59, Central Decimal File, File 762A.5, Box 3896, NARA. The name of the source was redacted on the cable.

120. For a more complete reading of the NSC-68 issue, see: Beisner, chapter 14 in *Life in the Cold War*, 236–51; Leffler, *Preponderance of Power*, 236–39; McMahon, *American World Order*, 108–10, 130–31; Wiggershaus, "West German Military Integration," 581–82; and Drew, *Strategy of Containment*.

121. Drew, *Strategy of Containment*, 9–10.

122. It was during this time that Secretary of Defense Johnson concluded that the State Department was conspiring against him to prevent him from keeping military spending down. He subsequently ordered that all contact with the State Department go through his office. By the time he assigned a good point of contact, NSC-68 had been finished. James Chace, *Acheson: The Secretary of State Who Created the American World* (New York: Simon & Schuster, 1998), 274–75.

123. Wells, "Sounding the Tocsin," 140.

124. McAllister, *No Exit*, 186.

125. These views are expressed by Wolfram Hanreider, *West German Foreign Policy 1949–1967: International Pressure and Domestic Response* (Stanford: Stanford University Press, 1967), 37; and Gunter Mai, *Westliche Sicherheitspolitik im Kalten Krieg: Der Korea-Krieg und die deutsche Wiederbewaffnung 1950* (Boppard am Rhine, Deu.: Boldt, 1977), 1. Stueck, *Rethinking*, 223.

126. Robert Endicott Osgood, *NATO: The Entangling Alliance* (Chicago: University of Chicago Press, 1962), 69.

127. Bonn 26, 14 July 1950, RG 59, Central Decimal Files, File 762A.5, Box 3896, NARA.

128. Wells, "Sounding the Tocsin," 126; Dean Acheson, "'Total Diplomacy' to Strengthen U.S. Leadership for Human Freedom," *Department of State Bulletin* 22, no. 559 (20 March 1950): 427; and Acheson, "Tensions between the United States and the Soviet Union," *Department of State Bulletin* 22, no. 560 (27 March 1950): 478. By late 1953, lower level State Department officials were telling their Department of Defense counterparts that they too, favored NATO over EDC (European Defence Community) for the FRG. Richard M. Leighton, ed., *Strategy, Money, and the New Look: 1953–1956*, vol. 3 of *History of the Office of the Secretary of Defense*, ed. Alfred Goldberg (Washington, DC: Historical Office, 2001), 574.

129. Office Memorandum, Hay-Lewis, Subject: Policy on Remilitarization of Western Germany, 17 July 1950, RG 59, Central Decimal Files, File 762A.5, Box 3896, NARA. Quotes in original. On 25 July, Byroade met with General Schuyler and mentioned that Harriman was one of many in the department who

believed Germany should be rearmed. Byroade also mentioned that the department had given full approval to the immediate formation of a ten-thousand-person police force. Memorandum for General Gruenther, Subject: Discussion with Col Byroade on German Rearmament, 25 July 1950, RG 319, TS Decimal File, 091 Germany, Box 21, NARA.

130. Acheson, *Present at the Creation*, 566; and Schwartz, *America's Germany*, 128.

131. Acheson, *Present at the Creation*, 567.

132. Meeting with the President, 30 July 1950, Item 2: The Position of Germany in the Defense of Western Europe, 1950, RG 59, Central Decimal Files, File 762A.5, Box 3896, NARA; and Kenneth W. Condit, *1947–1949*, vol. 2 of *History of the Joint Chiefs of Staff: The Joint Chiefs of Staff and National Policy* (Washington, DC: Office of Joint History, 1996), 194.

133. Dean Acheson, *The Struggle for a Free Europe* (New York: W.W. Norton & Company, 1971), 132.

134. McMahon, *American World Order*, 103; and McLellan, *State Department Years*, 180. McLellan says Acheson only enunciated this concept in February 1950, while McMahon puts it around the time of the first Soviet nuclear test in August 1949.

135. Beisner, *Life in the Cold War*, 127, 357. Acheson was well aware of the many military studies and papers that had been written advocating the rearmament of the FRG and he himself stated that the State Department had "not yet gotten that far." He also felt early on that the French attitude opposing German rearmament was wrong. Acheson, *Struggle for a Free Europe*, 124, 130.

136. Acheson, *Present at the Creation*, 442.

137. US Department of State, "United States High Commissioner for Germany (McCloy) to the Secretary of State," in *Foreign Relations of the United States, 1950*, 3:180–82.

138. Alfred Grosser, *The Western Alliance: European-American Relations since 1945*, trans. Michael Shaw (London: Macmillan, 1980), 125. See also Carter, *Forging the Shield*, 178. Another similar quotation from an unknown source was to "arm the Germans sufficiently to deter the Russians but not scare the Belgians."

139. "An Approach to the Formation of a European Army," RG 59, Records of the Bureau of European Affairs, Subject Files Relating to European Defense Arrangements, 1948–1954, Lot File 55 D 258, Box 1, NARA. The paper and its cover cable, dated 4 August 1950, are in RG 59, Central Decimal Files, File 740.5/8-450, NARA. See also: US Department of State, "Deputy Under Secretary of State (Matthews) to Assistant to the Secretary of Defense for Foreign Military Affairs and Military Assistance (Burns)," in *Foreign Relations of the United*

States, 1950, 3:211–19; and Trachtenberg and Gehrz, "America, Europe, and German Rearmament," 8–9.

140. "Summary of Telegrams," 2 August 1950, Papers of Harry S. Truman, PSF: Subject File, 1940–1953, Conference File, Box 141, HSTL.

141. Secretary of State Memos to President (12 August 50 and 16 August 50), RG 59, Lot 53 D 444, Box 4, Folder Aug 1950, NARA.

142. "My Dear Mr. Secretary," 26 August 1950, Papers of Harry S. Truman, PSF: Subject File, 1940–1953, Conference File, Box 141, HSTL.

143. Memorandum for S/S, 30 August 1950, Dean Acheson Papers, Memoranda of Conversations File, Box 67, HSTL. For the JCS response and its amendment, see: Memorandum for the Secretary of Defense, 30 August 1950, Subject: Position on Recommendations to be Submitted to the President Regarding a European Defense Force and Related Matters; and Proposed Joint Reply to the President's Letter of 26 August 1950, 7 September 1950, both in RG 59, General Records of the Department of State, Subject Files Relating to European Defense Arrangements, 1948–1954, Lot 55 D 258, Box 1, NARA.

144. Adenauer, *Memoirs, 1945–1953,* 279.

145. Ibid., 280. A second memo that same day to McCloy stated that the FRG now felt it necessary to restructure its relationship with the occupiers on a new basis (i.e., end the state of war, repurpose the occupation to protect against external dangers, and make the relationship contractual). See also Hans-Jürgen Rautenberg and Norbert Wiggershaus, *Die Himmeroder Denkschrift vom Oktober 1950: politische und militärische Überlegungen für einen Beitrag der Bundesrepublik Deutschland zur westeuropäischen Verteidigung* (Karlsruhe, Deu.: Braun, 1985), 13, 35–36.

146. John Foster Dulles Papers, Box 47, Seeley G. Mudd Manuscript Library, Princeton University.

147. Acheson, *Present at the Creation,* 568–71; Acheson, *Struggle for a Free Europe,* 133; Condit, *1947–1949,* 200–203; Martin, "American Decision to Rearm," 655-60; Thomas Alan Schwartz, "The 'Skeleton Key' – American Foreign Policy, European Unity and German Rearmament, 1949–1954," *Central European History* 19, no. 4 (December 1986): 375–77; McAllister, *No Exit,* 187–92; and Trachtenberg and Gehrz, "America, Europe, and German Rearmament," 11–16.

148. James Reston, "Arms Tie to Atlantic Pact Being Debated in Capital; One Group Sees Military Aid as Separate Issue – Other Links It to Treaty," *New York Times,* 3 March 1949, 3. Quoted in Osgood, *NATO: Entangling Alliance,* 37.

149. Trachtenberg and Gehrz, "America, Europe, and German Rearmament," 17–22; McMahon, *American World Order,* 11–17, 48; McLellan, *State Department Years,* 329; and McAllister, *No Exit,* 188–92. See appendix E, this book, for additional comment on this issue.

150. Trachtenberg and Gehrz, "America, Europe, and German Rearmament," 12.

151. Leighton, *The New Look*, 553.

152. Melvyn Leffler, in personal conversations with me, disagreed. He felt that leadership was retained by "nudging and persuading," but I would argue that nudging is not leading—one does not lead from behind.

Chapter 3: The Military Path to 12 September 1950

1. Carl von Clausewitz, *On War*, ed. and trans. Michael Howard and Peter Paret (Princeton: Princeton University Press, 1976), 636–37.

2. Dwight David Eisenhower, *Crusade in Europe* (Garden City, NY: Doubleday & Company, 1952), 429.

3. Weigley, *History of the United States Army*, 486. The point system that had been established to determine rotation eligibility was dropped and all men with two years' service were rapidly discharged.

4. "Statement by General of the Army Dwight D. Eisenhower, Chief of Staff, U.S. Army, Supplementing His Remarks on Demobilization Made to Members of Congress in the Auditorium, Library of Congress, 10:00AM, EST, Tuesday, January 15, 1946," Papers of Harry S. Truman, PSF: General File, 1945–1953, 5, Box 102, HSTL. See also Report to the President by Robert F. Patterson, Secretary of War, 11 June 1946, Papers of Harry S. Truman, PSF: Subject File, 1940–1953, Box 155, HSTL. Lord Ismay gives the total of US forces in Europe on VE Day as three million one hundred thousand. Hastings Lionel Ismay, *NATO: The First Five Years, 1949–1954* (Utrecht, Nld.: Bosch, 1956). Jonathan House describes the demobilization thus: "In the rush to demobilize, entire divisions dissolved without even a ceremony to mark their passing, leaving their equipment unsupervised and unmaintained." House, *Military History*, 78. William Mako has called the demobilization at the end of the war "an organized rout." Mako, *U.S. Ground Forces*, 6.

5. Trachtenberg, *A Constructed Peace*, 87; Condit, *1947–1949*, 187; and Christian Greiner, "The Defense of Western Europe and the Rearmament of West Germany, 1947–1950," in Riste, *Western Security*, 158. Almost 400,000 military vehicles in 1947 were unserviceable and of the 28,000 tanks in 1945, only 6,000 were on hand in 1950. By 1946, the navy's fleets also suffered major reductions, going from 99 aircraft carriers to 26 and from 412,000 aircraft to only 24,000. House, *Military History*, 78–80.

6. Condit, *1947–1949*, 152–53. (A hardcover version with slightly different pagination published in Wilmington, DE, by Michael Glazier in 1979 has also been used and will be identified with the addition "1979 ed.") The Joint Strategic Survey Committee (JSSC) believed the USSR would keep 5.5 million

men under arms. Walter S. Poole, "From Conciliation to Containment: The Joint Chiefs of Staff and the Coming of the Cold War, 1945–1946," *Military Affairs* 42, no. 1 (February 1978): 13. It should be pointed out, however, that US divisions were larger than Soviet divisions.

7. Russia was considered capable of overrunning Europe in six months. The risk of war was considered sufficient to warrant time and adequate preparations. Drew, *Strategy of Containment*, 27. At the time of the Czech coup, the effective combat strength of the US Army was but two and one-third divisions. The coup convinced President Truman that he had to address the ever-decreasing size of the army. As a result, a new draft law went into effect in 1948. Weigley, *History of the United States Army*, 506; and House, *Military History*, 110–11.

8. Leffler, *Preponderance of Power*, 40–46. At the very top, Edward Stetinius Jr. was replaced by Joseph Grew who was in turn replaced by James F. Byrnes as secretary of state, Henry Stimson was replaced by Robert Patterson as secretary of war, General George C. Marshall was replaced by General Dwight D. Eisenhower as army chief of staff, and Admiral Ernest J. King was replaced by Admiral Chester W. Nimitz as chief of naval operations.

9. Ibid., 104.

10. Poole, "From Conciliation to Containment," 13–15. See also Norman A. Graebner, Richard Dean Burns, and Joseph M. Siracusa, *America and the Cold War, 1941–1991: A Realist Interpretation* (Santa Barbara: Praeger, 2010), 106; and Bohlen, *Witness to History*, especially 235, 249–52, and 261.

11. Condit, *1947–1949* (1979 ed.), 284–86. House writes that conflict within the Truman administration in 1947, as well as within the ACC and the Council of Foreign Ministers created a "diplomatic deadlock" that precluded coherent guidance and prompted military leaders to make numerous decisions on their own. House, *Military History*, 115.

12. Freedman, *Evolution of Nuclear Strategy*, 48.

13. At the end of 1945, only forty-six B-29 bombers were configured to deliver an atomic bomb, but there were fewer bombs and not enough ground crews trained to assemble them. House, *Military History*, 78–82. Rosenberg gives the numbers of atomic bombs for the end of 1945: 2, July 1946: 9, July 1947: 13, July 1948: 50. All were Mark 3 "Fat Man" implosion bombs, were disassembled and required 39 men and two days to assemble, and could only be carried in specially configured B-29 bombers. Rosenberg, "Origins of Overkill," 13–14.

14. Freedman, *Evolution of Nuclear Strategy*, 51–52; and Condit, *1947–1949*, 283–84.

15. Condit, *1947–1949*, 285–87.

16. Condit, *1947–1949* (1979 ed.), 291–92.

17. Ibid., 295–96.

18. Ibid., 287–89, 294; and Freedman, *Evolution of Nuclear Strategy*, 52.

19. By 31 December 1949, the ever-decreasing size of the US Army left it with fewer troops (638,824) than on 30 June 1947 (683,837). Condit, *1947–1949*, Appendix 1, 301. In fact, HALFMOON and OFFTACKLE and the previous plans represented a "trip-wire" strategy in which, as Abenheim writes, the "*ultima ratio* rested in the B-29 and B-36 bombers of the Strategic Air Command." Abenheim, *Reforging the Iron Cross*, 42.

20. Trachtenberg, *A Constructed Peace*, 100–101. Once the Soviet Union had acquired a number of atomic bombs, this option , staging a "return"—a Normandy-like invasion of the European continent—was no longer open. The mass of troops and ships needed for such an assault would have made an excellent atomic target and would have thus been unthinkable after 1949. Thanks to Professor Jon Sumida, University of Maryland, for this insight.

21. Letter to Senator Robert A. Taft from Forrest Davis [representative of Secretary of War Robert Patterson], 29 January 1947, RG 319, Records of the Army Staff, Plans and Ops Division Decimal File 1946–48, P&O 091 Germany (Section I) (Cases 1-20), NARA.

22. US Department of State, "United States Assistance to Other Countries from the Standpoint of National Security," *Foreign Relations of the United States, 1947*, 1:740.

23. Coordination of United States – West European Military Resources to Counter Soviet Communism, TS Staff Study for the Joint Strategic Planning Committee, 2nd draft, 1948, RG 218, Entry UD7, 092 Geographic Files – Western Europe, 1948–1950, Sec 1, NARA.

24. For Western Union objectives, see Greiner, "Defense of Western Europe," 151. For JSSC thoughts, see Report by the Joint Strategic Survey Committee (on its own initiative) to the Joint Chiefs of Staff on Strategy, 5 April 1948, RG 218, Entry UD7, 092 Geographic Files – Western Europe, 1948–1950, Sec 1, NARA.

25. JCS 1811/12, 1 December 1947, Memorandum by the Chief of Staff, United States Army to the Joint Chiefs of Staff on the Military Implications of an Early Withdrawal of Occupation Forces from Germany, RG 218, Entry UD4, Geographic Files 1946–1947, 092 Germany, Sect. 19, NARA.

26. JSPC 876, 21 April 1948, United States Military Alliance, NARA.

27. JSM-496, 17 April 1948, RG 218, Records of the Joint Chiefs of Staff, Geographic File, 092 Western Europe, 1948–1950, Box 89, NARA.

28. JSPC 876, 21 April 1948, United States Military Alliance, NARA. See also JSPC 880, 22 April 1948, Policy Governing the Extent and Nature of Military

Planning to be Discussed with Representatives of France and Benelux, RG 218, Entry UD7, Geographic Files, 092 Western Europe, Sect. 2, NARA.

29. JSPC 877/4, 15 May 1948, Planners Conference, RG 218, Entry UD7, Geographic Files, 092 Western Europe, Sect. 2, NARA.

30. As late as July 1950, there were only two combat-ready US divisions on the continent and they were in West Germany. Walter S. Poole, *1950–1952*, vol. 4 of *History of the Joint Chiefs of Staff: The Joint Chiefs of Staff and National Policy* (Washington, DC: Office of Joint History, 1998), 187.

31. As an aside, it should be noted that on 20 March 1948, in response to the creation of the Brussels Treaty Organization three days earlier, the USSR removed Marshal Sokolovsky from the ACC, effectively ending the wartime Four-Power Alliance. Winkler, *1933–1990*, 120.

32. The text of General Wedemeyer's study (Dept of Army, P&O, Study, 19 March 1948, RG 59, Central Decimal Files, File 840.00, Box 5651) is dated 19 March 1949 and the JCS version of that paper is dated 18 March 1948. I am unable to account for the discrepancy in the dates of the two papers but it is obvious that the JCS paper was derived from General Wedemeyer's staff study. It appears from the available archival documentation that this study became JSPC 876, 21 April 1948, United States Military Alliance, NARA. Emphasis added.

33. US Department of State, "NSC 9: The Position of the United States with Respect to Support for Western Union and Other Related Free Countries," *Foreign Relations of the United States, 1948*, 3:86. NSC 9 was based on an earlier policy planning staff paper (PPS 27/1, 23 March 1948) that recommended the US conclude a mutual defense agreement under the UN charter, which was itself based on the Truman Doctrine of supporting free nations. NSC 9 was, thus, a precursor to the North Atlantic Treaty.

34. JCS 1868/4, 1 May 1948, RG 218, Records of the Joint Chiefs of Staff, Geographic File, 092 Western Europe, 1948–50, Box 89, NARA.

35. JCS 1868/6, 19 May 1948, Memorandum by the Chief of Naval Operations to the Joint Chiefs of Staff on the Position of the United States with Respect to Support for Western Union and other Free Countries, RG 218, Records of the Joint Chiefs of Staff, Geographic File, 092 Western Europe, 1948–50, Box 89, Sect. 2, NARA. See also Martin, "American Decision to Rearm," 648.

36. The Vandenberg Resolution (SR 239) was a resolution framed by Senator Arthur H. Vandenberg (R-MI), then chairman of the Senate Foreign Relations Committee, and Lovett that endorsed "association of the United States, by constitutional process, with such regional and other collective arrangements as are based on continuous and effective self-help and mutual aid, and as affect its national security." Leffler, *Preponderance of Power*, 211–12. See also US Department

of State, "Senate Resolution 239 (Vandenberg Resolution), June 11, 1948," in *Foreign Relations of the United States, 1948*, 3:135–36 for the wording of the resolution; and US Department of State, "NSC 9/3: The Position of the United States with Respect to Support for Western Union and Other Related Free Countries," *Foreign Relations of the United States, 1948*, 3:141n.

37. DELWU 2, 22 July 1948, RG 218, Chairman's File, Admiral Leahy 1942–1948, Box 5, Folder: Western Union, July–Oct 1948, NARA. The Western Union members were: Air Vice Marshall Hudleston (UK), Major General Ely (FR), Major General DeLeval (BE), Major General Doorman (NL), and Major Albrecht (LU).

38. (TS) 091752Z NCR 17175, 9 July 1948, RG 218, Chairman's File, Admiral Leahy 1942–1948, Box 5, Folder: Western Union, Jul–Oct 1948, NARA. DELWU 4, 23 July 1948, RG 218, Box 5, NARA indicated that Canada would also participate as a nonmember.

39. Condit, *1947–1949* (1979 ed.), 366–67. See also London NIACT 3216, 15 July 1948, RG 59, Central Decimal File, File 840.00, Box 5649, NARA. The acceptance of the invitation to participate in the Western Union Military Committee can be found in Department of State Outgoing Telegram 2765, 16 July 1948, RG 59, Box 5649, NARA.

40. Paris 3646, 29 June 1948, RG 218, Chairman's File, Admiral Leahy 1942–1948, Box 6, Folder: Western Union, 1948, NARA.

41. Memorandum of Conversation, General Wedemeyer-Mr. Draper, 26 June 1948, RG 218, Chairman's File, Admiral Leahy 1942–1948, Box 6, Folder: Western Union, 1948, NARA.

42. Teitgen's request for a guarantee is due to the fact that France is a nation governed by Roman law, making written and signed guarantees of extreme importance.

43. (TS) L-1370, 11 July 1948, RG 218, Chairman's File, Admiral Leahy 1942–1948, Box 5, Folder: Western Union, July–Oct 1948, NARA. A 17 June report by the British Joint Services Mission on the result of talks with the US JCS confirmed the British determination to hold the Rhine but stated that the United States planned withdrawal to the Pyrenees in order to retain a foothold on the continent. JSM-496, 17 June 1948, RG 218, Joint Chiefs of Staff, Geographic Files, 092 Western Europe, Box 89, NARA.

44. (TS) WAR 86482, 27 July 1948, RG 218, Chairman's File, Admiral Leahy 1942–1948, Box 5, Folder: Western Union, July–Oct 1948, NARA.

45. DELWU 9, 31 July 1948, RG 218, Chairman's File, Admiral Leahy 1942–1948, Box 5, Folder: Western Union, July–Oct 1948, NARA.

46. Enclosure to SM10699, 16 August 1948, Memorandum for Admirals Leahy and Denfield and Generals Bradley and Vandenberg,; and attachment to SM

10764, 24 August 1948, Memorandum for the JCS Chiefs of Staff, both in RG 218, Chairman's File, Admiral Leahy 1942–1948, Box 6, NARA.

47. Newport Meeting Minutes, 20–22 August 1948, RG 335, Undersecretary of the Army (Draper/Voorhees) Decimal File, Box 10, NARA.

48. The authorization was contained in WAR 85967, 16 July 1948, RG 218, Chairman's File, Admiral Leahy 1942–1948, Box 6, Folder: Germany, NARA. See also the attachment to Memorandum for the JCS, Command Structure for Western Europe, 30 September 1948, RG 218, Box 6, Folder: Germany, NARA.

49. WARX 89860, 24 September 1948, RG 218, Chairman's File, Admiral Leahy 1942–1948, Box 5, Folder: Western Union, July–Oct 1948, NARA.

50. See, for example, WARX 81100, 7 December 1948, RG 218, Chairman's File, Admiral Leahy 1942–1948, Box 5, Folder: Western Union, July–Oct 1948, NARA.

51. (TS) DELWU 70, 6 October 1948; and DELWU 72, 7 October 1948, both in RG 218, Chairman's File, Admiral Leahy 1942–1948, Box 5, Folder: Western Union, July–Oct 1948, NARA.

52. For the acceptance of the invitations to participate in the Western Union Chiefs of Staff and Equipment and Armament Committees, see: London, 4525, 15 October 1948; Letter, Robert E. Lovett and James Forrestal, 22 October 1948, RG 59, Box 5649, NARA; Letter, Robert E. Lovett and James Forrestal, 27 October 1948; Letter, Robert E. Lovett and James Forrestal, 16 November 1948; Letter, Robert E. Lovett and James Forrestal, 18 December 1948; Letter, Robert E. Lovett and James Forrestal, 4 January 1949; and Department of State Outgoing Telegram 4741, 23 December 1948, all in RG 59, Central Decimal Files, File 840.00, Box 5649, NARA. At the first meeting of the Chiefs of Staff Committee, General Jean de Lattre de Tassigny said, "It is an indication of courage and an act of faith in itself that the CinC's Committee are meeting to plan a defense for which they have not the means." DELWU 75, 13 October 1948, RG 218, Geographic File, 092 Western Europe, Box 91, NARA.

53. (TS) DELWU 94, 1 November 1948, RG 218, Chairman's File, Admiral Leahy 1942–1948, Box 5, Folder: Western Union, Nov–Dec 1948, NARA.

54. These assumptions and the following are found in The Defense of Western Europe, 10th draft, 27 September 1948, RG 335, Records of the Undersecretary of the Army (Draper/Voorhees), Decimal Files, 1947–1950, Box 10, NARA.

55. A breakdown of these 78 divisions is as follows: United Kingdom: 12, France: 30, Belgium and Luxembourg: 7, United States in W. Germany: 1½, Switzerland: 5, Italy: 10, Spain: 5, and United States in Austria and Trieste: ½. Combined, this would make 16 armored divisions, 52 infantry divisions, 4 airborne divisions, and 6 reinforced mountain divisions.

56. The total buildup was predicted to be seventy divisions by 1 January 1949, seventy-six divisions by 1 January 1950, eighty divisions by 1 January 1951, eighty-six divisions by 1 January 1952, and finally ninety-six divisions by 1 January 1953. This is very close to the Lisbon Force Goals of ninety-two divisions set at the 1952 NATO summit in Portugal.

57. The Western Union report is C.O.S.(48) 200 (0), "Short Term Strategic Aims in Europe at the Outbreak of War," 8 September 1948, RG 218, Joint Chiefs of Staff, Geographic File 092 Western Europe, 1948–50, Box 90, NARA. See also: JSPC Memorandum to General Gruenther, 1 November 1948; and A.B.A.I.S.5 (American-British Agreed Intelligence), 9 November 1948, both in RG 218, Joint Chiefs of Staff, Geographic File 092 Western Europe, 1948–50, Box 90, NARA. It should be noted, however, that in June 1948, three months after he became chairman of the Western Union Commanders-in-Chief Committee, Field Marshall Montgomery told British foreign minister Bevin that West Germany had to be included in the Western Union. House, *Military History*, 210

58. "Things to Do on Trip," 9 December 1948, RG 335, Undersecretary of the Army (Draper/Voorhees) Decimal File 1947–50, Box 8, NARA.

59. Hodges, "Formula for Peace," 5–6. The three commissioners were the author General Hodges (US), Engineer General Etienne Paskiewcz (France), and Major General V. J. E. Westropp (UK). See also Marguerite Higgens, "Disarming of Germans Set Up," *New York Herald Tribune*, 31 December 1948; and RG 335, Undersecretary of the Army (Draper/Voorhees) Decimal File 1947–50, Box 8, Folder 334 Misc/MilSecBd, NARA.

60. Memorandum for Director, Plans and Operations Division, Subject: German Police Force for Western Zones, 26 October 1948; and Letter, Personal to Clay from SAOUS, 10 December 1948, both in RG 335, Undersecretary of the Army (Draper/Voorhees) Decimal File 1947–50, Box 10, NARA.

61. The first members of NATO were Belgium, Canada, Denmark, France, Iceland, Italy, Luxembourg, the Netherlands, Norway, Portugal, the United Kingdom, and the United States. Ismay, *First Five Years*, 11.

62. Schwartz, *America's Germany*, 113.

63. Paul Nitze, "The Development of NSC 68," *International Security* 4, no. 4 (1980): 171.

64. Poole, *1950–1952* (1980 ed.), 180–83. See, for example, the NATO organizational chart as of December 1949 in Ismay, *First Five Years*, 26. NATO really did not become an "organization" until it was reorganized in 1951.

65. (TS) SX 1498, 10 February 1949; and (TS) DELWU 65, 1 March 1949, both in RG 218, Chairman's File, Admiral Leahy 1942–1948, Box 5, NARA.

66. Schwartz, *America's Germany,* 115–16. For an excellent account of Congress, MDAP, and German rearmament, see Birtle, *Rearming the Phoenix.*

67. Condit, *1947–1949* (1979 ed.), 373.

68. 3 August 1949, Agenda for Discussion with British Chief of Staff, RG 218, Central Decimal Files, Box 132, Folder CCS 337 (7-22-48) S. 1, NARA.

69. 4 Oct 49-DM-205, U.S.-UK-Canadian Planning Matters; and 5 October 1949, Meeting between CJCS Bradley and Air Marshall Lord Tedder, both in RG 218, Central Decimal Files, Box 132, Folder CCS 337 (7-22-48) S. 1, NARA. See also Poole, *1950–1952* (1980 ed.), 162–63.

70. For two of the exceptions, see Greiner, "Defense of Western Europe," 150–58; and Oliver Palkowitsch, "Westliche Verteidigungsstrategie," *Militärgeschichte* Heft 4 (2005): 18–21.

71. Tab A, "U.S. Policy Respecting the Disarmament and Demilitarization of the Federal German Republic," RG 319, Army - Operations Decimal File 1950–1951, Box 20, NARA.

72. Ibid.

73. Ironically, although much effort was put into assuring the Allies that former Nazis would not become part of the new German military, this never became a concern for either the US or British military staffs. The Germans also set up a personnel screening board (*Personalgutachterausschuss*) and an acceptance organization (*Annahme Organization*) to vet applicants. Corum, "Founding of the Bundeswehr," 45–48. See also John L. Sutton, "The Personal Screening Committee and the Parliamentary Control of West German Armed Forces," *Journal of Central European Affairs* 19 (January 1960): 389–401.

74. Tab A, "Respecting the Disarmament and Demilitarization," NARA.

75. Staff Study, "Possible Contributions by Germany to Her Own Security," 7 April 1950, G-3/Plans Division/International Branch, RG 319, Assistant Chief of Staff, G-3, Decimal File, 1950–1951, Box 94, NARA.

76. Memo, JSSC to Director, Joint Staff, 18 April 1950, RG 218, Central Decimal Files, Box 134, NARA.

77. "Tab A, Comment on Modification of U.S. Policy with Respect to German Disarmament," 21 April 1950, RG 218, Central Decimal Files, 1950–1951, Box 20, NARA.

78. Enclosure A of JCS 2124/2, 10 May 1950, RG 319, Assistant Chief of Staff/G-3, Operations, Records Section, Decimal File, March 1950–51, Box 94, NARA. Emphasis added.

79. Ibid. These previously expressed views referred to the JCS's recommendations to rearm Germany and modify export controls that advantaged Soviet bloc war matériel that had been voiced in responses to several Secretary of Defense memoranda.

80. Memo to the Chief of Staff, U.S. Army, Subject: The Problem of Germany (JCS 2124/2), 10 May 1950, RG 319, Assistant Chief of Staff/G-3, Operations, Records Section, Decimal File, March 1950–51, Box 94, (Sec. I-C) (Book I) (Case II Only), NARA.

81. NSC 71, 8 June 1950, PSF: Subject File, National Security Council - Meetings File, Box 180, HSTL. The JCS had urged approval of the federal police force on 17 May 1950.

82. Memorandum for Rear Admiral A. C. Davis, 30 June 1950, RG 218, Chairman's File, General Bradley 1949–53, Box 1.

83. Enclosure A of JCS 2124/2, 10 May 1950, NARA.

84. NSC 71/1, July 3, 1950, can be found in either RG 218, Geographic File 1948-50, 092 Germany (5-4-49) Sec. 1-4) Box 25 or RG 319, Army Operations, General Decimal File 1950–1951, 091. Germany, Box 21, NARA. Kennan was never happy with the idea of rearming West Germany, even after it was admitted to NATO. Kennan, *1950–1963*, 238.

85. Memorandum for Mr. Jessup, 14 June 1950, NARA.

86. Ibid.

87. Memorandum for the Secretary of Defense, Subject: U.S. Policy toward Germany (NSC 71, NSC 71/1), 6 July 1950, RG 319, Army Operations, General Decimal File 1950–1951, 091. Germany, Box 22, NARA.

88. Letter, General Handy to General Collins, 19 July 1950, RG 319, Army Operations, General Decimal File 1950–1951, From 091. France to 091. Germany, Box 20, NARA.

89. Ibid.

90. Ibid. The attachment shows that there were 8,075 industrial police and 13,456 labor service units. It also indicates that action was underway to arm all 5,375 technical service personnel (a subset of the labor service) with carbines, except those assigned medical and chaplain duties.

91. Note, General Handy to General Collins, 19 July 1950, RG 319, Army Operations, General Decimal File 1950–1951, From 091. France to 091. Germany, Box 20, NARA. The first of the three cables mentioned contains the gist of a report to McCloy and the French high commissioner François-Poncet from the British high commissioner Kirkpatrick of a discussion he had with Chancellor Adenauer regarding the need for some form of defensive capability for West Germany. Kirkpatrick raised the issue of an effective auxiliary force and François-Poncet responded that German service troops (labor service) integrated with the US Army could be increased and trained to fight in an emergency.

92. Letter, Colonel Byroade to General J. Lawton Collins, 20 July 1950, RG 319, Army Operations, General Decimal File 1950–1951, From 091. France to 091. Germany, Box 20, NARA.

93. JCS 2124/9, 20 July 1950, RG 319, Army Operations, General Decimal File 1950–1951, 091, Germany, Box 21, NARA. This is a further rendition of the original "Problem of Germany."

94. Ibid.

95. Ibid.

96. Memorandum for General Gruenther, Subject: Discussion with Col Byroade, 25 July 1950, NARA.

97. Ibid.

98. JCS 2124/11, 27 July 1950, RG 319, Army Operations, General Decimal File 1950–1951, 091, Germany, Box 21, NARA. The only available copy of this document has pencil markings on the left and right sides indicating that additional changes may have been made to subparagraphs b and c, so that they would have read

b.   The United States Government should immediately press for a controlled rearmament of Western Germany and for the organization of an adequate federal police force *of at least 25,000 men* for Western Germany as the initial phase of its rearmament program; and

c.   The question at this time is not one of whether we should risk the success of our political objectives vis-à-vis Western Germany, but rather whether or not we can afford to jeopardize the security of the United States *and of Western Europe* by not utilizing all of the forces that are available to us.

99. Memorandum for: General Gruenther, Subject: Rearmament of Western Germany, 1 August 1950, RG 319, Army - Operations, General Decimal File 1950–1951, Box 21, 091-Germany (Sect. 1C)(Book 1)(Case 12), NARA. In a handwritten note dated 5 August, on the bottom of the first page of the memo, General Gruenther wrote to General Schuyler, "In view of your current discussions with State I assume you will notify me when it is again appropriate to raise this subject with JCS."

100. Ibid.

101. Memorandum for General Schuyler, Subject: Record of Conference Attended, 5 August 1950, RG 319, Army - Operations, General Decimal File 1950–1951, Box 21, 091-Germany (Sect. 1C)(Book 1)(Case 12), NARA.

102. Byroade's concept for a European army, worked out with McCloy, is discussed in chapter 2, this book. A comparison of his plan and the G-3 plan was attached to Memorandum for General Gruenther, Subject: Rearmament

of Germany, 10 August 1950, RG 319, Army - Operations, General Decimal File 1950–1951, Box 21, 091-Germany (Sect. 1C)(Book II)(Case 12), NARA, stamped "NOT USED."

103. Letter, General Thomas T. Handy, Commander in Chief, EUCOM to General J. Lawton Collins, Chief of Staff, U.S. Army, 9 August 1950, RG 319, Army - Operations, General Decimal File 1950–1951, Box 22, 091-Germany, NARA.

104. Ibid.

105. Memorandum for Record, Subject: Conversations with State Department on German Rearmament, 10 August 1950, RG 319, Army - Operations, General Decimal File 1950–1951, Box 22, 091-Germany, NARA.

106. Ibid.

107. Enclosure to JCS 2124/12, 15 August 1950, RG 319, Army - Operations, General Decimal File 1950–1951, Box 21, 091-Germany, (Sect IC)(Book II)(Case12), NARA.

108. The paper was received by Major General James H. Burns, assistant to the secretary of defense for foreign military affairs, and sent to the JCS as Annex to Appendix 'A,' Note by the Secretaries to the Joint Chiefs of Staff on Establishment of a European Defense Force, JCS 2124/13, 18 August 1950, RG 319, Army - Operations, General Decimal File 1950–1951, Box 21, 091-Germany, NARA. Secretary of Defense Johnson's initial 17 August response was included in this paper but can also be found in RG 218, Geographic File, 1948–1950, 092 Germany (5-4-49) Sec. 1-4, Box 25, NARA.

109. Annex to Appendix 'A,' Note by the Secretaries, JCS 2124/13, 18 August 1950, NARA.

110. Ibid.

111. JCS 2124/16, 26 August 1950, 151, RG 218, Geographic File, 1948–1950, 092 Germany (5-4-49) Sec. 1-4, Box 25, NARA. Italics added to indicate the addition.

112. JCS 2124/11, 27 July 1950, NARA.

113. Memorandum for the Chief of Staff, U.S. Army, Subject: Identical Letters from the President to the Secretaries of State and Defense, on the U.S. Position with Respect to the Defense of Europe and the Nature of the Contribution by Germany to this Defense (SM 2012-50), 28 August 1950, RG 319, Army - Operations, General Decimal File 1950–1951, Box 20, 091-Germany, NARA.

114. JCS 2124/18, 1 September 1950, RG 319, Army - Operations, General Decimal File 1950–1951, Box 21, 091-Germany, (Sect IC)(Book II)(Case 12), NARA.

115. Ibid.

116. Appendix to JCS 2124/18, 1 September 1950, NARA.

117. Ibid.

118. JCS 2124/20, 6 September 1050, RG 218, Geographic File 1948–1950, 092 Germany (5-4-49) Sec. 1-4, Box 25, NARA.

Chapter 4: From EDF to EDC to NATO

1. Doris M. Condit, *The Test of War, 1950–1953*, vol. 2, *History of the Office of the Secretary of Defense* (Washington, DC: Historical Office, Office of the Secretary of Defense, 1988), 319. This response subsequently became NSC 82.

2. Ibid. See also JCS 2116/30, 8 September 1950, RG 319, Army - Operations, General Decimal File 1950–1951, Box 21, 091-Germany, (Sect IC)(Book III) (Case 12), NARA.

3. "Statement by the President," 9 September 1950, George Elsey Papers, Folder: Harry S. Truman, Foreign Relations—Western European Defense, Box 65, HSTL. See also Condit, *Test of War*, 320.

4. Acheson, *Present at the Creation*, 568–71. See also Condit, *1947–1949*, 200–203; Martin, "American Decision to Rearm," 655–60; Schwartz, "'Skeleton Key,'" 375–77; and Trachtenberg and Gehrz, "America, Europe, and German Rearmament," 11–16.

5. Among those who have covered these meetings and the proceedings of the Pleven Plan and EDC are: McGeehan, *German Rearmament Question*; Large, *Germans to the Front*; Schwartz, *America's Germany*; McAllister, *No Exit*; Birtle, *Rearming the Phoenix*; Trachtenberg, *A Constructed Peace*; and Fursdon, *European Defense Community*, to name just a few.

6. US Department of State, "The Secretary of State to the Embassy in France," *Foreign Relations of the United States, 1950*, 3:261. The text of the cable (Telegram 1124) was addressed solely to Ambassador Bruce in Paris. A footnote states that a similar eyes-only cable (Telegram 1197) was also sent to Ambassador Douglas in London.

7. McMahon, *American World Order*, 135.

8. Personal Message from Mr. Bevin to Mr. Acheson, 5 September 1950, RG 59, Decimal File 1950–1954, Box 3428, NARA. In this paper, Bevin stated that the British chiefs of staff had recommended that the German contribution consist of local naval forces, a balanced army of 20 divisions with a reserve of 10 divisions, a tactical air force of 1,100 aircraft, an air defense force of 1,000 fighters and a "substantial anti-aircraft force equipped with guided weapons."

9. Mawby, *Containing Germany*, 38. The British chiefs had proposed twenty German divisions, a number previously rejected. Bevin and the Foreign Ministry insisted that the expanded gendarmerie was needed for disturbances and sabotage.

10. Mr. Bevin to Mr. Acheson, 5 September 1950, NARA.

11. September Foreign Ministers Meeting, Communiqué on Germany, SFM D 4/6, 8 September 1950, RG 43 Records of the Council of Foreign Ministers, Box 48, NARA.

12. Poole, *1950–1952* (1980 ed.), 209–10. The JCS reaction to Marshall's attempts to relax the criteria was quite clear: German participation was absolutely essential, otherwise the US contribution to European defense should be reexamined.

13. Minutes of the Tripartite Meeting, 12 September 1950 (Dean Acheson), Memos of Conversation (Sept. 1949–Sept. 1950), Lot 53D444, Box 13, NARA.

14. SECTO 2, 12 September, 11:59 PM, RG 43, Records of the Council of Foreign Ministers, Box 50, NARA.

15. SECTO 8, 14 September, 10:32 AM, Papers of Harry S. Truman, PSF: Subject File, 1940–1953, Conferences File, Box 141, HSTL.

16. General Hays wrote McCloy that he had passed McCloy's message to Adenauer, who was grateful for the information regarding the communiqué but unhappy with statements allegedly made by Schuman that Germany would not be permitted combat troops but would work as auxiliaries such as labor forces and truck drivers. Adenauer stood by his secret offer to contribute to the European Defense Force but preferred that the Conference of Foreign Ministers put that question to the Federal Republic to put him in a stronger position vis-à-vis the Bundestag. See Bonn 149 and Bonn 150, 17 September 1950, both in RG 43, Records of the Council of Foreign Ministers, Box 50, NARA.

17. Minutes of the Meeting of the Three Foreign Ministers, New York, 14 September 1950, RG 59, Records of the Executive Secretariat (Dean Acheson), lot53D444, Box 13, NARA.

18. SECTO 13, 14 September 1950, 12:15 AM, RG 43, Records of the Council of Foreign Ministers, Box 50, NARA. Acheson stated that he was dictating the cable himself so that the president would know precisely what Acheson was thinking and advise him on any points the president disagreed with. At Acheson's private meeting with Bevin on 15 September, Bevin agreed to German participation but advised that some time should lapse before putting the decision into effect. Private Meeting with Mr. Bevin, 2:40 PM, September 15, 1950, RG 59 – General Records of the Department of State, Records of the Executive Secretariat (Dean Acheson), Lot 53D444, Box 13, NARA.

19. Verbatim Record No. 2, C5-VR/2 (Part), North Atlantic Council, Fifth Session, New York, 15 September 1950, RG 43, Records of the Council of Foreign Ministers, Box 50, NARA. See also SECTO 18, 16 September 1950, Papers of Harry S. Truman, PSF: subject File 1940–1953, Conference Files, Box 141, HSTL.

20. Verbatim Record No. 2, C5-VR/2 (Part), North Atlantic Council, Fifth Session, New York, 15th September 1950, RG 43, Records of the Council of Foreign Ministers, Box 50, NARA.

21. Memo for Admiral Robbins, 16 September 1950, RG 319, Army Operations, General Decimal File, 1950–1951, Box 22, NARA.

22. Bolte to CINCEUR, Routine Cable, 19 September 1950, RG 319 Army - Operations, General Decimal File, 1950–1951, Box 20, NARA.

23. Memorandum for the Secretary of Defense, CJCS 091 Germany, 21 September 1950, RG 218, Chairman's File, General Bradley, 1949–1953, Box 01, NARA.

24. Memorandum for General Marshall, 21 September 1950, RG 218, Chairman's File, General Bradley, 1949–1953, Box 01, NARA. The steps suggested in the second memo were approved on 23 September 1950. USDEL Minutes 3, Third Special Meeting of the Foreign and Defense Ministers of France, the United Kingdom, and the United States, New York, 23 September 1950, 10:00 AM, RG 43, Records of International Conferences, Commissions and Expositions, Records of the Council of Foreign Ministers, Box 48, NARA. It was also sent out as SECTO 45, 23 September 1950, RG 218, Records of the U.S. Joint Chiefs of Staff, Geographic File 1948–50, Box 25, NARA. On 27 September, McCloy cabled Acheson to express his displeasure that German Länder police would have armored motorized and engineer units. This, to him, was a halfway measure that constituted the nucleus of a German army. It compromised propaganda against the East and played in to the hands of those who wished to avoid any definite alignment with the West, such as Gustav Heineman, Ulrich Noack, and Pastor Martin Niemoller. RG 218, Records of the U.S. Joint Chiefs of Staff, Geographic File, 1948–50, Box 25, NARA.

25. Memorandum to Mr. Spofford, Safeguards on German Contribution, 22 September 1950, RG 59, Department of State Decimal Files, 762A.5/9-2250, Box 3896, NARA.

26. Ibid.

27. US Department of State, "The Ambassador in France (Bruce) to the Secretary of State," *Foreign Relations of the United States, 1950*, 3:337–38. It should be noted that Defense Minister Jules Moch, whose son had been garroted by the Nazis, threatened to resign and bring down the government if Germans were allowed to participate in the defense of Western Europe. Carter, *Forging the Shield*, 177. Mayne writes that Moch, along with other Frenchmen, wondered if the United States actually welcomed the Korean War as a pretext to push Europe and Germany toward rearmament. Mayne, *Recovery of Europe*, 239.

28. "Integrated Force under Centralized Command to Defend Western Europe," *Department of State Bulletin* 23 (9 October 1950): 588. See also Ismay, *First Five Years*, 33.

29. Memorandum for ACS/G-3, 28 September 1950, RG 319, Army Operations , General Decimal Files, 1950–51, Box 21, 091 Germany (Sect. i-C)(Book III)(Case 12), NARA.

30. Letter, General Burns to Admiral Davis, 2 October 1950, RG 218, Geographic File, 1948–50, 092 Germany (5-4-49) Sec. 1-4, Box 25, NARA.

31. TS Letter, Henry A. Byroade to the Secretary, 9 October 1950, RG 59, Decimal File, 1950–54, File 762A.5/10-750, Box 3896, NARA.

32. Ibid.

33. "Notes Growing Out of My Talk with Mr. Lovett," 10 October 1950, RG59, Records of the Department of State, Records of the Bureau of European Affairs, Subject Files Relating to European Defense Arrangements, 1948–1954, Lot File 55D258, Box 4, NARA.

34. Letter, Major General Kohler to General Gruenther, 4 October 1950, Gruenther Papers, TS Correspondence (2), HSTL

35. Tom Connally, "Reviewing American Foreign Policy since 1945," *Department of State Bulletin* 23 (9 October 1950): 564.

36. The McCloy cable is Frankfurt 2919, 8 October 1950, RG 218, Geographic File 1948–50, Box 25, NARA.

37. Memorandum of Conversation, Participation of Germany in European Defense Force, 11 October 1950, RG 218, Geographic File 1948–50, Box 25, NARA.

38. The Bevin-Schuman letter is an attachment to ODM-1-2, RG 218, Geographic File 1948-50, Box 25, NARA. What is of interest in the Bevin-Schuman letter is Bevin's statement that he did not accept German participation in the integrated force with any more enthusiasm than France. His attitude, he stated, reflected that of the Cabinet. That said, he did admit that Western Europe was defenseless and that a defense line in Germany meant it was "unavoidable that Germany must play a part." He wrote, "It is certain that we shall not get the contribution from the U.S.A., which is absolutely essential for the defence of Europe unless we are prepared to accept that conclusion." He concluded that they both had "a duty to ensure the immediate defence of Western Europe" and hoped that France would "be persuaded to agree" that Europe could not be defended from the USSR "without acceptance of the principles that German units should be incorporated in the integrated force."

39. SX 2848, 11 October 1950, RG 319, Army - Operations, General Decimal File, 1950–1951, Box 20, NARA.

40. JCS 2124/24, 12 October 1950, Report by the Joint Strategic Plans Committee on German Contribution to an Integrated Defense, RG 319, Army - Operations, General Decimal File, 1950–1951, Box 21, NARA. JCS 2124/24 was approved as amended and the memorandum for the secretary of defense was forwarded separately on 13 October 1950. The recommendation to the NAC was submitted as ODM - 1/3 (Final), 18 October 1950, RG 218, Geographic File, 1948–50, 092 Germany (5-4-49) Sec. 1-4, Box 25, NARA. 'Bolte also wrote Collins and recommended against raising the issue of authorizing German tactical aviation at the October NATO defense ministers meeting. Bolte argued that every effort should be expended to secure French agreement to the contribution of German ground forces. Memorandum for the Army Chief of Staff, German Contribution to an Integrated Defense, 13 October 1950, RG 319, Army - Operations, General Decimal File, 1950–1951, 091 Germany (Sect I-C)(Book III) (Case 12), Box 20, NARA.

41. Ismay, *First Five Years*, 33. For an interesting perspective on the birth of the Pleven Plan, as the French plan for the European army was first known, see Jean Monnet, *Memoirs*, trans. Richard Mayne (Garden City: Doubleday & Company, 1978), 345–50. Additional information on the Pleven Plan can be found in Hitchcock, *France Restored*, 141–44; McGeehan, *German Rearmament Question*, 75–80; and Large, *Germans to the Front*, 91–95.

42. Pleven's proposal stated, "The contingents supplied by the participating States would be incorporated in the European Army *at the level of the smallest possible unit*." Monnet, *Memoirs*, 347. Italics in original.

43. According to notes written by Acheson for his Princeton seminars, the French Council of Ministers said, "The formation of German divisions or the establishment of a German ministry of defense would lead inevitably sooner or later to the reconstitution of a national army and in this way to the resurrection of German militarism." Dean G. Acheson Papers, Princeton Seminars File, 1953–1970, Section Towards SHAPE (Page 3), Box 78, HSTL.

44. Memorandum for General Marshall, 27 October 1950, RG 218, Chairman's File, General Bradley, 1949–52, 092.2 North Atlantic Treaty, Box 2, NARA.

45. Thomas A. Schwartz, "Eisenhower and the Germans," in *Eisenhower: A Centenary Assessment*, ed. Günter Bischof and Stephen E. Ambrose (Baton Rouge: Louisiana State University Press, 1995), 214.

46. Ismay, *First Five Years*, 34.

47. Poole, *1950–1952*, 211–12.

48. Memorandum for the Record, 30th and 31st October Meetings of the North Atlantic Defense Committee, 1 November 1950, RG 319, Army - Operations General Decimal File 1950–1951, 091 Germany, Box 22, NARA. The disagreement

lay in the fact that the US proposal was a military one that sought immediate action, while the French proposal was a political one that required time to solve the political issues before addressing the military issues. A few days later, on 6 November, Netherlands ambassador Von Reijan gave H. Freeman Matthews a paper written by Dutch prime minister Dirk Stikker in which he related that the French were unhappy with the United States regarding the September Foreign Ministers meeting, as Schuman was totally surprised and completely unprepared for discussion of German participation (Acheson had sent a cable to Ambassador Bruce in Paris to give to Schuman outlining his thoughts for the meeting around 9 September). Schuman was also upset that the United States had not taken impending French elections, in which the Pleven government's chances appeared uncertain, into consideration. French fear of a revived German militarism was such that no solution other than the French plan was conceivable. However, despite the opposition of the French defense minister, France was prepared to work out a formula. Stikker said that Schuman did not like the plan's final form—he was not a Federalist—but that he believed the French proposal regarding smaller units would not hinder negotiations. RG 59, Records of the Department of State, Records of the Bureau of European Affairs, Subject Files Relating to European Defense Arrangements, 1948–1954, Lot File 55D258, Box 4, NARA.

49. Bonn 284, 8 November 1950, RG 59, Department of State Decimal File 762.00/11-850, NARA.

50. G-4 Memorandum for the Chief of Staff, U.S. Army on JCS2124/25, 10 November 1950; JCS 2124/25, Decision on Logistics Aspects of German Rearmament, 15 November 1950; and unnumbered cable, G-3 (Bolte) to USCINCEUR, 17 November 1950, all in RG 319, Army - Operations General Decimal File, 091 Germany, 091-GE-TS (Sect 1-C)(Book IV)(Case 12), Box 21, NARA. A RCT is approximately five to six thousand men strong.

51. Summary of Telegrams, Western Europe, 10 November 1950, Papers of Harry S. Truman, PSF: Subject File, 1940–1953, Conferences File, Box 141, HSTL. President Truman wrote "approved" and put his initials next to the segment of the 10 November summary.

52. Summary of Telegrams, Western Europe, 20 November 1950, Papers of Harry S. Truman, PSF: Subject File, 1940–1953, Conferences File, Box 141, HSTL.

53. Memorandum for Chief of Staff, U.S. Army, Telecon 3 December 1950, Between State and Defense Representatives and Mr. Spofford, 4 December 1950, RG 319, Army - Operations General Decimal File, 091 Germany, 091-GE-TS (Sect 1-C)(Book V)(Case 12), Box 22, NARA.

54. Adenauer, *Memoirs, 1945–1953*, 280–81, 300–302. This "relaxation" of occupation controls was something Adenauer had been asking for and was addressed

in his memorandum on 29 August 1950. Ending the occupation would strengthen Adenauer against the opposing Social Democratic Party, but more importantly, would inform the West Germans that they were, in fact, free.

55. Enclosures A and B to JCS 2124/29, 4 December 1950, Report by the Joint Strategic Survey Committee on European Defense Arrangements including German Participation, RG 218, Geographic File 1948–1950, Box 26, NARA. Also enclosed was a personal letter from Acheson to Schuman in which Acheson pushed Spofford's compromise proposal, which sought to separate German participation from the creation of an integrated force and the buildup of the political entity sought in the Pleven Plan.

56. Meeting of the President and the Prime Minister, 3:30 M, 6 December 1950, in the Cabinet Room, Papers of Harry S. Truman, PSF: Subject File, 1940–1953, Box 142, HSTL. Minutes of this meeting can also be found in RG 43, Records of International Conferences, Commissions and Expositions, Records of the Council of Foreign Ministers, New York, Tripartite Meeting, September 1950, Box 52, Folder: US, UK, Washington, DC, 1950, US Minutes, NARA.

57. Memorandum of Telephone Call (Acheson to Lovett), 6 December 1950, Dean G. Acheson Papers, Secretary of State File, 1945–1972, Memoranda of Conversations File, 1949–1953, Box 68, HSTL.

58. Memorandum for the Chief of Staff, U.S. Army (Bolte to Collins), German Rearmament Developments 4–6 December, 7 December 1950, RG 319, Army - Operations General Decimal File, 091 Germany, 091-GE-TS (Sect 1-C) (Book V) (Case 12), Box 22, NARA. Some suggest that the US refusal to negotiate German issues with the USSR between 1949 and 1954 was to avoid having these negotiations present a platform for the Soviets to offer West Germany a settlement, such as unification in return for neutrality or, at a minimum, nonalignment with the West. What is forgotten, however, is that Adenauer, who saw West German salvation only in the west, would have refused such an offer. See Joseph B. Egan, "The Struggle for the Soul of Faust: The American Drive for German Rearmament 1950–1955" (PhD diss., University of Connecticut, 1985), 3.

59. Memorandum for the Chief of Staff, U.S. Army, Telecon, 8 December, with Mr. Spofford, RG 319, Army - Operations General Decimal File, 091 Germany, 091-GE-TS (Sect 1-C) (Book V) (Case 12), Box 22, NARA. Emphasis added.

60. Memorandum of Telephone Conversation with Under Secretary Lovett, 15 December 1950, Dean G. Acheson Papers, Secretary of State File, 1945–1972, Memoranda of Conversations File, 1949-1953, Box 68, HSTL.

61. RG 43, Records of International Conferences, Commissions and Expositions, Records of the Council of Foreign Ministers, Box 48, NARA; and Confidential Press Release, 18 December 1950, Papers of Harry S. Truman, PSF:

General File, 1945–1953, Box 102, HSTL. See also 6th Session of the NAT Council, Minutes of the 1st and 2nd Meetings, 18 December 1950; Brussels 983, 985, and 986, 18 December 1950; and Brussels 996 and 1002, 19 December 1950, all in RG 43, Records of International Conferences, Commissions and Expositions, Records of the Council of Foreign Ministers, New York, Tripartite Meeting, September 1950, Box 53, NARA. When Eisenhower left on his trip to Europe as the new SACEUR, he was instructed by Acheson to demonstrate American determination to build strength in Europe but also accept that the Allies must also do what is necessary. Beisner, *Life in the Cold War*, 453.

62. Briefing Notes for President at the 11 Dec NSC Meeting, 9 December 1950, RG 43, Records of International Conferences, Commissions and Expositions, Records of the Council of Foreign Ministers, Box 53, Folder: US, UK, Washington December 1950 Miscellaneous, folder 1 of 2, NARA.

63. NIE-17, "Probable Soviet Reactions to a Remilitarization of Western Germany," 27 December 1950, RG 263, Records of the Central Intelligence Agency, National Intelligence Estimates Concerning the Soviet Union, 1950–1961, Box 1, NARA.

64. Ibid.

65. The EDC concept officially came into being when its treaty was signed on 27 May 1952. It is not my intent, however, to retell the negotiations over the EDC that lasted almost four years before it was rejected by the French in August 1954.

66. Birtle *Rearming the Phoenix*, 91. For additional discussion regarding not wanting unwilling German contingents, see Onslow, "West German Rearmament," 483.

67. Schwartz, "Case of German Rearmament," 307; and Monnet, *Memoirs*, 358–59.

68. ALO 208, 18 July 1951, attachment to NSC 115, August 2, 1951, RG 273, Records of the National Security Council (NSC), Policy Papers 110-117, Entry 1, Box 15, NARA. It can also be found in US Department of State, "The Ambassador in France (Bruce) to the Secretary of State," in *Foreign Relations of the United States, 1951*, vol. 3, *European Security and the German Question*, part 1 (Washington, DC: US Government Printing Office, 1951): 838–39.

69. Fursdon, *European Defense Community*, 119. In a later letter to Secretary of Defense Marshall on 3 August, Eisenhower again stated that he was initially "firm in [his] refusal to get tied up in the project because it seemed, almost inherently, to include every kind of obstacle, difficulty, and fantastic notion that misguided humans could put together in one package." He also wrote that the "plan was not above suspicion that it may have been put forward in the certainty that it could not be achieved." Putting his hopes on the new French government, he

was shifting his beliefs, however, because he saw that (1) most of the governments involved were sincere in their efforts to develop the European Army; (2) a spectacular accomplishment was "vitally necessary" to get the whole security program moving and generate confidence in Europe and America; (3) the plan offered the only immediate hope, acceptable to other Europeans, of developing "the German strength that [was] vital"; and (4) there will be no progress toward European unity except through "specific programs of this kind." Attachment to Letter from Marshall to the President, 27 August, 3 August 1951, HSTL Student Research File, (B File) North Atlantic Treaty Organization, #34A, Box 1 of 2, HSTL.

70. NSC 115, 2 August 1951, RG 273, Records of the National Security Council (NSC), Policy Papers 110-117, Entry 1, Box 15, NARA.

71. Birtle, *Rearming the Phoenix*, 94.

72. Memorandum for the Chief of Staff, U.S. Army, Size of German Military Contribution to the Defense of Western Europe, 13 January 1951, RG 319, Army – Operations General Decimal file, 1950–1951, 091. Germany, Box 22, NARA. The figure of 195,000 was broken down as follows: 165,000 army (12 RCTs with support and service troops), 25,000 air force and 5,000 navy. Naval vessels were limited to mine, patrol, and harbor craft only.

73. Memorandum for the Chief of Staff, U.S. Army, Negotiations on German Military Contribution to the Defense of Western Europe, 12 January 1951, RG 319, Army - Operations General Decimal File, 1950–1951, 091 - Germany (TS) (Sect II)(Cases 21-40), Box 22, NARA; and Memorandum for the Chief of Staff, Size of German Military Contribution, 13 January 1951, NARA.

74. The limitations were part of NATO Document C6-D/1, 13 December 1950, and were sent in a memo to Bromley Smith at state by Ridgeway B. Knight, advisor to Ambassador Bruce, on 26 January 1951. Memorandum for Mr. Bromley Smith, Negative Limitations Concerning German Participation in the NATO Defense Structure for Western Europe, RG 59 – General Records of the Department of State, Bureau of European Affairs, Records Relating to the European Defense Community 1951–1954, Lot File 56D38, Box 34, NARA.

75. Bonn 468, 18 January 1951, RG 218, Geographic File 1948–1950, Box 26, NARA. This cable was also part of JCS 2124/33, 23 January 1951, RG 319 - Army Operations, General Decimal File 1950–1951, Box 23, 091- Germany (TS) (Section II-D)(Book I)(Case 38).

76. Enclosure B, JSPC 965/4, 1 February 1951, German Participation in European Defense Arrangements, RG 218, Geographic File 1948–1950, Box 26, NARA. This JSPC document was finalized and distributed as JCS 2124/40 on 15 February 1950 and the actual letter to the US representative on the standing committee was dispatched as SM-536-51, 28 February 1951, RG 319, Army

262 Operations, General Decimal File 1950–1951, Box 23, 091- Germany (TS) (Section II-D)(Book I)(Case 38), NARA. The JCS envisioned ten to fifteen German divisions maximum for implementation of the NATO Medium Term Defense Plan (App A to JCS 2124/24), but as divisions were forbidden during the transition period, JCS wanted ten to fifteen division equivalents by 1 July 1951 (ten division equivalents = thirty RCTs or "groupements," which in turn would comprise 13,000 men in an infantry RCT, 12,600 in an armored RCT, and 12,600 in a mechanized RCT). RG 319, Army Operations, General Decimal File 1950–1951, Box 23, 091- Germany (TS) (Section II-D)(Book I)(Case 38), NARA. At some point in late February or early March, however, the number of RCTs was reduced to 24. SM-678-51, 14 March 1951, Enclosure A to JCS 2124/43, 4 April 1951, RG 218, Geographic File 1951–53, Box 17.

77. Enclosure B, JSPC 965/4, 1 February 1951, NARA.

78. See, for example, the numerous memoranda of conversations with the foreign ministers of Belgium, the Netherlands, Luxembourg, and Great Britain found in Dean G. Acheson Papers, Secretary of State File, 1945–1972, Memoranda of Conversations File, 1949–1953, Box 71, HSTL.

79. G-3 Memo to Chief of Staff, Army, 21 August 1952, RG 319 - Army Operations, General Decimal File 1950–51, 091 Germany (TS), (Section II-D) (Case 30), Box 12, NARA. See also JSPC 956/24, 7 August 1952, RG 319 - Army Operations, Box 12, NARA.

80. North Atlantic Council, C9-D/19, Resolution on German Participation in Western Defense, 22 February 1952, RG59 – Records of the Department of State, Records of the Bureau of European Affairs, Subject Files Relating to European Defense Community, 1951–1954, Lot File 56D38, Box 31, NARA.

81. Memo, 26 March 1952, RG 319, Army - Operations General Decimal File 1952, 091 Germany (TS)(Section II-A)(Book I)(Case 21 only), Box 115, NARA. The secretary's representative found the German estimates too high, much to the dismay of the Germans and the de facto but unofficial defense minister, Theodor Blank.

82. Enclosure to JCS 2099/212, 8 July 1952, RG 319, Army - Operations General Decimal File 1952, 091 Germany (TS), (Section IV-A) (Case 61), Box 11, NARA. JCS 2099/205, sent on 4 June 1952, contained an earlier, similar request from the State Department for information on whether Germany was eligible for arms assistance on a reimbursable basis. This document cited NSC 115, which established the fact that the ability of Germany to defend itself or participate in the defense of Western Europe was important to the security of the United States.

83. Memorandum for the Secretary of Defense, Implementation of Possible Military Assistance to Western Germany, 16 July 1952, RG 319, Army - Operations General Decimal File 1952, 091 Germany, Box 116, NARA.

84. Memorandum for the Secretary of Defense, Implementation of Possible Military Assistance to Western Germany, 22 August 1952, RG 319, Army - Operations General Decimal File 1952, 091 Germany, Box 116, NARA. The directive to USCINCEUR, based on Memorandum from the Assistant Chief of Staff, G-3, for the Chief of Staff, US Army, same subject, and attached to this memorandum, appears to have been contained in JCS 2099/226, as amended on 22 August 1952. G-3 recommended approval and mentioned that the navy and air force were also recommending approval. See chapter 5, this book.

85. Memorandum of Conversation, 28 September 1952, RG 319 - Army Ops General Decimal File 1952, 091 Germany (TS) (Section IV-A)(Case 61), Box 12, NARA. See, for example, Frank M. Buscher, "The U.S. High Commission and German Nationalism, 1949–52," *Central European History* 23, no. 1 (March 1990): 57–75.

86. Letter, John Ferguson to Paul Nitze, 26 September 1952, RG 59 – General Records of the Department of State, Records of the Policy Planning Staff 1947–1953, Box 16 (folder 1), NARA.

87. Memorandum of Meeting at the White House between President Truman and General Eisenhower, 18 November 1952, Dean G. Acheson Papers, Secretary of State File, Memoranda of Conversations File, 1952, HSTL.

88. In February 1952, the NATO ministers met in Lisbon, Portugal, and adopted a series of force proposals that called for a total of fifty combat-ready divisions (and forty reserve divisions), four thousand aircraft, and "strong" naval forces by the end of 1952. *The North Atlantic Treaty Organization: Facts and Figures* (Brussels: NATO Information Service, 1989), 41. See also "NSC 135 No. 3: The Mutual Security Program," in *Foreign Relations of the United States, 1952–1954*, vol. 1, *General: Economic and Political Matters*, part 1 (Washington, DC: Government Printing Office, 1952–1954), 516–18, which reported on the shortfall of 15 divisions and 90m aircraft, as well as other deficiencies from the NATO European countries; and Osgood, *Entangling Alliance*, 87–91, which includes a brief rationale of why the British and French were economically forced to abandon the Lisbon Force Goals.

89. Toward the end of 1952, three-time prewar Radical prime ministers Édouard Herriot and Édouard Daladier had denounced the EDC, placing France's ratification of the EDC Treaty in a precarious position. Memorandum of Conversation with Mr. Eden, Secretary of State for Foreign Affairs, European Items Raised by Mr. Eden in New York, 12 November 1952, Dean G. Acheson Papers, Secretary of State File, 1945–1972, Memoranda of Conversations File, 1949–1953, Box 71, HSTL.

90. Memorandum of Meeting at the White House, 18 November 1952, HSTL.

91. Bonn 3204, 12 January 1953, 8 m., RG 59 – General Records of the Department of State, Bureau of European Affairs, Records Relating to the European Defense Community, Entry A1 1601-G, Box 33, NARA. (For a description of the EDC-IC, see chapter 5, this book.) Six months later, on 2 July 1953, the US high commissioner in Bonn wrote Dulles informing him that French intransigence and refusal on the Military Security Board to allow defense items to be produced in Germany was jeopardizing the entire program. The United States needed to tell France they could no longer veto such issues in the MSB and must allow production of up to $150 million in 1954 if they wished to obtain their share of the program. RG 59, Records of the Department of State, Records of the Bureau of European Affairs, Subject Files Relating to European Defense Community, 1951–1954, Lot File 56D38, Box 32, NARA.

92. DUSM-12-53, 14 January 1953, Memorandum for the Joint Chiefs of Staff, Re-examination of Position on Participation of the German Federal Republic in Western European Defense, Enclosure to JCS 2124/79, 15 January 1953, RG 218, Records of the JCS, Geographic File, 1951–1953, Box 18, NARA. The NAC document is C-6-D/1.

93. Ibid.

94. Kevin Ruane, "Agonizing Reappraisals: Anthony Eden, John Foster Dulles, and the Crisis of European Defence, 1953–54," *Diplomacy and Statecraft* 13, no. 4 (December 2002): 156–57.

95. Ronald W. Preussen, "Cold War Threats and America's Commitment to the European Defense Community: One Corner of a Triangle," *Journal of European Integration History*, Spring 1996, 65; and Chris Tudda, "'The Devil's Advocate': Robert Bowie, Western European Integration, and the German Problem, 1953–1954," in Anna Kasten Nelson, *The Policy Makers: Shaping American Foreign Policy from 1947 to the Present* (Lanham, MD: Rowman and Littlefield Publishers, 2009), 29.

96. Mako, *U.S. Ground Forces*, 13–14. The emphasis on nuclear weapons, strategic airpower, and the "long haul" was the same rationale Churchill used to explain Great Britain's inability to meet the Lisbon Force Goals, leaving NATO far short of what was needed to meet a Soviet "major assault." Osgood, *Entangling Alliance*, 88–89.

97. Dwight D. Eisenhower, *Mandate for Change, 1953–56: The White House Years* (New York: Signet Books, 1965), 184–85.

98. Unnumbered Bonn cable sent via pouch, 6 February 1953, RG59, Records of the Department of State, Records of the Bureau of European Affairs, Subject Files Relating to European Defense Community, 1951–1954, Lot File 56D38, Box 32, NARA. One week after the Eisenhower administration took office in January 1953, Dulles asked General Bradley about alternatives to EDC

in the event that it was not approved. Aside from telling him that the JCS had always seen full NATO membership for the FRG as preferable, Bradley repeated the need for twelve German divisions to force the Soviets to concentrate their forces: "I don't have enough atomic weapons," he said, "to plaster all of Europe." Leighton, *The New Look*, 553.

99. Reexamination of Position on Participation of the German Federal Republic in Western European Defense, 20 February 1953, RG 218, Records of the JCS, Geographic File, 1951–53, 092 Germany (5-4-49) Sec. 8-14, Box 18, NARA. This was a response to JCS 2124/83 (not found), which apparently included a reply to Admiral Davis from the JSSC. While the JCS preferred unlimited German participation in NATO, EDC was accepted as the best way to implement its forward strategy. Brian R. Duchin, "The 'Agonizing Reappraisal': Eisenhower, Dulles, and the European Defense Community," *Diplomatic History* 16, no. 2 (April 1992): 205.

100. Participation of the German Federal Republic, 20 February 1953, NARA.

101. RG 59 – General Records of the Department of State, Records of the Policy Planning Staff, Lot 64D563, Box 16, Folder 3, NARA.

102. Ibid.

103. JCS 2124/84, 6 March 1953, RG 218, Records of the JCS, Geographic File 1951–53, 092 Germany (5-4-49) Sec. 15 to 387 Germany (12-17-43) Sec. 16, Box 19, NARA. JCS's concerned stemmed from the fact that no German forces could be raised until the EDC Treaty was ratified.

104. SM-609-53, 20 March 1953, RG 218, Records of the JCS, Geographic File 1951–53, 092 Germany (5-4-49) Sec. 15 to 387 Germany (12-17-43) Sec. 16, Box 19, NARA.

105. Eyes Only, TS, "Discussion at the 138th Meeting of the National Security Council on Wednesday, March 25, 1953," 26 March 1953, Ann Whitman File, Papers as President, 1953–1961, NSC Series, Box 4, Dwight David Eisenhower Library (hereafter DDEL).

106. The "load" in regard to Southeast Asia was multifaceted. George Armstrong Kelly writes, "Since 1947, the [French] Army had been engaged in a war without allies and without the sympathy or support of many Frenchmen. The government had given orders to fight the wars and win them but had not furnished either the means or the appropriate political direction." Kelly, *Lost Soldiers: The French Army and Empire in Crisis 1947–1962* (Cambridge, MA: MIT Press, 1965), 8. In addition, the French government was confronted on the home front by efforts to sabotage the war effort by the Communist Party (Parti Communiste Française, or PCF) and the Labor Party (Confédération Générale du Travail, or CGT), with the former writing congratulatory letters to Ho Chi Minh on his

successes and assuring him the support of the French working class. John Stuart Ambler, *The French Army in Politics, 1945–1962* (Columbus: Ohio State University Press, 1966), 107–8.

107. Eyes Only, TS, "138th Meeting of the National Security Council," 26 March 1953, DDEL.

108. Bonn A - 1507, 9 April 1953, RG 319, Army - Operations, General Decimal File 1953, 091. G, Box 34, NARA..

109. Ibid. As a matter of fact, an itemized (but still incomplete) list was provided to the FRG on 22 November 1954.

110. RG 59 – General Records of the Department of State, Records of the Policy Planning Staff, RG 59, Lot 64D563, Box 16, Folder 3, NARA.RG 59, Box 16, Folder 3, NARA.

111. Duchin, "'Agonizing Reappraisal,'" 203fn3.

112. Stephen E. Ambrose, *Eisenhower*, vol. 2, *The President* (New York: Simon and Schuster, 1983), 120; and Ambrose, *Eisenhower: Soldier and President* (New York: Simon & Schuster, 1990), 334.

113. Dwight D. Eisenhower, "The Chance for Peace," *Department of State Bulletin* 28 (27 April 1953): 600.

114. Note, John C. Ausland to Mr. Coburn Kidd, The President's Speech and German Unity, 17 April 1953, RG 59, Office of German Affairs, Subject Files 1949–1960, Box 14, NARA. The note indicated, however, that Eisenhower did not make clear which countries comprised the European community other than the FRG and Western Europe.

115. Undated "personal and secret" letter, Eisenhower to Churchill, Ann Whitman File, Dulles-Herter Series, Box 1, DDEL.

116. Undated paper, "Main Difference between GER and S/P drafts," RG 59 – General Records of the Department of State, Records of the Policy Planning Staff 1947–1953, Lot 64D563, Box 16, NARA. A handwritten annotation on the paper indicates it was used for discussing the German paper on 23 June 1953 in RB offices.

117. Letter, Chancellor Adenauer to Secretary of State John Foster Dulles, 8 July 1953, RG 59 – General Records of the Department of State, Office of German Affairs, "Subject Files," 1949–1960, Lot 63D166, Box 06, NARA; "Communiqué, No. 379, July 14, 1953," Ann Whitman File, Dulles-Herter Series, Box 1, DDEL; and ACofS, G-3, Plans Div to ACofS, G-2, Intelligence Estimate (Germany) , G-3 091 Germany (24 July 1953), RG 319, Army - Operations, General Decimal Files 1953, 091. G, Box 34, NARA.

118. JCS 2124/87, "Memorandum for the Secretary of Defense," 30 July 1953, RG 218, Records of the Joint Chiefs of Staff, Geographic File 1951–53, 092 Germany (5-4-49) Sec. 15 to 387 Germany (12-17-43) Sec. 16, Box 19, NARA.

119. NSC 160/1 "United States Policy with Respect to Germany," 17 August 1953, RG 273, Records of the National Security Council (NSC), Policy Papers 159-160, Entry 1, Box 23, NARA.

120. Ibid. The reference to a European community obviously refers to the initiation of talks among the EDC signatories on the parallel European Political Community (EPC).

121. Letter, Conant to Dulles, 28 October 1953, RG 59 – General Records of the Department of State, Records of the Policy Planning Staff 1947–1953, Lot 64D563, Box 16: (Folder 2), NARA.

122. Letter, Conant to Dulles, 13 November 1953, RG 59 – General Records of the Department of State, Records of the Policy Planning Staff 1947–1953, Lot 64D563, Box 16: (Folder 2), NARA.

123. Letter, Dulles to Adenauer, 20 November 1953, Alfred M. Gruenther Papers, 1941–1983, Box 1, DDEL. That same day, Dulles also wrote Conant that Conant's concerns troubled him as well. He stated that the key to EDC ratification was solving the Saar problem—an issue beyond the scope of this narrative—and that Adenauer should go to the extreme to reach a settlement with France on that problem.

124. John Foster Dulles, "A Report on the North Atlantic Treaty Organization," *Department of State Bulletin* 30, no. 758 (January 1954): 5.

125. US Department of State, "Statement by the Secretary of State to the North Atlantic Council," in *Foreign Relations of the United States, 1952–1954*, 5p1:463. This latter phrase, somewhat reorganized, was repeated later that day in a press conference given by Dulles. US Department of State, "Statement by the Secretary of State," in *Foreign Relations of the United States, 1952–1954*, 5p1:468. For an excellent summary of the US position vis-á-vis Europe and the EDC, see Duchin, "'Agonizing Reappraisal,'" 201–21.

Chapter 5: 1954–55

1. (TS) DULTE 83, 16 February 1954, Ann Whitman File, Dulles Herter Series, Box 2, DDEL.

2. "United States Assurances to the EDC with Proposed Changes Indicated" in "Memorandum for the President," 19 March 1954, Ann Whitman File, Dulles-Herter Series, Box 2, DDEL. One month earlier, General Gruenther had written the president of a visit by a group of French industrialists who appeared to favor EDC. One, Rene Fould, "the big noise in steel in France," told Gruenther the following: "If the U.S. could give us a satisfactory guarantee that they will stand by France, I think I could promise you here and now that France will approve EDC promptly." Letter from General Gruenther to the President, 14 February 1954, Ann Whitman File, Dulles-Herter Series, Box 2, DDEL.

3. (TS) DULTE 2, 22 April 1954, Eyes Only for the President, Ann Whitman File, Dulles-Herter Series, Box 2, DDEL.

4. (TS) DULTE 9, 23 April 1954, Ann Whitman File, Dulles-Herter Series, Box 2, DDEL.

5. (TS) DULTE 8, 23 April 1954, Ann Whitman File, Dulles-Herter Series, Box 2, DDEL.

6. For more on the French defeat in Indochina and the political situation in France in 1954 see: Jean-Pierre Rioux, *The Fourth Republic, 1944–1958*, Cambridge History of Modern France 7 (Cambridge: Cambridge University Press, 1987), 217–18; and Kelly, *Lost Soldiers*, 51.

7. JCS 2124/119, 24 June 1954, "EDC Alternative Planning," RG 218, Records of the Joint Chiefs of Staff, Geographic File, 1954–56, 092 Germany (5-4-49) Sec. 22-30, Box 23, NARA.

8. Undated Memorandum by the Chief of Staff, U.S. Air Force on EDC Alternative Planning, RG 218, Records of the Joint Chiefs of Staff, Geographic File, 1954–56, 092 Germany (5-4-49) Sec. 22-30, Box 23, NARA.

9. Ibid.

10. Letter, James B. Conant to Livingstone Merchant, 18 June 1954 with enclosure attached to Note from Robert Murphy to Admiral Radford, 25 June 1954, RG 218, Records of the U.S. Joint Chiefs of Staff, Chairman's File, Admiral Radford, 1953–57, Box 9, NARA. Ironically, Conant's letter was written the same day as a message from Ambassador Bruce, the US observer to the EDC Interim Committee, to the Department of State reporting on a dinner conversation with Belgian foreign minister Spaak the previous night. Spaak discussed "French-inspired" rumors that the United States and United Kingdom were seeking alternatives to the EDC Treaty. He told Bruce that if France wanted to renegotiate the treaty before voting on it (which had been intimated by Mendés-France), Belgium would refuse to take part in such negotiations and he believed he spoke as well for Luxembourg and the Netherlands. Spaak wanted the United States and the United Kingdom to take a strong stand against any attempt to modify the treaty until France had voted on it. Furthermore, Spaak said that if France voted against EDC, Benelux and the FRG would seek only one alternative: full FRG membership in NATO without discrimination. US Department of State, "The United States Observer to the Interim Committee of the European Defence Community (Bruce) to the Department of State: Coled 281," in *Foreign Relations of the United States, 1952–1954*, vol. 3, *United Nations Affairs*, ed. William Z. Slany (Washington, DC: Government Printing Press, 1952–1954), 975. See also Paris 4946, 21 June 1954, Ann Whitman File, Papers as President, 1953–1961, Dulles-Herter Series, Box 3, DDEL.

11. Memorandum for the Secretary of Defense, "Subject: EDC Alternative Planning," 25 June 1954, RG 218, Records of the U.S. Joint Chiefs of Staff, Geographic File, 1954–56, 092 Germany (5-4-49) Sec. 22-30, Box 23, NARA.

12. US Department of State, "Agreed United States–United Kingdom Secret Minute on Germany and the EDC," in *Foreign Relations of the United States, 1952–1954*, 3:988.

13. 205th Meeting of the National Security Council, 1 July 1954, Ann Whitman File, Papers as President, 1953–1961, NSC Series, Box 5, DDEL.

14. "Note by the Secretaries," 9 July 1954, RG 218, Records of the U.S. Joint Chiefs of Staff, Geographic File, 1954–56, 092 Germany (5-4-49) Sec. 22-30, Box 23, NARA.

15. "U.S. Position on German Defense Contribution in Event of EDC Delay or Rejection," retyped 20 July 1954, RG 59, General Records of the Department of State, Office of the Legal Advisor, Office of the Assistant Legal Advisor for Special Functional Problems, Subject and Country Files, Committee on Occupational; Deferment to Johnson Act, Entry A1 3071, Box 2, NARA. On that same day, Secretary of State Dulles was in France for the Geneva Conference on Korea and Indochina and spoke with Prime Minister Mendés-France, telling him that if the EDC did not happen soon, "it would be better to write off what [they had] tried to do to build up the defensive strength of Western Europe as a noble but unproductive experiment." Memorandum of Conversation, 13 July 1954, Ann Whitman File, Papers as President, 1953–1961, Dulles-Herter Series, Box 3, DDEL.

16. "EDC Delay or Rejection," 20 July 1954, NARA.

17. Ibid.

18. Senate Resolution, 27 July 1954, Ann Whitman File, Papers as President, 1953–1961, Dulles-Herter Series, Box 3, DDEL.

19. Revised draft, "Interim Measure for German Rearmament in the Event of French Failure to Act on EDC Prior to Recess," 4 August 1954, RG 218, Records of the U.S. Joint Chiefs of Staff, Geographic File, 1954–56, 092 Germany (5-4-49) Sec. 22-30, Box 23, NARA.

20. Copy of message from Anthony Eden to Secretary Dulles, 23 August 1954, Ann Whitman File, Papers as President, 1953–1961, Dulles-Herter Series, Box 4, DDEL. What Mendés-France was speaking about was a plan dubbed "little NATO" that included Great Britain, the EDC countries, and Germany with some restrictions. Hitchcock, *France Restored*, 195–97.

21. Memorandum for the President, 24 August 1954, Ann Whitman File, Papers as President, 1953–1961, Dulles-Herter Series, Box 3, DDEL; and copy of message from Sir Winston Churchill to Secretary Dulles, 24 August 1954, Box 4, DDEL.

22. Cable from Ambassador Bruce (forwarded by Bedell Smith to the president), Capitol Ref 542 (no date), Ann Whitman File, Papers as President, 1953–61, Dulles-Herter Series, Box 4, DDEL.

23. Paraphrase of Eden Message, 27 August 1954, Ann Whitman File, Papers as President, 1953–61, Dulles-Herter Series, Boxes 3 and 4, DDEL.

24. EDC's defeat was due to a complex set of internal French politics, among which was the view that support for EDC meant that France was doing America's bidding in rearming Germany. For a comprehensive discussion of French objections to EDC and the events leading to its demise, see Hitchcock, chapter 6, in *France Restored*, 169–203.

25. Rolf Steininger, "John Foster Dulles, the European Defense Community, and the German Question," in *John Foster Dulles and the Diplomacy of the Cold War*, ed. Richard H. Immerman (Princeton: Princeton University Press, 1990), 104. See also US Department of State, "Memorandum by Leon W. Fuller of the Policy Planning Staff to the Director of that Staff (Bowie)," in *Foreign Relations of the United States, 1952–1954*, 5p1:863–65; and US Department of State, "NSC 160/1: United States Position with Respect to Germany," paragraph 11.b. in *Foreign Relations of the United States, 1952–1954*, vol. 7, *Germany and Austria*, ed. William Z. Slany, part 1 (Washington, DC: Government Printing Press, 1952–1954), 515–16.

26. Duchin, "Agonizing Reappraisal," 209; and Steininger, "John Foster Dulles," 2.

27. "JCS Agreed Statement Submitted to the Secretary of Defense as of Possible Use to the Secretary of State," 15 September 1954, RG 218, Records of the U.S. Joint Chiefs of Staff, Chairman's File, Admiral Radford, 1953–57, Box 9, NARA.

28. US Department of State, "NCS 5433: Immediate U.S. Policy toward Europe," in *Foreign Relations of the United States, 1952–1954*, 5p2:1205.

29. Memorandum of Discussion at the 215th Meeting of the National Security Council, Friday, September 24, 1954, Ann Whitman File, File, Papers as President, NSC Series, Box 6, DDEL. Also in US Department of State, "Memorandum of Discussion at the 215th Meeting of the National Security Council, Friday, September 24, 1954," *Foreign Relations of the United States, 1952–1954*, 5p2:1263–71. Steininger writes that Dulles believed the JCS plan was unworkable but also feared that discussion of any alternative, including "peripheral defense," would be interpreted as a weakening of support for EDC. Neither he nor President Eisenhower saw admitting West Germany to NATO as an alternative and Dulles felt that EDC had been the only means for achieving a German defense contribution. He was also not in favor of offering a commitment. Steininger, "John Foster Dulles," 82, 92, 93, 97, 106.

30. The British also preferred the NATO option. In a telegram to President Eisenhower, Churchill called the EDC a "sludgy amalgam" and said he didn't

"blame the French for rejecting EDC but only for inventing it." Message from the Prime Minister to the President, 18 September 1954, Ann Whitman File, Dulles-Herter Series, Box 4, DDEL.

31. 215th Meeting of the National Security Council, 24 September 1954, DDEL.

32. Hitchcock, *France Restored*, 192–93; and Trachtenberg, *A Constructed Peace*, 124. According to Hitchcock, Mendés-France called upon Alexandre Parodi, Georges Boris, and André Gros to find a compromise solution. According to both Hitchcock and Trachtenberg, it was Mendés-France who came up with the essential elements of a plan to solve the German question, dubbed "little NATO." Mendés-France allegedly passed this idea to the British and it was put into motion by Eden through the Brussels Treaty Organization. See also Leighton, *The New Look*, 575.

33. Ruane, *Rise and Fall*, 111. Professor Ruane's book parallels mine in method as it is the result of a great deal of research in the British archives. The larger part of this latter section is derived from part 3 of his work, for which I am deeply indebted.

34. Ruane, "Agonizing Reappraisals," 157, 160–61.

35. Ruane, *Rise and Fall*, 162; and Ruane, "Agonizing Reappraisals," 154. Large adds that Adenauer's offer was qualified: the promise was that these weapons would not be produced on German territory, which did not stand in the way of Germany possessing them. Adenauer had always insisted in full military equality with the other NATO nations. Large, *Germans to the Front*, 218.

36. Duchin "'Agonizing Reappraisal,'" 217; and Ruane, "Agonizing Reappraisals," 166. Eden's plan was similar to that proposed by Mendés-France in footnote 20, this chapter. According to Trachtenberg, the British had gone along with EDC out of loyalty to the United States but never really wanted it. Trachtenberg states that Mendés-France had no problem with the British presenting this plan as their own. Trachtenberg, *A Constructed Peace*, 124.

37. Ruane, "Agonizing Reappraisals," 164. Emphasis added.

38. Ibid., 167–68.

39. Prime Minister to the President, 18 September 1954, DDEL. Richard H. Immerman writes that Dulles was "unenthusiastic in no small measure" because the United States had ceded the initiative to the British. Immerman, *John Foster Dulles: Piety, Pragmatism, and Power in U.S. Foreign Policy* (Wilmington, DE: Scholarly Resources, 1999), 105; Hitchcock, *France Restored*, 196; and Leighton, *The New Look*, 575.

40. Ruane, "Agonizing Reappraisals," 169. One month earlier, shortly before the French rejected EDC, Churchill had proposed a new NATO without France. The British Chiefs of Staff, however, feared that a NATO without France would

cause the loss of French territory and the supply ports on the channel and Atlantic, totally disrupting the lines of communication. They also concluded that while the German contribution would, over time, replace France's contribution, both contributions were needed and Germany should not be seen as a substitute for France. Steininger, "John Foster Dulles," 94, 99.

41. FRUS 1952–1954:5, 1268.

42. The nine-power London portion took place from 28 September to 3 October 1954 and the Paris portion from 20 to 23 October. Participants were the United Kingdom, France, Belgium, the Netherlands, Luxembourg, Italy, the Federal Republic of Germany, Canada, and the United States. US Department of State, "B. Nine-Power and Four-Power Conferences at London, September 28–October 3, 1954: 1. Proceedings of the Meetings," in *Foreign Relations of the United States, 1952–1954*, 5p2:1294–332; and US Department of State, "D. Nine-Power, Four-Power, and North Atlantic Council Ministerial Meetings at Paris, October 20–23, 1954: 1. Proceedings of the Meetings," in *Foreign Relations of the United States, 1952–1954*, 5p2:1404–25. See also Eisenhower, *Mandate for Change*, 488.

43. (TS) DULTE 3, 28 September 1954, Dulles to the President, the Summer White House, Ann Whitman File, Dulles-Herter Series, Box 2, DDEL. Dulles also told Eisenhower in this note that the British commitment would probably make the nine-power conference succeed, as long as the United States reaffirmed the assurances it had given previously to maintain forces in Europe as long as needed. The reaffirmation of these assurances was given on 1 February 1955.

Epilogue

1. On 2 December 1953, the three US services were advised that on 23 November 1953, the FRG became eligible for reimbursable military assistance under the MDAA. "Memorandum for the Chief, Foreign Aid Division, G-4," 2 December 1953, RG 319, Army - Operations General Decimal Files 1953, 091, G, Box 34, NARA. See also Wolfgang Schmidt, "Von der 'Befehlsausgabe' zum 'Briefing': Der Amerikanisierung der Luftwaffe Während der Aufbau phase der Bundeswehr," *Militärgeschichte* 11, Heft 3 (2001): 44.

2. For example, postwar archival documentation for Commander, Naval Forces Germany (COMNAVFORGER) is, as of this writing, still classified and not available to the public.

3. Edward F. Fisher, *USAREUR Planning for German Army Assistance (U)* (Washington, DC: US Army Europe, Historical Division, 1955), 4. USAFE says it was Secretary of Defense Charles Wilson who asked for a new German rearmament plan. *USAFE's Assistance to Create a New German Air Force* (Wiesbaden, Deu.: Historical Division, Office of Information Services, 1956), 50–56. Courtesy of the

Air Force Historical Office, Bolling Air Force Base, Washington, DC.

4. Robert J. Watson, *1953–1954*, vol. 5 of *History of the Joint Chiefs of Staff: The Joint Chiefs of Staff and National Policy* (Washington, DC: Office of Joint History, 1998), 315. All the JCS recommendations were contained in JCS 2124/142, which is no longer available.

5. Ibid., 3–5. See also *History of Headquarters*, 1:101n22.

6. Fisher, *USAREUR Planning*, 7.

7. The official, proper name for Amt Blank and Dienststelle Blank was Dienststelle des Bevollmächtigten des Bundeskanzlers für die mit der Vermehrung der alliierten Truppen zusammenhängenden Fragen, or "Plenipotentiary for the Federal Chancellor for Questions Regarding the Reinforcement of Allied Troops."

8. Fisher, *USAREUR Planning*, 30–32. This "obstacle" could also be seen as an unintentional consequence of a lack of planning and foresight on the part of the US military authorities, who had known for a long time that discussions with the Germans requiring disclosure of classified information would be necessary.

9. Despite Allied objections to the formation of a German federal police force, a West German border police (*Bundesgrenzschutz*) was organized in 1951 and equipped with light arms and machine guns. Regular communication and coordination with US Army units began almost immediately. The border police were subsequently outfitted with 60 mm mortars and light M-8 armored vehicles, supplied by EUCOM after approval from the Department of the Army in November 1951. Carter, *Forging the Shield*, 173.

10. For a description of the Himmerod Conference, its participants, and its purpose, see appendix E.

11. Schmidt, "Von der 'Befehlsausgabe' zum 'Briefing,'" 43.

12. James Corum, "Building a New Luftwaffe: The United States Air Force and Bundeswehr Planning for Rearmament, 1950–1960," *Journal of Strategic Studies* 27, no. 1 (March 2004): 94–97.

13. David R. Snyder, "Arming the 'Bundesmarine': The United States and the Build-Up of the German Federal Navy, 1950–1960," *Journal of Military History* 66, no. 2 (April 2002): 479, fn 6. See also Friedrich Ruge, "The Postwar German Navy and Its Mission," *U.S. Naval Institute Proceedings* 83, no. 10 (October 1957): 1038. The German armaments industries, including all ship building and construction facilities, were completely dismantled.

14. Douglas C. Peifer, *The Three German Navies: Dissolution, Transition, and New Beginnings, 1945–1960* (Gainesville: University Press of Florida, 2002), 153–55. Peifer's book utilizes only German sources. LSU (A) was the German Liaison Office. LSU (C), with a strength of 171 men, was under the US Navy's Rhine River Patrol, and LSU (B) consisted of "three flotillas employing thirty-three

minesweepers, three fast patrol boats, and a plethora of support craft manned by 850 officers and ratings." Peifer, "Origins of the East and West German Navies: From the Kriegsmarine to the Volksmarine and Bundesmarine" (PhD diss., University of North Carolina, 1996).

15. Snyder, "Arming the 'Bundesmarine,'" 480; and Peifer, "East and West German Navies," 157.

16. Snyder, "Arming the 'Bundesmarine,'" 482. Peifer states that the initial NHT proposal was for a minimum force of 12 larger torpedo boats, 36 fast attack boats, 24 small submarines (U-boats), 12 convoy escorts, 12 small antisubmarine warfare (ASW) boats, 36 patrol boats, and 36 landing craft and 144 naval aircraft. A revised proposal, which became the German negotiating position at the HICOM Conference in Bonn, added 2 minelayers, 1 net layer, 9 escort vessels, 30 airplanes, 30 helicopters, 3 air bases, 3 weapons depots, 2 coastal artillery sections, a signals section, and a headquarters. It also increased personnel requirements from approximately 15,000 to over 20,000. Peifer, "East and West German Navies," 176.

17. Snyder, "Arming the 'Bundesmarine,'" 484, 486–88. Friedrich Ruge lists 182 ships of various types and 58 planes that were "originally planned" for delivery to the German navy. Among them were 18 destroyers and 12 submarines, vessels strenuously objected to by the French. Ruge, "Postwar German Navy," 1038.

18. Peifer, "East and West German Navies," 177.

19. RG 549, Records of the U.S. Army, Europe, USAREUR Assistant Chief of Staff (G-3) OPOT, School Section Classified General Correspondence, 1951–1952, Box 210, Folder: Training Branch, School Section 092.2-352, NARA.

20. Fisher, *USAREUR Planning*, 9.

21. Letter, ACS G-3 to CINCEUR, RG 319, Army Operations - General Decimal File, Box 34, (Section I)(Case 1-20), NARA. Detachment A had been established as a small staff earlier by General Ridgeway (CINCEUCOM) to maintain liaison with the EDC-IC. Carter, *Forging the Shield*, 179.

22. Fisher, *USAREUR Planning*, 8–9. Surveys of installations and training areas were taken throughout 1953 and into 1954 to find barracks and training areas that could be made available to German forces. Carter, *Forging the Shield*, 180–81.

23. Letter, ACS G-3 to CINCEUR, NARA.

24. Fisher, *USAREUR Planning*, 1–3.

25. Ibid., 2–3. Referencing Amembassy TOPOL 2256, State made it clear that it was also upset with the negative French attitude, as France had been setting the tempo for the EDC-IC's work, which was extremely slow in regard to planning for the German contribution. State told Paris to make clear to Hervé Alphand , France's permanent representative to the NAC, that that attitude had made a very "unfortunate impression" with the State Department. Unnumbered outgoing

State cable, 23 May 1953, RG 59, General Records of the Department of State, Bureau of European Affairs, Lot Files 56D389, Records Relating to the European Defense Community, Entry A1 1601G, Box 32, NARA.

26. EUCOM Letter to Chief of Staff, Department of the Army, 12 December 1953, Establishment of an Advanced Planning Group, Military Assistance Division, Headquarters US EUCOM, RG 319, Army - Operations General Decimal Files 1953, 091, G, Box 34, NARA. See also Fisher, *USAREUR Planning*, 8.

27. Fisher, *USAREUR Planning*, 13–15.

28. Ibid., 16–19. See the air force section below. APG is also called APG/MAAG or APG (Bonn) in some USAREUR documents.

29. Ibid., 13; and Memo (Maj. Gen Roberrt G. Gard, Dep Ch of Staff for Opns, for Asst Chiefs of Staff), subj: Planning in USAREUR for Assistance in the Formation of the German Army, 2 September 1954, RG 549, Entry 2105, USAREUR General Correspondence, NARA. See also Carter, *Forging the Shield*, 184.

30. Ibid., 21–23.

31. Ibid., 26–28.

32. Ibid., 34.

33. Ibid., 35–36.

34. Under the new NATO organization, LANDCENT, later changed to AFCENT (Allied Forces Central Europe), was headquarters, while NORTHAG and CENTAG were the two subordinate commands.

35. Fisher, *USAREUR Planning*, 37–38. USAREUR was responsible for only the first twelve months of the thirty-six-month training period. See also outgoing telegram, Bonn 4617, 19 March 1953, RG 59, General Records of the Department of State, Bureau of European Affairs, Lot Files 56D38, Records Relating to the European Defense Community, 1951–1954, Entry A1 1601-G, Box 33, NARA.

36. Fisher, *USAREUR Planning*, 38.

37. Ibid., 40.

38. Ibid., 38–41.

39. Ibid., 45.

40. "USAREUR German Army Assistance Plan," RG 319, Records of the Army Staff, ACS/Ops (G-3), Security Classified Correspondence, Box 44, NARA

41. Corum, "Founding of the Bundeswehr," 38–44.

42. General Norstad became CINCUSAFE in October 1950 and commander in chief , Allied Air Forces Central Europe (COMAAFCE) in April 1951. In July 1953 he became deputy SACEUR, and on 20 November 1956 he was made SACEUR, a position he held until his retirement in January 1963. He was a major supporter of the German Air Force. US Air Force, "General Lauris

Norstad," updated July 1960, http://www.af.mil/AboutUs/Biographies/Display/ tabid/225/Article/106085/general-lauris-norstad.aspx.

43. *USAFE's Assistance*, 5.

44. Ibid., 6.

45. Building a German armed force was a "monumental planning task." Not only had Germany been disarmed and its armaments industry completely destroyed, it also lacked a basis for organizing and equipping an armed force. Everything, including a federal office to develop policy and administer military matters, had to be built from the ground up. Ibid., 8n19. See also Corum, "Building a New Luftwaffe," 94.

46. *History of Headquarters*, 1:97–98; and *USAFE's Assistance*, 7–8.

47. *History of Headquarters*, 1:98; and *USAFE's Assistance*, 9–10. The figures presented by Heusinger were forty-six thousand front line troops, including three thousand flight personnel, thirty thousand ground staff, six thousand antiaircraft personnel, and six thousand communications personnel. See also Corum, "Building a New Luftwaffe," 98.

48. Tate initially envisioned a program similar to that run by the army's Historical Division with ex-Wehrmacht officers, but that was not accepted.

49. *USAFE's Assistance*, 10–12. See also Corum, "Building a New Luftwaffe," 98–99.

50. Despite numerous requests to disclose classified information, authority was not given until August 1953. The authorization provided an exception to the National Disclosure Policy, allowing "restricted" military information to be released to the FRG on a need-to-know basis. In December 1953, the authorization was amended to include disclosure of certain categories of "confidential" information. *USAFE's Assistance*, 12–13.

51. Ibid., 13–14; and *History of Headquarters*, 1:98. According to the USAFE history, this was the first indication the USAF had that these meetings had been taking place.

52. *History of Headquarters*, 1:98–99; and *USAFE's Assistance*, 13–15.

53. *USAFE's Assistance*, 15.

54. Ibid., 16.

55. Corum, "Building a New Luftwaffe," 93.

56. Ibid., 90, 93–94, 99–100.

57. *USAFE's Assistance*, 16–17.

58. Schmidt, "Von der 'Befehlsausgabe' zum 'Briefing,'" 46. Steinhoff was a highly decorated pilot, having flown 993 missions with 176 victories. He was severely burned when his ME-262 crashed following a blown tire on takeoff. He is credited with helping build the German Air Force within NATO and served, among various other positions, as chief of staff of the German Air Force and chairman of the NATO Military Committee.

59. Ibid.

60. Corum, "Building a New Luftwaffe," 100.

61. *USAFE's Assistance*, 17.

62. Ibid., 19.

63. Ibid., 19–21.

64. Ibid., 22–23.

65. *History of Headquarters*, 1:99–100.

66. *USAFE's Assistance*, 23. Prestocking aircraft for Germany prior to ratification of the EDC Treaty had been prohibited, but with the establishment of the training group, aircraft deliveries could begin. James S. Corum, "Starting from Scratch: Establishing the *Bundesluftwaffe* as a Modern Air Force, 1955–1960," *Air Power History* 50, no. 2 (2003): 19.

67. *USAFE's Assistance*, 27.

68. Corum, "Building a New Luftwaffe," 102.

69. *USAFE's Assistance*, 28–29.

70. Ibid., 31.

71. Ibid., 29–31. The pilot-to-aircraft ratio was set at 1.25:1 for all tactical aircraft, 1.5:1 for all-weather interceptors, and 2:1 for transport aircraft.

72. Schmidt, "Von der 'Befehlsausgabe' zum 'Briefing,'" 47.

73. *History of Headquarters*, 1:100–101, 103; and *USAFE's Assistance*, 32. EDC, for example, required each unit to be 100 percent manned at peacetime strengths at activation, with all personnel fully trained and combat status achieved three months after activation. USAFE, however, provided for a phased buildup over four years with combat readiness dependent on pilot-to-aircraft ratios, aircraft deliveries, and flying time that would accrue over time until the unit attained its specified numbers of aircraft and pilots. Similarly, EDC expected that the full complement of 1,326 aircraft would be available by the end of the third year. USAFE's manning procedures were tied to the USAF delivery schedule, which was to provide the full complement of aircraft by the end of the fourth year. According to James S. Corum, the plan called for a total of 1,326 aircraft as follows: 6 fighter-bomber wings and 8 day fighter wings (75 aircraft each), 2 all-weather interceptor wings (36 aircraft each), 2 reconnaissance wings (54 aircraft each), and 2 transport wings (48 aircraft each). Corum, "Starting from Scratch," 19.

74. *History of Headquarters*, 1:103–4.

75. *USAFE's Assistance*, 34n110.

76. Ibid., 35.

77. Ibid., 37.

78. Ibid., 35–39, 49–50. The author of this book was present and participated in the ceremony when Fürstenfeldbrück was turned over to the German Air Force in October 1957.

79. Corum, "Building a New Luftwaffe," 101.

80. Corum, "Starting from Scratch," 19.

81. *History of Headquarters*, 1:105; and *USAFE's Assistance*, 49

82. For an excellent essay on four critical areas of German-US defense cooperation and personal and matériel American aid for West German rearmament and its impact on the character of the Bundeswehr, see Ingo Wolfgang Trauschweizer, "Learning with an Ally: The U.S. Army and the Bundeswehr in the Cold War," *Journal of Military History* 72, no. 2 (April 2008): 477–508.

Appendix A

1. Bellush, *He Walked Alone*, 193. See also: US Department of State, "Summary of the Proceedings of the Fourth Session of the Tripartite Conference, October 22, 1943, 4 p.m.," in *Foreign Relations of the United States Diplomatic Papers, 1943*, vol. 1, *General* (Washington, DC: Government Printing Office, 1943), 604; US Department of State, "Conference Document No. 6," in *Diplomatic Papers, 1943*, 1:705–8; US Department of State, "Conference Document No. 7," in *Diplomatic Papers, 1943*, 1:708–10; US Department of State, "Conference Document No. 8," in *Diplomatic Papers, 1943*, 1:710–11; US Department of State, "Annex 2: European Advisory Commission," in *Diplomatic Papers, 1943*, 1:756–57; US Department of State, "Conference Document No. 20," in *Diplomatic Papers, 1943*, 1:720–23; and US Department of State, "Report on the Work of the European Advisory Commission," in *Foreign Relations of the United States: Diplomatic Papers, 1945*, vol. 3, *European Advisory Commission, Austria, Germany* (Washington, DC: Government Printing Office, 1945), 544–58. For a history of the precursor to and beginning of the EAC, see Bruce Kuklick, "The Genesis of the European Advisory Commission," *Journal of Contemporary History* 4, no. 4 (October 1969): 189–201.

2. US Department of State, "Report on the Work," in *Diplomatic Papers, 1945*, 3:545–46.

3. For a detailed history of the negotiations on this document see Wellig, chapter 2 in *History of the Civil Affairs Division*, Book 6, *Germany*, 1–155.

4. Pogue, *Supreme Command*, 485.

5. US Department of State, "Annex 2: Unconditional Surrender of Germany," in *Foreign Relations of the United States Diplomatic Papers, 1944*, vol. 1, *General* (Washington, DC: Government Printing Office, 1944), 257; and US Department of State, "Article 2," in *Diplomatic Papers, 1945*, 3:211.

6. Pogue, *Supreme Command*, 488.

7. "Declaration Regarding the Defeat of Germany and the Assumption of Supreme Authority by Allied Powers; June 5, 1945," The Avalon Project at Yale Law School, http://avalon.law.yale.edu/wwii/ger01.asp.

8. US Department of State, "Agreement between the Governments of the United States of America, the Union of Soviet Socialist Republics and the United Kingdom and the Provisional Government of the French Republic on Certain Additional Requirements to be Imposed on Germany," in *Foreign Relations of the United States: Diplomatic Papers: The Conference of Berlin (the Potsdam Conference), 1945* (Washington, DC: Government Printing Office, 1945), 2:1012. This document was repeated on 20 September 1945 as Allied Control Council Proclamation No. 2 (CONL/P/(45)26), www.loc.gov/rr/frd/Military_Law/Enactments/01LAW01.pdf, 81.

9. US Department of State, "Agreement between the Governments," in *Conference of Berlin*, 2:1012.

10. Ibid., 1014–15.

11. US Department of State, "Draft Summary of the Agreement between the Governments of the Union of Soviet Socialist Republics, the United Kingdom, the United States of America, and the Provisional Government of the French Republic on Control Machinery in Germany," in *Diplomatic Papers, 1945*, 3:264–65. See also JCS 1130/3, March 1945, 33-34, RG 260, Entry 13/A1, Box 23, Folder JCS 1130, NARA.

12. US Department of State, "Communiqué: Report on the Tripartite Conference of Berlin," in *Conference of Berlin*, 2:1501.

13. US Department of State, "Report on the Work," in *Diplomatic Papers, 1945*, 3:544–58.

14. US Department of State, "The Work of the European Advisory Commission (January 1944–July 1945): A Summary Report," in *Foreign Relations of the United States: Diplomatic Papers: The Conference of Berlin (the Potsdam Conference), 1945* (Washington, DC: Government Printing Office, 1945), 1:292–94.

15. For an account of Winant's frustrations, see Bellush, *He Walked Alone*, 192–210.

16. According to a list of the US draft directives, only twenty-three directives were circulated. US Department of State, [untitled note], *Diplomatic Papers, 1945*, 3:537–39. Winant stated that the lack of agreement on these directives was due to the failure of the Soviet government to provide instructions to its delegation to negotiate on them. US Department of State, "European Advisory Commission," in *Conference of Berlin*, 1:294. See appendix C, this book, for a list of the seven approved US directives.

Appendix B

1. Appendix A, Ltr, Supreme Hq AEF, AG 381-1 GBI-AGM, 6 May 1945, RG 331, Entry NM8/11, Box 6, NARA. No record of memoranda 2 or 3 has been found.

Appendix C

1. Supreme Headquarters Allied Expeditionary Force, "Eradication of Nazism," in *Handbook for Military Government in Germany*, part 2, chap. 2, http://www.history. army.mil/reference/Finding%20Aids/Mil_gov.pdf. A listing of all the Enactments and Approved Papers of the Control Council and Coordinating Committee can be found at: https://www.loc.gov/rr/frd/Military_Law/enactments-home.html.

2. RG 260, Records of the Adjutant General, Records Relating to Government Laws, 1945–1949, Box 634, NARA.

3. Ibid., Box 635.

4. Military Gazette, Issue C, April 1947, 2–8, RG 260, Records of the Adjutant General, Civil Administration and Political Affairs Branch, 1945–1949, Box 73.

5. RG 260, Records of the Adjutant General, Records Relating to Government Laws, 1945–1949, Box 638, NARA.

6. Supreme Headquarters Allied Expeditionary Force (SHAEF), "Military Government—Germany: Supreme Commander's Area of Control; Ordinance No. 1: Crimes and Offences," in *Handbook for Military Government*, part 1, chap. 4.

7. RG 260, Entry (A1) 44, Records of the Adjutant General, Military Government Regulations, 1946–1948, Box 694, NARA.

8. Legal Division, "Allied Control Council Law No. 8: Elimination and Prohibition of Military Training," in *Enactments and Approved Papers of the Control Council and Coordinating Committee*, vol. 1, *1945*, https://www.loc.gov/rr/frd/Military_Law/Enactments/Volume-I.pdf, 223–24.

9. Legal Division, "Allied Control Council Law No. 23: Prohibition of Military Construction in Germany," in *Enactments and Approved Papers of the Control Council and Coordinating Committee*, vol. 3, *1 March 1946 – 30 June 1946*, https://www.loc.gov/rr/frd/Military_Law/Enactments/Volume-III.pdf, 83.

10. Legal Division, "Allied Control Council Law No. 25: Control of Scientific Research," in *Enactments and Approved Papers*, 3:103–11.

11. Legal Division, "Allied Control Council Law No. 34: Dissolution of the Wehrmacht," in *Enactments and Approved Papers of the Control Council and Coordinating Committee*, vol. 4, *1 July 1946 – 30 September 1946*, https://www.loc.gov/rr/frd/Military_Law/Enactments/Volume-IV.pdf, 63.

12. Legal Division, "Control Council Law No. 43: Prohibition of the Manufacture, Import, Export , Transport or Storage of War Materials," in *Enactments and Approved Papers of the Control Council and Coordinating Committee*, vol. 5, *1 October 1946 –31 December 1946*, https://www.loc.gov/rr/frd/Military_Law/Enactments/Volume-V.pdf, 194–202.

13. Legal Division, "Control Council Law No. 46: Abolition of the State of Prussia," in *Enactments and Approved Papers of the Control Council and Coordinating*

Committee, vol. 6, *1 January 1947 – 31 March 1947*, https://www.loc.gov/rr/frd/ Military_Law/Enactments/Volume-VI.pdf, 28.

14. Legal Division, "Control Council Directive No. 16: Arming of the German Police," in *Enactments and Approved Papers*, 1:182–83.

15. Legal Division, "Control Council Directive No. 18: For Disbandment and Dissolution of the German Armed Forces," in *Enactments and Approved Papers*, 1:188–90.

16. Legal Division, "Control Council Directive No. 22: Clearance of Minefields and Destruction of Fortifications, Underground Installations and Military Installations in Germany," in *Enactments and Approved Papers*, 1:228–29.

17. Legal Division, "Control Council Directive No. 23: Limitation and Demilitarization of Sport in Germany," in *Enactments and Approved Papers*, 1:304–5.

18. Legal Division, "Control Council Directive No. 28: Reports on Disposal of German War Material in Germany," in *Enactments and Approved Papers*, 3:91–96.

19. Legal Division, "Control Council Directive No. 30: Liquidation of German Military and Nazi Memorials and Museums," in *Enactments and Approved Papers*, 3:134–36. The amended version is Legal Division, "Control Council Directive No. 30: Revision of Article IV of Directive No. 30 on the Liquidation of German Military and Nazi Memorials and Museums," in *Enactments and Approved Papers*, 4:10.

20. Legal Division, "Coordinating Committee Directive No. 32: Disciplinary Measures against Managing and Administrative Staffs of Educational Institutions, Teaching Staff, and Students Guilty of Militaristic, Nazi, or Anti-Democratic Propaganda," in *Enactments and Approved Papers*, 3:183–84.

21. Legal Division, "Control Council Directive No. 39: Liquidation of German War and Industrial Potential," in *Enactments and Approved Papers*, 5:1–6.

Appendix D

1. RG 260, Entry A2 B1 C3, Box 363, NARA.

Appendix E

1. Hans Jürgen Rautenberg and Norbert Wiggershaus, *Die Himmeroder Denkschrift vom Oktober 1950: politische und militärische Überlegungen für einen Beitrag der Bundesrepublik Deutschland zur westeuropäischen Verteidigung*, special ed. (Karlsruhe, Deu.: G. Braun, 1985), 36–60. See also Large, *Germans to the Front*, 97–103. The officers who attended the conference were: from the army, Colonel General Heinrich von Vieringhoff-Scheel, General Frido von Senger und Etterlin, General Herman Foertsch, General Hans Röttiger, Lieutenant General Adolf Heusinger, Lieutenant General Dr. Hans Speidel, Colonel Eberhard Graf von

Nostitz, Colonel Johann Adolf Graf von Kielmansegg, and Major Wolf Graf von Baudissin; from the air force, General Dr. Robert Knauss, General Rudolf Meister, and Major Horst Krüger; from the navy, Admiral Walter Gladisch, Captain Schulze-Hinrichs, and Vice Admiral Friedrich Ruge. Of these fifteen, seven obtained the rank of general in the Bundeswehr, six died before or during the creation of the Bundeswehr, and two obtained high positions in the Bundesnachrichtendienst, the Federal Intelligence Service. Interestingly, James S. Corum writes that only one air force officer, General Knauss, attended the conference. Corum "Starting from Scratch," 16–29; and Corum, "Building a New Luftwaffe," 89–113. See also David Clay Large's discussion of the Himmerod Memorandum in *Germans to the Front,* 97–103.

2. Rautenberg and Wiggershaus, *Himmeroder Denkschrift vom Oktober,* 42.

3. Ibid., 47. There is an addition mistake in the original note in footnote 210. The total number of aircraft was actually 831 versus the 821 given.

4. Ibid., 48–49.

5. G-3/Plans Div/Int'l Br, 091 Germany TS German Contribution to the Defense of Western Europe, 14 June 1951, RG 319, Army - Operations General Decimal File 1950–1951, 091. Germany, Box 23, NARA. It should be noted that in a cable from Acheson to Ambassador Bruce, repeated to ambassador s Gifford and Spofford in London and General Hays, the deputy high commissioner in Frankfurt, Acheson wrote that as serious difficulties over the Bonn Report were expected from France, and if tripartite agreement on the report was not possible, he was prepared to send it to the NAC without such agreement. Deptel 6898, 21/7 PM Jun 1951, Enclosure A to JCS 2124/47, 30 June 1951, RG 319, Army - Operations General Decimal File 1950–1951, 091. Germany, Box 23, NARA.

6. SX 5322, 241001Z June 1951, RG 218, Geographic File 1951–53, 092 Germany (5-4-49) Sec. 8-14, Box 18, NARA. On 2 July, General Handy weighed in on the Bonn Report with a five-page, detailed letter to the army chief of staff..

7. JCS 2124/52, 6 August 1951, Appendix "A" to Enclosure "A," RG 319, Army - Operations General Decimal File, 1950–1951, 091. Germany, TS, (Section II-D)(Book II)(Case 38 Only), Box 23, NARA. It appears that this submission was withdrawn until the Foreign Ministers Conference on 12 September 1951.

8. Ibid.

9. JCS 2124/59, 1 September 1951, RG 319, Army - Operations, General Decimal File 1950–1951, 091- Germany (TS) (Section II-D)(Book IV)(Case 38), Box 23, NARA.

10. Enclosure A, JCS 2124/59, 1 September 1951, NARA. The Conference for the Organization of a European Defence Community took place in Paris from January 1951 until May 1952 when the EDC Treaty was signed. These views and

views on a State Department–drafted position paper for the Washington Foreign Ministers (Tripartite) Talks (which the Pentagon considered inadequate) were sent to the secretary of defense. Memorandum for the Secretary of Defense, Washington Foreign Ministers Meeting (Tripartite Talks) Draft Position Paper (WFM T-4/2a), 8 September 1951, "European Defense Forces and the Question of German Contribution to Defense," 12 September 1951, RG 319, Army - Operations, General Decimal File 1950–1951, 091- Germany (TS) (Section II-D)(Book IV) (Case 38), Box 23, NARA.

11. Appendix B to Enclosure A, JCS 2124/59, 1 September 1951, NARA. The E-boat's actual designation is S-Boot for *Schnell* (fast) boat. The Allies used the designation "E" to identify the vessel as an enemy fast attack boat. On 18 October 1951, the Military Committee of the Conference for the Organization of a European Defense Community agreed on the basic unit size for the various "groupements" of the European Defense Force and settled on peacetime/wartime strengths as follows: Infantry – 14,500/17,000; Armored – 12,500/14,500; and Mechanized – 12,700/14,700. This agreement resolved the long-standing differences between the French and the Germans, as the French had initially insisted that any German formation larger that an RCT of 4,000–6,000 personnel was politically impossible. To soothe French sensibilities, however, the term 'division' was avoided. Attachment to Paris 2269, October 18, 6 m., RG 59, General Records of the Department of State, Bureau of European Affairs, Lot 56D38, Records Relating to the European Defense Community, 1951–1954, Entry A1, Box 32, NARA.

Appendix F

1. Acheson, *Present at the Creation*, 568–71; and Acheson, *Struggle for a Free Europe*, 133. See also Condit, *1947–1949*, 200–203; Martin, "American Decision to Rearm," 655–60; Schwartz, "Skeleton Key," 375–77; McAllister, *No Exit*, 187ff; and Trachtenberg and Gehrz, "America, Europe, and German Rearmament," 11–16.

2. Acheson, *Present at the Creation*, 593–94; McAllister, *No Exit*, 188; and Mc-Geehan, *German Rearmament Question*, 41.

3. Tobias Hecht, *Die Haltung der USA zur NATO Erwieterung: Strategie, Pragmatik und Weltordnung in den Jahren nach dem Ost-West-Konflikt* (Halle on the Saale, Deu.: Universitätsverlag Halle-Wittenberg, 2014), 48.

4. McMahon, *American World Order*, 132–33.

5. McLellan, *State Department Years*, 329. For the JCS response and its amendment, see Memorandum for the Secretary of Defense, 30 August 1950, Subject: Position on Recommendations, NARA; and Proposed Joint Reply, 7 September 1950, NARA.

6. Memorandum for S/S, 30 August 1950, HSTL.

7. Trachtenberg and Gehrz, "America, Europe, and German Rearmament," 17–22; and McMahon, *American World Order*, 11–17, 48. See also McAllister, *No Exit*, 187–92. General Bradley called Acheson "an uncompromising hawk," but left no personal or official papers that describe the 30 August meeting or indicate he forced the German rearmament issue on Acheson. Omar Bradley and Clay Blair, *A General's Life: An Autobiography* (New York: Simon & Schuster, 1983), 519; and e-mail correspondence between this author and archivists at the US Army Military Historical Institute, Carlisle Barracks, December 2010. McMahon doesn't even mention the Bradley meeting and states that Acheson took the "lead role" in developing this single package. McMahon, *American World Order*, 137. For an excellent article that supports this thesis, see also Christopher Gehrz, "Dean Acheson, the JCS and the 'Single Package': American Policy on German Rearmament," *Diplomacy and Statecraft* 12, no. 1 (March 2001): 135–60.

8. Beisner, *Life in the Cold War*, 363.

9. US Department of State, "To the Embassy in France," *Foreign Relations of the United States, 1950*, 3:262.

10. Memorandum of Conversation, 28 September 1950, RG 59, General Records of the Department of State, Records of the Executive Secretariat (Dean Acheson), Lot 53D444, Box 13, NARA.

11. Trachtenberg and Gehrz, "America, Europe, and German Rearmament," 12.

12. US Department of State, "To the Embassy in France," *Foreign Relations of the United States, 1950*, 3:261–62. A footnote states that a similar cable, DEPTEL 1197, was sent to London.

Appendix G

1. David R. Kepley, "The Senate and the Great Debate of 1951," *Prologue* 14, no. 4 (Winter 1982): 213–26. See also McLellan, chapter 17 in *State Department Years*, 327–46.

2. Acheson, *Present at the Creation*, 634–40.

3. Chace, *Acheson: The Secretary of State*, 326.

4. Ibid., 327.

5. "The President's News Conference," 11 January 1951, The American Presidency Project, http://www.presidency.ucsb.edu/ws/?pid=14050.

6. Acheson, *Present at the Creation*, 638–39.

7. Dean G. Acheson, "The Great Debate and Troops to Europe, December 1950–April 1951," Synopsis H, 6, Dean G. Acheson Papers, Princeton Seminar File, 1953–1970, Box 78, HSTL. Acheson writes that Eisenhower also testified

to a closed joint session of the Senate Armed Services and Senate Foreign Affairs committees, after which the debate became focused on the more specific question of what, if any, contribution the United States should make to the defense of Western Europe. Acheson, "The Great Debate," 7.

8. Acheson, *Present at the Creation,* 638–39.

9. Statement of General Marshall before Senate Foreign Relations and Senate Armed Services Committees Thursday, 15 February 1951 at 10 A.M. (EST), Student Research File (B File), the Integration of Western Europe, Box 1 of 1, HSTL. The statement can also be found in *Department of State Bulletin* 24 (26 February 1951): 327–30.

10. Ibid.

11. Acheson, *Present at the Creation,* 638–40. See also US Department of State, "Editorial Note," *Foreign Relations of the United States, 1951,* 3p1:22–24. Acheson's, Marshall's and Bradley's main statements can be found in *Department of State Bulletin* 24 (26 February 1951): 323–27, 327–30, and 330–32, respectively.

12. S. Res 99, 82nd Congress, 1st Session, "Assignment of Ground Forces of the United States to Duty in the European Area," Papers of George M. Elsey, Harry S. Truman Administration, Speech File, Box 55, HSTL. It is of interest to note that McLellan writes that in mid-August 1950, the State Department "set before the Pentagon a proposal . . . combined with the dispatch of four to six divisions to reinforce American ground forces in Europe." He argues further that this gave the Pentagon a "voice in U.S. policy on that subject." McLellan, *State Department Years,* 328. McLellan does not, however, provide any source for that statement and I have found nothing in either State Department archives or the Acheson papers that supports his assertion.

Bibliography

Primary Sources

ARCHIVES

Center for Military History, Ft. McNair, Washington, DC

Dwight D. Eisenhower Presidential Library, Abilene, KS

    Papers of Dwight D. Eisenhower

        Pre-presidential Papers

        Ann Whitman File

        CD Jackson Papers

        Eleanor Lansing Dulles Papers

        Alfred M. Gruenther Papers

        General Walter Bedell Smith Papers

        Harold R. Bull Papers

        John Foster Dulles Papers

        Edward E. "Swede" Hazlitt Papers

        William E. Robinson Papers

        Supreme Headquarters, Allied Expeditionary Force, Office of the Secretary, General Staff

        White House Central File, Confidential File

        Central File, Official File

Germany under Reconstruction, University of Wisconsin Digital Collection. http://digital.library.wisc.edu/1711.dl/History.GerRecon.

Harry S. Truman Presidential Library, Independence, MO

    Papers of Harry S. Truman

    Dean G. Acheson Papers

    Papers of George M. Elsey

Papers of Howard Trivers

Henry Byroade Oral History

Theodore Achilles Oral History

Library of Congress, online

Militärgeschichtliches Forschungsamt, Potsdam, Germany

National Archives and Records Administration, College Park, MD

RG 38

RG 43

RG 59

RG 80

RG 84

RG 216

RG 218

RG 260

RG 263

RG 313

RG 319

RG 330

RG 331

RG 335

RG 341

RG 407

RG 466

RG 549

World War I Document Archive. Edited by Richard Hacken. Brigham Young University Library. http://wwi.lib.byu.edu.

BOOKS

von Clausewitz, Carl. *On War.* Edited and translated by Michael Howard and Peter Paret. Princeton: Princeton University Press, 1976.

Cline, Ray S. *Washington Command Post: The Operations Division.* US Army in World War II series. Washington, DC: Center of Military History, US Army, 2003.

Coles, Harry L., and Albert K. Weinberg. *Civil Affairs: Soldiers Become Governors.* United States Army in World War II Series. Washington, DC: Office of the Chief of Military History, 1964.

Condit, Doris. *The Test of War, 1950–1953.* Vol. 2, *History of the Office of the Secretary of Defense.* Washington, DC: Historical Office, Office of the Secretary of Defense, 1988.

Condit, Kenneth W. *1947–1949.* Vol. 2 of *History of the Joint Chiefs of Staff: The Joint Chiefs of Staff and National Policy.* Washington, DC: Office of Joint History, 1996. http://www.jcs.mil/Portals/36/Documents/History/Policy/Policy_V002.pdf.

———. *1947–1949.* Vol. 2 of *History of the Joint Chiefs of Staff: The Joint Chiefs of Staff and National Policy.* Wilmington, DE: Michael Glazier, 1979.

Eisenhower, Dwight David. *Crusade in Europe.* Garden City: Doubleday and Company, Inc., 1952.

Fisher, Edward. F. *USAREUR Planning for German Army Assistance.* Washington, DC: Historical Division, US Army Europe, 1955.

———. *USAREUR Training Assistance to the West German Army (U).* Washington, DC: Historical Division, US Army Europe, 1958.

Frederickson, Oliver J. *The American Military Occupation of Germany, 1945–1953.* Darmstadt, Deu.: Historical Division, Headquarters, United States Army, Europe, 1953.

Hastings Cassidy, Velma, comp. *Germany, 1945–1949: The Story in Documents.* European and British Commonwealth Series 9. Washington, DC: Government Printing Office, 1950.

History of Headquarters United States Air Force in Europe, 1 July – 31 July 1957. Redacted. Wiesbaden, Deu.: Historical Division, Office of Information Services, 1956. Courtesy of the Air Force Historical Office, Bolling Air Force Base, Washington, DC.

Kasten Nelson, Anna, ed. *State Department Policy Planning Staff Papers 1947–1949.* 3 vols. New York: Garland, 1983.

Legal Division. *Enactments and Approved Papers of the Control Council and Coordinating Committee.* Vol. 1, *1945.* https://www.loc.gov/rr/frd/Military_Law/Enactments/Volume-I.pdf.

———. *Enactments and Approved Papers of the Control Council and Coordinating Committee.* Vol. 3, *1 March 1946 – 30 June 1946.* https://www.loc.gov/rr/frd/Military_Law/Enactments/Volume-III.pdf.

———. *Enactments and Approved Papers of the Control Council and Coordinating Committee.* Vol. 4, *1 July 1946 – 30 September 1946.* https://www.loc.gov/rr/frd/Military_Law/Enactments/Volume-IV.pdf.

———. *Enactments and Approved Papers of the Control Council and Coordinating Committee.* Vol. 5, *1 October 1946 –31 December 1946.* https://www.loc.gov/rr/frd/Military_Law/Enactments/Volume-V.pdf.

———. *Enactments and Approved Papers of the Control Council and Coordinating Committee.* Vol. 6, *1 January 1947 – 31 March 1947.* https://www.loc.gov/rr/frd/Military_Law/Enactments/Volume-VI.pdf.

Leighton, Richard M., ed. *Strategy, Money, and the New Look: 1953–1956.* Vol. 3 of *History of the Office of the Secretary of Defense*, edited by Alfred Goldberg. Washington, DC: Historical Office, 2001.

Merriam, Ray, ed. *History of COSSAC (Chief of Staff to Supreme Allied Commander), 1943–1944.* Bennington, VT: Merriam Press, 2000.

Militärgeschichtliches Forschungsamt, ed. *Von der Kapitulation bis zum Pleven-Plan.* Bd. 1 von *Anfänge westdeutscher Sicherheitspolitik: 1945–1956.* Munich: R. Oldenbourg, 1982.

———. *Die EVG-Phase.* Bd. 2 von *Anfänge westdeutscher Sicherheitspolitik: 1945–1956.* Munich: R. Oldenbourg, 1982.

NATO Handbook. Brussels: NATO Office of Information and Press, 1995.

The North Atlantic Treaty Organization: Facts and Figures. Brussels: NATO Information Service, 1989.

Notter, Harley A. *Postwar Foreign Policy Preparation, 1939–1945.* Department of State Publication 3580, General Foreign Policy Series 15. Washington, DC: Government Printing Office, 1949.

Pogue, Forrest C. *The Supreme Command.* US Army in World War II, European Theater of Operations Series. Washington, DC: Center of Military History, 1996.

Poole, Walter S. *1950–1952.* Vol. 4 of *History of the Joint Chiefs of Staff: The Joint Chiefs of Staff and National Policy.* Washington, DC: Office of Joint History, 1998.

———. *1950–1952.* Vol. 4 of *History of the Joint Chiefs of Staff: The Joint Chiefs of Staff and National Policy.* Wilmington, DE: Michael Glazier, 1980.

Rautenberg, Hans Jürgen, and Norbert Wiggershaus. *Die Himmeroder Denkschrift vom Oktober 1950: politische und militärische Überlegungen für einen Beitrag der Bundesrepublik Deutschland zur westeuropäischen Verteidigung.* Special ed. Karlsruhe, Deu.: G. Braun, 1985.

Schnabel, James F. *1945–1947.* Vol. 1 of *History of the Joint Chiefs of Staff: The Joint Chiefs of Staff and National Policy.* Washington, DC: Office of Joint History, 1996.

Starr, Joseph R. *U.S. Military Government in Germany: Preparations for the Posthostilities Period.* Karlsruhe, Deu.: Historical Division, European Command, 1950.

Supreme Headquarters Allied Expeditionary Force. "Eradication of Nazism." In *Handbook for Military Government in Germany*, part 2, chap. 2. http://www.history.army.mil/reference/Finding%20Aids/Mil_gov.pdf.

———. "Military Government—Germany: Supreme Commander's Area of Control; Ordinance No. 1: Crimes and Offences." In *Handbook for Military Government*, part 1, chap. 4.

US Army, European Command, Historical Division. *Disarmament and Disbandment of the German Armed Forces*. Occupation Forces in Europe Series, 1945–1946. Frankfurt-am-Main, Deu.: Office of the Chief Historian, European Command, 1947.

———. *The First Year of the Occupation*. 3 vols. Occupation Forces in Europe Series, 1945–46. Frankfurt-am-Main, Deu.: Office of the Chief Historian, European Command, 1947.

———. *Planning for the Occupation of Germany*. Occupation Forces in Europe Series, 1945–46. Frankfurt-am-Main, Deu.: Office of the Chief Historian, European Command, 1947.

———. *The Second Year of the Occupation*. 7 vols. Occupation Forces in Europe Series, 1945-46. Frankfurt-am-Main, Deu.: Office of the Chief Historian, European Command, 1947.

US Department of State. *A Decade of American Foreign Policy: Basic Documents, 1941–1949.* Washington, DC: Government Printing Office, 1950.

———. *Foreign Relations of the United States, 1946.* Vol. 2, *Council of Foreign Ministers.* Washington, DC: Government Printing Office, 1946.

———. *Foreign Relations of the United States, 1947.* Vol. 1, *General; The United Nations.* Washington, DC: Government Printing Office, 1947.

———. *Foreign Relations of the United States, 1947.* Vol. 3, *The British Commonwealth; Europe.* Washington, DC: Government Printing Office, 1947.

———. *Foreign Relations of the United States, 1948.* Vol. 1, *General; The United Nations.* Washington, DC: Government Printing Office, 1948.

———. *Foreign Relations of the United States, 1948.* Vol. 2, *Germany and Austria.* Washington, DC: Government Printing Office, 1948.

———. *Foreign Relations of the United States, 1948.* Vol. 3, *Western Europe.* Washington, DC: Government Printing Office, 1948.

———. *Foreign Relations of the United States, 1949.* Vol. 3, *Council of Foreign Ministers; Germany and Austria.* Washington, DC: Government Printing Office, 1949.

———. *Foreign Relations of the United States, 1950.* Vol. 3, *Western Europe*, edited by S. Everett Gleason and Fredrick Aandahl. Washington, DC: Government Printing Office, 1950.

———. *Foreign Relations of the United States, 1950.* Vol. 4, *Central and Eastern Europe; The Soviet Union.* Washington, DC: Government Printing Office, 1950.

———. *Foreign Relations of the United States, 1951.* Vol. 3, *European Security and the German Question*, part 1. Washington, DC: Government Printing Office, 1951.

————. *Foreign Relations of the United States, 1952–1954*.Vol. 1, *General: Economic and Political Matters*, part 1. Washington, DC: Government Printing Office, 1952–1954.

————. *Foreign Relations of the United States, 1952–1954*.Vol. 3, *United Nations Affairs*, edited by William Z. Slany. Washington, DC: Government Printing Press, 1952–1954.

————. *Foreign Relations of the United States, 1952–1954*.Vol. 5, *Western European Security*, edited by William Z. Slany. 2 parts. Washington, DC: Government Printing Office, 1952–1954.

————. *Foreign Relations of the United States, 1952–1954*.Vol. 7, *Germany and Austria*, edited by William Z. Slany. Part 1. Washington, DC: Government Printing Press, 1952–1954.

————. *Foreign Relations of the United States: The Conferences at Washington, 1941–1942, and Casablanca, 1943*. Washington, DC: Government Printing Office, 1943.

————. *Foreign Relations of the United States Diplomatic Papers, 1943*.Vol. 1, *General*. Washington, DC: Government Printing Office, 1943.

————. *Foreign Relations of the United States Diplomatic Papers, 1944*.Vol. 1, *General*. Washington, DC: Government Printing Office, 1944.

————. *Foreign Relations of the United States: Diplomatic Papers, 1945*.Vol. 3, *European Advisory Commission, Austria, Germany*. Washington, DC: Government Printing Office, 1945.

————. *Foreign Relations of the United States: Diplomatic Papers: The Conference of Berlin (the Potsdam Conference), 1945*. 2 vols. Washington, DC: Government Printing Office, 1945.

————. *Occupation of Germany: Policy and Progress, 1945–1946*. Department of State Publication 2783. Washington DC: Government Printing Office, 1947.

————. *The United States and Germany, 1945–1955*. Washington, DC: Government Printing Office, 1955.

US Senate Committee on Foreign Relations. *Documents on Germany, 1944–1970*. Washington, DC: Government Printing Office, 1971.

USAFE's Assistance to Create a New German Air Force. Wiesbaden, Deu.: Historical Division, Office of Information Services, 1956. Courtesy of the Air Force Historical Office, Bolling Air Force Base, Washington, DC.

Watson, Robert J. *1953–1954*.Vol. 5 of *History of the Joint Chiefs of Staff: The Joint Chiefs of Staff and National Policy*. Washington, DC: Office of Joint History, 1998.

Wellig, Richard M. *History of the Civil Affairs Division, War Department Special Staff, World War II to March 1946*. Book 6, *Germany*. Unpublished draft manuscript.

ARTICLES AND CHAPTERS

Acheson, Dean. "Tensions between the United States and the Soviet Union." *Department of State Bulletin* 22, no. 560 (27 March 1950): 478.

——. "'Total Diplomacy' to Strengthen U.S. Leadership for Human Freedom." *Department of State Bulletin* 22, no. 559 (20 March 1950): 427.

Connally, Tom. "Reviewing American Foreign Policy since 1945." *Department of State Bulletin* 23 (9 October 1950): 563–87.

Dulles, John Foster. "A Report on the North Atlantic Treaty Organization." *Department of State Bulletin* 30, no. 758 (January 1954): 3–7.

Eisenhower, Dwight D. "The Chance for Peace." *Department of State Bulletin* 28 (27 April 1953): 599–603.

Fett, Kurt. "Der Grundlagen der militärischen Planungen." In Buchheim, *Aspekte der deutschen Wiederbewaffnung*, 169–84.

"Integrated Force under Centralized Command to Defend Western Europe." *Department of State Bulletin* 23 (9 October 1950): 588.

"Restatement of U.S. Policy on Germany." *Department of State Bulletin* 15, no. 376 (September 1946): 496–501.

Volkman, Hans-Erich. "Adenauers Politik der militärischen Westintegration 1950–1956." *Militärgeschichte* 5 (1990): 419–32.

MEMOIRS

Adenauer, Konrad. *Memoirs, 1945–1953.* Translated by Beate Ruhm von Otten. Chicago: Henry Regnery Company, 1965.

Acheson, Dean. *Present at the Creation: My Years in the State Department.* New York: Norton, 1969.

——. *The Struggle for a Free Europe.* New York: W.W. Norton and Company, 1971.

Bohlen, Charles E. *Witness to History, 1929–1969.* New York: W.W. Norton and Company, 1973.

Bradley, Omar, and Clay Blair. *A General's Life: An Autobiography.* New York: Simon and Schuster, 1983.

Clay, Lucius D. *Decision in Germany.* Melbourne: William Heinemann, 1950

Eisenhower, Dwight D. *Mandate for Change, 1953–56: The White House Years.* New York: Signet Books, 1965.

——. *The Papers of Dwight David Eisenhower.* Vols. 1–5 edited by Alfred D. Chandler Jr. Vols. 7–9 edited by Louis Galambos. Baltimore: Johns Hopkins Press, 1970.

Ismay, Hastings Lionel (Lord Ismay). *NATO: The First Five Years, 1949–1954.* Utrecht, Nld.: Bosch, 1956.

Monnet, Jean. *Memoirs.* Translated by Richard Mayne. Garden City, NY: Doubleday and Company, 1978.

Speier, Hans. *From the Ashes of Disgrace: A Journal from Germany, 1945–1955.* Amherst: University of Massachusetts Press, 1981.

————. *German Rearmament and Atomic War: The Views of German Military and Political Leaders.* Evanston, IL: Row, Peterson and Company, 1957.

Secondary Sources
BOOKS

Abenheim, Donald. *Reforging the Iron Cross: The Search for Tradition in the West German Armed Forces.* Princeton: Princeton University Press, 1988.

Ahmann, R., Adolf M. Birke, and Michael Howard, eds. *The Quest for Stability: Problems of West European Security, 1918–1957.* London: Oxford University Press.

Ambler, John Stuart. *The French Army in Politics, 1945–1962.* Columbus: Ohio State University Press, 1966.

Ambrose, Stephen E. *D-Day, June 6, 1944: The Climactic Battle of World War II.* Touchstone ed. New York: Simon and Schuster, 1995.

————. *Eisenhower.* Vol. 2, *The President.* New York: Simon and Schuster, 1983.

————. *Eisenhower: Soldier and President.* Touchstone ed. New York: Simon and Schuster, 1990.

Barzini, Luigi, *The Europeans.* New York: Simon and Schuster, 1983.

Beisner, Robert L. *Dean Acheson: A Life in the Cold War.* New York: Oxford University Press, 2006.

Bellush, Bernard. *He Walked Alone: A Biography of John Gilbert Winant.* The Hague: Mouton, 1968.

Birtle, Andrew J. *Rearming the Phoenix: U.S. Military Assistance to the Federal Republic of Germany, 1950–1960.* New York: Garland Publishing Inc., 1991.

Bischof, Günter, and Stephen E. Ambrose, eds. *Eisenhower: A Centenary Assessment.* Baton Rouge: Louisiana State University Press, 1995.

Buchheim, Hans, ed. *Aspekte der deutschen Wiederbewaffnung bis 1955.* Boppard am Rhine, Deu.: Harold Boldt Verlag, 1975.

Carter, Donald A. *Forging the Shield: The U.S. Army in Europe, 1951–1962.* Washington, DC: Center of Military History, 2015.

Chace, James. *Acheson: The Secretary of State Who Created the American World.* New York: Simon and Schuster, 1998.

Cornish, Paul. *British Military Planning for the Defence of Germany, 1945–1950.* New York: St. Martin's Press, 1996.

Corum, James S., ed. *Rearming Germany.* Leiden, Nld.: Brill, 2011.

Craig, Gordon A. *From Bismark to Adenauer: Aspects of German Statecraft*. New York: Harper and Row, 1958.

———. *The Politics of the Prussian Army, 1640–1945*. New York: Oxford University Press, 1964.

D'Este, Carlo. *Eisenhower: A Soldier's Life*. New York: Henry Holt, 2002.

Delaforce, Patrick. *Invasion of the Third Reich, War and Peace: Operation Eclipse*. Stroud, Eng.: Amberly, 2011.

Diefendorf, Jeffrey M., Axel Frohn, and Hermann-Josef Rupieper, eds. *American Policy and the Reconstruction of West Germany, 1945–1955*. Washington, DC: German Historical Institute, 1993.

Doering-Manteuffel, Anselm. *Adenauerzeit: Stand, Perspectiven und methodischen Aufgaben der Zeitgeschichtsforshung (1945–1967)*. Bonn: Bouvier, 1993.

———. *Die Bundesrepublik Deutschland in der Ära Adenauer: Aussenpolitik und innere Entwicklung, 1949–1963*. Darmstadt, Deu.: Wissenschaftliche Buchgesellschaft, 1983.

Doering-Manteuffel, Anselm, and Hans-Peter Schwarz. *Adenauer und die deutsche Geschichte*. Bonn: Bouvier, 2001.

Dockrill, Michael, and John W. Young. *British Foreign Policy, 1945–56*. New York: St. Martin's Press, 1989.

Dockrill, Saki. *Britain's Policy for West German Rearmament, 1950–1955*. Cambridge Studies in International Relations 13. Cambridge: Cambridge University Press, 1991.

———. *Eisenhower's New-Look National Security Policy, 1953–1961*. New York: St. Martin's Press, Inc., 1996.

Drew, S. Nelson, ed. *NSC-68: Forging the Strategy of Containment*. Washington, DC: National Defense University, 1994.

Entmilitarisierung und Aufrüstung in Mitteleuropa 1945–1956. Herford, Deu.: E. S. Mittler and Sohn, 1983.

Etzold, Thomas H., and John Lewis Gaddis, eds. *Containment: Documents on American Policy and Strategy, 1945–1950*. New York: Columbia University Press, 1978.

Freedman, Lawrence. *The Evolution of Nuclear Strategy*. 3rd ed. Basingstoke, Eng.: Palgrave Macmillan, 2003.

Frei, Norbert. *Adenauer's Germany and the Nazi Past: The Politics of Amnesty and Integration*. Translated by Joel Golb. New York: Columbia University Press, 2002.

Fursdon, Edward. *The European Defense Community, a History*. New York: St. Martin's Press, 1980.

Gaddis, John Lewis. *The Cold War: A New History*. New York: Penguin Press, 2005.

———. *The Long Peace: Inquiries into the History of the Cold War*. New York: Oxford University Press, 1987.

————. *Strategies of Containment: A Critical Appraisal of American National Security Policy during the Cold War*. Oxford: Oxford University Press, 1982.

————. *The United States and the Origins of the Cold War, 1941–1947*. New York: Columbia University Press, 1972.

————. *We Now Know: Rethinking Cold War History*. Oxford: Oxford University Press, 1997.

Gildea, Robert. *France since 1945*. Oxford: Oxford University Press, 1997.

Graebner, Norman A., Richard Dean Burns, and Joseph M. Siracusa. *America and the Cold War, 1941–1991: A Realist Interpretation*. Santa Barbara: Praeger, 2010.

Grosser, Alfred. *The Colossus Again: Western Germany from Defeat to Rearmament*. Translated by Richard Rees. New York: Praeger, 1955.

————. *Germany in Our Time: A Political History of the Postwar Years*. Translated by Paul Stephenson. New York: Praeger, 1971.

————. *The Western Alliance: European-American Relations since 1945*. Translated by Michael Shaw. London: Macmillan, 1980.

Halle, Louis J. *The Cold War as History*. New York: Harper and Row, 1967.

Hanrieder, Wolfram F. *Germany, America, Europe: Forty Years of German Foreign Policy*. New Haven, Eng.: Yale University Press, 1989.

————. *West German Foreign Policy 1949–1967: International Pressure and Domestic Response*. Stanford: Stanford University Press, 1967.

Harper, John Lamberton. *American Visions of Europe: Franklin D. Roosevelt, George F. Kennan, and Dean G. Acheson*. Cambridge: Cambridge University Press, 1996.

Hecht, Tobias. *Die Haltung der USA zur NATO Erwieterung: Strategie, Pragmatik und Weltordnung in den Jahren nach dem Ost-West-Konflikt*. Halle on der Saale, Deu.: Universitätsverlag Halle-Wittenberg, 2014.

Hitchcock, William L. *France Restored: Cold War Diplomacy and the Quest for Leadership in Europe*. Chapel Hill: University of North Carolina Press, 1998.

————. *The Struggle for Europe: The Turbulent History of a Divided Continent, 1945–2002*. New York: Doubleday, 2003.

Hoffernaar, Jan, Dieter Krüger, and David T. Zabeki, eds. *Blueprints for Battle: Planning for War in Central Europe*. Lexington: University of Kentucky, 2012.

Holborn, Hajo. *American Military Government: Its Organization and Policies*. Washington, DC: Infantry Journal Press, 1947.

House, Jonathan M. *A Military History of the Cold War 1944–1962*. Campaigns and Commanders series 34. Norman: University of Oklahoma Press, 2012.

Immerman, Richard H., ed. *John Foster Dulles and the Diplomacy of the Cold War*. Princeton: Princeton University Press, 1990.

————. *John Foster Dulles: Piety, Pragmatism, and Power in U.S. Foreign Policy*. Wilmington, DE: Scholarly Resources, 1999.

Ireland, Timothy P. *Creating the Entangling Alliance: The Origins of the North Atlantic Treaty Organization.* Westport, CT: Greenwood Press, 1981.

Isaacson, Walter, and Evan Thomas. *The Wise Men: Six Friends and the World They Made.* New York: Simon and Schuster, 1986.

Joffe, Josef. *The Limited Partnership: Europe, the United States, and the Burdens of Alliance.* Cambridge, MA: Ballinger Publishing Company, 1987.

Jordan, W. M. *Great Britain, France, and the German Problem, 1918–1939: A Study of Anglo-French Relations in the Making and Maintenance of the Versailles Settlement.* London: Oxford University Press, 1943.

Judt, Tony. *Postwar: A History of Europe since 1945.* New York: Penguin Press, 2005.

Kaplan, Lawrence S. *The Long Entanglement: NATO's First Fifty Years.* Westport, CT: Praeger, 1999.

———. *A Community of Interests: NATO and the Military Assistance Program, 1948–1951.* Washington, DC: Historical Office, Office of the Secretary of Defense, 1980.

Kaplan, Lawrence S., Denise Artaud, and Mark R. Rubin, eds. *Dien Bien Phu and the Crisis of Franco-American Relations: 1954–1955.* Wilmington, DE: SR Books, 1990.

Kelly, George Armstrong. *Lost Soldiers: The French Army and Empire in Crisis 1947–1962.* Cambridge, MA: MIT Press, 1965.

Kennan, George F. *Memoirs.* Vol. 1, *1925–1950.* Boston: Little, Brown and Company, 1967.

———. *Memoirs.* Vol. 2, *1950–1963.* Boston: Little, Brown and Company, 1972.

Kissinger, Henry. *Nuclear Weapons and Foreign Policy.* Garden City, NY: Doubleday and Co., 1958.

———. *The Troubled Partnership: A Re-appraisal of the Atlantic Alliance.* Garden City, NY: Anchor Books, 1966.

LaFeber, Walter. *America, Russia, and the Cold War, 1945–1996.* 8th ed. New York: McGraw-Hill, 1997.

Large, David Clay. *Germans to the Front: West German Rearmament in the Adenauer Era.* Chapel Hill: University of North Carolina Press, 1996.

Layne, Christopher. *The Peace of Illusions: American Grand Strategy from 1940 to the Present.* Ithaca: Cornell University Press, 2006.

Leffler, Melvyn. *A Preponderance of Power: National Security, the Truman Administration, and the Cold War.* Stanford: Stanford University Press, 1992.

Lider, Julian. *Problems of Military Policy in the Konrad Adenauer Era (1949–1966).* Stockholm: Swedish Institute of International Affairs, 1984.

Lowry, Montecue J. *The Forge of West German Rearmament: Theodor Blank and the Amt Blank.* New York: Peter Lang, 1990.

Lundestad, Gier. *"Empire" by Integration: The United States and European Integration, 1945–1997*. Oxford: Oxford University Press, 1998.

Mai, Gunther. *Westliche Sicherheitspolitik im Kalten Krieg: Der Korea-Krieg und die deutsche Wiederbewaffnung 1950*. Boppard am Rhine: Harald Boldt Verlag, 1977.

Mako, William P. *U.S. Ground Forces and the Defense of Central Europe*. Studies in Defense Policy. Washington, DC: The Brookings Institution, 1983.

Matloff, Maurice. *Strategic Planning for Coalition Warfare, 1943–1944*. Washington, DC: Office of the Chief of Military History, 1959.

Mawby, Spencer. *Containing Germany: Britain and the Arming of the Federal Republic*. New York: St. Martin's Press, 1999.

Mayne, Richard. *The Recovery of Europe: 1945–1973*. Garden City, NY: Anchor Books, 1973.

McAllister, James. *No Exit: America and the German Problem, 1943–1954*. Ithaca: Cornell University Press, 2002.

McGeehan, Robert. *The German Rearmament Question: American Diplomacy and European Defense after World War II*. Urbana: University of Illinois Press, 1971.

McLellan, David S. *Dean Acheson: The State Department Years*. New York: Dodd, Mead and Company, 1976.

McMahon, Robert J. *Dean Acheson and the Creation of an American World Order*. Washington, DC: Potomac Books, 2009.

Mitchell, Otis C. *The Cold War in Germany: Overview, Origins, and Intelligence Wars*. Lanham MD: University Press of America, 2005.

Morgan, Roger. *The United States and West Germany, 1945–1973: A Study in Alliance Politics*. London: Oxford University Press, 1974.

Nelson, Anna Kasten, ed. *The Policy Makers: Shaping American Foreign Policy from 1947 to the Present*. Lanham: Rowman and Littlefield Publishers, 2009.

Nelson, Walter Henry. *Germany Rearmed*. New York: Simon and Schuster, 1972.

Ninkovich, Frank A. *Germany and the United States: The Transformation of the German Question since 1945*. Updated ed. New York: Twayne Publishers, 1995.

Offner, Arnold A. *Another Such Victory: President Truman and the Cold War, 1945–1953*. Stanford: Stanford University Press, 2002.

Osgood, Robert Endicott. *NATO: The Entangling Alliance*. Chicago: University of Chicago Press, 1962.

Peifer, Douglas C. *The Three German Navies: Dissolution, Transition, and New Beginnings, 1945–1960*. Gainesville: University Press of Florida, 2002.

Rioux, Jean-Pierre. *The Fourth Republic, 1944–1958*. Cambridge History of Modern France 7. Cambridge: Cambridge University Press, 1987.

Riste, Olav, ed. *Western Security: The Formative Years: European and Atlantic Defence 1947–1953*. New York: Columbia University Press, 1985.

Ruane, Kevin. *The Rise and Fall of the European Defence Community: Anglo-American Relations and the Crisis of European Defence, 1950–55.* New York: St. Martin's Press, 2000.

Ruhm von Oppen, Beate. *Documents on Germany Under the Occupation, 1945– 1954.* London: Oxford University Press, 1955.

Schwartz, Thomas Alan. *America's Germany: John J. McCloy and the Federal Republic of Germany.* Cambridge, MA: Harvard University Press, 1991.

Searle, Alaric. *Wehrmacht Generals, West German Society, and the Debate on Rearmament, 1949–1959.* Westport, CT: Praeger, 2003.

Smith, Jean Edward. *The Papers of General Lucius D. Clay, Germany 1945–1949.* Vol. 1. Bloomington: Indiana University Press, 1974.

Smith, Joseph. *The Cold War.* Historical Association Studies. 2nd ed. Oxford: Blackwell Publishers, 1998.

Stein, Harold, ed. *American Civil-Military Decisions: A Book of Case Studies.* Tuscaloosa: University of Alabama Press, 1963.

Steininger, Rolf. *The German Question: The Stalin Note of 1952 and the Problem of Reunification.* Edited by Mark Cioc. Translated by Jane T. Hedges. New York: Columbia University Press, 1990.

Stirk, Peter M. R., and David Willis, eds. *Shaping Postwar Europe: European Unity and Disunity, 1945–1957.* New York: St. Martin's Press, 1991.

Stoler, Mark A. *Allies and Adversaries: The Joints Chiefs of Staff, the Grand Alliance, and the U.S. Strategy in World War II.* Chapel Hill: University of North Carolina Press, 2000.

Stueck, William. *Rethinking the Korean War: A New Diplomatic and Strategic History.* Princeton: Princeton University Press, 2002.

Tönnies, Norbert. *Der Weg zu den Waffen.* Köln, Deu.: Erich Pabel Verlag, 1961.

Trachtenberg, Marc. *A Constructed Peace: The Making of the European Settlement, 1945–1963.* Princeton: Princeton University Press, 1999.

———. *History and Strategy.* Princeton Studies in International History and Politics. Princeton: Princeton University Press, 1991.

Trauschweizer, Ingo. *The Cold War U.S. Army: Building Deterrence for Limited War.* Lawrence: University of Kansas Press, 2008.

Truman, Harry S. *Memoirs.* Vol. 1, *Year of Decisions.* Garden City, NY: Doubleday and Co., 1955.

———. *Memoirs.* Vol. 2, *Years of Trial and Hope.* Garden City, NY: Doubleday and Co., 1956.

Urwin, D. W. *Western Europe since 1945: A Short Political History.* 3rd ed. New York: Longman, 1981.

Vaughan, Richard. *Twentieth Century Europe: Paths to Unity*. New York: Barnes and Noble Books, 1979.

Weigley, Russell F. *History of the United States Army*. New York: Macmillan Publishing Co., 1967.

Wettig, Gerhard. *Entmilitarisierung und Wiederbewaffnung in Deutschland, 1943–1955*. München: R. Oldenburg Verlag, 1967.

Wheeler-Bennett, John W. *The Nemesis of Power: The German Army in Politics, 1918–1945*. 2nd ed. New York: Palgrave Macmillan, 2005.

White, Theodore H. *Fire in the Ashes: Europe in Mid-century*. New York: Sloane, 1953.

Wiggershaus, Norbert, and Roland G. Foerster. *The Western Security Community: Common Problems and Conflicting National Interests during the Foundation Phase of the North Atlantic Alliance*. Oxford: Berg, 1992.

Williams, Geoffrey. *The Permanent Alliance: The European-American Partnership 1945–1984*. Leiden, Nld.: A. W. Sijthoff, 1977.

Williams, Phil. *The Senate and U.S. Troops in Europe*. New York: St. Martin's Press, 1985.

Willis, F. Roy. *France, Germany and the New Europe, 1945–1967*. Rev. ed. Oxford: Oxford University Press, 1968.

Winkler, Heinrich August. *Germany: The Long Road West*. Vol. 2, *1933–1990*. Oxford: Oxford University Press, 2007.

Yergin, Daniel. *Shattered Peace: The Origins of the Cold War and the National Security State*. Boston: Houghton Mifflin, 1977.

Young, John W. *Britain, France and the Unity of Europe, 1945–1951*. Leicester: Leicester University Press, 1984.

Ziemke, Earl F. *The U.S. Army in the Occupation of Germany, 1944–1946*. Washington, DC: Center of Military History, 1975.

Zubok, Vladislav, and Constantin Pleshakov. *Inside the Kremlin's Cold War: From Stalin to Krushchev*. Cambridge, MA: Harvard University Press, 1996.

Zurcher, Arnold J. *The Struggle to Unite Europe, 1940–1958: An Historical Account of the Development of the Contemporary European Movement from Its Origin in the Pan-European Union to the Drafting of the Treaties for Euratom and the European Common Market*. Washington Square: New York University Press, 1958.

ARTICLES AND CHAPTERS

Allen, Diane Manchester. "Development of Postwar Policy in Germany." *Western Political Quarterly* 17, no. 1 (March 1964): 109–16.

Artaud, Denise. "France between the Indochina War and the European Defense Community." In Kaplan, Artaud, and Rubin, *Dien Bien Phu*, 251–68.

Barnes, Trevor. "The Secret Cold War: The C.I.A. and American Foreign Policy in Europe, 1946–1956. Part I." *Historical Journal* 24, no. 2. (June 1981): 399–415.

———. "The Secret Cold War: The C.I.A. and American Foreign Policy in Europe, 1946–1956. Part II." *Historical Journal* 25, no. 3. (September 1982): 649–70.

Baylis, John. "Britain, the Brussels Pact and the Continental Commitment." *International Affairs* 60, no. 4 (Autumn 1980): 615–30.

———. "Britain and the Dunkirk Treaty: The Origins of NATO." *Journal of Strategic Studies* 5, no. 2 (June 1982): 236–47.

Bischof, Günter. " Eisenhower, the Summit, and the Austrian Treaty, 1953–1955." In Bischof and Ambrose, *Centenary Assessment*, 136–61.

Brands, H. W. "The Age of Vulnerability: Eisenhower and the National Insecurity State." *American Historical Review* 94, no. 4 (October 1989): 963–89.

Buchheim, Hans. "Adenauers Sicherheitspolitik, 1950–1951." In Buchheim, *Aspekte der deutschen Wiederbewaffnung*, 119–33.

Buhite, Russell D., and Wm. Christopher Hamel. "War for Peace: The Question of an American Preventive War against the Soviet Union, 1945–1955." *Diplomatic History* 14, no. 3 (Summer 1990): 367–84.

Buscher, Frank M. "The U.S. High Commission and German Nationalism, 1949–52." *Central European History* 23, no. 1 (March 1990): 57–75.

Carpenter, Ted Galen. "United States' NATO Policy at the Crossroads: The 'Great Debate' of 1950–1951." *International History Review* 8, no. 3 (August 1986): 389–415.

Corum, James S. "Adenauer, Amt Blank, and the Founding of the Bundeswehr 1950–1956." In Corum, *Rearming Germany*, 29–52.

———. "American Assistance to the New German Army and Luftwaffe." In Corum, *Rearming Germany*, 93–116.

———. "Building a New Luftwaffe: The United States Air Force and Bundeswehr Planning for Rearmament, 1950–1960." *Journal of Strategic Studies* 27, no. 1 (March 2004): 89–113.

———. "Starting from Scratch: Establishing the Bundesluftwaffe as a Modern Air Force, 1955–1960." *Air Power History* 50, no. 2 (2003): 16–29.

Craig, Gordon A. "Germany and NATO: The Rearmament Debate, 1950–1958." In *NATO and American Security*, edited by Klaus Knorr, 236–59. Princeton: Princeton University Press, 1959.

———. "NATO and the New German Army." In *Military Policy and National Security*, edited by William W. Kaufmann, 194–232. Princeton: Princeton University Press, 1956.

Creswell, Michael. "'With a Little Help from Our Friends': How France Secured an Anglo-American Continental Commitment, 1945–54." *Cold War History* 3, no. 1 (October 2002): 1–28.

Creswell, Michael, and Marc Trachtenberg. "France and the German Question, 1945–1955." *Journal of Cold War Studies* 5, no. 3 (Summer 2003): 5–28.

Croft, Stuart. "British Policy towards Western Europe 1945–1951." In Stirk and Willis, *Shaping Postwar Europe*, 77–89.

Dilks, David. "The British View of Security: Europe and a Wider World." In Riste, *Western Security*, 25–59.

Dockrill, Saki. "Britain and the Settlement of the West German Rearmament Question in 1954." In Dockrill and Young, *British Foreign Policy*, 149–72.

———. "The Evolution of Britain's Policy towards a European Army 1950-1954." *Journal of Strategic Studies* 12, no. 1 (March 1989): 38–62.

Duchin, Brian R. "The 'Agonizing Reappraisal': Eisenhower, Dulles, and the European Defense Community." *Diplomatic History* 16, no. 2 (April 1992): 201–22.

Duroselle, J. B. "The Turning-Point in French Politics: 1947." *Review of Politics* 13, no. 3 (July 1951): 302–28.

Fontaine, Andre. "Potsdam: A French View." *International Affairs* (RUSI) 46, no. 3 (July 1970): 466–74.

Fish, M. Steven. "After Stalin's Death: The Anglo-American Debate over a New Cold War." *Diplomatic History* 10, no. 4 (Fall 1986): 333–56.

Folly, Martin H., "Breaking the Vicious Circle: Britain, the United States, and the Genesis of the North Atlantic Treaty." *Diplomatic History* 12, no. 1 (Winter 1988): 59–78.

Gaddis, John Lewis. "The Emerging Post-revisionist Synthesis on the Origins of the Cold War." *Diplomatic History* 7, no. 3 (Summer 1983): 171–90.

———. "The Tragedy of Cold War History." *Diplomatic History* 17, no. 1 (Winter 1993): 1–16.

Gehrz, Christopher. "Dean Acheson, the JCS and the 'Single Package': American Policy on German Rearmament, 1950." *Diplomacy and Statecraft* 12, no. 1 (March 2001): 135–60.

Gildea, Robert. "Myth, Memory and Policy in France since 1945." In *Memory and Power in Post-War Europe: Studies in the Presence of the Past*, edited by Jan-Werner Müller, 59–75. Cambridge: Cambridge University Press, 2002.

Grabbe, Hans-Jürgen. "Konrad Adenauer, John Foster Dulles, and West German-American Relations." In Immerman, *Diplomacy of the Cold War*, 109–32.

Greenwood, Sean. "Ernest Bevin, France, and 'Western Union': August 1945–February 1946." *European History Quarterly* 14, no. 3 (July 1984): 319–37.

———. "Return to Dunkirk: The Origins of the Anglo-French Treaty of March 1947." *Journal of Strategic Studies* 6, no. 4 (December 1983): 49–65.

Greiner, Christian. "The Defense of Western Europe and the Rearmament of West Germany, 1947–1950." In Riste, *Western Security*, 150–80.

Guillen, Pierre. "France and the Defence of Western Europe: From the Brussels Pact (March 1948) to the Pleven Plan (October 1950)." In Wiggershaus and Foerster, *Western Security Community*, 125–48.

Hammond, Paul Y. "Directives for the Occupation of Germany: The Washington Controversy." In Stein, *American Civil-Military Decisions*, 311–464.

Hampton, Mary. "NATO at the Creation: U.S. Foreign Policy, Germany and the Wilsonian Impulse." *Security Studies* 4, no. 3 (Spring 1995): 610–56.

Harper, John L. "Friends Not Allies: George F. Kennan and Charles E. Bohlen." *World Policy Journal* 12, no. 2 (Summer 1995): 77–88.

Henrikson, Alan K. "The Creation of the North Atlantic Alliance, 1948-1952." *Naval War College Review* 33, no. 3 (1980): 4–39.

Herring, George B., and Richard H. Immerman. "Eisenhower, Dulles, and Dien Bien Phu: 'The Day We Didn't Go to War' Revisited." In Kaplan, Artaud, and Rubin, *Dien Bien Phu*, 81–103.

Hershberg, James G. "'Explosion in the Offing': German Rearmament and American Diplomacy, 1953–1955." *Diplomatic History* 16, no. 4 (Fall 1992): 511–49.

Hodges, John P. "Formula for Peace – Military Security Board." *Information Bulletin*, no. 161 (17 May 1949): 5–6.

Hogan, Michael J. "The Search for a 'Creative Peace': The United States, European Unity, and the Origins of the Marshall Plan." *Diplomatic History* 6, no. 3 (Summer 1982): 267–86.

Immerman, Richard H. "Confessions of an Eisenhower Revisionist." *Diplomatic History* 14, no. 3 (Summer 1990): 267–85.

Jervis, Robert. "The Impact of the Korean War on the Cold War." *Journal of Conflict Resolution* 24, no. 4 (December 1980): 563–92.

Johnston, Andrew M. "Mr. Slessor Goes to Washington: The Influence of the British Global Strategy Paper on the Eisenhower New Look." *Diplomatic History* 22, no. 3 (Summer 1998): 361–98.

Joffe, Josef. "Europe's American Pacifier." *Foreign Policy* 54 (Spring 1984): 64–82.

Jones, Howard, and Randall B. Woods. "The Origins of the Cold War: A Symposium." *Diplomatic History* 17, no. 2 (Spring 1993): 251–76.

Kaplan, Lawrence S. "The United States, NATO, and French Indochina." In Kaplan, Artaud, and Rubin, *Dien Bien Phu*, 229–50.

———. "Western Union and European Military Integration 1948–1950 – An American Perspective." In Wiggershaus and Foerster, *Western Security Community*, 45–68.

Karber, Phillip A., and Jerald A. Combs. "The United States, NATO, and the Soviet Threat to Western Europe: Military Estimates and Policy Options 1945–1963." *Diplomatic History* 22, no. 3 (Summer 1998): 399–430.

Kelly, George A. "The French Army Re-enters Politics 1940–1955." *Political Science Quarterly* 76, no. 3 (September 1961): 367–92.

Kepley, David R. "The Senate and the Great Debate of 1951." *Prologue* 14, no. 4 (Winter 1982): 213–36.

Kuklick, Bruce. "The Genesis of the European Advisory Commission." *Journal of Contemporary History* 4, no. 4 (October 1969): 189–201.

Large, David Clay. "Grand Illusions: The United States, The Federal Republic of Germany, and the European Defense Community." In Diefendorf, Frohn, and Rupieper, *Reconstruction of West Germany*, 375–94.

Leffler, Melvyn P. "American Conception of National Security and the Beginnings of the Cold War, 1945–48." *American Historical Review* 89, no. 2 (1984): 346–400.

———. "The Cold War: What Do 'We Now Know'?" *American Historical Review* 104, no. 2 (April 1999): 501–24.

———. "The Emergence of an American Grand Strategy." In *The Cambridge History of the Cold War*, vol. 1, *Origins*, edited by Melvyn P. Leffler and Odd Arne Wested, 67–89. Cambridge: Cambridge University Press, 2010.

———. "Inside Enemy Archives: The Cold War Reopened." *Foreign Affairs* 75, no. 4 (July–August 1996): 120–35.

Lundestad, Geir. "Empire by Invitation? The United States and Western Europe, 1945–1952." *Journal of Peace Research* 23, no. 3. (September 1986): 263–77.

Maier, Klaus A. "The Federal Republic of Germany as a 'Battlefield' in American Nuclear Strategy, 1953–1955." In Diefendorf, Frohn, and Rupieper, *Reconstruction of West Germany*, 395–410.

Martin, Laurence W. "The American Decision to Rearm Germany." In Stein, *American Civil-Military Decisions*, 645–65.

Mastny, Vojtech. "Imagining War in Europe: Soviet Strategic Planning." In *War Plans and Alliances in the Cold War: Threat Perceptions in the East and West*, edited by Vojtech Mastny, Sven Haltemark, and Andreas Wenger, 15–45. London: Routledge, 2006.

May, Ernest R. "The American Commitment to Germany, 1949–1955." *Diplomatic History* 13, no. 4 (Fall 1989): 431–60.

———. "The Impact of Nuclear Weapons on European Security 1945–1957." In Ahmann, Birke, and Howard, *Quest for Stability*, 513–32.

de Maizière, Ulrich. "Zur Plannung und Vorbereitung eines westdeutschen Verteidigungsbeitrages." In Fischer, *Entmilitarisierung und Aufrüstung*, 80–92.

McCreedy, Kenneth O. "Planning the Peace: Operation Eclipse and the Occupation of Germany." *Journal of Military History* 65, no. 3 (July 2001): 713–39.

McLachlan, Donald H. "Rearmament and European Integration." *Foreign Affairs* 29, no. 2 (1951): 276–86.

Meisner, Boris. "Die Vereinbarungen der Europäischen Beratenden Kommission über deutschland von 1944–45." *Aus Politik und Zeit Geschichte* 46, no. 70 (November 1970): 3–14.

Messer, Robert L. "Paths Not Taken: The United States Department of State and Alternatives to Containment, 1945–1946." *Diplomatic History* 1, no. 4 (Fall 1977): 297–319.

Messerschmidt, Manfred, Christian Greiner, and Norbert Wiggershaus. "West Germany's Strategic Position and Her Role in Defence Policy as Seen by the German Military, 1945–1949." In *Power in Europe?: Great Britain, France, Italy and Germany in a Postwar World, 1945–1950*, edited by Josef Becker and Franz Knipping, 353–67. Berlin: Walter de Gruyter, 1986.

Meyer, Georg. "Die Entmilitarisierung in der amerikanischen, britischen und französisichen Besatzungszone sowie in der Bundesreublik Deutschland von 1945 bis 1950." In *Entmilitarisierung und Aufrüstung*, 11–36.

Meyer, Steven E. "Carcass of Dead Policies: The Irrelevance of NATO." *Parameters* 33, no. 4 (Winter 2003–4): 83–97.

Miscamble, Wilson D. "Rejected Architect and Master Builder: George Kennan, Dean Acheson and Postwar Europe." *Review of Politics* 58, no. 3 (Summer 1996): 437–68.

Mosely, Philip E. "The Dismemberment of Germany." *Foreign Affairs* 28, no. 3 (April 1950): 487–98.

———. "The Occupation of Germany." *Foreign Affairs* 28, no. 4 (July 1950): 580–604.

Nelson, Anna K. "The Importance of Foreign Policy Process: Eisenhower and the National Security Council." In Bischof and Ambrose, *Centenary Assessment*, 111–25.

Nitze, Paul. "The Development of NSC 68." *International Security* 4, no. 4 (1980): 170–76.

Noack, Paul. "Militärpolitische Entscheidungen nach dem Scheitern der Europäischen Verteidigungsgemeinschaft." In Buchheim, *Aspekte der deutschen Wiederbewaffnung*, 149–63.

Nobleman, Eli E. "Quadripartite Military Government Organization and Operations in Germany." *American Journal of International Law* 41, no. 3 (July 1947): 650–55.

Onslow, C. G. D. "West German Rearmament." *World Politics* 3, no. 4 (July 1951): 450–85.

Palkowitsch, Oliver. "Westliche Verteidigungsstratagie." *Militärgeschichte* Heft 4 (2005): 18–21.

Peifer, Douglas H. "Establishing the Bundesmarine: The Convergence of Central Planning and Pre-existing Maritime Organizations, 1950–1956." In Corum, *Rearming Germany*, 117–33.

———. "Origins of the East and West German Navies: From the Kriegsmarine to the Volksmarine and Bundesmarine, 1944–1956." PhD diss., University of North Carolina, 1996.

Pomerin, Reiner. "The United States and the Armament of the Federal Republic of Germany." In *The American Impact on Postwar Germany*, edited by Reiner Pomerin, 15–33. Providence: Berghahn Books, 1995.

Poole, Walter S. "From Conciliation to Containment: The Joint Chiefs of Staff and the Coming of the Cold War, 1945–1946." *Military Affairs* 42, no. 1 (February 1978): 12–16.

Preussen, Ronald W. "Cold War Threats and America's Commitment to the European Defense Community: One Corner of a Triangle." *Journal of European Integration History*, Spring 1996, 51–69.

Rearden, Steven L. "Paul H. Nitze and NSC-68: 'Militarizing' the Cold War." In Nelson, *Policy Makers*, 5–28.

Rosenberg, David Alan. "American Atomic Strategy and the Hydrogen Bomb Decision." *Journal of American History* 66, no. 1 (June 1979): 62–87.

———. "The Origins of Overkill." *International Security* 7, no. 4 (1983): 3–71.

———. "U.S. Nuclear Stockpile, 1945 to 1950." *Bulleting of the Atomic Scientists* 38, no. 5 (May 1982): 25–30.

Ruane, Kevin. "Agonizing Reappraisals: Anthony Eden, John Foster Dulles and the Crisis of European Defense, 1953–54." *Diplomacy and Statecraft* 13, no. 4 (December 2002): 151–85.

Ruge, Friedrich. "The Postwar German Navy and Its Mission." *U.S. Naval Institute Proceedings* 83, no. 10 (October 1957): 1035–43.

Schmidt, Gustav. "'Tying' (West) Germany into the West – But to What? NATO? WEU? The European Community?" In *Western Europe and Germany: The Beginnings of European Integration*, edited by Clemens A. Wurm, 137–74. Oxford: Berg Publishers, 1995.

Schmidt, Wolfgang. "Von der 'Befehlsausgabe' zum 'Briefing': Der Amerikanisierung der Luftwaffe während der Aufbauphase der Bundeswehr." *Militärgewschichte* 11, Heft 3 (2001): 43–52.

Schuker, Stephen A. "Reflections on the Cold War: A Comment." *Diplomacy and Statecraft* 12, no. 4 (December 2001): 1–9.

Schultz, Heinz. "The Dilemma of German Rearmament after the Second World War." *Army and Defence Journal* 110, no. 2 (1980): 189–204.

Schuman, Robert. "France and Europe." *Foreign Affairs* 31, no. 3 (April 1953): 349–60.

Schwabe, Klaus. "The Cold War and European Integration, 1947–63." *Diplomacy and Statecraft* 12, no. 4 (December 2001): 18–34.

———. "The United States and European Integration: 1947–1957." In Wurm, *Western Europe and Germany*, 115–36.

Schwartz, Thomas Alan. "The Case of German Rearmament: Alliance Crisis in the 'Golden Age.'" *Fletcher Forum* 8 (Summer 1984): 296–309.

———. "Eisenhower and the Germans." In Bischof and Ambrose, *Centenary Assessment*, 206–21.

———. "The 'Skeleton Key' – American Foreign Policy, European Unity and German Rearmament, 1949–1954." *Central European History* 19, no. 4 (December 1986): 369–85.

Sisk, Thomas M. "Forging the Weapon: Eisenhower as NATO's Supreme Allied Commander, 1950–1952." In Bischof and Ambrose, *Centenary Assessment*, 64–85.

Simpson, Benjamin M., III. "The Rearming of Germany 1950–1954: A Linchpin in the Political Evolution of Europe." *Naval War College Review* 23, no. 9 (May 1971): 76–90.

Slusser, Robert M. "The Opening Phases in the Struggle for Germany." *Slavic Review* 38, no. 3 (September 1979): 473–80.

Snyder, David R. "Arming the 'Bundesmarine': The United States and the Build-Up of the German Federal Navy, 1950–1960." *Journal of Military History* 66, no. 2 (April 2002): 477–500.

Soutou, Georges-Henri. "France and the Cold War, 1944–63." *Diplomacy and Statecraft* 12, no. 4 (December 2001): 35–52.

———. "France and the German Rearmament Problem 1945–1955." In Ahmann, Birke, and Howard, *Quest for Stability*, 487–512.

Steininger, Rolf. "John Foster Dulles, the European Defense Community, and the German Question." In Immerman, *Diplomacy of the Cold War*, 79–108.

Sutton, John L. "The Personal Screen Committee and the Parliamentary Control of West German Armed Forces." *Journal of Central European Affairs* 19 (January 1960): 389–401.

Trachtenberg, Marc. "Melvyn Leffler and the Origins of the Cold War." *Orbis* 39, no. 3 (Summer 1995): 439–55.

———. "New Light on the Cold War?" *Diplomacy and Statecraft* 12, no. 4 (December 2001): 10–17.

———. "The Nuclearization of NATO and U.S.-West European Relations." In *NATO, The Founding of the Atlantic Alliance and the Integration of Europe*, edited by Francis H. Heller and John R. Gillingham, 413–30. New York: St. Martin's Press, 1992.

———. "The United States, France, and the Question of German Power, 1945–1960." In *Deutschland und Frankreich vom Konflikt zur Aussöhnung: Die Gestaltung der westeuropäischen Sicherheit 1914–1963*, edited by Stephen Schuker with Elisabeth Müller-Luckner, 235–48. Schriften des Historischen Kollegs, Kolloquien 46. Munich: Oldenbourg, 2000.

Trachtenberg, Marc, and Christopher Gehrz. "America, Europe, and German Rearmament, August–September 1950: A Critique of a Myth." In *Between Empire and Alliance: America and Europe during the Cold War*, edited by Marc Trachtenberg, 1–32. Lanham: Rowman and Littlefield, 2003.

Trauschweizer, Ingo Wolfgang. "Learning with an Ally: The U.S. Army and the Bundeswehr in the Cold War." *Journal of Military History* 72, no. 2 (April 2008): 477–508.

Tudda, Chris. "The 'Devil's Advocate': Robert Bowie, Western European Integration, and the German Problem, 1953–1954." In Nelson, *Policy Makers*, 29–57.

Uhl, Matthias. "Soviet and Warsaw Pact Military Strategy from Stalin to Brezhnev." In Hoffernaar, Krüger, and Zabeki, *Blueprints for Battle*, 33–53.

Varsori, Antonio. "Italy and the European Defence Community: 1950–1954." In Stirk and Willis, *Shaping Postwar Europe*, 100–111.

Weigall, David. "British Perceptions of the European Defense Community." In Stirk and Willis, *Shaping Postwar Europe*, 90–99.

Wells, Samuel F., Jr. "The First Cold War Buildup: Europe in United States Strategy and Policy, 1950-1953." In Riste, *Western Security*, 181–97.

———. "The Origins of Massive Retaliation." *Political Science Quarterly* 96, no. 1 (Spring 1981): 31–52.

———. "Sounding the Tocsin: NSC-68 and the Soviet Threat." *International Security* 4, no. 2 (Autumn 1979): 123–24.

Wiggershaus, Norbert. "Aussenpolitische Voraussetzungen für den Westdeutschen Verteidigungsbeitrag." In *Wiederbewaffnung in Deutschland nach 1945*, edited by Alexander Fischer, 63–77. Berlin: Duncker and Humblot, 1986.

———. "The Decision for a West German Defense Contribution." In Riste, *Western Security*, 198–214.

———. "The Problem of West German Military Integration." In Wiggershaus and Foerster, *Western Security Community*, 375–412.

————. "Die Überlegungen füer einen westdeutschen Verteidigungsbeitrag von 1948 bis 1950." In Fischer, *Entmilitarisierung und Aufrüstung*, 93–115.

Young, John. "Churchill's Bid for Peace with Moscow, 1954." *History* 73, no. 239 (October 1988): 425–48.

Ziemke, Earle F. "The Formulation and Initial Implementation of U.S. Occupation Policy in Germany." In *U.S. Occupation in Europe after World War II*, edited by Hans A. Schmitt, 27–44. Lawrence: Regents Press of Kansas, 1978.

MISCELLANEOUS

Army List (UK), Biographical List of Officers, p. 860. Date, publisher unknown. Provided to the author by the archivists at the Gloucester Regimental Museum.

Budde, Dieter. "Abrüstung, Entwaffnung und Rüstungskontrolle unter Berücksichtigung politischer und strategisher Aspekte und ihre Auswirkung auf Deutschland." PhD diss., Universität der Bundeswehr München, 2000.

"Brigadier Grazebrook, T.N., C.B.E., D.S.O., D.L., Obituary." *The Back Badge*, Gloucester Regimental Journal, 1967. Provided to the author by the archivists at the Gloucester Regimental Museum.

Cockman, Terry L. "West German Rearmament: From Enemy to Ally in Ten Short Years." MA thesis, Indiana University, 1988.

Chatham House Study Group. *Defence in the Cold War: The Task for the Free World*. London: Royal Institute of International Affairs, 1950.

Documents on Germany, 1944–1959: Background Documents on Germany, 1944–1959, and a Chronology of Political Developments Affecting Berlin, 1945–1956. Washington, DC: Government Printing Office, 1959. http://digital.library.wisc.edu/1711.dl/History.BackgrndDocs.

Edinger, Lewis J. *West German Armament*. Maxwell AFB, AL: Documentary Research Division, Research Studies Institute, Air University, 1955.

Egan, Joseph B. "The Struggle for the Soul of Faust: The American Drive for German Rearmament, 1950–1955." PhD diss., University of Connecticut, 1985.

McCreedy, Kenneth O. *Waging Peace: Operation Eclipse I and II – Some Implications for Future Operations*. Carlisle Barracks, PA: US Army War College, 2004.

Naef, Charles Robert. "The Politics of West German Rearmament, 1950–1956." PhD diss., Rutgers University, 1979.

Porter, Jack J. "Military Institutions, Democracy and the Pursuit of Responsibility: The Rearming of the Federal Republic of Germany 1949–1955." Paper prepared for the Annual Conference of the American Political Science Association, Boston, Massachusetts, 28 August–1 September 2002.

310

"Washington's Farewell Address (1796)." In *American Historical Documents: 1000–1904.* Vol. 43 of *Harvard Classics*, edited by Charles William Elliot. New York: P. F. Collier and Son, 1909. http://www.bartleby.com/43/24.html.

Willenz, Eric. "Early Discussions regarding a Defense Contribution in Germany (1948–1950)." Santa Monica: Rand Corporation, RM-968, 15 October 1952.

Index